Tourism and Indigenous Peoples: Issues and Implications

Tourism and Indigenous Peoples: Issues and Implications

Editors

Richard Butler and Tom Hinch

AMSTERDAM • BOSTON • HEIDELBERG • LONDON • NEW YORK • OXFORD • PARIS •
SAN DIEGO • SAN FRANCISCO • SINGAPORE • SYDNEY • TOKYO
Butterworth-Heinemann is an imprint of Elsevier

Butterworth-Heinemann is an imprint of Elsevier
Linacre House, Jordan Hill, Oxford OX2 8DP, UK
30 Corporate Drive, Suite 400, Burlington, MA 01803, USA

First edition 2007

Notice
No responsibility is assumed by the publisher for any injury and/or damage to persons
or property as a matter of products liability, negligence or otherwise, or from any use or
operation of any methods, products, instructions or ideas contained in the material herein.
Because of rapid advances in the medical sciences, in particular, independent verification
of diagnoses and drug dosages should be made.

British Library Cataloguing in Publication Data
A catalogue record for this book is available from the British Library

Library of Congress Control Number:
A catalogue record for this book is available from the Library of Congress

ISBN-10: 0750664460
ISBN-13: 9780750664462

For information on all publications visit our web site at
http://books.elsevier.com

Typeset by Charon Tec Ltd (A Macmillan Company), Chennai, India
www.charontec.com
Printed and bound in the Great Britain

Working together to grow
libraries in developing countries

www.elsevier.com | www.bookaid.org | www.sabre.org

ELSEVIER   BOOK AID
            International   Sabre Foundation

Contents

List of figures   viii

In memoriam   x

Acknowledgements   xi

Biographies   xii

1   Introduction: revisiting common ground   1
    Tom Hinch and Richard Butler

Part One Indigenous Knowledge and Tourism

2   Traditional ecological knowledge and indigenous tourism   15
    Caroline F. Butler and Charles R. Menzies
3   Doing it the 'Pacific Way': indigenous
    education and training in the South Pacific   28
    Tracy Berno
4   Building a triangulated research foundation for
    indigenous tourism in BC, Canada   40
    Peter W. Williams and Beverley O'Neil
5   Aboriginal tourism research in Australia   58
    Joc Schmiechen and Alicia Boyle

Part Two Indigenous Commerce in Tourism

6   The market perspective of indigenous tourism:
    opportunities for business development   73
    Alison J. McIntosh and Chris Ryan
7   Indigenous tourism and poverty reduction   84
    Harold Goodwin

Contents

8 Indigenous owned casinos and perceived local community
   impacts: Mohegan Sun in South East Connecticut, USA   95
   Barbara Anne Carmichael and Jan Louise Jones

Part Three Indigenous Environment and Tourism

9 Māori nature tourism businesses: connecting with the land   113
   Anna Carr
10 The effects of tourism development on indigenous
   populations in Luang Namtha Province, Laos   128
   Wantanee Suntikul
11 Conservation, wildlife and indigenous tourism:
   longhouse communities in and adjacent to
   Batang Ai National Park, Sarawak, Malaysia   141
   Oswald Bratek, Pat Devlin and David Simmons

Part Four Indigenous Culture and Tourism

12 Tourism and culture in Mongolia: the case of the
   Ulaanbaatar Naadam   161
   Kevin O'Gorman and Karen Thompson
13 Sami perspectives on indigenous tourism in northern Europe:
   commerce or cultural development?   176
   Robert Pettersson and Arvid Viken
14 The Aboriginal people of Taiwan: discourse and silence   188
   Chris Ryan, Janet Chang and Tzung-Cheng (T.C.) Huan

Part Five Indigenous Community-Based Tourism

15 Merging two disparate worlds in rural Namibia:
   joint venture tourism in Torra conservancy   205
   Mai Salole
16 Indigenous ecotourism's role in community
   development: the case of the Lennox Island First Nation   220
   John Colton and Scott Harris
17 Local level institutions in tourism management
   in Nepal's Annapurna region   234
   Sanjay K. Nepal

Part Six Indigenous Tourism: Policies and Politics

18 Tourism in Iran: central control and indigeneity   251
   Kevin O'Gorman, L.R. McLellan and Tom Baum
19 Indigenous minorities of China and effects of tourism   265
   Trevor Sofield and F.M. Sarah Li
20 Indigenous Australia in the bittersweet world: the power of
   tourism in the projection of 'old' and 'fresh' visions of
   Aboriginality   281
   Keith Hollinshead

21 Politics, power and indigenous tourism   305
    Michael Hall

Conclusions

22 Conclusions: Key themes and issues in indigenous
    tourism   319
    Richard Butler and Tom Hinch

References   *333*
Index   *377*

List of figures

1.1   Indigenous tourism defined   6
1.2   The indigenous tourism system   7
4.1   Distribution of BC Aboriginal cultural tourism operations by industry sector   46
4.2   Challenges confronting Aboriginal cultural tourism operations by economic performance   47
4.3   Product–market match assessment summaries for select Aboriginal cultural tourism development options   50
8.1   Location of Mohegan Sun and Foxwoods Casinos (Southeast Connecticut)   98
8.2   Mohegan Sun Casino and Resort Hotel   101
9.1   Cultural references in eco-cultural tourism promotional material   121
11.1   Location of Batang Ai National Park among other protected areas of Sarawak   143
11.2   Location of longhouses and tourist routes in Ulu Batang Ai   144
12.1   Nadaam stadium   170
12.2   Horse racing venue   172
12.3   Levels of satisfaction with attributes of the Naadam Festival   173
12.4   Magnitude of between groups differences on satisfaction variables   174
13.1   Map showing Sápmi in northern Europe   178
14.1   Embankment at Maolin   194
14.2   The indigenous tourism system   200
14.3   Framework of indigenous tourism   201
16.1   Lennox Island   222
16.2   Four C's of Aboriginal community development   223
16.3   Impact of Lennox Island ecotourism on community development   228
17.1   Location of the Annapurna region in Nepal   237
18.1   Caravanserai 'Zeineldin': exterior view   257

18.2   Caravanserai 'Zeineldin': interior view   257
18.3   Inbound tourism of Iran   260
20.1   Changes in cultural values in the Western world:
        related to engagement with other populations
        through tourism   285
20.2   Principal perspectives in applied anthropology
        upon traditional/primal peoples   288
20.3   Precepts to guide future research and management
        of indigenous tourism in Australia   298

In memoriam

Dr. Michael J. Troughton, (1939–2007)
Professor of Geography, University of Western Ontario, Canada.

A highly respected colleague, mentor and friend of many years, who will
be greatly missed.

Acknowledgements

Our first acknowledgement has to be to our fellow contributors to this volume, who responded courteously and fairly promptly to our sometimes demanding requests, and who have provided the bulk of this volume. We hope that they consider their efforts worthwhile and are satisfied with the final outcome.

We are grateful to the staff at Elsevier for their support and assistance with the preparation and publication of the volume, in particular Sally North, who has patiently stuck with us for a rather longer time and larger volume than anticipated initially.

Finally, we thank our families, who have put up with absences and disrupted holidays, including Christmas, and despite this, have helped with contributions and editing, and always provided support for us and this project.

Biographies

Tom Baum is Professor of International Tourism and Hospitality Management in the University of Strathclyde, Glasgow. He has primary and masters degrees from the University of Wales and a PhD from Strathclyde. Tom has worked extensively in tourism across a number of countries and contributed widely to the published literature in international tourism.

Tracy Berno is an Associate Professor in Tourism and Head of Department – Tourism and Hospitality at the University of the South Pacific in Fiji. Tracy has worked and lived in the South Pacific region for over 15 years. Her interests, along with sitting on nice tropical beaches and eating mangoes, include tourism in the South Pacific, tourism education and cross-cultural aspects of tourism.

Alicia Boyle has worked in VET/TAFE education and training for over 20 years. She has been in Darwin, Australia with the Charles Darwin University since 1999 in both academic teaching and research positions. She is the Education Coordinator for the Desert Knowledge Cooperative Research Centre and the Northern Territory Network Coordinator for the Sustainable Tourism Cooperative Research Centre. Alicia works extensively in applied research with key interests in education and industry development.

Oswald Braken is a Senior Manager in the Protected Areas and Biodiversity Conservation Unit of Sarawak Forestry, Sarawak, Malaysia, responsible for the management and conservation of biodiversity in Sarawak. He was Person In-Charge of the National Parks and Wildlife Office in the Northern Region of Sarawak from 1986 to 1994, responsible for the management, development and protection of the national parks including tourism activities and protection wildlife in the region. His major interests are in nature, tourism and wildlife conservation.

Richard Butler is Professor of International Tourism in the Department of Hospitality and Tourism Management at the University of Strathclyde in Glasgow. He is a past president of the International Academy for the Study of Tourism, and of the Canadian Association for Leisure Studies. After 30 years in Canada he returned to the UK in 1997 and continues his research interests in destination development, tourism in islands and peripheral regions, sustainability and the links between literature and tourism.

Caroline Butler did her postgraduate work in anthropology at the University of British Columbia and is currently Adjunct Professor of Anthropology at the University of Northern British Columbia. She has collaborated with First Nations communities in British Columbia, researching natural resource use and employment, Aboriginal fishing rights, Indigenous knowledge and traditional resource management, and has also worked with commercial fishers and loggers on the north coast of British Columbia exploring issues of resource regulations and local knowledge.

Barbara Anne Carmichael is an Associate Professor in the Department of Geography and Environmental Studies and Associate Director of NEXT Research Centre in the School of Business and Economics at Wilfrid Laurier University, Waterloo, Ontario, Canada. Her research interests include tourist choice behavior, casino impacts, market segmentation, special events and resident attitudes toward tourism.

Anna Carr is a senior lecturer at the Department of Tourism, University of Otago. Prior to her career in academia she worked for the Department of Conservation and was co-owner of two adventure tourism businesses. Her research interests include ecotourism, adventure tourism operations, wilderness management and visitor interpretation/education. She affiliates to NgaPuhi and Ngati Ruanui *iwi*.

Janet Chang is Associate Professor of the Graduate Institute and Department of Tourism Management, School of Business, Chinese Culture University, Taipei, Taiwan. Dr. Chang spent a few years working in international chain hotels in US and Taiwan prior to commencing her academic career. She has produced scholarly publications in numerous leading journals including *Annals of Tourism Research, Tourism Management and Journal of Business Research*. She is a member of the Editorial Board of Tourism Management. Her current research interests include aboriginal tourism, tourism and hospitality marketing and tourist behavior.

John Colton is an Associate Professor at Acadia University's School of Recreation Management and Kinesiology in Wolfville, Nova Scotia where he is Coordinator of the Outdoor Recreation and Sustainable Tourism Program. His research interests include aboriginal tourism, nature based tourism, and sustainable community development. He lectures in tourism studies, global issues, and sustainable community development.

Pat Devlin's career began in science and outdoor/environmental education as a lecturer at Christchurch Teacher's College and as a seasonal ranger/naturalist at Tongariro National Park. He established the programme for

National and Rural Park Management at Lincoln University and since retirement, he has continued involvement with postgraduate supervision and in teaching park management subjects in Sarawak (Eastern Malaysia).

Harold Goodwin is Director of the International Centre for Responsible Tourism and Professor of Responsible Tourism Management at Leeds Metropolitan University as well as a member of the Pro-Poor Tourism Partnership. He wrote the first discussion paper for the British government on *Sustainable Tourism and Poverty Elimination* in 1998, the Pro-Poor Tourism Partnership has subsequently produced a series of case studies and reports (www.pptpartnership.org) and he directed an implementation project in The Gambia which secured increased living standards for local guides, craft workers and fruit and juice vendors.

Michael Hall is Professor in Marketing in the College of Business and Economics, University of Canterbury, Christchurch, New Zealand and Docent in the Department of Geography, University of Oulu, Finland. He is co-editor of Current Issues in Tourism and regional editor for Tourism Geographies. He has published widely in the tourism, environmental history and heritage fields. Current interests focus on temporary human mobility and regional development policies, tourism and international business, global environmental change and gastronomy.

Scott Harris holds a BA from the University of Victoria in Geography and Economics. Soon after completing his undergraduate studies, Scott worked for the Kwakiutl District Council on Vancouver Island, British Columbia as a resource planner (1994–2001). In 2003 he completed his MA focusing on aboriginal ecotourism in Prince Edward Island. He currently resides in British Columbia where he works as a resource planner for several aboriginal communities.

Tom Hinch is a Professor and the Associate Dean Undergraduate Programs with the Faculty of Physical Education and Recreation at the University of Alberta in Edmonton, Canada. In addition to his work related to tourism and indigenous peoples, Tom has an active research program that focuses on the nexus between sport and tourism.

Keith Hollinshead was originally a 'Marketing' specialist, but since obtaining his Ph.D. in the USA has become an eclectic theorist drawing insight from Anthropology, Political Science, Cultural Studies, Human Communications, and Continental Philosophy amongst a wide mix of domains. His background includes a period as Promotions Manager of the Yulara International Tourist Resort (at Uluru [Ayers Rock] in Central Australia) in 1983–4, and then Convenor of the Second Australian National Folklore Conference in Sydney. He is currently a Professor at the University of Bedfordshire and his current research interests generally concern the axial and collaborative role of tourism in the political manufacture of the public culture of places.

Tzung-Cheng (T.C.) Huan is a Professor at National Chaiyi University (NCYU) and has additional appointments with NCYU's Taiwan Indigenous Education and Enterprise Development Center and Taiwan Farmers' Management Association. He has been the interface with Taiwan's Indigenous people and farmers in other capacities. He participates in eco-tourism development at Alishan, one of the most famous indigenous tourism destinations in Taiwan. He is on the editorial review boards of *Annals of Tourism Research and Tourism Management*. He publishes papers and contributes to books in areas including cultural/heritage tourism, international travel, benefits sought, travel behavior, environmental education, trip satisfaction, and tourism marketing.

Jan Louise Jones is an Assistant Professor in the Department of Recreation and Leisure Services at the University of Maine at Presque Isle. She is also a member of the Eastern Woodland Métis Nation in Nova Scotia, Canada. Her research interests include the socio-cultural impacts of tourism and casino developments in both local and international travel destinations.

Sarah Li is a specialist on tourism policy, planning and development issues in China and has undertaken more than 15 research projects and consultancies in that country over the past decade. She is a graduate of the University of Surrey, UK (MSc in Tourism) and Murdoch University, Western Australia (PhD in Tourism). Previously appointed to the University of Tasmania she is currently an independent consultant based in Cambodia, where she has been working for the Asian Development Bank on tourism education and training while undertaking various short term assignments in China.

Rory MacLellan is a Senior Lecturer in Tourism at the University of Strathclyde in Glasgow. He has an MA in Geography from the University of Aberdeen and an MSc in Tourism from the University of Strathclyde. His teaching and research interests cluster around tourism and the natural environment, particularly in Scotland. These include rural tourism, sustainable tourism, eco-tourism, wildlife tourism and outdoor activities. He has published on aspects of tourism and the Scottish natural environment including articles on wildlife holidays, sustainable tourism and has co-edited a book titled 'Tourism in Scotland'. He has also carried out research on aspects of Scottish tourism for a number of agencies including Scottish Enterprise, Scottish Natural Heritage, the Scottish Parliament and Scottish Environment LINK.

Alison McIntosh is Associate Professor at the Department of Tourism & Hospitality Management, University of Waikato, New Zealand. Her main research interests are in tourists' experiences of heritage and culture, and the sustainable development of indigenous tourism. Alison has published in leading journals such as *Annals of Tourism Research, Journal of Travel Research* and *Tourism Management*.

Charles Menzies is an Associate Professor of Socio-Cultural Anthropology in the Department of Anthropology at the University of British Columbia and is a member of the Ts'msyeen Nation. His primary research interests are natural resource management (primarily fisheries related), political economy, contemporary First Nations' issues and maritime anthropology. He has conducted field research in north coastal British Columbia (Canada), Brittany (France) and Donegal (Ireland).

Sanjay Nepal is an Assistant Professor at the Department of Recreation, Park and Tourism Sciences, Texas A&M University, College Station, Texas, USA. His research interests include exploring the relationship between tourism, protected areas and local communities, participatory conservation, tourism impacts on the environment and mountain tourism.

Kevin O'Gorman is currently completing his PhD in the Department of Hospitality and Tourism Management, University of Strathclyde, in Glasgow; after completing seven years postgraduate study, of theology, philosophy and the classics, in Italy and Spain. His research interests comprise of the history and philosophy of hospitality and tourism and his PhD research is an analysis of ancient, classical, mediaeval texts both in their original languages and modern commentaries on them, to establish the true origins of hospitality and tourism.

Beverley O'Neil is a citizen of the Ktunaxa First Nation in British Columbia, Canada, and owner of O'Neil Marketing & Consulting, and Numa Communications Ltd. Prior to starting her businesses, she was the Director of Community Economic Development for the Ktunaxa/Kinbasket Tribal Council. Her current work focuses on community economic development that fosters Aboriginal community, cultural and corporate relationship building especially as they relate to women and youth initiatives.

Robert Pettersson works at the European Tourism Research Institute, ETOUR, and is head of the tourism department at the Mid-Sweden University in Östersund, Sweden. His research interests include Sami tourism and other forms of nature and culture-based tourism in peripheral areas. He also lectures in human geography and tourism studies.

Chris Ryan is Professor of Tourism at the Department of Tourism & Hospitality Management, University of Waikato, New Zealand, editor of *Tourism Management*, a Fellow of the International Academy for the Study of Tourism and an Honorary Professor of the University of Wales. Chris has published in leading journals such as *Annals of Tourism Research, Tourism Management, Journal of Travel Research, Journal of Sustainable Tourism* and *The Journal of Travel and Tourism Marketing*.

Mai Salole was born in Norway. She grew up in Ethiopia and has since lived in Norway, the U.K, Italy, Ethiopia, Zimbabwe, the Netherlands, South Africa, and Belgium . She has a first degree from the University of Lund and an MSc in Tourism Management from the University of Surrey. She is currently working as a tourism consultant with Southern Africa and Ethiopia as special areas of interest.

David Simmons is the leader of Lincoln University's tourism programme and a founding staff member of the Social Science, Parks, Recreation and Tourism Group. He has been at Lincoln University since 1978 and his research interests focus on how 'places' evolve vis à vis tourism. Recently, his research has focused on pathways to sustainability, including the public (policy/planning) and private (business practice) sector nexus. He has worked on the 2nd Sarawak Tourism Master plan and various implement-ation projects since 1992.

Joc Schmiechen is the Indigenous Tourism Research Fellow at the Charles Darwin University, Alice Springs, Australia. He has over 30 years involve-ment in outdoor education, expedition leadership, Aboriginal education, environmental management, cross cultural and eco tourism encompassing some of the remotest and wildest locations in Australia and Antarctica, with extensive government and industry experience in the Aboriginal and Special Interest tourism sectors throughout Australia. He has developed a particular interest in small businesses and their operators working in remote locations coupled with an ongoing concern about tourism impacts and developing sustainable practices. He recently completed a 2-year project on Heritage Tourism in the Lake Eyre Basin.

Trevor Sofield is Foundation Professor of Tourism at the University of Tasmania. With his first degree in social anthropology and a forty year career interest in indigenous peoples in a number of countries throughout the Asia Pacific Region, he has specialized in China studies over the past 12 years. He is currently Team Leader for the Mekong Tourism Development Project which has community based tourism programs in Cambodia, Laos and Vietnam.

Wantanee Suntikul is a post-doctoral fellow at the School of Hotel and Tourism Management at the Hong Kong Polytechnic University. She obtained her Masters Degree in Tourism Marketing from the University of Surrey, UK and a PhD in Tourism from the same university. Her research interests include tourism planning and development, politics and tourism, tourism and political transition, tourism in national protected areas, pro-poor tourism and community-based tourism. Her primary geographical area of research focus is Southeast Asia. She is currently working intensively on tourism in Laos.

Karen Thompson is a Lecturer in Tourism Management at the University of Strathclyde in Glasgow, UK. Her principal research interest is in visitor behaviour, in particular the use of destination transport networks by tourists. Karen's other main interest is in tourism development in Soviet Central Asia, and she has written on ecotourism and the use of heritage and cultural events in tourism development within that geographical region. A recent research exercise on visitor behaviour and motivation at the Ulaanbaatar Naadam festival allowed the two above interests to be combined.

Arvid Viken is an Associate Professor in Tourism at Finnmark University College, Alta, Norway. He has done research on indigenous tourism, Arctic tourism, nature-based tourism and edited and written a series of articles and books within the sociology of tourism, heritage tourism and tourism and environment.

Peter Williams is Director of the Centre for Tourism Policy and Research, and a Professor in the School of Resource and Environmental Management at Simon Fraser University in British Columbia, Canada. He conducts behavioral and policy research related to use of natural and cultural resources for sustainable tourism development purposes.

CHAPTER 1

Introduction: revisiting common ground

Tom Hinch and Richard Butler

Introduction

Indigenous cultures have become a powerful attraction for tourists and as such they have drawn the attention of tourism entrepreneurs, government agencies and academics. Since the publication of *Tourism and Indigenous Peoples* (Butler and Hinch, 1996) over a decade ago, debates about indigenous tourism have flourished including those as fundamental as whether indigenous tourism represents an opportunity for indigenous people to gain economic independence and cultural rejuvenation to whether it presents a major threat of hegemonic subjugation and cultural degradation. A parallel range of opinions exist at operational levels inclusive of debates about the size of indigenous tourism markets, the appropriateness of various marketing practices and the business models that are most suitable for indigenous tourism operations. The continued existence of these debates is due in part to an ever-changing world environment characterized by powerful forces for the integration of indigenous people into a global culture on one hand while encouraging indigenous communities to protect and enhance local advantages that may give them a competitive advantage in this global economy on the other (Notzke, 2006). For indigenous people, the essence of this advantage lies in their distinctive cultures and in the increasing fascination of non-indigenous people in things indigenous.

Given the complexities of globalization, indigenous cultures and tourism, the range of debate that surrounds indigenous tourism is not surprising. The reality is that there are a range of both opportunities and threats that indigenous people may encounter if they choose to become involved in tourism. The exact blend of these opportunities and threats tend to be unique in time and space although some common patterns and themes exist. They are influenced both by external factors over which indigenous people have little control and by internal factors over which indigenous people have at least some opportunity to influence.

This book is meant to build on the 1996 publication of *Tourism and Indigenous People*. While that publication tended to focus on the impacts of the involvement of indigenous people in tourism, this volume is meant to explore the dynamics of their active involvement. In order to fulfill this objective, a broad range of scholars with active programs in indigenous tourism were invited to contribute and were encouraged to capture indigenous voices in their contributions. The articulation of these voices was perhaps easier for those authors who were in fact indigenous (see bibliographies), but non-indigenous authors have incorporated direct native voices where possible and have done their best to accurately interpret indigenous perspectives albeit with inescapable cultural filters. These non-indigenous contributions are not seen as a limitation of the book in as much as they reflect the cross-cultural reality of indigenous tourism both in terms of the typical host–guest relationship and in terms of the operational environment in which indigenous tourism operates.

In re-establishing the common ground for this book, the introductory chapter of the 1996 publication of *Tourism and Indigenous Peoples* is revisited and modified to reflect an evolving understanding of indigenous tourism, a new set of authors, and an increased focus on the dynamics of the active involvement of indigenous people in tourism. The rationale for indigenous tourism opens the chapter followed by a discussion of the definition of indigenous tourism as employed by the editors. These sections draw heavily upon Hinch and Butler (1996). They are followed by the presentation of an indigenous tourism system model that represents a significant departure from the framework presented in 1996 as it captures emerging perspectives on the cultural underlay upon which indigenous tourism lies. Finally, the topical structure of the book is presented along with concluding comments.

Rationale for indigenous tourism

Western-based economic rationale remains the primary motivation for engaging in the business of indigenous tourism. Essentially, tourism is seen as a way to address the many economic, social and cultural challenges facing indigenous people (IUOTO, 1963; Zinder, 1969; UN, 1999). The essence of this argument is that income generated through tourism represents a fair exchange of value for value between indigenous and non-indigenous people. It is argued that increased economic independence will be accompanied by a higher degree of self-determination and cultural pride as the shackles imposed by poverty and social welfare are broken. In contrast to many other forms of economic activity, such as clear cutting timber from traditional indigenous lands in rain forest regions, appropriately managed tourism is seen as a sustainable activity that is generally consistent with indigenous values about the sanctity of the land and people's relationship to it. Moreover, from an economic perspective, indigenous people are seen as having a competitive tourism advantage based on their unique cultures (Notzke, 2004), the fundamental place of hospitality within many of these cultures (McIntosh et al., 2002) and their increasingly valuable traditional lands (Stevens, 1997). A symbiotic relationship is possible to the extent that cultural survival contributes to economic success and economic success contributes to cultural survival. Notwithstanding this apparent convergence of interests between indigenous and non-indigenous components in the tourism industry, there remain several fundamental issues that challenge the long-term viability of indigenous tourism initiatives (see concluding chapter).

The participation of indigenous people in tourism is also driven by the belief that such cross-cultural interaction promotes understanding between indigenous and non-indigenous people (D'Amore, 1988). This argument assumes that much of the harm that has been perpetuated by dominant societies on indigenous people has been, and continues to be, based on ignorance. From this perspective, increased exposure to non-indigenous people in the positive circumstances associated with tourism increases the mainstream population's understanding and appreciation of the plight of indigenous peoples. Similarly, indigenous people are advantaged by their glimpse of a more humanistic dimension of their non-indigenous counterparts. In both cases, indigenous and non-indigenous participants disseminate their new knowledge throughout their home communities. Increased understanding results in changed attitudes and behaviors that lead, in turn, to a more just and equitable relationship between indigenous and non-indigenous peoples (D'Amore, 1988). In contrast to many other types of contact, the fact that tourism can be planned and managed implies that indigenous people can influence the nature of the economic and cultural exchange. Based on the centrality of the cultural attraction and increased indigenous ownership, indigenous people can, at least in theory, negotiate their involvement in tourism from a position of strength.

Critics of indigenous tourism would argue that the rationale just described is fallacious or at the very least, naïve. Early critics of tourism development pointed out that the industry was dominated by outside interests who retained most of the benefits and left the host destinations to suffer the costs (e.g., Bryden, 1973; Turner and Ash, 1975; MacCannell, 1976; De Kadt, 1979). Over the past two decades, however, ecotourism activities (Fennell, 1999; Weaver, 2001, community-based approaches (Murphy, 1985), and more generally, sustainable approaches (Sofield, 2003) have gained popularity. These approaches attempt to mitigate the negative impacts of tourism and accentuate the positive ones with the goal of ensuring a net positive impact along with a fair distribution of these impacts. Clearly, however, this nirvana has yet to be achieved and there are systemic causes for this failure (Mowforth and Munt, 1998). Rather than suggesting that there is a magic set of principles or strategies that can provide a universal guarantee of success in the context of indigenous tourism, the contributing authors in this book examine indigenous tourism in the unique contexts of place and time. They adopt critical scholarly perspectives, attempt to reflect native voices in their work and try to make sense of complex situations and events related to tourism and indigenous peoples.

Questions of definition

A variety of terms are used in the literature to describe the different groups that fall under the indigenous concept adopted in this book. A sampling of terminology includes Indian (Csargo, 1988; Hollinshead, 1992), Aboriginal (Altman, 1989; Altman and Finlayson, 1993; Parker, 1993), native (Tourism Canada, 1988), indigenous (Ryan and Aicken, 2005) and first nations (Reid, 1993). In certain contexts broader terms such as cultural (Robinson and Boniface, 1999) and ethnic (Swain, 1993) tourism have also been used to encompass the indigenous tourism dimensions in whole or in part. Over the past 10 years, however, there has been a general coalescing of terms in the tourism literature with the most frequent references being to Aboriginal and indigenous peoples. The choice of a particular term is normally based on: the geographic context, the specific group that is the focus of the publication and the way that this group refers to their own ethnicity, and the sensibilities of the target audience for the publication.

While the terminology used by each author in this collection varies according to the nuances of the study or argument being presented, the umbrella term of indigenous tourism is used by the editors of this volume. It should be noted, however, that the term indigenous is also contested which is not surprising given the distinctive rights and restrictions that indigenous peoples face throughout the world. In contrast to the more general definition of indigenous used by Butler and Hinch (1996) and in keeping with other recent publications on this topic (e.g., Ryan and Aicken, 2005), the definition for indigenous provided by the United Nations Development Program (UNDP) (http://www.undp.org/csopp/NewFiles/ipadoutdef.html) has been adopted. In essence, classifying a group as indigenous implies that this group was present and occupied a given area prior to the creation of modern states and borders. Indigenous groups are also typically seen to be distinct in terms of their cultural and social identities and institutions relative to dominant groups in society. Key characteristics include:

(i) self-identification and identification by others as being part of a distinct indigenous cultural group, and the display of desire to preserve that cultural identity;
(ii) linguistic identity different from that of the dominant society;
(iii) social, cultural, economic, and political traditions and institutions distinct from the dominant culture;
(iv) economic systems oriented more toward traditional systems of production than mainstream systems;
(v) unique ties and attractions to traditional habitats and ancestral territories and natural resources in these habitats and territories.
(United Nations Development Program, 2004)

One of the limitations of this definition is that culture is dynamic and while the UNDP definition emphasizes tradition, it must also be recognized that there is an ever-changing contemporary dimension to these groups that does not invalidate their indigenous status although it may complicate it. The use of 'indigenous' in this book is therefore meant to be inclusive rather than exclusive. While some readers may prefer tighter parameters they will hopefully be receptive to the common cultural, economic, environmental and political issues that are faced by groups who are both at the core and on the peripheries of this definition.

Indigenous tourism refers to tourism activities in which indigenous people are directly involved either through control and/or by having their culture serve as the essence of the attraction. The factor of control is a key in any discussion of development (an issue referred to again in the concluding chapter). Whoever has control or exercises power generally determines such critical factors as the scale, pace, nature, and indeed, the outcomes of development. Similarly, given the centrality of attractions in tourism, the extent to which the attraction is a manifestation of indigenous culture is also a primary indicator of indigenous tourism. Figure 1.1 illustrates these two key dimensions by way of a matrix. The horizontal axis represents the range of control that indigenous people have over a given tourism activity. At the left

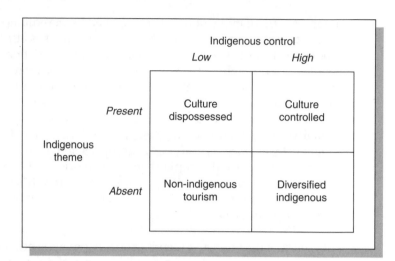

Figure 1.1
Indigenous tourism
defined (Hinch and
Butler, 1996, p.10)

end of the continuum indigenous groups have no control at all, while at the right end they have total control in terms of ownership and management interests. In between these extremes, a number of graduations exist including the participation of indigenous people as employees, advisory board members, and formal partners in development. The vertical axis represents the degree to which the tourist attraction is based on indigenous culture. These themes range from being focused totally on indigenous culture to a complete absence of an indigenous theme.

Tourism enterprises which are both controlled by indigenous people and which feature an indigenous themed attraction clearly fall within the scope of the definition for indigenous tourism (culture controlled). Just as clearly, tourism activity which is neither controlled by indigenous people nor which features an indigenous theme, lies outside the purview of this book (non-indigenous tourism) and it should be recognized that this type of activity dwarfs the volume of activity in the other three quadrants in actual practice. Tourism enterprises which are controlled by indigenous interests but which do not feature a central attraction that is based on indigenous culture represent part of the middle ground between the two extremes just noted (diversified indigenous). Examples of this type of activity include casinos owned by indigenous groups (see chapter by Carmichael and Jones, Editors' Note) or ecotourism enterprises like Whale Watch Kaikoura (Curtin, 2003) which emphasizes a western-based marine biology interpretative presentation but is owned by the Maori interests. While the costs and benefits of running these operations obviously has a direct impact on indigenous peoples, the values, management styles and unique legal rights of these groups may also have a bearing on the nature of the tourism experience that is produced as well as the sustainability of the enterprise. Finally, there is a substantial level of tourism activity that is developed around indigenous attraction themes but in which indigenous people themselves have little or no controlling interest (Culture

Dispossessed). Activities that fall into this latter category have become increasingly controversial and generate heated debates about cultural expropriation, indigenous intellectual property rights and copyright infringement.

The indigenous tourism system

There are a variety of components and relationships that underpin indigenous tourism. In reality, each indigenous tourism experience is unique in terms of time, space and participants. A similar claim could be made of virtually all types of tourism experiences but to hide behind this fact is to ignore common, albeit not universal, patterns which exist and which provide insight into a variety of issues that arise in the context of indigenous tourism.

Hinch and Butler (1996) presented a framework for indigenous tourism that served to highlight some of the key components of indigenous tourism but it was of limited value in terms of identifying the relationships between these components. The revised model presented in Figure 1.2 is meant to address this shortcoming and to highlight the central role of culture as a dynamic within this system. It has been influenced by a variety of sources including the basic geographic dimension of Leiper's (1990) tourism system and the important role of media as highlighted by Ryan and Trauer (2005) (see chapter by Ryan, Chang and Huan, Editors' Note). At the heart of this

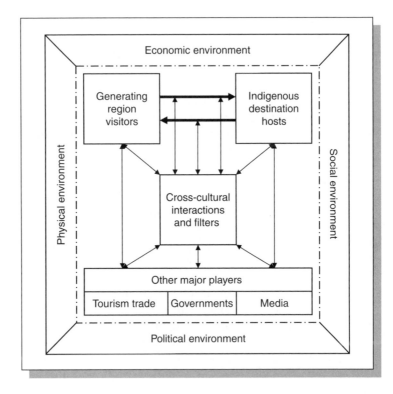

Figure 1.2
The indigenous
tourism system

model is the basic travel dynamic between the generating region where the tourists reside and the destination region where the hosts, in this case the indigenous hosts, are found. By definition, there is a physical flow of tourists from the generating region to the indigenous destination and back again (Leiper, 1990). This flow in human traffic is accompanied by a variety of additional flows including financial resources, information and images. While the heavily marked arrows on the model symbolize an equal flow of tourists traveling to the destination area and then back home, the ancillary flows are not necessarily equal and therein lie many of the controversies surrounding indigenous tourism. In general, the intent of the hosts is to have a net inflow of money into the destination and to export positive images of the destination and themselves.

One of the distinguishing features of an indigenous tourism system relative to a tourism system in general is the emphasis on culture. In the Culture Controlled quadrant of Figure 1.2 there is often a very conscious intent to feature, and indeed commodify, the 'otherness' of the hosts as the essence of the attraction. Variations of such cultural attractions are limitless but include: interpretive centers, performances, festivals, home-stays, guided tours and a range of other offerings that feature indigenous culture that is in some way packaged and sold to the visitors. But the cultural overlay found in the indigenous tourism system is much more encompassing than its tangible manifestation in a culturally based attraction. It is also reflected in basic values and principles that are infused in the way an enterprise is operated. An example of this would be the unique forms of hospitality found in indigenous destination communities.

There are multiple cultures interacting in an indigenous tourism context. Basic categories of these cultures include those associated with: (1) the host indigenous culture found in a specific destination; (2) the mainstream culture that dominates the national–political region in which the destination exists; (3) the global culture that increasingly characterizes the international and national tourism industries of which the indigenous tourism industry is but a part and (4) the multiple cultures that make up the international market for indigenous tourism. Each of these cultural groups can again be broken down into a multitude of cultural components. For example, often the indigenous hosts will consist of a complex array of tribal and family groups. As a result of this cultural complexity, there are a variety of filters that come into play during any of the multiple interactions that occur in indigenous tourism. These filters are used by the interacting individuals to understand and interpret the multiple values and practices that characterize indigenous tourism interactions. Moreover, these cultural filters are unique for each participant. As a result of this cultural complexity, indigenous tourism tends to require more complex negotiation than many other types of tourism.

While the main players in indigenous tourism are the tourists and the hosts, a number of other influential groups exist. Leading this group are the various intermediaries that make up the travel trade. Key elements include: (1) travel agents in the origin; (2) transportation companies that facilitate the physical travel of the tourist and (3) outbound and inbound tour operators that develop a range of tour packages. The travel trade is dominated by an increasingly global culture that operates at a worldwide scale and responds to shareholder interests. Operators who specialize in indigenous tourism represent a very small segment of this group and must normally work within the operating parameters of the tourism industry as a whole if they hope to remain solvent. Governments also tend to be active participants in indigenous tourism. Their involvement is found in the normal tourism functions – often concentrated in the area of marketing – of national, state and local governments but is especially noteworthy compared to that in other forms of tourism due to the active participation of government agencies with mandates in development or addressing the needs of indigenous peoples. These government agencies often see tourism as a potential agent for indigenous economic and social development and actively support indigenous tourism through policy initiatives, consultant services and financial assistance. Media, in all of its manifestations, is also a major player in the indigenous tourism system. Because of the newsworthiness of indigenous issues, indigenous tourism tends to generate considerable attention in the media. This attention plays an important role in the development of tourist images of indigenous products and indeed the development of identity of the indigenous hosts.

The final component of the indigenous tourism system is the broader environmental context. This component of indigenous tourism system reflects the reality that tourism is not a closed system. Indigenous tourism is impacted by trends in the economic, social, political and physical world. These trends represent external influences largely beyond the control of either the indigenous or global tourism industries but which have a direct bearing on their performance. A brief examination of these factors in the context of indigenous peoples highlights key operating considerations for indigenous tourism.

Economic environment

Economic considerations are recognized as a driving force in tourism. Strong economic performance in the tourist market areas will result in higher levels of discretionary spending for travel and more trips. Weak economic performance in destination areas often results in tourism actively supported as an alternative to struggling primary or secondary industries. Mainstream governments, anxious to reverse the dependency of indigenous people on social assistance, may encourage indigenous tourism development. While a communal approach to economic development is often associated with traditional indigenous communities, the success rate of this approach has come into question in places like Australia (see chapter by Schmiechen and Boyle, Editors' Note). Increasingly, private entrepreneurial approaches are being pursued in indigenous communities (Wuttunee, 1992; Altman and Finlayson, 1993). Such trends may reflect the growing corporatization of the global economy in combination with evolving generational differences and changing socio-political structures and programs found in indigenous communities.

Social environment

Indicators of the social demographic characteristics of many indigenous people throughout the world have contributed to the view that one of the shared features of indigenous people is the 'culture of poverty' in which they live (Frideres, 1988). As Goodwin points out in his chapter, 'Poverty means a lack of basic capacity to participate effectively in society. It means not having enough to feed and clothe a family, not having a clinic or school to go to, not having the land on which to grow one's food or a job to earn one's living, not having access to credit' (IMF and IDA, 1999, p. 5). These are the conditions that indigenous peoples tend to exist in much more frequently than non-indigenous peoples. Given these depressing conditions, it is not surprising that the constraints to tourism and the resulting development goals of indigenous communities often vary from the goals of non-indigenous communities. For example, a study in Alberta, Canada found that indigenous communities are much more likely to identify tourism development objectives related to the improvement of basic infrastructure and service upgrading than are non-indigenous communities (Hinch, 1994).

Political environment

Indigenous people continue to become increasingly politically aware and active. Despite the substantial constraints that they face, indigenous people have become more informed of their legal and political rights and they have increasingly exercised them. There has been a general increase in land claim settlements, which has resulted in financial gain and increased resource management roles (Hinch, 2001). A good example of these gains in a tourism context is the growth in indigenous owned casino development throughout the US and Canada based on legal challenges by indigenous groups (Stansfield, 1996). These gains are not uniformly distributed however, as Hollinshead and Hall point out in their respective chapters in this volume. There continues to be conflict between indigenous and non-indigenous peoples. Such conflict tends to suppress demand for indigenous tourism products even where the destination is far removed from the site of conflict.

Political differences are also a significant aspect of the internal politics of indigenous groups. Given the cultural diversity of indigenous people, it is not surprising that there is rarely a unified voice speaking on their behalf. The internal politics of the international, national, regional and local indigenous organizations are very dynamic and at times confusing. Such volatility is not attractive to the mainstream tourism trade, which prefers predictability and stability within its operating environments. Often there are two levels of governance in indigenous communities: one imposed by the dominant culture and one imbedded in the traditional practices of the community. Decisions made in the imposed governance structure are not always consistent with those made by traditional governing structures. Tourism operators must therefore deal with the reality of dual governing structures: one of which is an elected body while the other looks to the traditional guidance of elders, taking into account valued communal and kinship bonds, and processes of consensus building within the community. A good example of the problems that can arise from such a situation was presented by Sofield (1996).

Natural environment

The widespread destruction of natural areas throughout the world resulting from urbanization, pollution and unsustainable agriculture and resource extraction practices is actually increasing the value of many traditional indigenous lands (Stevens, 1997). Much of the traditional indigenous land near core development areas has been lost to expropriation, and indigenous people were often displaced to peripheral places that have since gained considerable value. By virtue of their undeveloped state, these lands are increasingly being prized as scarce resources that are attractive for nature-based tourism. They are likely to increase in value if the trend of worldwide environmental degradation is not dramatically reversed.

The traditional relationship between indigenous people and the land compared to non-indigenous people and the land is also distinct (Notzke, 2006). While most indigenous people 'believe they are conjugated inseparably with nature' non-indigenous people tend to see the land as a resource for human use (Gray, 1991; Hollinshead, 1992).

Many attempts to integrate indigenous people into prevailing wage economies have led to their alienation from the land with its consequent negative impacts. The ongoing settlement of Aboriginal land claims in many countries has resulted in increasing indigenous control of traditional lands. Greater control of the land base has allowed indigenous people to pursue land-based tourism as an attractive compromise between involvement in a wage economy and traditional subsistence practices tied to the land. Given the importance of this environment to indigenous people, any changes in environmental quality or control have significant implications on the practice of indigenous tourism (Gardner and Nelson, 1988).

Conclusion

One of the challenges for the editors of a collected volume of papers such as this is to capture the synergies so that the whole is greater than the sum of the parts. A variety of strategies have been used in this volume to capture these synergies. First, approximately one third of the papers contained in this volume were written by authors who contributed to the 1996 book. The majority of these authors have revisited and updated the topics and cases that they addressed at that time. Second, the introductory chapter highlights the common ground in terms of definitions and themes that are explored in more detail in the following chapters. Third, cross-references to other chapters have been inserted by the editors where they are seen to be particularly relevant. Fourth, a concluding chapter has been added to this book, giving the editors the opportunity to integrate the contributions of the individual chapters by highlighting the common implications, noting areas of concern not previously covered in the literature, addressing discrepancies that arise from the different contributions, and speculating on future issues and problems that bear consideration in the further development of indigenous tourism. A fifth strategy to capture the synergies of this collection of contributions is the organization of the volume into six key topical areas, each of which features a short introduction preceding each section. These sections are not exclusive but the contributions have been organized based on the editors' view of the key themes that emerge. These sections include: (a) indigenous knowledge and tourism; (b) indigenous commerce in tourism; (c) indigenous environment and tourism; (d) indigenous culture and tourism; (e) indigenous community-based tourism and (f) indigenous tourism: policies and politics.

This chapter has established a common ground for the chapters that follow. It accomplished this by drawing on the common ground established in *Tourism and Indigenous Peoples* (Butler and Hinch, 1996) and by extending it to reflect the evolution of this area of study since 1996. The rationale for studying indigenous tourism and the definition of indigenous tourism employed by the editors remains consistent with that provided in the 1996 publication. However, considerable modifications have been made to the indigenous tourism system model that forms a key part of the common ground outlined in this chapter. At the heart of these modifications is an increased emphasis on the role of culture and the cultural filters that create complexity thereby giving rise to the numerous debates that characterize indigenous tourism. In many ways, the chapters that follow are manifestations of these debates. Although each contribution represents a perspective that is specific to a particular time and place, there are common underlying themes, patterns and lessons that provide insight into indigenous tourism. Therein lies the primary contribution of this book.

This volume does not provide definitive truths about indigenous tourism, as given its complexity, few universal truths exist. It does, however, provide a diverse range of examples of indigenous tourism practices and perspectives from across the globe. Yet despite the geographic, cultural and topical diversity that is exhibited, common challenges and strategies for indigenous tourism emerge. Individual contributors to this volume provide a wealth of insight in their respective areas. As the editors, we have tried to organize and discuss the chapters in a way that captures the synergistic insights found in this collection of perspectives on tourism and indigenous peoples.

Part One

Indigenous Knowledge and Tourism

Introduction

Knowledge and values are the cornerstones for decision making in tourism development whether the decisions that must be made are as fundamental as whether or not to pursue tourism as a development option, or more of an operational nature such as how to implement tourism in an optimal and desired manner. Knowledge in this context is not only knowledge of indigenous peoples, as many non-indigenous groups are also involved in decisions about tourism. In the light of this, it is of critical importance for public sector agencies at all levels, as well as private sector operators and intermediaries, to be knowledgeable of the needs, preferences, and priorities of indigenous peoples. As well, it is equally important for indigenous peoples to be informed about tourism, as this is often a new experience for many, and the whole concept of tourism and travelling for pleasure may be strange to them (Berno, 1996). This section contains four chapters that examine cross-cultural perspectives of indigenous knowledge, research, and education as they relate to tourism. In the first chapter Butler and Menzies define traditional ecological knowledge and then go on to address the challenges and processes of incorporating this into tourism development. They use the example of First Nations in British Columbia and illustrate the ways in which such knowledge could be utilized in both the use and conservation of traditional resources and how traditional knowledge can itself serve as an attraction for tourists, while preserving the traditional values of the people involved. The second chapter by Berno builds on her chapter in the first volume and describes the issues involved in presenting tourism programmes in education and training to indigenous populations in the context of the South Pacific, an area where tourism pressure has been growing rapidly in the past decade. These first two chapters are followed by two chapters which deal with the problem of identifying research needs and development options for the public sector in terms of becoming involved in indigenous tourism. A key issue in this regard is how to successfully incorporate indigenous voices into tourism research upon which to build policy and planning for indigenous tourism, which is addressed by Williams and O'Neil in the context of British Columbia. The final chapter by Schmeichen and Boyle examines a similar problem in Australia, and reviews the progress made in this area over recent years in producing an appropriate and acceptable research programme to serve the needs of Aboriginal tourism. Both programmes are also concerned with the problems relating to developing culturally appropriate education and training programmes that disseminate this knowledge in appropriate and meaningful ways. Incorporating the indigenous voice and knowledge into these research programmes has been an essential feature in both examples.

CHAPTER 2

Traditional ecological knowledge and indigenous tourism

Caroline F. Butler and Charles R. Menzies

The dominance of Western knowledge in general, and modern science in particular, has come under increasing scrutiny and pressure during the last two decades. There is growing recognition that Western ways of knowing are socially constructed and influenced (Latour, 1999) and thus claims of greater objectivity and empiricism fail to support Western knowledge's continuing eclipse of alternative epistemologies. At the same time, there has been significant dissatisfaction regarding Western ways of understanding and managing the environment, accentuated by environmental crises and resource declines (see Rogers, 1995; Neis et al., 1999). The cultural and political rights of indigenous peoples have also been increasingly recognized both legally and in the public consciousness. These shifts have been influencing academic thought, the politics of knowledge and resource governance, and the practicalities of resource management. While scholars have long been interested in indigenous relationships with the environment, during the last two decades these practices and understandings have been studied more formally as traditional ecological knowledge (TEK), and explored as a source of alternative management and conservation approaches. This chapter will discuss the political and practical links between TEK and indigenous communities' participation in tourism.

Johnston asserts that 'many institutional barriers exist for indigenous communities innovating tourism products which *incorporate and/or support* the continued application of indigenous knowledge and technologies' (2000, p. 95, emphasis added). For tourism to be sustainable and amenable to indigenous priorities, its relationship to and incorporation of TEK is a critical issue. As ecotourism and indigenous cultural tourism gain increasing popularity in both alternative and mainstream tourism markets, questions of sovereignty and of environmental responsibility become increasingly pertinent. The unique relationship between an indigenous group and their territory, and the intimate knowledge the community has developed about their lands and resources, should serve as the basis for any environmentally sustainable and culturally appropriate tourism development.

To explore these issues and relationships, we will discuss the TEK and traditional management systems of the Gitxaała, a coastal Tsimshian nation in northern British Columbia, Canada. Menzies is a member of the Tsimshian nation and both authors have been working with the Gitxaała community since 2001. Five collaborative research projects have documented the ecological knowledge, and conservation and management practices of the Gitxaała people, in the prehistorical, historical, and contemporary eras. The Gitxaała, like other First Nations in British Columbia currently negotiating land claims, are exploring their economic development options, including tourism opportunities. We will argue that there are critical ways that Gitxaała TEK can and should provide a foundation for tourism development in the north coast of British Columbia.

Understanding TEK

The recent scholarly engagement with epistemological hierarchies has resulted in literature exploring the concepts of indigenous knowledge (IK), TEK, local knowledge (LK), and other similar terms labelling knowledges that have a subaltern relationship with Western 'modern' scientific knowledge. It is important not to overstate the differences between Western science and other knowledges, or to reify Western science, and therefore it is critical to emphasize the role of power in defining these categories. As Agrawal argues, IK is less substantively than structurally different from Western knowledge, and its locality is 'primarily derived from its peripheral relations to power' (1995, p. 187). Thus, the environmental knowledge of local lay persons, small-scale fishers, indigenous peoples is studied and discussed similarly in terms of its opposition to Western (scientific) knowledge. We can therefore understand the multiple acronyms, IK, TEK, LK, as part of a larger body of work developing 'alternative knowledge theory' (Butler, 2005, p. 8).

The increasing specific interest in indigenous and LK of the environment is the result of both political change and resource crises. Nygren links the development of LK research to globalization and increasing distinction between local and global as categories of experience (1999, p. 268). Blaikie and Brookfield suggest that the interest in local-level environmental knowledge is connected to the rise of political ecology as a theoretical movement (1987, p. 17). In Canada, research on indigenous-environment relations is directly linked to the recognition of indigenous rights; most early TEK studies occurred in northern regions for use in land claim negotiations (see Nadasdy, 2003). Research with the James Bay Cree, during the 1970s in the context of a major hydroelectric development that would flood their territory, made important links between cosmology and management practices (see Tanner, 1979; Salisbury, 1986). Land use and occupancy studies in Canadian arctic established the persistence of indigenous practices in contemporary management contexts. The value of local environmental knowledge research was reinforced by the collapse of the east coast cod in the early 1990s, as it became clear that small-scale fishers had identified the problem before government stock assessments called for a fishing moratorium (Finlayson and McCay, 2000).

Berkes (1999) defines IK as the LK held by indigenous peoples, with TEK as the ecological subset of IK, the land-based, practical knowledge of resource and the beliefs regarding human interaction with the ecosystem. He suggests that 'local knowledge' is a useful referent for more recent (non-indigenous) knowledge (Berkes, 1999, p. 8), and LK is often used when discussing small-scale fisheries (i.e., Ruddle, 1994).

While the comparative opposition of TEK and Western science tends to oversimplify the differences between these two ways of understanding the world, a summary of the lists of contrasting characteristics that have been generated by scholars in the field can aid in understanding the general tendencies of each approach, and the ways in which they become opposed politically in management settings. TEK is often characterized as qualitative, holistic, oral, intuitive, practical, and cyclical, whereas Western science is portrayed as quantitative, reductionist, textual, analytical, theoretical, and linear (see Wolf et al., 1991; Berkes, 1993; Berneshawi, 1997; Grenier, 1998). Such lists help us to grasp what differentiates TEK from the mainstream, dominant way of relating to the environment; however, it is important to note the more complicated aspects of these questions and to engage with emerging critiques of the early TEK literature.

While general traits of TEK can be identified, it is misleading to discuss it in this monolithic way. TEK is always embedded in a particular cultural and ecological context. Thus there are many traditional knowledges, and each one, while it may share traits with other traditions, reflects a unique way of understanding the world. Furthermore, Nadasdy (2003) argues that knowledge is a problematic term to use in the discussion of First Nations peoples' understandings of their world, constructing it as something that can be made separate from the social and cultural relations which shape it. One of the problems with research labelled as 'TEK' is that it constructs ecological knowledge as something discrete – which can be 'distilled' into a product that can be 'integrated' with Western science (see Nadasdy, 2003). Discussions of TEK and tourism must recognize the larger sociocultural and political context in which TEK is embedded – that knowledge is 'a way of life' (*op. cit.*, p. 63) and is based on both cosmology and experience. This is particularly important in the context of tourism planning and development with or by indigenous peoples.

Rather than focus on the 'traditional' nature of indigenous-environmental knowledge, a term that tends to relegate such knowledge to the past, it is important to emphasize that TEK is long term, cumulative, and contemporary. It is an ever-growing body of knowledge that develops over many generations and expands as new experiences are added to the community's tradition. TEK is dynamic: while its roots lie in a traditional lifestyle and practices, it adapts to changing circumstances and absorbs both new information and technology. Non-IK can be incorporated into TEK, expanding its scope (Ruddle, 1994), and each season of resource use increases the depth of this knowledge (Clayoquot Sound Scientific Panel, 1995).

TEK can adapt to new environmental, political, or economic circumstances and is thus 'an embodied practice directly rooted in everyday livelihood activities' (Menzies, 2006, p. 88). Furthermore, not only can IK provide the basis for tourism land use in a region, tourism can also impact that knowledge. Indigenous communities will develop and acquire new knowledge based on their experience of and the demands of the tourism industry.

The dynamic nature of TEK makes it historical; in a colonial setting like Canada it provides a historical understanding of the environmental changes that have resulted from industrial development during the last two to four centuries (see Butler, 2006). On the north coast of British Columbia, experience of a pre-European contact landscape is only three generations past – fairly recent in the deep oral history of the region. Pre-industrial levels of resource abundance and the impacts of changing technologies are part of the

TEK of this area. The difference between an 80-year-old person's fishing experience and a 20-year-old person's fishing experience can detail the significant environmental change wrought by the rapid expansion of the commercial fishery, for example.

This brings us to the issue of TEK differentiation. While scholars understand traditional knowledge to be the cumulative result of generations of local resource use, and thus having a communal nature, it is critical to recognize that knowledge is not homogeneous, even within the smallest indigenous communities. Social position, age, gender, personal history of resource use, area of harvesting, and other factors influence the particular knowledge held by an individual (see Butler, 2004, p. 38). Individuals thus draw upon the communal, cumulative knowledge of their people as transferred socially, the knowledge transferred to them directly by their family and community members, and the knowledge they develop through their own resource use practices. Thus, both elders and young people hold important but different TEK, as do men and women. It is important to address this knowledge differentiation when approaching TEK as a basis for tourism development, and as a resource for particular activities, such as guiding.

TEK is increasingly turned to for the improvement of resource management approaches as sustainability and conservation are inherent to traditional harvesting practices (Osherenko, 1988; Kuhn and Duerden, 1996). TEK's local specificity and detail can provide more successful and scale-appropriate management systems (Ruddle, 1994; Neis et al., 1999), as opposed to dominant structures which are externally imposed and rarely site specific. During the past decades TEK has become a mandatory information source for many government resource management structures in Canada, reflecting an increased recognition of indigenous sovereignty, despite the limits of these concessions (see Nadasdy, 2003; Butler, 2005). However, it is important to recognize that traditional knowledge systems have been impacted by the history of colonialism in all indigenous territories. In Canada and elsewhere, IK persists despite assimilationist government policies and the territorial dispossession of Aboriginal peoples, but such systems of belief and resource management have not been left unscathed by the changes brought by colonial settlement and governance. Felt, in his analysis of Newfoundland fishers' salmon knowledge, argues that researchers must pay close attention to the circumstances of knowledge production and the context of its use (1994). TEK cannot be approached as an apolitical issue. TEK research must recognize and explore the colonial impacts on indigenous territories and knowledge (Butler, 2006). The power relations between IK and Western science must be interrogated (Nadasdy, 2003). And finally, the investigation and utilization of TEK is a political act which recognizes indigenous sovereignty in land use and governance, and in education and research.

Thus, the inclusion of TEK in tourism planning and development can be decolonizing, supporting the expression of sovereignty and cultural revitalization in economic development. Engaging with indigenous environmental priorities, ecological knowledge and resource use practices can both improve tourism products and enhance the benefits to the community. Ignoring TEK and local resource management priorities and practices continues the pattern of dispossession and displacement associated with external development, by tourism as well as other forms of economic activity. TEK should be accepted as a critical component of environmentally sustainable, culturally appropriate, and politically progressive tourism development.

Gitxaała TEK

The following discussion provides a brief case study illustrating the potential links between TEK research and tourism planning. We explore the historical and contemporary use of TEK in an Aboriginal community in northwestern Canada and its relevance to the regional tourism industry. The material is drawn from a series of linked research projects with the Gitxaała First Nation, in collaboration with community elders and active resource harvesters. The names of research participants have been changed to protect their privacy.

The territories of the Tsimshian peoples stretch along the northern third of the coast of British Columbia, an inland approximately 150 kilometres. Tsimshian people live in the seven contemporary reserve communities of Lax Kw'Alaams, Metlakatla, Kitsumkalum, Kitasoo, Kitselas, Gitga'at, and Gitxaała; many also reside off-reserve in the northern towns of Prince Rupert and Terrace, and throughout British Columbia. Members of these communities share the common language of Sm'algyax. Each community manages its relationship with the state through an elected chief and council, but a traditional hereditary system of governance still thrives. The four matrilineal tribes, *Laxgibuu* (Wolf), *Gispudwada* (Killer Whale), *Laxsgiik* (Eagle), and *Ganhada* (Raven), are further divided into house groups or *wilp*, corporate units that own and manage the interlocking territories which tend to coincide with the watersheds surrounding salmon-bearing streams. The system of clan and house group ownership provides a structure for resource management based on hereditary rights.

Gitxaała territories stretch across a coastal archipelago, south of the town of Prince Rupert. Gitxaała people continue to use both the marine and terrestrial resources for commercial, trade, and subsistence uses. Their resource use is premised upon a conservative, need-based level of exploitation, which is supported by an intimate understanding of the local ecosystem. Harvest controls and intra- and inter-community distribution networks, combined with active habitat management and enhancement, have resulted in long-term sustainable relationships between human populations and local species and ecosystems. The Gitxaała people describe the social basis of sustainability through the concept of *'syt guulm goot'*, being of one heart. This type of social connection and interdependence is mirrored by an equivalent environmental ethic:

Certain fish camps caught certain fish [species of salmon] – some pinks, some dogs (chum), etc. Back in the village they would barter with each other so their diet was balanced. So they just took so much out of each creek.

Sam Campbell, 50 years of age

Before I leave, I find out who I want to help, who I want to give to. That tells me how much I need . . . you don't shoot animals you have no use for.

Jake Kinson, 28 years of age

Current tourism developments within Gitxaała territory are emerging out of the context of the diminishing local economic relevance and social transformation of the natural resource extraction industry. Developing in ways antagonistic towards Gitxaała approaches, British Columbia's industrial fishing and forestry industries of the past century and a half focused upon maximizing the rate of financial return at the expense of ecological sustainability. Recent economic and political changes have resulted in a significant decline in employment in these sectors that, coupled with rising 'green' sentiments globally, has created a favourable context for tourism development in the Gitxaała territories. The resulting tourism developments in the Gitxaała territories can be grouped into three basic forms: wilderness-based tourism (including sport fishing and ecotourism), heritage tourism (a focus upon indigenous and industrial history), and mass tourism (cruise ships).

Gitxaała TEK, which emphasizes social and environmental interdependence, and which promotes sustainable community-based resource use through the governance and management of small ecological units, can provide the basis for the development of positive tourism experiences in their territory. We have identified three key aspects of Gitxaała TEK which can shape and maintain sustainable tourism development: conservation, observation, and holistic resource use. These components of Gitxaała TEK can be linked to three forms of tourism in Gitxaała territory identified above.

Conservation

Gitxaała TEK, embedded in the social structure of property ownership and community cooperation, provides the basis for local conservation and sustainable resource use.

During the salmon fishing season, the number of fish harvested has always been tuned to the amount of spawners arriving at the mouth of the stream. The salmon-bearing streams were closely managed by the *smoogyit* (house leader, often translated as chief), who cleared debris from the streams before each season to improve the passage and spawning habitat. These practices continued well into the twentieth century, despite significant disruption from the imposition of colonial fishing regulations. Fish were traditionally harvested through the use of tidal traps at the mouth of creeks which allowed selective harvest by species and size, and according to abundance:

At the west coast of Banks Island they put a gate across a creek. They waited until the fish pooled and then let them up. Then they fished, and then they closed it again. They monitored – they counted the fish so they were taking a specific percentage of the run. At Lowe Inlet they walked up to the spawning beds to check constantly.

Leo Galbraith, 55 years old

Similarly, deer are targeted or left to increase, based on the community's reading of the population dynamics and rate of harvest. Wolves are culled if they are overly impacting the deer population, and deer have been transplanted to a predator-free island to create a population for future harvest:

I take does if I think there are too many for one area. I'll take some out. That's a deadly thing – too many does. It causes disease. I keep track of the number of bucks and does. How wide the valley is – is it big enough for all those does to survive?

Jake Kinson

My grandfather moved deer from Banks Island. We do that too. If we get small crabs in the trap, we put them in the lagoon there, trying to build it up. Me and my cousin have been doing that for a while. We throw the females over too.

Ben Smith, 35 years old

The tide line is used as a conservation boundary, and the harvest of many shellfish species is prohibited while they are under water to limit the percentage of the stock that is impacted by use. Spawning avoidance and other seasonal restrictions further reduce pressure on each resource.

Gitxaała TEK can provide the basis for the development of sustainable tourism in their territory. Specifically, consumptive tourist activities such as sports fishing and hunting that are part of wilderness-based tourism in the region can be informed by Gitxaała management practices and conservation priorities. There is a problem with the term 'wilderness' in that it presupposes a 'natural' landscape untouched by human hands. The term emerges from a European/Euro-American worldview that contrasts land that has been modified by direct human intervention with land that has not (or at least not apparently) been modified by human intervention. As our research in Gitxaała and that of others (see e.g., Deur and Turner, 2006; Langdon, 2006) has shown, the landscapes of Aboriginal North America were not 'pristine,' 'untouched' lands but rather were in large part the outcome of several millennia of human–environment interaction. The use of the term wilderness as untouched by human hands thus implies – for many non-indigenous people – the absence of any meaningful First Nations engagement with shaping the landscape. Despite these problems we have kept the term as it is one that non-indigenous people use to identify areas not obviously touched by European style developments. We would ask the reader to keep in mind that when we say wilderness we are fully aware that these lands were shaped and formed by several thousand years of indigenous practices.

Wilderness-based tourism in Gitxaała territories includes the commercial sport fishery, guided hunting, and ecotourism activities such as whale watching. For most of the twentieth century there has been some form of sport fishery in region; however, since the mid- to late 1980s this fishery has shifted from a family-oriented recreational fishery to a commercial charter fishery in which clients are recruited from across the USA and Europe. Within the sport fishing sector two primary modes of commercial sport fishery can be identified: luxury fishing lodges and charter boats operating from Prince Rupert.

Guided hunting, while not as prominent in the region as sport fishing, does play a modest role in the forms of tourism extant. Most hunting, however, remains an individual recreational practice and provides food for a range of households in the region (see Mattson et al., 2004). The primary trophy hunting enterprises tend to be based further in the interior of the province.

Ecotourism, the other major variant of wilderness-based tourism practiced in the region, has also been growing since the mid-late 1980s. Tours are primarily conducted by boat, with some kayaking expeditions, visiting wildlife sanctuaries to view grizzly bears, Kermode bears ('spirit bears' – the rare white variant of the common black bear), and orcas and humpback whales.

All of these tourist activities can benefit from the application of Gitxaała TEK. For consumptive activities, harvest limits can be set according to Gitxaała estimates of species abundance and vulnerability to predation. Extraction practices can be managed and regulated according to traditional structures, such as tideline conservation and in-season monitoring of harvest levels. Active management, such as creating or enhancing resource populations for harvest, can ensure sustainability of consumptive activities. The Gitxaała ethic of respect and non-interference can be applied to ecotourism and wildlife-viewing activities. Finally, the Gitxaała community members, particularly active food harvesters, are extremely knowledgeable regarding wildlife behaviour and movement patterns in their territories. They are well positioned to guide and advise the practice of all of these activities. Furthermore, participation in these activities can contribute to the ongoing accumulation and dissemination of TEK. Brody notes that for beaver (Dunne-Za) hunters in northeastern British Columbia, guiding 'requires and reinforces' many traditional skills (1988, p. 207).

Observation

A critical source of TEK and an aspect of its ongoing development and practice is the observation of the environment. Gitxaała people continue to closely monitor ecosystem health and resource abundance in their territories. They have observed cyclical changes of weather and climate, and the more dramatic changes resulting from industrial development in their territory during the last two centuries.

Gitxaała community members have worked with us to document environmental change resulting from both colonialism and climate change. Harvesters note that the seaweed season is beginning earlier in the year, due to warmer winters, and many suggest a similar pattern in the herring roe fishery. The length of the season for picking tidal resources has shortened, with cockles and clams spawning earlier. It has been observed that mussels have become more difficult to locate in Gitxaała territory in the last few years, and cockles have declined during the last two decades. In fact, most species harvested from the shore on a low tide have declined in abundance, and harvesters must travel further and further to supply their needs of clams, sea cucumbers, abalone, and octopus. Commercial harvesting of some of the resources by scuba diving is identified by Gitxaała people as the major issue in abalone decline and is considered a threat to other resources.

Gitxaała environmental observation can provide crucial monitoring of the impact of tourism and other industries on the north coast. The ecological impacts of increased boat traffic, including cruise ships and whale-watching tours, of ever increasing harvests of fish by recreational fishers, and of the establishment of fishing lodges in local waters will be noticed by the resources users who travel within their territory throughout the year. Recent agreements between coastal First Nations, including the Gitxaała First Nation, and fish farming enterprises working within their territory include clauses which require the farm to be removed if the community observes any negative environmental impacts. Tourism developments could be made subject to similar restrictions, requiring activities to cease or be modified should the traditional owners of the territory identify any reductions in resource abundance.

The application of TEK to monitor the environmental impacts of tourism is particularly relevant to the consumptive activities discussed in the previous section and also to the mass tourism that is a growing part of the regional economy. The development of cruise ship-based tourism is a relatively recent phenomenon in northern British Columbia, with cruise ships beginning to stop in Prince Rupert in 2003. In addition to the environmental impacts of the large ships themselves, there is an increase in day tours, by bus on the mainland and by boat (sports fishing and whale-watching tours) which also merits careful monitoring.

Holistic resource use

The ability to harvest and process local marine and terrestrial resources has been a critical part of Gitxaała TEK. Gitxaała families moved between several harvesting sites throughout the course of the year. The seasonal round began with herring roe harvest in March. Kelp and tree branches were placed in the water for the herring to spawn on, and the product was later dried. At this time other species were harvested including tidal resources, sea birds, seals, and sea lions. A major relocation was made in May to the seaweed camps on the outer islands, where seaweed was picked and dried, and halibut fishing was done. In June, extended families moved to the salmon fishing camps located at particular creek mouths, focusing on both subsistence and commercial salmon harvesting. Fish were smoked and dried, and later canned; berries were harvested in abundance, native plants were gardened, and deer and mountain goat were hunted. The fall was spent at the traplines, trapping fur-bearing animals such as mink, marten, and beaver, and hunting large animals such as moose, deer, and bear. The winter months were spent in the village, feasting and managing social responsibilities. While impacted by colonialism and industrial development in the region, most of these harvesting activities persist.

The relationship between Gitxaała people and their environment can form the basis for cultural tourism to the area. The wide variety of traditional foods, the fascinating means of harvest, and unique processing technologies will appeal to visitors with an interest in indigenous culture and to outdoor enthusiasts (see discussion of dual track tourism below). The contemporary diet of village residents includes significant amounts of food harvested from the neighbouring land and sea; this is TEK in practice, which can be observed, participated in, and indeed tasted, by visitors. A tour through an active smokehouse and sampling *woks* (dried halibut) or a nature tour exhibiting the deadfall technology used to trap marten can highlight Gitxaała traditional knowledge and practices, and their ongoing importance to contemporary community members.

Heritage tourism and particularly Aboriginal tourist products are an increasing focus of regional tourism enterprises. The North Pacific Cannery Museum is located on the site of a former salmon cannery in the mouth of the Skeena River, just outside of Prince Rupert. The museum, while facing chronic funding shortfalls, attempts to present the history of the cannery community and the industrial work process in a way that reflects historical accuracy and might appeal to the influx of summer tourists. There has been an increasing focus on Aboriginal material in the museum displays, recently including First Nations performances that portray indigenous connections to the river, rather than the participation of First Nations people in the canning industry. This First Nation programme interestingly reflects a shift towards TEK in the tourism product. As the museum plays to the interests of the increasing number of European and American tourists, including cruise boat passengers, indigenous histories and practices begin to eclipse the industrial history of salmon canning as a preferred attraction.

The Museum of Northern British Columbia has undergone a more complete transformation. Prior to the 1970s the museum was a classic curio cabinet museum with a combination of natural history and human history objects, later evolving through the introduction of dioramas of early European businesses and homes. The museum is now housed in a northwest coast style cedar plank and timber building in downtown Prince Rupert with a new focus on highlighting displays of local First Nations' history and culture.

Finally, new First Nations heritage tours are being developed in conjunction with the Museum of Northern British Columbia. Visitors can choose from a Feasting and Storytelling tour in a longhouse building, an archaeological walking tour of nearby island, and a kayaking tour that leaves from the dock of the Metlakatla First Nation reserve community across the harbour from Prince Rupert. These tours highlight the importance and relevance of First Nations culture in the region, and the latter two in particular draw on the TEK of the Tsimshian peoples.

Here Gitxaała environmental observation will provide crucial monitoring of the impact of tourism and other industries on the north coast. The ecological impacts of increased boat traffic, including cruise ships, of ever increasing harvesting of salmon, halibut, and rockfish by recreational harvesters, the establishment of fishing lodges in local bays, and whale watching stand to have a significant impact on the environment and the capacity of Gitxaała people to continue harvesting their customary foods. As tourism continues to expand and development it becomes ever more important that Gitxaała and other First Nations are directly involved in all aspects of the tourism trade.

Conclusion

There is an important opportunity for the people of the north coast of British Columbia to link tourism development with Gitxaała TEK. As we have documented in this chapter Gitxaała TEK contains values and principles of conservation, it involves processes of holistic resource use and relies upon an intimate observational relationship with the environment. This aspect of Gitxaała TEK creates an important pathway towards the economic development of unique tourism opportunities. By linking these values to the development of tourism, appropriate decisions can be made over the types of tourism to support that will employ Gitxaała people, support the continued use and development of their TEK, and result in ecologically sustainable economic development. The application of TEK in this location has obvious implications for indigenous tourism development in many other areas, with significant mutual benefits to both tourists and indigenous peoples. A report commissioned by Tourism British Columbia identifies a growing market for Aboriginal Cultural Tourism (Research Resolutions Consulting, 2004) (see also chapter by Williams and O'Neil, Editors' Note). The research indicates that 65% of such tourists desire experiences in remote settings, with wildlife viewing being the most popular outdoor activity for this market segment (ibid, p. 94). Other activities enjoyed by this group include hiking, whale watching, fishing, and wilderness camping (ibid, p. 97). Tourists with a focus on outdoor activities also show a desire to participate in Aboriginal Cultural Activities (ibid, p. 29). These trends have been identified as 'Dual Track' tourism, a market niche for Aboriginal tourism development in British Columbia (O'Neil Marketing and Consulting et al., 2005) and is an area where TEK can be easily utilized. Dual Track travellers seek both outdoors and cultural experiences (Research Resolutions Consulting, 2001, p. 2) and show an interest in natural wonders, historic sites, adventure activities, and other ways of life (O'Neil Marketing and Consulting et al., 2005, p. 11). This combination of interests and activities is ideally suited to the incorporation of TEK into tourism planning and the highlighting of TEK in the touristic experience.

The inclusion of TEK into tourism planning and development has both practical and political benefits. As suggested by the case study, on the north coast of British Columbia, Gitxaała environmental observation can provide crucial monitoring of the impact of tourism and other industries on the north coast. The ecological impacts of increased boat traffic, including cruise ships and whale-watching tours, of ever increasing harvesting of salmon, halibut, and rockfish by recreational harvesters, the establishment of fishing lodges in local bays, stand to have a significant impact on the environment and the capacity of Gitxaała people to continue harvesting their customary foods. As tourism continues to expand and develop it becomes ever more important that Gitxaała and other First Nations are directly involved in all aspects of the tourism trade to ensure environmental sustainability. The intimate knowledge of their territories positions Gitxaała people as the ideal guides and interpreters for visitors to the area, especially those with an interest in wildlife viewing and/or harvesting, and in the ways in which indigenous peoples have coexisted with the resources for millennia.

Finally, the recognition of and incorporation of TEK into tourism planning and development is crucial to ensuring that such developments are culturally sustainable, respectful of indigenous rights, and supportive of indigenous ways of life. Tourism, like other forms of extractive industries, contains within it positive and negative potentials for First Nations and the region. We use the term 'extractive industries' to deliberately draw a parallel with the region's history of resource extraction industries. While tourism is not classically about extracting natural resources for industrial processing it is 'extracting' experiences from the environment, local history, and local cultures in ways that necessarily transform them. Using TEK and indigenous rights as a basis for tourism planning can ensure that the industry is a decolonizing rather than recolonizing force of change, by establishing tourism enterprises that are based on indigenous values, priorities, understandings, and which provide direct cultural and economic benefits to communities.

CHAPTER 3

Doing it the 'Pacific Way': indigenous education and training in the South Pacific

Tracy Berno

> Educational programs for development must be placed in the context of their societies' needs and be interconnected with well conceived development plans. . . The onus is therefore placed on the hospitality and tourism education programs to demonstrate that knowledge benefits not only the individual who acquires it, but also the society of which he or she is a part (Hegarty, 1990, p. 41, quoted in Lewis, 2005, p. 5).

Introduction

To fulfil the human resource needs resulting from the growth of tourism demand, many developing countries have established tourism and hospitality training programs and institutes. In many instances, 'Western' models of education have been imported from Europe or North America (Theuns and Go, 1992; Craig-Smith, 2005; Lewis, 2005). This has led to programs that are oriented towards the management of 'Western-style' tourism and hospitality facilities, but applied to an indigenous context.

It could be argued that as tourism is an international 'industry' this primarily 'Western' perspective is appropriate for tourism education in both developed and developing countries. However, does this approach address the needs of sustainability, empowerment and self-determination of indigenous people? Is tourism education (both in terms of content and delivery) an etic (universal) field of knowledge, or does there need to be consideration given to the socio-cultural context in which it is delivered? This chapter considers these critical issues in relation to tourism development and indigenous people by addressing the need to consider the 'indigenous voice' in relation to tourism and hospitality education in the South Pacific region. This will be achieved through the consideration of the following: the South Pacific cultural and geographical context; how tourism training and education is currently structured in the region; characteristics of human resource development (HRD) and tourism education that are particular to the region; and the cumulative effect of these characteristics in providing a context from which a 'Pacific Way' for tourism education can be shaped.

In considering this push for indigenous tourism education in the South Pacific, emphasis will be placed on the need to include tourism education as part of a holistic and integrative planning approach. It is also suggested that within this framework, tourism education must be compatible with Pacific styles of teaching and learning, as well as balancing content and level of delivery to achieve a type of indigenous tourism education that supports the aspirations of Pacific Island people.

The South Pacific context

The island nations of the South Pacific are spread across 33 million square kilometres of the Pacific Ocean and include countries from all three of the major communities of interest: Polynesia, Micronesia and Melanesia. The close to 2 million inhabitants of the region represent a broad range of cultural, ethnic and linguistic backgrounds. These island states and nations also represent a cross-section of types and levels of development, colonial heritage, population types and densities, and physical geographies. In many ways, their only common feature is that they reside within the tropical belt of the Pacific Ocean.

In global terms, the South Pacific as a whole accounts for only 0.15% of the world's international tourist arrivals. This small number is enough for tourism to be the mainstay of the region's economy and to support an approximate 1,500 core tourism businesses. Despite the downturn in visitation to the Solomon Islands, Papua New Guinea and more significantly, to Fiji in 2000 and 2001 (and again in 2006, Editors' Note) (all due to political unrest), there were still approximately 1,180,000 international visitor arrivals to the region in 2004. Fiji and French Polynesia host the vast majority of these visitors with smaller, relatively inaccessible countries such as Tokelau and Tuvalu receiving a minimal number of visitors (Hopkins, 2004).

The World Tourism Organization is predicting continued growth in tourist arrivals to the region, with an expectation that arrivals will grow by 5% a year (World Tourism Organization, 2006). Concomitant with this growth in arrivals will be an on-going need for workers in every level of industry. Potentially, this increased need for human resources could provide the vehicle for enhanced educational and economic opportunities for Pacific Island peoples. However, to date, this has not been the reality for many indigenous people in the region.

Tourism education, human resources development and capacity building in the region

The state of HRD for the tourism sector in the region has been reviewed on several occasions (see for example Medlik, 1989; Dowse, 1994; King, 1994, 1996; TCSP, 1995, 1999; Burns, 1999; SPTO, 2002). Continuing interest in HRD needs in the region is indicative of the inherent challenges in trying to implement tourism training and education throughout such a large and diverse cultural and geographical area.

The South Pacific region requires a system of training and education that addresses the needs of the estimated 36,171–213,025 current employees in the travel and tourism industry (Milne, 2005), as well as the future needs of tourism. These wide-ranging estimates reflect the fact that there were no reliable secondary sources of data on tourism employment in member countries of the South Pacific Tourism Organisation (SPTO). In addition to the demand for labour, consideration must also be given to the large range of diversity in the region and the challenges of delivering the training across huge geographical distances.

Due to the vast distances between countries, limited transportation to some and limited access to communication technology outside of the main centres, strong connections between the public and private sector can be difficult to establish and maintain on a regional basis. Given the scope and scale of the region, no single organization can afford to employ enough educators to meet all the disparate needs of all areas of the tourism industry. Limitations to communications also pose significant challenges. Additionally, it cannot be forgotten that regionality itself is potentially problematic. On one hand, it is desirable to work collaboratively and collectively to optimize the use of training and education resources, but on the other hand, there is a sense that destinations are competing against each other for tourists. Notwithstanding any inherent concern about competition, given the particularities of the regional context, a cooperative approach to tourism training and education is required (Berno, 2001; SPTO, 2002).

The University of the South Pacific (USP), based in Suva, Fiji, is the only regional tertiary level educational provider in the South Pacific Region. The University's Charter, states that, 'The objects of the University shall be the maintenance, advancement and dissemination of knowledge by teaching, consultancy and research and otherwise, and the provision at appropriate levels of education and training responsive to the well-being and needs of the communities of the South Pacific' (USP, 2006).

The University, through regional stakeholder consultation, has identified the development of the tourism and hospitality field as one of the key strategic directions for the institution (USP, 1999). In order to ensure the provision of 'appropriate levels of [tourism and hospitality] education and training . . . to the communities of the South Pacific', it is essential to assess those needs.

Current tourism training and education in the South Pacific

Despite the importance of tourism to the region and the increasing demand for human resources, there exists a limited public awareness of the current and potential benefits of tourism. As such, there are relatively low levels of tourism training and education activities throughout the region.

The quality of the facilities and training across the region varies. Although there has been some improvement since a Tourism Council of the South Pacific (TCSP, now the South Pacific Tourism Organization – SPTO) study on HRD needs was undertaken in 1995, seven countries (American Samoa, Kiribati, Marshall Islands, Nauru, Niue, Solomon Islands and Tuvalu) still lack formal forms of tourism education, other than visits in the past from the SPTO mobile team (SPTO, 2002) and distance study through the USP.

Much of the tourism training in the region is undertaken at the pre-degree level in hospitality and catering schools and in polytechnics. This training focuses on the acquisition of vocational and trade skills, rather than a critical social scientific perspective or management concepts applied to the context of tourism. This 'front line' does little to address the serious shortage of regional management staff, and maintains the current status quo – a reliance on expatriates to fill these positions, with the majority of sub-managerial positions being filled by Pacific Islanders.

Most national tourism organizations (NTOs) also offer some form of tourism training and many major resorts offer in-house training to staff. Several countries in the region also have national training councils (NTCs) that offer short-course vocational training for the tourism industry.

Additionally, several national non-governmental organizations (NGOs) such as the Fiji Ecotourism Association (FETA), and regional organizations such as the South Pacific Regional Environmental Programme (SPREP) and the Pacific Asia Travel Association (PATA) offer short courses and workshops for the tourism industry. Finally, bilateral aid agencies (such as NZAid and AusAID) also play a role in the provision of community-based tourism training in the region (SPTO, 2002).

Characteristics of HRD and tourism education in the South Pacific

Irrespective of the level of delivery, or the agency by which it is delivered, there are particular contextual issues in the South Pacific that need to be considered in any discussion of tourism education and training. On the surface, the relevance of these issues to tourism education is not always readily apparent. However, they are issues that are integral to creating opportunities and equity for indigenous people in the tourism industry in the South Pacific. The nature of landownership in the Pacific is one such issue, as is the collectivist nature of Pacific society.

Land ownership in the Pacific is based on a collective model. Unless a rare freehold property is obtained, lands are leased from the collective ownership, with leases ranging from a few years to more than 75 years. Leases are encumbered with a range of conditions that vary depending on the particular country and the aspirations of the Land Owning Community (LOC). One of the areas that may be affected by this form of land tenure is employment, which is related to training and education. National law or local conventions may result in the situation where staff for tourism operations on leased land are recruited from the local LOC. Leases often have job rights attached guaranteeing the LOC jobs at the resorts and/or operations.

Although these contractual arrangements facilitate employment opportunities for indigenous people in the tourism industry, they may also act as barriers to employment at higher levels. For example, as jobs are available by right, motivation to attend pre-employment and in-service training can be negatively affected (SPTO, 2002). This lack of training can result in indigenous staff being concentrated at lower levels of the employment hierarchy. Additionally, even if staff are motivated to undertake pre-employment training, the remoteness of villages or offshore islands (where many tourism operations are situated) restricts access to training opportunities. Potentially, these contextual issues limit labour mobility and could impact on who will benefit from education and training (TCSP, 1992). Differing authority structures at the workplace and in the villages may lead to tensions. As a result, employees may also be reluctant to undertake additional training to enable them to move on to supervisory positions as it may challenge traditional village lines of authority (TCSP, 1992).

The cultures of the South Pacific are for the most part, collectivist, rather than individualistic in nature. These collectivist characteristics can exert additional constraints on opportunities for indigenous people in the tourism industry. For those in paid employment, there is often significant social pressure to share wealth with the extended family, or in some cultures, to make financial contributions to the church. These demands grow proportionally with increases in income. This pressure to provide financial support may at times act as a disincentive for indigenous people to take up paid employment in the tourism industry or to undertake additional training and education to support job advancement (TCSP, 1992).

If 'Western' models of tourism education and HRD are adopted without adequate consideration of these socio-cultural characteristics and the cultural context (an 'imposed etic') (Berno, 1996), there is a danger that indigenous people will fail to reach their full potential and achieve their aspirations. However, if the context in which the tourism education is to be delivered is considered, tourism training and education can become a means for the empowerment of indigenous people, as well as a means to contribute to self-determination and support the overall sustainability of tourism in the region.

Tourism education and 'The Pacific Way'

As discussed above, the need for HRD and capacity building in South Pacific tourism has been the subject of discussion and research for some time now. In response to these HRD needs of the industry, a range of providers exist throughout the region who offer tourism and hospitality education. Although this supply of educational programs helps to address the issue of sufficient capacity, the issue of how the current tourism and hospitality education curriculum can meet the deeper needs of the indigenous people of the region for sustainability, empowerment and self-determination still needs to be considered.

In her discussion of tourism educational needs in the small island developing states (SIDS) of the Caribbean, Lewis (2005) argues that SIDS present a distinct context for tourism education, and as such, the challenge presented is how to develop a tourism curriculum that responds to the threats and challenges posed by globalization in SIDS, whilst at the same time placing the curriculum in the socio-economic and cultural contact of the island destination. Conlin and Baum (1994) extend this challenge by suggesting that not only does the particular socio-cultural context need to be accounted for, in order to optimize opportunities for indigenous people within the tourism industry, a comprehensive, holistic approach to planning for tourism needs to be applied – one which integrates HRD and career planning as well as education. The following discussion will consider the need to position indigenous tourism education in the South Pacific within this broader planning context.

A holistic, integrative approach to indigenous tourism education

The case for the inclusion of indigenous people in the tourism planning process is well documented in the tourism literature. However, much of the emphasis of this inclusion has been to support a sympathetic understanding of the importance of tourism within the local community, often with the end objective to ensure tourism's success at the destination (Conlin and Baum, 1994). Conlin and Baum suggest that the positive impact of employment and career development for members of the local community often appears to be peripheral to the planning process, and when planning does incorporate considerations of employment, it is often restricted to the recommendation of the provision of education and training for the tourism industry. They go on to suggest that the emphasis on training for the development of lower-level skills and abilities for indigenous people in tourism and hospitality fails to take into account cultural and traditional barriers which could mitigate against indigenous people entering the tourism industry. Their argument warns that such an approach does not lead to empowerment and self-determination of indigenous people within tourism. In fact, somewhat paradoxically, it supports the status quo.

They suggest that there is a need for a holistic, comprehensive process to plan for the development of indigenous human resources in island tourism, one that considers and integrates five areas:

1 the tourism environment
2 tourism and the labour market
3 tourism and education
4 human resource practice in the industry
5 tourism and the community

Liu and Wall (2006) echo this call for the integration of tourism human resources in the context of policy trends within planning paradigms, suggesting that future tourism plans in developing countries should give greater prominence to the development of human resources in a way that enables indigenous people to participate in and benefit from tourism development in their region. They too suggest that HRD in tourism in less developed countries has been constrained by attempts to meet international service standards with a disregard for cultural sensitivity and adequate adaptation to local societal and cultural contexts (p. 169). This limitation has been reflected in on-going calls for greater involvement of indigenous people in directing, participating in and benefiting from tourism development. They go as far as to suggest that '[i]f tourism is really to be a "passport to development" and a means to enhance the lives of destination residents, then greater attention must be given in tourism plans to their needs and capabilities' (p. 169).

In the South Pacific, the lack of integration of tourism education, HRD requirements and tourism planning is evident in the wide variation in courses, content, hours and methods for delivery of the tourism training and education currently available. Each of the institutions that offers tourism qualifications sets their own competency standards and awards their own certificates, degrees and diplomas. There is a lack of consistency on both national and regional levels for these qualifications. This lack of standards limits labour mobility in the region, as well as creates barriers to academic progression from lower levels through to degree level. The problem is further exacerbated by a lack of coordination between government agencies (such as Ministries of Tourism and NTOs) and the Ministries of Education as to who holds responsibility for tourism education and training (SPTO, 2002).

Looking at it from a human resource perspective, one of the positive outcomes of adopting and applying an integrative planning process (both at the national and regional levels) is the development 'of' Pacific communities and not just 'in' them (Conlin and Baum, 1994). Such an approach provides the platform from which tourism training and education can be prioritized within the national budget and the national educational and tourism plans. As a result, the opportunity to enhance indigenous participation in tourism through broader educational opportunities is improved (TCSP, 1992).

Teaching and learning the South Pacific Way

Providing the opportunity for 'home grown' tourism and hospitality education within the South Pacific region is not adequate to address issues of low levels of indigenous participation. Cognizance must be given to the particular context in which the education occurs. Educators in the Pacific acknowledge large gaps between the culture of formal education, which is based mainly on colonial models, and the culture of the majority of indigenous students. This dissonance has resulted in teaching and learning difficulties, and in many cases, under-achievement. It is estimated that in most Pacific Islands countries, at least 80% of those who start secondary school in Form 1 do not achieve a school leaver's qualification by the end of Forms 5 or 6 (Thaman, 1993, 1997, 2000).

To address this gap, Thaman (2000) suggests that Pacific island teachers and students must 're-claim their education by looking towards the sources of their identities and developing philosophies and teaching and learning strategies that are rooted in their cultural values and practices' (p. 49). To achieve this, she suggests that higher education programs in the South Pacific need to take into account the culture from which students come – the ways in which they were raised and socialized – and value the knowledge that students bring to the educational setting (Thaman, 2000, 2004; see chapter by Butler and Menzies, Editors' Note).

In relation to tourism and hospitality education, the starting point for this consideration needs to be the very definition and experience of tourism and hospitality. As discussed by Berno (1996, 1999), institutionalized tourism is not an indigenous practice in the South Pacific. The way in which many indigenous people define or understand tourism, therefore, differs from what is commonly accepted in 'Western' tourism and hospitality curricula. Many, if not most, tourism students in the South Pacific have never been a tourist themselves. Many have never flown on a plane, eaten in a restaurant or entered a hotel lobby. However, there are traditional concepts of leisure, ceremony, celebration, travel and hospitality, which can be utilized to bridge the gap (Blanton, 1981). Using indigenous understandings of hospitality and personal experience as a platform, students can develop an understanding of tourist behaviour, the institutionalization and commercialization of hospitality, the nature of tourist–host interactions and cross-cultural differences (both tourist–host differences as well as national ones) (Blanton, 1981; Berno, 1996, 1999), as a means of understanding 'tourism' as practiced and experienced by visitors to the region. As suggested by an informant in Blanton's 1981 research, '. . .[in a developing country], one should start housekeeping training with the *concept* of a bed, not how to make it' (p. 111).

Balanced content: education *for* tourism and education *about* tourism

A holistic approach to tourism planning that integrates education with strategic HRD for empowerment of indigenous people, provides a platform from which the specific educational context of the South Pacific can be considered. However, the question of what general approach to tourism and hospitality education is the most appropriate for the South Pacific remains.

Botterill (1992) suggests that at the heart of the disappointment that many people have with tourism's relationship with education is the distinction that is made between education *for* tourism as opposed to education *about* tourism (p. 2). To make the distinction between these two approaches, the former, education for tourism, emphasizes courses in skill related areas of the tourism industry, typically with a management focus. The latter, education about tourism, considers the broader role and impact of tourism as a social phenomenon. This approach considers tourism as a tool for economic development, issues of cross-cultural understanding and the impacts of human activity in tourism on the socio-cultural and natural environments.

In a region such as the South Pacific, a strong argument can be made that there is a need for education both for and about tourism as part of the tourism curriculum. As King (1994) suggests, a blend of business studies and social sciences are helpful in developing an understanding of the impacts of tourism, as well as the techniques for the provision of high quality service at the destination. More importantly, however, a balanced mix of educational platforms addresses the critical issue of empowerment and self-determination for indigenous people in tourism. By providing business management education for tourism, indigenous people are empowered by the skills and abilities to plan, develop and manage their own tourism product. It helps avoid what Burns (1992) criticizes as '. . .education in developing countries. . .[that aims]. . .at producing compliant employees for an industry dominated by expatriate managers and transnational corporations' (p. 8).

By providing education about tourism that addresses critically the broader context of tourism as a social phenomenon, indigenous people are further empowered through the skills to promote self-determination in the context of tourism. Specifically, as Burns (1992) suggests in his consideration of the development of a new tourism curriculum in Papua New Guinea, '[i]f we recognize that tourism can sow the seeds of its own destruction, then we must also see that tourism education has the power to act as a regulating factor. . . [alerting] students to the problems of tourism while placing the problems in a specific cultural context. . .[thus challenging] the tourism myths which masquerade as convention wisdom' (p. 8). Burns goes on to suggest that this type of curriculum model, one which emphasizes culture and the fulfilment of indigenous needs, could be used as a paradigm for the evaluation and reorganization of other programs of study.

Education for empowerment: public awareness, vocational and professional, entrepreneurial

To further support the empowerment and self-determination of indigenous people in tourism, tourism and hospitality education should address four separate, but not mutually exclusive, levels of tourism education: public awareness; vocational skills training; professional management education and entrepreneurial development (Echtner, 1995; Kwmae, 1997).

Public awareness • • •

In the Pacific Island countries, like many other developed and developing nations, the tourism industry is not generally considered to be a mainstream career opportunity. It is often viewed as a short-term, transient type of work, with minimal financial and psychological benefits. This cynical view is exacerbated in many developing countries by the practices of multi-nationals, who give preference to expatriates for management positions, relying on indigenous personnel to fill low-level vocational positions (Conlin and Baum, 1994). Additionally, there is often little appreciation by locals of the importance of tourism to their region, and career opportunities within the industry. In the Pacific, this is exacerbated by a tendency to regard employment in the public sector and the professions as the preferred option for advancement. Tourism is not generally seen as a means to achieve the same ends (TCSP, 1992). To address these issues, Kwmae (1997) suggests that tourism education in the school system can play an important role in creating public awareness of tourism in general, its importance to a region, and it can provide an opportunity for moulding positive attitudes towards the industry and careers within it.

The Tourism Council of the South Pacific (1992) also suggests that tourism awareness should be incorporated into the primary and secondary curricula in the South Pacific as a means for not only increasing awareness and understanding of tourism in the region, but as a means to develop employment skills such as languages and traditional art forms (arts and crafts, dancing and similar cultural activities). It has also been suggested (South Pacific Forum Secretariat, 1998) that the foundation of a skilled workforce in tourism and hospitality is dependent on basic education. As such, they too have emphasized the need to address tourism education at the school level, both as a tourism awareness exercise, as well as reinforcing core skills to support HRD needs in industry.

Vocational and professional training • • •

With the rapid growth of tourism, in many developing countries, including those of the Pacific, there is a critical shortage of trained indigenous people, both on the front line as well as supervisory positions. Vocational training is essential to build a labour pool in support of these positions. As a complement to vocational training, there is a need for higher-level education (e.g., degree level) to afford indigenous people the opportunity to rise to management levels – positions that currently are often filled by expatriates.

Irrespective of whether it is vocational or professional tourism education, it is important that the content and delivery be contextualized and positioned within the culture and characteristics of the South Pacific. For example, the content of courses needs to recognize the unique socio-political and cultural aspects of the region as they relate to tourism. This is not just a focus on nationality or regionality. It needs to be a comprehensive consideration and incorporation of the developmental issues relevant to the region (Thaman, 2004). As Craig-Smith (2005, p. 369) suggests, 'Whilst in a global economy many skills and much knowledge should be, and is universal, an industry, and particularly the tourism industry, should be quick to adopt the "image" and "speciality" of the [South Pacific] locale.'

Entrepreneurial • • •

The forms of tourism education discussed above, public awareness, vocational and professional, are all concerned for the most part with developing the skills and knowledge required to *work for someone else* (Echtner, 1995). The last component of tourism education, therefore, addresses the development of skills and knowledge to *work for oneself*. It has been suggested that one of the most critical needs for tourism in developing countries is the fostering of entrepreneurship (Nehrt, 1987, cited in Echtner, 1995).

Echtner (1995) provides a range of salient benefits associated with indigenous entrepreneurship in developing countries. Along with the broader empowerment of indigenous people, these benefits include: greater economic payback and local control; greater use of local supplies; less negative socio-cultural impacts; more effective response to market changes, and cumulatively, the opportunity to enhance community stability.

That said however, there are contextual issues in the South Pacific in relation to entrepreneurship education that need to be considered. The characteristics of South Pacific entrepreneurs differ from those of their Western counterparts (Saffu, 2003). Saffu, using Hoefstede's cultural dimensions as a framework (including the dimensions of collectivism, power distance, masculinity/femininity and uncertainty avoidance), suggests that the set of characteristics for success in the Pacific is sufficiently different to that of the West that a different approach to entrepreneurial education is warranted.

Specifically, Saffu suggests that rather than teaching South Pacific entrepreneurs how to run their business as individualistic, risk-taking profit maximizing business people (the characteristics associated with successful entrepreneurship in the West), training should focus on providing skills that will help South Pacific entrepreneurs become more adept at manoeuvring the South Pacific cultural and business environment. An appropriately designed training programme should incorporate cultural nuances and norms, and focus on how entrepreneurs can be adaptable and flexible, with the ability to blend the modern and the traditional. Saffu also suggests that training should equip aspiring entrepreneurs with the skills that will enable them to meet traditional social and familial demands, while at the same time, meet their business goals.

Conclusion

Potentially, tourism in the South Pacific provides opportunities for indigenous people to engage in and benefit from the development process. A key issue underpinning this involvement, is the education and training they currently receive to support this engagement.

Like many countries in the developing world, the small island states of the South Pacific have been subject to educational systems adopted from previous colonial powers and/or external 'Western' models. Tourism and hospitality education is no exception. The continuing call for more indigenous involvement in the tourism industry is testament to the failure of the traditional methods of HRD and education to address the needs of indigenous people's aspirations.

This chapter has argued that providing tourism training and education alone is not enough to empower indigenous people in tourism. To fully support the aspirations of indigenous people, the education and training must build a platform of cultural and contextual understanding. In the South Pacific, this challenge involves establishing a 'Pacific Way' for the future of tourism education – one that supports the development of international skills and understanding, whilst at the same time inculcates and incorporates the unique features and characteristics of the South Pacific.

CHAPTER 4

Building a triangulated research foundation for indigenous tourism in BC, Canada

Peter W. Williams and
Beverley O'Neil

Introduction

North America has a long tradition of literature promoting travel to the far corners of the continent to experience the unique cultures of Aboriginal peoples (Albers and James, 1983; CTC, 1998). While such promotions have generated substantial revenues for many regions and businesses, most have created mixed and sometimes controversial outcomes for indigenous entrepreneurs and their communities (Laxson, 1991; Parker, 1992; Mercer, 1995; Butler and Hinch, 1996; Johnston, 2006). In Canada, market studies have empirically confirmed that learning about and/or experiencing Aboriginal and other indigenous cultures are of interest to a significant proportion of Canada's domestic and international travelers (Williams and Dossa, 1995; Williams and Stewart, 1997; Lang Research, 2000; Price Waterhouse Coopers, 2000). However, the extent to which this interest has translated into actual Aboriginal tourism incidence rates and market penetration is low (Williams and Dossa, 1999). The reasons behind this situation are complex, but relate to a lack of a comprehensive and co-ordinated commitment to developing and delivering such services. There is growing recognition that sustainable Aboriginal tourism development depends on establishing a realistic product–market match between what consumers want, what the travel trade believes is marketable, and what host communities and their entrepreneurs feel is supportable (Notzke, 2004).

This chapter describes a product–market match research program that shaped the foundation for a recently developed comprehensive *Aboriginal Cultural Tourism Blueprint Strategy for BC* (ATBC, 2006). It outlines a triangulated set of consumer, travel trade, tourism operator, and community-based research procedures and subsequent findings that informed the Strategy's development. In doing so, it contributes to a growing literature on emerging forms of Aboriginal tourism development in Canada and elsewhere (see chapter by Schmiechen and Boyle, Editors' Note).

Canadian context

Aboriginal tourism in Canada has longed been viewed as a source of potential economic growth and independence for many indigenous people (Native Council of Canada, 1987; Csargo, 1988; Tourism Canada, 1988; Government of Canada, 1989; Hinch, 1995; ISTC, 1996). However, in recent years the urgency of this perspective has been emphasized in both overriding public policy and tourism-specific planning initiatives.

At a national level, shifts in Aboriginal policy (e.g., Royal Commission on Aboriginal People, 1996) and Supreme Court of Canada legal decisions (e.g., Government of Canada, 1997) have quickened the devolution of power and responsibility for economic and social development from centralized government bureaucracies to more Aboriginally based institutions. Some of these Aboriginal stakeholders have flagged tourism as a vehicle for diversifying and strengthening traditionally remote and narrowly focused resource-based economies. They view it as a route to strengthening traditional values and creating new social opportunities for their people (Grinder, 1992; ABC, 1998; Doucette, 2000).

Complementing this growing interest, numerous policies and programs centered on building the capacity of Aboriginal peoples to develop, market, and deliver culturally appropriate tourism products and services have emerged. While little research has systematically assessed the efficacy of these programs, a growing academic and practitioner discourse suggests that Aboriginal tourism's long-term sustainability is dependent on the development of products and services that not only match with market preferences, but are also delivered by well-trained native operators and their partners in culturally sensitive ways (Angus Reid Group, 1993; Haywood et al., 1993; ATTC, 1996; O'Neil, 1996; Notzke, 2004). This involves creating an appropriate product–market match (ISTC, 1992).

Understanding what aspects of culture attract visitors, and what types of cultural products and services Aboriginal communities are prepared and able to provide is central to achieving an appropriate product–market match. From a demand side perspective, Aboriginal cultural tourism involves visitor attendance at cultural attractions (e.g., historic or heritage buildings, sites, monuments, displays; landscaped art or craft workshops or galleries; festivals/fairs; performing arts; and museums) controlled and managed by Aboriginal people. From a supply side viewpoint, it entails providing opportunities for learning about and/or experiencing local traditions, social customs, religious practices, and cultural celebrations. This includes supplying opportunities for first-hand interactions with consenting and informed Aboriginal people, obtained by either visiting their land or observing or participating in local customs, rituals, and other traditional activities (Conference Board of Canada et al., 1997).

British Columbia context

The province of British Columbia (BC) is known for the quality of its spectacular natural environment and increasingly for its diverse cultural mix – especially that associated with its rich Aboriginal heritage. For several decades, the province's destination marketing organizations have recognized the potential importance of this culture for tourism purposes (DREE, 1980; Nicholson Norris, 2001), but placed little priority on developing these opportunities in the marketplace. While there are 'success stories' illustrating that Aboriginal tourism can be systematically and beneficially integrated into the province's tourism management system, past levels of product development and associated market penetration are limited (Williams and Dossa, 1999; Mate, 2006). Most recently, increasing political momentum has encouraged Aboriginal, provincial, and federal government stakeholders to develop a research driven strategy capable of realizing the full potential of Aboriginal tourism in BC. The following sections describe how a combination of consumer, travel trade, tourism operator, and community-based research methods provided the information foundation needed for the development of this strategy.

Methods

A steering committee of Aboriginal and non-Aboriginal representatives from tourism industry organizations and government agencies in BC guided and monitored the entire research process. Chaired by the President of Aboriginal Tourism British Columbia (ATBC), it provided initial framing and scoping for the research, as well as on-going feedback concerning the outcomes and linkages between the various components of the investigation. Aboriginal members of this committee were especially valuable in identifying the most appropriate protocols and methods for accessing stakeholders who might 'sponsor' and/or facilitate the research process in specific Aboriginal regions. They also played prominent roles in identifying key issues to be explored in the data collection processes, and contextualizing the collective responses provided by Aboriginal respondents. The on-going dialog between this group and the research team produced a social learning environment in which all participants (steering committee and research team members) benefited.

The research team also was comprised of a mix of Aboriginal and non-Aboriginal members. The project manager and research team leader were both Aboriginals with extensive native tourism management experience. They worked closely with four non-native researchers familiar with policy, travel trade, marketing, and strategic planning issues confronting Aboriginal tourism development. Throughout the research process, the researchers used the services of a range of Aboriginals to organize and implement data collection procedures. This approach helped ensure the on-going trust and commitment of key Aboriginal stakeholders to the project's objectives.

The research employed a product–market match framework (ISTC, 1992) and triangulated research methods to establish priority actions for supporting Aboriginal tourism development in BC. The framework sequentially identified preferred Aboriginal tourism products and services as highlighted by tourists and the travel industry and, the willingness and capability of Aboriginal communities and entrepreneurs to deliver such experiences.

A triangulated approach to data collection and interpretation informed the research process (Opermann, 2000). Its selection came down to a question of pragmatism. No one method was capable of providing sufficient information to adequately confirm the most viable Aboriginal product–market matches. Through a combination of face-to-face interviewing, mail-back, and telephone surveying, as well as community and focus group dialoguing, a more comprehensive frame of reference for data gathering and interpretation emerged (Downward and Mearman, 2004)). The combined perspectives of the multiple observers using these methods helped to reduce the cultural biases and logistical limitations of single method forms of inquiry (Decrop, 1999). It also provided a practical means of cross checking one result with another, and increasing the trustworthiness of the findings (Decrop, 2004).

The product–market match frame necessitated that four interrelated research processes be conducted sequentially. Initially, the researchers conducted a two stage intercept and post trip follow-up survey of travelers in BC. This laddering method provided information on the trip planning, product preferences, trip behavior, product perceptions, future trip intentions, and socio-demographic traits of all travelers.

The initial intercept study collected the responses of 2,239 randomly selected travelers concerning their pre-trip, expected travel behaviors, and product preferences. Respondents completed face-to-face interviews using standardized questionnaires at a set of strategically selected Aboriginal and non-Aboriginal sites throughout the province. At Aboriginal intercept sites, indigenous interviewers informed the community about the survey objectives, schedule interviewing times, and collected questionnaire data.

Survey respondents (620) willing to participate in a post-trip follow-up 'online' or 'mail-back' survey provided information on their trip behaviors, exposure, and satisfaction with BC's Aboriginal tourism experiences, and intentions to include Aboriginal tourism activities in future provincial travels. Data collected identified Aboriginal tourism market penetration as well as consumer opinions of product awareness, preferences, satisfaction, and competitiveness.

The second research phase involved interviewing tour operators generating tourist traffic for BC from key domestic and international travel markets. These 34 tour operators were industry leaders selling pre-arranged travel packages directly via web based or traditional advertising, or indirectly through travel intermediaries. Their travel packages focused primarily on providing nature-based learning, cultural, and/or adventure-based products and services to travelers. Complementing the content of the consumer surveys, the standardized telephone interviews probed tour operator perspectives concerning Aboriginal products and services that might be internationally competitive and suited to integration into future tour operator marketing programs. This research phase also examined specific challenges and opportunities associated with incorporating BC-based Aboriginal tourism components into tour packages. These data provided critical perspectives concerning the requirements essential for integrating Aboriginal tourism into broader and influential travel marketing programs.

The third research phase identified the status of Aboriginal cultural tourism business development in BC. Indigenous interviewers collected data via telephone with Aboriginals owning and operating tourism businesses. The survey's standardized format probed the types of Aboriginal cultural products and services provided, operating and marketing practices, financial performance indicators, and prospects and constraints to development. Data collected from 85 Aboriginally owned businesses helped determine the 'market readiness' of existing Aboriginal tourism products and services, as well as identify the requirements to make them more economically and socially viable. Market readiness in this context referred to the extent to which existing tourism products and services met the expected standards of international tour operators interested in incorporating Aboriginal cultural tourism experiences into their travel packages.

Seven public forums and three Aboriginal tourism leader focus groups were conducted in various Aboriginal regions across the province in the final phase of the research. To encourage as much information sharing as possible, local Aboriginal family members arranged protocols and obtained permission to conduct the meetings, inform community stakeholders about research objectives and priorities, and encourage key informants to participate. These public forums attracted over 240 participants including a range of Aboriginal leaders, economic development officers, tourism operators, local government, and community representatives, as well as non-Aboriginal tourism destination marketing agencies, and human resource training personnel. The focus groups involved stakeholders (approximately 8–10 per session) representing Aboriginal business, cultural, and economic interests in each region. In all of these meetings, data collected from the preceding research phases informed the dialog that ensued. Following the completion of the formal forums and focus groups, less vocal stakeholders had opportunities to express their perspectives via fax, e-mail, and telephone venues.

Participants explored the overall willingness and readiness of Aboriginal stakeholders to embrace the development of specific forms of cultural tourism and identified issues and challenges to Aboriginal cultural tourism participation. The perspectives provided in these sessions offered valuable qualitative insights into the overall readiness of communities to develop products and services that matched with consumer preferences.

In combination, the diversity and wealth of data gathered via these multiple and complementary lines of inquiry informed the ensuing product–market match assessment. The following section highlights those findings that proved to be essential to the Aboriginal Cultural Tourism Blueprint Strategy's development.

Findings

Consumer perspectives

A full third of the travelers surveyed indicated they had either engaged in Aboriginal cultural pursuits during their visit and/or planned to do so within the next 3 years. This 'high-affinity' market segment included six niche markets expressing specific interest in various Aboriginal experiences related to heritage, outdoor adventure, festivals, handicraft and art, cuisine, and sport.

In combination, these 'high-affinity' travelers tended to seek unique destinations which increased their opportunities to experience and learn about different cultures, and enjoy pristine natural areas as part of larger touring trips. They expressed most satisfaction with those BC Aboriginal tourism experiences that involved viewing and purchasing authentic crafts, and touring museums and art galleries. Their most positive impressions were linked to opportunities to learn about the region's native cultures, experience the friendliness/receptiveness of Aboriginal people, and view and/or purchase Aboriginal arts and crafts. Compared to other Aboriginal destinations, they believed that primary competitive advantages of BC's native tourism experiences were linked to the quality and uniqueness of its Aboriginal arts, crafts, cuisine, and architecture; the willingness of Aboriginals to share their knowledge and culture; and the connections of Aboriginal culture to the region's natural environment. In contrast, they lamented the few opportunities that existed to experience Aboriginal performing arts, cuisine, languages, sporting events, and natural environments with native guides. Overall, they felt that opportunities to experience Aboriginal cultural tourism products and services were too limited.

Aboriginal cultural tourism business characteristics

The researchers identified 343 potential Aboriginal tourism enterprises in existing BC business directories. About 36% (123) of them participated in the telephone survey. Of these, 89% (110) were existing tourism businesses. About 77% (85) of them indicated that their businesses were at least 51% owned by Aboriginals and provided cultural tourism products and services as part of their operations. Several of these enterprises provided a range of cultural products and services within their operations. Aboriginal cultural components were most frequently associated with existing attraction (34%), adventure (31%), and tourism services (29%) operations (Figure 4.1).

Half (51%) of these businesses had incorporated cultural dimensions into their operations with formal approval from the appropriate band. In almost every case (90%), this approval was derived from 'elders' and/or other 'cultural keepers' in the community.

In the operating year preceding the survey, more than half these businesses (58%) reported they had earned a profit or broke even. Those businesses most likely to not have losses were attractions, owned by individuals, operating

Tourism industry sector	Percentage of Aboriginal cultural tourism operations providing sector products/services*
Transportation	13
Food and beverage	16
Travel trade	20
Events and conferences	22
Accommodations	24
Tourism services	29
Adventure	31
Attractions	34
n	85

Figure 4.1
Distribution of BC Aboriginal cultural tourism operations by industry sector

*Some business provided multiple products and services.

year round. Most operators were positive about their future prospects. Nearly 80% of them reported that their sales had remained the same or had increased since they started their businesses. A full three quarters (76%) of them indicated that they planned to expand their operations in the three years following the time of the interview.

The top three operating challenges they faced were related to limited marketing, human resources, and capital support (Figure 4.2). The challenges of limited human resource capacity were most apparent among businesses operating at a profit or breaking even. Limited access to capital was the leading impediment to economic success for businesses operating at a loss (Figure 4.2). Few of these businesses met market-ready travel trade business standards required for inclusion in broader marketing activities pursued by industry-based destination marketing organizations.

Travel trade perspectives

The business activities of the 34 tour operators interviewed were influential in generating about 50,000 visitors to BC in 2002. These travelers originated in Canada, United States, United Kingdom, Germany, Switzerland, Australia, New Zealand, Japan, and Mexico. While perspectives concerning Aboriginal tourism development opportunities and challenges varied between tour operators and the markets they served, several overriding commonalities were apparent. Those of most significance to the development of the Strategy related to trends in cultural tourism product preferences and marketing requirements.

Product preferences • • •

About 73% of the tour operators offered Aboriginal products and services in Canada. Almost 90% of them were favorable to expanding their portfolios to

Business challenge	Profit/ break even operations (%)	Loss operations (%)	Overall operations (%)
Limited human resources	69.2	57.9	65.5
Limited marketing	59.0	68.4	62.1
Limited capital	35.9	78.9	50.0
Limited business planning	23.1	5.3	17.2
Limited community/government support	20.5	21.1	20.7
Unfavorable Aboriginal business image	15.4	0.0	10.3
Unfavorable business location	12.8	15.8	13.8
Limited product development	5.1	5.3	5.2

Figure 4.2
Challenges confronting Aboriginal cultural tourism operations by economic performance

accommodate more of these products and services in BC. However, most (90%) indicated that this was contingent on such offerings matching the preferences of their clients, and the business expectations of their operations.

They believed their clients were seeking Aboriginal cultural tourism opportunities which incorporated:

- Guided adventures, wilderness, and wildlife viewing tours complemented with cultural interpretations provided by Aboriginal people.
- Authentic, hands-on, interactive tourism experiences incorporating opportunities to meet Aboriginal people engaged in the production of indigenous food and crafts; sample local foods; learn about community traditions, legends/mythology, art, culture, flora, fauna.
- 'Tastes' of Aboriginal culture incorporated into mainstream tours, as an enhancement and interpretation of broader travel experiences.

Marketing ● ● ●

Notwithstanding their optimism concerning market interest in Aboriginal cultural products and services, tour operators expressed considerable concern about the limited marketing sophistication of current Aboriginal tourism operations. They believed that opportunities to successfully deliver many of their potentially attractive product options were primarily constrained by limited:

- Aboriginal community and entrepreneurial awareness of the business requirements needed to be competitive in the cultural tourism marketplace.
- Tourist and travel industry marketplace awareness of available Aboriginal 'market-ready' products and services.
- Aboriginal human and technical capacity to respond to marketplace product inquiries and marketing requests in a professional and timely manner.
- Aboriginal strategic alliances with the 'mainstream' travel industry partners for product development and marketing activities.

Community forums and focus group perspectives

Participants in the community forums and focus groups were generally wary but predisposed to the development of Aboriginal tourism in their respective regions. Tourism development was viewed as a vehicle of providing opportunities for:

- *Economic development*: Offering communities and individuals opportunities for economic diversification, employment, entrepreneurship, training and education, and business linkages with external partners.
- *Cultural development*: Providing important means and motivations to care for and maintain local heritage and cultural practices, especially for Aboriginal youth.
- *Social development*: Offering their communities and society opportunities for cultural exchange, understanding, and learning.

- *Self-determination/control*: Providing younger Aboriginal people opportunities to pursue self-determination and control of their own economic and cultural destinies.
- *Political development*: Raising public awareness of issues and opportunities associated with on-going treaty negotiations associated with local governance, land ownership, wildlife and environmental management, and resource sharing.

Cultural product development opportunities deemed to be most in line with local capacities, cultural values, and community interests varied between regions. However, common interest existed for developing various forms of accommodation, authentic arts and crafts, heritage and cultural attractions, ceremonial events, eco and adventure tours, learning programs, performing arts, and cuisine for visitors.

Apprehensions concerning the development of such products and services in Aboriginal communities also emerged from these forums. The most prevalent evolved around the level of political and cultural will to undertake such initiatives, and overall community capacity to deliver market-ready products and services. From a political perspective, forum participants suggested that limited community understanding of travel market trends and product preferences, or tourism's potential benefits and costs existed. Focus group informants cited the challenges of intra-band politics and uncertain governance systems, as well as limited understanding of systematic methods for sharing culture in a tourism context as impediments to Aboriginal leadership approving the development of cultural tourism products and services.

From a capacity building perspective, community forum and focus group respondents collectively expressed concern over the currently limited ability of their Aboriginal communities to personally understand and share their cultures in appropriate ways; deal with the financial and bureaucratic requirements of banking and government institutions; attract and train staff to competently deliver competitive products; and arrange partnering alliances with broader tourism industry stakeholders. In response to these issues they suggested a range of policy and planning, management, and training-oriented capacity building initiatives that would improve their ability to meaningfully participate in Aboriginal cultural tourism.

Product–market match assessment

Using the preceding databases as a foundation, the researchers collectively conducted a product–market match assessment for each of the Aboriginal cultural tourism niches identified in the analysis of the consumer survey data. This iterative process involved highlighting and prioritizing areas for Aboriginal tourism product development and support. Figure 4.3 illustrates the strategic content included in this product–market assessment. In addition, a summary description of the festivals/events product–market assessment illustrates the reasoning behind priorities assigned to each product identified.

Product–market characteristics	Festivals/ events	Cuisine	Outdoor/ adventure
Market characteristics[a]			
Market preference for product (%)	79	74	71
Likely BC Aboriginal tourism trip within 3 years (%)	41	44	40
Top geographic market	Overseas 35%	Overseas 35%	Overseas 39%
Primary trip type	Touring 58%	Touring 58%	Touring 58%
Average daily trip party expenditure	$596	$525	$559
Recent trip use of generic Aboriginal tourism sites (%)	72	72	72
Frequency of 'high' satisfaction rating with overall Aboriginal tourism experience (%)	39	39	37
Average importance of specific product to future trip decision (scale scores ranges from 1=not important at all to 5=very important)	4.5	4.5	4.1
Average satisfaction with specific product experience (scale score ranges from 1=not at all satisfied to 5 = very satisfied)	3.5	2.9	3.1
Perceived limited availability of Aboriginal experiences (%)	56	58	55
Export-ready product characteristics			
Product abundance (L, M, H)[b]	L-M	L	M
Product geographic access	L	L	M
Reinforcement of product importance expressed in other market reports/databases	H	H	H
Travel trade compatibility			
Presence in current travel trade packages (L, M, H)[c]	L	L	M
Availability of product for future travel trade package development	M	L	M
Industry's perceived importance to future travel trade package development	H	H	M
Comparative advantage of product to options in competing jurisdictions	M	L	M
Aboriginal community compatibility			
Potential compatibility with community values (L, M, H)[d]	H	H	H
Potential compatibility with community economic development goals	M	H	H
Compatibility with community personnel capacity	H	H	M
Product–market match summary			
Overall importance to BC's future Aboriginal tourism competitiveness (L, M, H)[e]	H	H	M

[a]Based on data derived from BC Aboriginal Consumer Travel Market Surveys.
[b]Low (L), medium (M) and high (H) ratings based on BC Product Survey data, key informant interviews and document reviews.
[c]Low (L), medium (M) and high (H) ratings based on travel trade interviews, key informant interviews and document reviews.
[d]Low (L), medium (M) and high (H) ratings based on community focus groups, workshops, survey data, and document reviews.
[e]Low (L), medium (M) and high (H) ratings based on team assessment of overall compatibility with Aboriginal strategy goals.

Figure 4.3

Product–market match assessment summaries for select Aboriginal cultural tourism development options

Festivals/events product–market summary • • •

Aboriginal festivals/events product development options were assessed as being particularly compatible with the preferences of BC's Aboriginal tourism stakeholders. About 79% of the high-affinity Aboriginal travelers expressed an interest in experiencing such events during vacation trips to the province. They also spent comparatively more on their trips than other cultural market segments. While they placed relatively high importance on experiencing festivals/events, their satisfaction with the availability of such opportunities was much lower. Consumer perceptions of limited availability were reflected in the product survey findings. Festivals/events were associated with only 20% of the Aboriginal cultural tourism operations surveyed and were largely held in rural communities removed from most tourist travel routes. The fact that many events tended to occur during a single concentrated period early in the summer season, meant limited access by travelers. Furthermore, many of these festivals/events were not marketed to either tour or other travelers in a targeted fashion.

About two-thirds (63%) of the tour operators considered festivals/events to be important ingredients for future tour developments. In most cases, they were more interested in incorporating specialized events as opposed to festivals. Preferred options included visiting accessible Aboriginal communities and facilities where traditional dance, music, and food could be experienced in 2–4 hours programs. Tour operators had limited awareness of either current timing or public accessibility to such events. Most events were perceived by tour operators to be primarily for Aboriginal people.

Aboriginal communities and entrepreneurs expressed considerable interest in opening such festivals/events to broader markets. They felt this would provide community members with opportunities to share and promote their cultures within relatively controlled environments. From an economic perspective, they viewed such developments as a financially low-risk method for exploring the strengths and weaknesses of tourism for their communities; building up community infrastructure and personnel capacities; and, offering artisans more direct sales channels for their home-based products. Infrastructure development, human capacity building, and marketing costs were seen as primary constraints to developing and managing such events and festivals. Aboriginal stakeholders expressed a need for considerable capacity building support in order to realize the full potential of this cultural tourism product opportunity. Many of these perspectives were supported by Aboriginal festivals research findings conducted elsewhere (Hinch and Delamere, 1993).

Management implications

The triangulated approach used in this research not only identified a range of product and market opportunities that exist for Aboriginals in BC, but also a set of overriding management challenges that must be addressed before the full potential of tourism can be realized. These challenges relate to both product development and marketing initiatives. This section discusses these challenges and outlines elements of the Strategy which emerged to address them.

Product development

Travelers prefer Aboriginal products and services delivered within packages providing more individualized and spontaneous experiences. Ideally these experiences should be in areas with outstanding natural and cultural features, where opportunities to safely learn from Aboriginals in their 'own environment' exist. Many Aboriginal communities in BC have an abundance of the raw product ingredients needed for such packages. In some cases, they have already tied them together as innovative trip options (Coull, 1997). However, in many other cases, land and resource tenure, cultural understanding, and authenticity issues represent critical constraints to such product development.

Land and resource tenure • • •

The core attractiveness of Aboriginal tourism for most travelers involves experiencing local cultures in the context of outstanding natural areas. However, the ability of local Aboriginal communities to develop internationally competitive cultural tourism experiences in such environments is dependent on secure access and tenure to the land on which such products can be delivered (Hinch, 2001). In most cases, such tenure is uncertain due to on-going land claim negotiations. As a consequence, opportunities for Aboriginal product development are restricted. Settling land claims issues is a priority for sustainable Aboriginal tourism in BC (see chapter by Hall, Editors' Note). This research clearly indicates the importance of including tourism landscape values in negotiated settlements.

Cultural understanding • • •

Consumers and the travel trade express considerable interest in experiences which emphasize participation in interactive activities with Aboriginal people. Delivering such opportunities is a significant challenge for many Aboriginals. In too many cases, adult Aboriginals are still confronting and recovering from the effects of European colonization. Fortunately, the current generation of young Aboriginals demonstrate a strong and growing willingness to rebuild their confidence and rekindle many of their cultural traditions (McBride et al., 2002). Reconstructing these traditions and cultural value systems is not easily achieved. Much of their history is not captured in print. What is remembered tends to be recorded only in the oral traditions of a collective few. More must be done to sustain these collective memories so that the emerging youth in Aboriginal communities can clearly portray authentic depictions of their cultures to other community members and those travelers interested in understanding them (see chapter by Butler and Menzies, Editors' Note).

A growing number of these Aboriginal stakeholders supp
ment of a more holistic approach to cultural tourism – one wh
a combination of economic, social–cultural, environmen
dimensions. Typical product themes range along a contir...
which are primarily non-participatory in character (e.g., purchasing cratts,
clothing, and art from commercial galleries and studios), to those which entail
limited engagement (e.g., interpretation of heritage sites, villages, and events),
to those requiring full participation (e.g., wilderness hiking/hunting with an
Aboriginal guide and learning their customs, legends, and/or traditional
crafts by living in their communities). Those cultural tourism products which
require comprehensive participation have strong appeal with a small but committed proportion of the travel market, but are less attractive to the remaining
population. Less participatory forms of cultural tourism appeal to a wider
group of travelers and tour operators (Williams and Richter, 2002). Establishing an appropriate mix of temporally and geographically appropriate
cultural tourism experiences will require careful attention to the specific
capacities of the communities involved.

Authenticity • • •

A significant part of the market's appeal for Aboriginal cultural tourism rests
with its authentic dimensions. The market's preferences lay more with intimate and spontaneous cultural experiences as opposed to those which were
predominantly 'staged' and designed for larger audiences. This situation
places great responsibility on Aboriginal communities to protect the authenticity of what they offer to visitors.

In BC, most Aboriginal groups are guided in their collective actions by
principles linked to sacredness (spirituality), Mother Earth (natural environments), and elders (traditional wisdom) (Swinwood, 1998). Decisions concerning the development of cultural tourism experiences must be built on
these principles. In some cases, tribal elders have established that the marketing of crafts and artwork should be encouraged only when a 'certification
of authenticity' process has been put in place. In this way, an appropriate
'stamp of approval' indicating product quality and authenticity can be provided for all products offered for sale, and the integrity of the Aboriginal
tourism product and experience can be protected (Conference Board of
Canada et al., 1997).

Marketing

Current Aboriginal tourists seek:

- flexible travel packages that include options for varying levels of cultural
  engagement;
- tours that include but are not limited to indigenous destinations;
- trips they can plan prior to traveling;

- product information that creates awareness of the variety of safe, social, and adventuresome aspects of Aboriginal tourism;
- hassle free booking systems.

Currently, the capability and readiness of most Aboriginal communities to develop such marketing practices is constrained by limited awareness of product delivery expectations, scarce marketing capacity, and rare partnerships with competent and professional travel trade partners.

Reliability in product delivery • • •

For the most part, the marketplace wants meaningful interactions with personnel (preferably Aboriginal) who are well trained, educated, and experienced in working with tourists. From a purely administrative perspective, reliability means being able to provide rapid and responsive communication about product options and pricing, accommodation availability, and other more spurious travel planning information. Development of such communications capacities is an issue for most small- and medium-sized businesses, including those associated with Aboriginal cultural tourism. In many cases, cultural stakeholders are engaged in occupations and artistic endeavors which operate according to different rhythms and priorities – not necessarily linked to the needs of tourists. This is a challenge which only culturally appropriate customer-service-oriented training programs can address (White et al., 1998).

Aboriginal image realignment • • •

Stereotypical images of Aboriginal peoples and their lifestyles, which have little to do with current realities, still exist amongst many travelers. In some cases, these images create unrealistic expectations concerning the nature of the Aboriginal experiences visitors expect to encounter. Future marketing efforts should portray more realistic Aboriginal images which emphasize natural environment linkages and Aboriginal diversity (see chapters by Hollinshead for a further discussion on this issue, Editors' Note).

Natural environment linkages • • •

Amongst travelers, there is a strong affinity between the Aboriginal cultures and the natural environment. Images and activities linked to the use and management of the nature environment (e.g., canoeing, trekking, horseback riding, fishing, nature interpretation) and sustainable resource harvesting pursuits (e.g., fishing and forestry) create positive and contemporary images of Aboriginal peoples for visitors and local communities.

Aboriginal diversity • • •

There is a tendency for the travel industry to characterize all North American native groups with one broad stereotypical brush – similar values, beliefs, activities, and lifestyles. Future Aboriginal tourism positioning efforts should emphasize the distinctive lifestyles which characterize and individualize BC native groups. This will encourage travelers to increase their exposure and understanding to a range of Aboriginal experiences.

Strategic alliances • • •

Because of the often remote and frequently fledgling character of BC's Aboriginal tourism attractions, developing alliances with well-positioned, knowledgeable, and culturally sensitive tourism industry partners is important (Kelly, 2005). Such alliances shape the patterns of destination use, target markets attracted, and economic impact created for Aboriginal tourism operators and their communities. However, there is much debate concerning the distribution of power in such relationships. In some case, alliances may increase the risk of cultural commoditization and the loss of Aboriginal authenticity in tourism product offerings. This is especially the case when Aboriginal participation is viewed primarily as an 'added value' component of more mainstream tourism travel packages. Clearly, Aboriginal control over their land and cultural resources must be paramount, and the principles and values of the community must drive partnership relationships. The role of tribal elders in determining the extent and type of partnerships appropriate is critical for most Aboriginal communities.

Strategic directions

The *Aboriginal Cultural Tourism Blueprint Strategy for BC* (ATBC, 2006), emerging from the research summarized in this chapter, emphasizes the development and marketing of those options that match best with travel market preferences, Aboriginal community interests, and local capacities. It recognizes that capitalizing on such opportunities requires a long-term development program that is responsive to the needs of Aboriginal tourism communities and entrepreneurs. However, an overriding reality is that ultimately, appropriate matches between market preferences, community values, and local capabilities must be met before fully market-ready tourism businesses can be established.

The Strategy is driven by a vision of a '*vibrant and sustainable Aboriginal tourism industry that contributes to Aboriginal community health and well-being, respects First Nation's languages and culture, and ensures that the originators of the culture enjoy the benefits of Aboriginal tourism*' (ATBC, 2006). Strategic goals emanating from this vision focus on developing the capacities of Aboriginal communities and their stakeholders to establish and engage in businesses that offer culturally appropriate tourism products and services that are responsive to the needs of the travel industry marketplace. Recognizing the diversity in the quality and quantity of existing tourism experiences, the Strategy identifies specific product development, human resource capacity building, and marketing initiatives that should be implemented. The relative priorities of these programs vary depending on the extent to which regional and local Aboriginal tourism product development is at a 'Start-Up' (i.e., stakeholder interest in pursuing appropriate forms of development), 'Emerging' (i.e., appropriate business operating with clear product and management short-falls), or 'Market Ready' (i.e., appropriate business operating at travel market-place standards but requiring market development support) stage.

Conclusions

For most regions of Canada there exists only anecdotal and piecemeal information for building relevant Aboriginal tourism development strategies. Existing consumer market information provides a directional focus for planning and development at a macro level and is largely unsuited to regional or local application. Tourism travel trade expectations are similarly available at a national as opposed to provincial or regional level. Intelligence concerning the diversity of existing Aboriginal tourism businesses is growing, but is still undeveloped in terms of its marketplace competitiveness. Finally, the readiness and capacity of Aboriginal communities and their stakeholders to embrace Aboriginal tourism development is poorly understood.

The collective findings of this research suggest that as Aboriginal human and institutional capacity expands in BC, so will opportunities to capitalize on marketplace interest in Aboriginal cultural tourism. While a growing number of stakeholders are developing these capacities, still more must occur before the full potential of Aboriginal tourism can be realized. There is need to inform all stakeholders of the ways in which indigenous cultures and their landscapes create value for Aboriginals on and off reserve land.

From a methodological perspective, the triangulated research program described in this chapter provided at least three significant benefits to the Strategy development process. Firstly, the use of multiple lines of inquiry helped identify the existence of several reoccurring Aboriginal tourism development themes. By probing the same development issues with differing sets of informed stakeholders, greater clarity concerning 'marketplace' expectations, as well the extent to which existing Aboriginal community stakeholders were positioned to meet them emerged.

Secondly, the triangulated approach increased opportunities to gather pertinent information that has often been left uncovered in more traditional single research method applications. It required that data collection systems and schedules suited to the rhythms and preferences of travel trade, consumers, Aboriginal tourism operators, and local Aboriginal community stakeholders be employed. While this created some administrative challenges, in the end it generated a much richer and robust database than probably would have occurred using non-triangulated methods.

Finally, by selectively using a combination of Aboriginal and 'western' researchers to collect key components of the data, a greater and more comprehensive level of responses emerged. Several of these researchers were also engaged in the analysis and interpretation of the data. Their collective perspectives on the meaning of the data generated the critical insight and realism needed to effectively inform the Strategy's development.

Acknowledgments

This chapter is based entirely on research directed by a steering committee of individuals committed to the development of Aboriginal tourism in BC. Special thanks is extended to the Board of Directors of the Aboriginal Tourism Association of British Columbia led, respectively, by past and current Chairs Richard Krentz and Brenda Baptiste, and Executive Director Paula Amos. As well, the on-going commitment and professional support of Tourism British Columbia staff members Don Foxgord, Richard Porges, and Krista Morten, Project Coordinator Brian Payer, and Project Consultants Judy Karwacki, Kathy Holler, and David Russel were pivotal in keeping this research program focused, strategic, and credible. In addition, the authors thank the many Aboriginal stakeholders who graciously provided guidance and data collection support throughout this research program. Finally, special appreciation is extended to all of the respondents who unselfishly supplied invaluable information that formed the basis for the Strategy that emerged.

CHAPTER 5

Aboriginal tourism research in Australia

Joc Schmiechen and Alicia Boyle

Introduction

Aboriginal tourism research and development throughout Australian tourism jurisdictions has fluctuated markedly over the past 10 years. The Northern Territory was the first to recognise Aboriginal culture as a growing area of tourism interest, leading the way with the appointment of the first full time Aboriginal Tourism Development position in the Northern Territory Tourist Commission (NTTC) in 1984. Through the efforts of Chris Burchett, Aboriginal culture as a tourism product was exposed for the first time to international tourism markets. These efforts commenced with the International Tourism Bourse (ITB) in Berlin (1987–1991) and continued at the World Expo in Barcelona (1992), the World Congress on Tourism for Peace in Vancouver (1992) and with an Aboriginal Tourism road show to the USA (1993). Such exposure laid the foundation for the subsequent growing interest generated in Aboriginal tourism based in Australia.

The 1991 national report of the *Royal Commission into Aboriginal Deaths in Custody*, identified the tourism, cultural and pastoral industries as potential sources of economic growth and employment for Aboriginal people. The Northern Territory was again first to recognise the potential value of Aboriginal tourism and provided some of the first detailed analyses of the situation with a call for government action in *Aboriginal tourism in the Northern Territory – A discussion paper* (Northern Territory Tourist Commission and Northern Territory Office of Aboriginal Development, 1994). In 1994, the Federal Government dedicated fifteen million dollars towards the development of national Aboriginal tourism and cultural strategies, which after extensive stakeholder canvassing, were released in 1997. The resulting National Aboriginal and Torres Strait Islander Tourism Industry Strategy (NATSITIS) provided considerable focus on what was an emerging sector within the broader tourism industry.

NATSITIS provided the catalyst for a number of States developing their own Aboriginal tourism strategies and initiatives, with the Northern Territory, Queensland, South Australia and the Kimberley region of Western Australia leading the way. Soon it became apparent that the difficulties of developing appropriate product, the limited conversion from the market place and the tightening of available funding under a new Federal government would slow down the earlier momentum generated during the NATSITIS development process (Schmiechen, 2000).

The 2000 Olympics provided a resurgence of interest in Aboriginal tourism with the then Federal Tourism Minister, Jackie Kelly, lending strong personal support. Her commitment was mirrored by the leaders of peak industry bodies at the time such as the Tourism Council of Australia (TCA) and the Australian Tourism Commission (ATC). Focus on Aboriginal tourism became a significant feature of international trade shows such as the ITB in Berlin and the Australian Tourism Exchange (ATE). Aboriginal culture was increasingly recognised as one of the important features that differentiates Australia as a unique destination from its world competitors (Schmiechen, 1996, 2000; Morse, 2000).

In 2003 the Federal tourism minister, Joe Hockey commissioned a major review of the existing Federal tourism structures and directions. The result precipitated a significant restructure and a new strategy was detailed in *A Medium Long Term Strategy for Tourism – Tourism White Paper* (DITR, 2004a). This strategy identified Aboriginal tourism as a major special interest area and directed the new national tourism marketing body, Tourism Australia (TA), to take responsibility for leadership in this area. A key initiative was the establishment of Indigenous Tourism Australia (ITA) to spearhead a new national approach to furthering the development of Aboriginal tourism. The Department of Industry, Tourism and Resources (DITR) also retained some responsibilities for Aboriginal tourism and in 2005 initiated a $3.83 million mentoring programme, *Business Ready Program for Aboriginal Tourism* (DITR, 2004b).

At the 2000 Sydney National Aboriginal Tourism Forum the Sustainable Tourism Cooperative Research Centre (Sustainable Tourism CRC) recognised that there were considerable gaps in information, a lack of investment and little cohesion in Aboriginal tourism research. It saw a need to better harness the intellectual resources from both academia and industry to develop a clear strategic framework to address Aboriginal tourism research (Moore, 2000). This recognition commenced a process of consultation and collaboration with key stakeholders leading to the current initiative and the development of an Indigenous Tourism Research Agenda.

Aboriginal tourism has been subject to innumerable strategies and policy changes, most raising more hope than real action or outcomes. It remains an extremely fragile and tenuous sector of the tourism industry despite much of the marketing hype indicating otherwise (Schmiechen, 2000). In many ways a critical point has been reached as to how many of the fledgling and even established indigenous businesses can survive and become viable in an increasingly difficult tourism environment. There is now a greater need than ever for good leadership, clear vision, targeted support and a cohesive effort by all parties concerned to 'get it right,' and most importantly listen and act on the voices of those actually trying to do the business. Research has an important role to play in this endeavour.

The role of research

The value and importance of tourism research to provide strategic directions, underpin policy initiatives, guide marketing direction, evaluate products and performance has been well recognised by key government and industry organisations. In the past ten years this has been especially highlighted in the Aboriginal tourism sector (NTTC, 1996; Aboriginal and Torres Strait Islander Commission and Office of National Tourism, 1997a; Indigenous Tourism Leadership Group, 2003; Tourism Research Australia, 2004).

Boyle's scoping study on Aboriginal tourism research in 2001 and subsequent presentation at the Council for Australian University Tourism and Hospitality Education (CAUTHE) Con-ference in Fremantle, Western Australia in 2002, highlighted that there was a lack of research underlying the nature of

Aboriginal tourism in Australia (Boyle, 2002). The State, Commonwealth and Territory tourist agencies have focused primarily on product demand and visitor expectations with the main statistical information derived from the Bureau of Tourism Research (BTR) International Visitor Survey (IVS). These have proved to be imperfect tools at best (AGBMcNair, 1996; Aboriginal and Torres Strait Islander Commission and Office of National Tourism, 1997a; DITR, 2000; Indigenous Tourism Leadership Group, 2003; Colmar Brunton, 2004; Tourism Research Australia, 2004).

Most of the academic research has tended to be descriptive, mainly in the form of reports and conference papers with little in peer-reviewed journals (Boyle, 2002) and a small body of work in postgraduate dissertations. A common problem with this literature is that the research is often repetitive with a strong emphasis on evaluating visitor expectations and reactions to Aboriginal tourism experiences and most critically, few of the findings from these works are readily available or applied to the practical demands of doing the business of tourism. Boyle's study found that from 1992 to 2001 there were clearly identifiable gaps in providing further research or knowledge bases in the industry, agency and academic domains that needed to be addressed.

Above all there is a requirement for a more cohesive, cooperative and coordinated approach to meet the demand for accurate information. The Sustainable Tourism CRC and its partners aim to meet this need through the development and implementation of an Indigenous Tourism Research Agenda (see chapter by Williams and O'Neill, editors' note).

Consultation process

Boyle's definitive literature review in 2001 in the *Australian Indigenous Tourism Scoping Study* commissioned by the Sustainable Tourism CRC provided a comprehensive foundation underpinning the core priorities in this agenda. The literature review built on and made significant additions to Zeppel's earlier work (Zeppel, 1999) and the workshop report, discussion paper and final report brought together most of the past history of Aboriginal tourism research in Australia and engaged with a wide representation of the key stakeholders.

An Aboriginal tourism researchers meeting in Brisbane in 2004 also reiterated many of the key issues of concern and highlighted the growing interest in Aboriginal tourism research (Buultjens, 2004). Judy Bennett's (2005) authoritative work on Aboriginal tourism entrepreneurship also brought together many of the well-identified issues and focused on an area that had been much neglected. In combination, these contributions all provided the basis for the *Indigenous Tourism Research Issues Paper* (Schmiechen, 2005a) which extrapolated the key issues and provided additional information from current understanding and involvement with the Aboriginal tourism sector. This paper was circulated to representatives from the State Tourism Organisations (STOs) and other key agencies and organisations as well as a network of Aboriginal tourism researchers. The content was also presented at several Australian forums in 2005 including: CAUTHE Conference in Alice Springs in February

2005, Desert Knowledge Conference Alice Springs in February 2005, Australian Aboriginal Tourism Conference Perth in June 2005, Garma Festival Nhulunbuy in August 2005 and at the meeting of the Aboriginal Tourism Australia, STOs and agencies in Perth in June 2005.

Concurrently, an extensive consultation programme was undertaken with a range of Aboriginal tourism enterprises throughout Australia. This consultation process was often the first awareness Aboriginal people engaged in tourism had of what the research institutions were seeking to do for their benefit and that of the tourism industry. The key issues contained in the paper were discussed, explained and the feedback and comments recorded with additional follow-up taking place as required. This was a most important part of the project and provided the much needed connection to those actually engaged in the business of tourism.

A wide range of over 60 Aboriginal operators including community enterprises, family businesses and sole operators were consulted, both on a one-to-one basis and at a number of key industry forums, which helped establish sound links for future feedback and involvement. This direct input from Aboriginal operators addressed a major gap in the previous workshops and consultations during Boyle's 2001 scoping study. The comments and responses were used to articulate the *Draft Indigenous Tourism Research Agenda (unpublished)*. This draft document was presented for final comment and agreement at the meeting of STOs and agencies in Sydney in September 2005 as facilitated by TA.

Setting new directions

The *Indigenous Tourism Research Agenda* (Schmiechen, 2005b) sets out to provide a framework and direction to enable Aboriginal tourism researchers to focus their efforts on areas of need identified by a wide range of stakeholders with interests in the development and sustainability of Aboriginal tourism. In terms of timing, the agenda will be implemented over the next two years and then evaluated to determine its future directions and effectiveness.

The Sustainable Tourism CRC followed up its declaration at the Sydney 2000 National Aboriginal Tourism Forum to develop a cohesive national approach to Aboriginal tourism research. Partners in this venture included the Tropical Savannas Cooperative Research Centre (Tropical Savannas CRC), Desert Knowledge Cooperative Research Centre (Desert Knowledge CRC) and the NTTC. These partners bring with them strong existing networks and a commitment to furthering the social and economic development of Aboriginal people. Further partnerships and funding support will be actively sought to provide a truly national focus.

Resources of the key partners will be combined and directed to assist Aboriginal tourism researchers to deliver outcomes that directly benefit Aboriginal tourism enterprises. A key part of enacting this Agenda is to ensure greater participation and ownership by Aboriginal people in the research process and ensure there is ready dissemination of the findings to the 'grass roots' enterprises as well as to all key agencies and stakeholders seeking to support and advance this important component of the tourism industry. The Agenda builds on an extensive body of past work including a wide reaching consultation programme that identified the key issues. These have been grouped in a number of themes.

Research priorities

The following research priorities set out guidelines and direction for researchers seeking to engage with Aboriginal tourism research and draw on the support and resources of the primary stakeholders. It should be noted that the priorities are not meant to be prescriptive but rather to establish a framework for a more cohesive and targeted approach to research that will assist Aboriginal tourism businesses to deliver better business and commercial outcomes. In consultation with other major interest groups and organisations, it is hoped to make this framework the core of a national Indigenous Tourism Research Agenda.

In the consultation, all ten issues initially identified in the *Indigenous Tourism Research Issues Paper* (Schmiechen, 2005a) were deemed important and worthy of ongoing research. They are clustered into three broad themes covering the major issues of concern with some suggested areas for investigation. There are obviously linkages between each of the themes, indicative of the fact that Aboriginal tourism is highly dynamic with many complex parts that need to be considered as parts of a whole rather than examined in isolation. This approach is reflected by suggesting the need for a priority project to evaluate the present state of Aboriginal tourism through a series of selected strategic case studies.

These themes are by no means exhaustive and the proposed research should fall within the broader thematic parameters. The proposed framework will be appraised on its specific merit to deliver practical business outcomes to Aboriginal tourism ventures.

Theme 1: Land ownership, funding and value

Access to and control of the land are fundamental issues affecting many Aboriginal businesses and invariably they are directly linked to obtaining the capital resources to fund and sustain tourism ventures.

Land ownership • • •

Both the most recent consultation and ongoing comment from Aboriginal tourism operators associated with the development of the NATSITIS in 1997, stressed land ownership structures as the major issue inhibiting tourism development. The many different types of land tenure and their unique nature have generally restricted the levels of collateral available and led to a lack of access to finance that affects most business ventures (Burchett, 1993b; Finlayson, 1993; Turner, 1993; NTTC 1995; Boyle, 2001a).

In response to this issue, suggested areas for research investigation include: gaining an improved understanding of how the nature of current Aboriginal land tenure and ownership systems are acting as inhibiting factors for tourism businesses in their desire to seek access to capital for enterprise development and growth; evaluating alternative financing models; and determining how the uncertainty and short time frames for joint ventures on Aboriginal trust lands hamper potential investment.

Funding and value • • •

Most Aboriginal tourism businesses have been largely supported by funding through the Community Development Employment Program (CDEP), Aboriginal Torres Strait Islander Commission (ATSIC) grants and a range of Department of Employment, Education and Training (DEET) training funds (Boyle, 2001a; Bennett, 2005). Only a very small number of Aboriginal tourism businesses could survive and continue to trade without this assistance. This dependence places them in an extremely precarious position and takes little account of broader social values that may be the major return for this investment in what otherwise would be business ventures that are not commercially viable.

Investigating this issue would require examining a number of key areas including: the role of and inadequacies of the CDEP and how the programme could be enhanced and better utilised; the expectation by funding agencies that Aboriginal tourism businesses can and should be self-sustaining and determining what should be realistic time frames to achieve this; and gaining an improved understanding and recognition of the social benefits (better health, social and cultural outcomes) that society receives from government investment in Aboriginal tourism enterprises.

Theme 2: Business structures and skills

Community versus family and sole operator enterprises • • •

Tourism potential, aspirations and initiatives are seen as major factors in gaining greater economic independence, especially in rural and remote areas. Government funding support for Aboriginal tourism development has been almost exclusively directed towards community enterprises, which have had a very low rate of success (Altman and Finlayson, 1993; Burchett, 1993b; Pitcher et al., 1999; Bennett, 2005; Schmiechen (anecdotal information), 2005).

On the other hand, very little resource or support has been provided to family units or sole operators engaged in tourism. Most of these businesses have struggled with very limited assistance and virtually no access to government financial support, yet have shown much higher success rates than the community-based enterprises (Altman and Finlayson, 1993; Rooke, 1993; NTTC, 1995; Pitcher et al., 1999; Schmiechen (anecdotal information), 2005).

Bennett, in her recent work on Aboriginal tourism entrepreneurship states that,

> between 1988 and 1991 an average expenditure of $54 million was specifically directed towards community-based enterprises annually, and under ATSIC, during 1988–1989, 76.9% of funds released went to community-based projects' (Bennett, 2005, p. 25, cited in Arthur, 1991). 'This state of affairs persisted despite the numerous problems encountered with communal ownership. These included issues surrounding decision-making, limited accountability, and too many potential beneficiaries given the small scale of most enterprises and the tendency for community enterprises to be driven by social as well as economic objectives.
>
> (Bennett 2005, p. 25)

The apparent imbalance between the support provided to communities as opposed to sole operators or family enterprises has been voiced at numerous forums and in numerous strategies (Rook, 1993; NTTC, 1995; ATSIC, 1997a; Pitcher et al., 1999) and was further endorsed in the consultation process with Aboriginal operators.

This ongoing concern suggests the need to undertake a critical evaluation of Aboriginal community tourism enterprises. The reasons for their lack of success must be identified and guidelines developed to ensure their sustainable operation. Factors that have helped sole operators and/or family tourism enterprises in establishing successful tourism enterprises may provide some insights. Guidelines would assist policy makers and funding organisations to apply better business and funding models to Indigenous tourism enterprises most likely to succeed.

Ensuring succession, increasing participation and capacity in Aboriginal tourism enterprises ● ● ●

Many Aboriginal tourism ventures started with the underlying premise that the youth would follow and take up the running of the business. This was seen both as a means of cultural continuity and at times revival, as well as forging a better economic base to generate more sustainable and rewarding lifestyles. In many instances this has not been the case and numerous enterprises have faltered and closed because there was no viable ownership and management succession. Bill Haney's Land of the Lightning Brothers tour operation in the Victoria River District of the Northern Territory and Herman and Mavis Malbunka at Ipolera in Central Australia are typical examples. This has especially been the case where committed elders have not been able to recruit the next generation to take on leadership roles in the businesses created.

Even where Aboriginal groups have ownership, control or involvement in major tourism assets and locations there has been a very poor record of Aboriginal involvement in operations or management of the various aspects of those businesses. The Jawyon enterprise at Nitmiluk (Katherine Gorge) in the Northern Territory, Kooljamon Resort on the Dampier Peninsula in North West Western Australia and the Gagudju Association's hotel and tour operations in Kakadu National Park in the Top End of the Northern Territory are some prime examples of such difficulties (Schmiechen, 2000).

There is a need to examine the reasons and key factors that have led to the lack of succession by younger generations in tourism enterprises. The structural, educational, social and cultural factors that inhibit greater participation by younger people in Aboriginal tourism enterprises need to be investigated along with the role of mentoring, support and training programmes in order to determine the main factors that will help to gain better long term sustainability of Aboriginal tourism businesses. Researching the availability and relevance of tourism awareness and training programmes at primary and secondary school levels would be needed to further develop appropriate strategic guidelines to assist Aboriginal tourism enterprises to overcome these barriers (see chapter by Berno, Editors' Note).

Theme 3: Understanding the market

Engaging the domestic market and increasing its participation ● ● ●

Traditionally the main documented and acknowledged interest area for Aboriginal tourism has been the international market although this market is relatively small and location specific. Given this focus on external markets, there exists a lack of depth in understanding of the domestic market which, despite displaying limited interest *a priori*, provides a far greater number of tourists spread over a much broader regional footprint. Great gains could be made from better conversion of the domestic market which over the years has been believed to have an adverse reaction to engaging directly with Aboriginal tourism products (Miller, 2000; Perry, 2000; Tourism Queensland, 2000; Boyle, 2001a). This state of affairs has been exacerbated by the large degree of fragmentation in the efforts to provide a place for Aboriginal culture in conventional spaces visited by domestic tourists and recognise their overwhelming connections with mainstream holiday destinations and tourist routes (Schmiechen, 2004; Desert Knowledge Australia, 2005).

It is necessary to determine the key factors that are inhibiting greater engagement of the domestic traveller with Aboriginal tourism products. In the first instance, this insight would reveal what these consumers want and if this matches product availability. It is also important to examine the appropriateness of current marketing efforts, for the sake of adjusting messages about Indigenous tourism according to varying degrees of general awareness and information regarding living conditions, expectations and protocols regulating cultural exchanges in different locations. The latter would also inform the management and interpretation of Aboriginal cultural heritage, encompassing main cultural sites along the major domestic tourism flow routes and provide directions for specialised segments such as the four wheel drive market and the opportunities these present especially in the remote regions.

Accessing niche markets • • •

There has been a strong push in recent years to 'mainstream' Aboriginal tourism and encourage participation in the broader tourism opportunities rather than focus on the cultural dimensions (Boyle, 2001a; Indigenous Tourism Leadership Group, 2003; Miller, personal comments and conference presentations). Although the investigation of mainstream opportunities remains a relevant direction for Aboriginal tourism, the predominant opportunities are associated with the niche or special interest sub-markets (Burchett, 1993c; Schmiechen, 1996, 1997; Martin, 1997; TA, 2005). With the right location, good marketing and sound financial backing, Aboriginal tourism experiences can provide excellent opportunities, especially for the much sought after low volume/high yield market. This is exemplified by the success of Putjimira safari camp on the Tiwi Islands north of Darwin in the Northern Territory in the early 1990s and the current profile and success of the Gunya Tourism joint venture at Titjikala near Alice Springs in Central Australia.

Niche market penetration could be improved by assessing past efforts in markets such as the 'Not For Profits In Travel' market in the USA. Current trends and opportunities suggest that strategic targeting could be beneficial. It would also be constructive to examine the linkages between Aboriginal art and performance activities and develop a programme to capitalise on their exposure to entice travellers to experience the locations in which these originate; and to examine the opportunities presented by educational learning markets and devise means to devise appropriate product configurations for these specialised travellers.

Image presentation and definition • • •

The marketing of what is deemed to be an Aboriginal product, experience or 'flavour' often distorts and impedes the development of a wider range of Aboriginal tourism products by stereotyping a traditional cultural image that is not indicative of what is most readily available to visitors (Hollinshead, 1996; Schmiechen, 2000). The feeling that the 'real Aboriginal experience' is only available in the north of Australia remains a contentious issue and belies the fact that the natural environment is the most predominant tourism attractor (NTTC, 1995; Boyle, 2001a). Aboriginal tourism enterprises are more likely to gain better market share and recognition by adding value to the prime attraction of the unique Australian landscape and its exotic wildlife and presenting their special perspective on land, life and art (see chapter by Carr, Editors' Note).

Operators in various research forums and consultations consistently expressed their concerns with the way that imagery is used to market Aboriginal tourism. Typically, promotional materials present clichéd and stylised images that rarely reflects the diversity or the contemporary approach that characterizes a range of Aboriginal touring experiences (NTTC, 1995; 1996; Ahoy, 2000; Schmiechen, 2000, see also chapter by Hollinshead, Editors' Note).

As a result, there is a need to undertake a critical review and evaluation of current marketing images used by Federal, State and Territory tourism agencies and major product providers, and to determine guidelines for presenting a more balanced and accurate representation of what Australian Aboriginal tourism is and what it offers. This research should assess the nature, effect and impacts of how Aboriginal Australia is presented in various media, including newspapers, journals, magazines, film, video, guide books, as well as art and performance and explore how a more realistic and acceptable image could be presented to the public.

Accurately appraising the nature, extent and demand for Aboriginal tourism to differing consumer sectors • • •

The figures and statistics continually presented about the interest in Aboriginal tourism merit much greater scrutiny and need to be confronted with the actual commercial performance of sector players. The degree of proclaimed interest has never been reflected in actual uptake in established Aboriginal tourism businesses. The much used '80% interest in Aboriginal culture' for marketing to the international market is not reflected in the degree of visitation to even well-established Aboriginal tourism enterprises in Australia (Burchett, 1993b; Freeman, 2000; Pitterle, 2000; Boyle, 2001a; Schmiechen, 2004; Tremblay et al., 2005).

Obtaining accurate information requires: an analysis of the current methods of obtaining both qualitative and quantitative data for assessing interest and participation in Aboriginal tourism with a view to developing more appropriate methods and assessing the accuracy of these statistics against 'ground truthing' with major Aboriginal products. It would be useful to undertake comparative research on how the characteristics of the Aboriginal tourism experience in Australia relate to similar situations in other countries such as New Zealand, Canada and the USA. Special emphasis should be given to the relationship between data collection methods with perceptions of Aboriginal tourism interest and degree of uptake in relevant locations so as to develop more appropriate data collection methods.

Evaluating the current state and nature of Aboriginal tourism

A major outcome of the scoping study and workshops conducted by Boyle (2001a, b) has been the need to evaluate the present state of Aboriginal tourism at a National, State/Territory and local level and establish what has worked and what has not worked, the current stage of development, funding and finance issues, marketing strategies, technology use, skill base and capacity that resides within the businesses and, effectiveness of training and mentoring programmes.

The *Scoping Study Workshop Participants* (Boyle, 2001b) identified the lack of a clear benchmark picture of the actual state of Aboriginal tourism in Australia, especially which areas of enterprise have the best opportunities and viability in the present tourism environment. This has been further reiterated in 2005 at meetings conducted by TA with the STOs and key agencies. Little work has been done to evaluate the efforts of the past ten years in a cohesive manner and provide a real base of information to work with for the future development and sustainability of Aboriginal tourism.

Equally important is the lack of information and analyses on the ability of Aboriginal tourism businesses to become financially self-sustaining juxtaposed against the need for ongoing support that takes into account the positive social and cultural benefits such enterprises have for individuals and the wider community.

Case studies are seen as one approach to address this area of inquiry. Although this approach is not new, case studies constitute an important research tool, the value of which is enhanced if they are designed so as to provide comparable analytical methods and an integrated knowledge base. To address concerns such as those voiced by the Scoping Study workshop participants, the Indigenous Tourism Research Agenda ought to facilitate a series of strategic case studies using such a unified methodology and supporting the same business issues perspective. This case study programme ought to be managed with a tightly coordinated approach in order to provide a generic understanding of the essential factors that affect the viability and sustainability of Aboriginal tourism businesses. Identification of the primary drivers of business performance and sustainability in various Aboriginal contexts, could lead to the development of a nationally applicable 'diagnostic tool' for achieving better business outcomes for existing and future Aboriginal tourism development.

The next steps

The Federal Government in *A Medium Long Term Strategy for Tourism – Tourism White Paper* (DITR, 2004a) formed a new national tourism marketing body, TA. This body was given the task of helping ITA to spearhead a new national approach to furthering the development of Aboriginal tourism (Information about ITA can be found on their website at www.indigenoustourism. australia.com). This new body is currently engaged in discussion with key stakeholders at government and industry levels to formulate a new direction for Aboriginal tourism. Research has been identified as a major plank in developing this new initiative commencing with an Australia wide product audit and development of a more accurate national product database. It is essential that the directions taken by the University research sector be closely aligned with ITA's objectives through the Indigenous Tourism Research Agenda.

The Sustainable Tourism CRC is also engaged in developing a National Cultural Heritage Tourism Research Strategy and a National Sustainable Tourism Resources Programme as well as providing ongoing research support for Ecotourism. All have relevance and can overlap with Aboriginal tourism. It is desirable to adopt a coordinated approach linking tourism research in these areas.

Part of the Aboriginal tourism research project aims at maintaining and expanding an Aboriginal tourism research network that emerged in 2004. It is intended to take this effort beyond the boundaries of tourism faculties into other related disciplines such as natural resource management, business, social sciences as well as areas of interest outside the university sector. Such a network will become an important conduit for information exchange and a major vehicle in supporting the Indigenous Tourism Research Agenda.

To achieve a truly national approach it is imperative to engage with other key organisations and groups that have important roles in furthering Aboriginal interests even if they have no specific connections with tourism or even business development. The Australian Institute of Aboriginal and Torres Strait Islander Studies, the Australian Aboriginal Training Advisory Council and the Centre for Aboriginal Economic Policy Research at the Australian National University are a few examples of organizations holding relevant capabilities and research interests.

The wider tourism industry, as well as key sectors of corporate Australia, have ongoing interests in improving the quality and uptake of Aboriginal tourism initiatives and the consequent benefits this can have in improving Aboriginal livelihoods and wealth creation. Their support will be actively sought to provide resources and assistance to help achieve practical outcomes for Aboriginal tourism enterprises through the Indigenous Tourism Research Agenda.

Last but most importantly, the voice of Aboriginal tourism operators need to be an integral part in driving the Indigenous Tourism Research Agenda forward. The initial contacts established through the consultation period need to be developed and nurtured with sound feedback and honest interactive exchanges to achieve better outcomes for Aboriginal tourism.

The challenge is in large part for existing and future researchers with interests in tourism or in Aboriginal economic development to use a more coordinated approach while applying their capabilities, knowledge, skills and resources to build a more integrated research base relating to the issues discussed above. As the Indigenous Tourism Research Agenda is explicitly concerned with business aspects of cultural and economic Aboriginal life, it is critical to ensure that research outcomes find their way to industry and further the viability of Aboriginal enterprises involved in tourism thereby contributing to the sustainability of the wider Australian tourism industry.

Part Two

Indigenous Commerce in Tourism

Introduction

As many tourism texts state, tourism is a major economic activity at the global scale, and its economic benefits are what drive most efforts focusing on the development of tourism. It can be a powerful tool in national, regional and local development, and as noted in the introductory chapter to this volume, may be one of the very few ways of allowing some indigenous groups to become economically empowered and thus move towards control of their own destiny. While tourism may be proposed as offering a variety of benefits and costs, it must be remembered that it is a commercial activity and indigenous tourism, like every other form of tourism, is characterised by basic issues of commerce. The scales at which such operations exist vary widely, as do the markets and impacts. The first chapter in this section explores the nature of tourist demand for indigenous tourism in New Zealand. McIntosh and Ryan examine the elements that make up this demand, commenting on the relative lack of useful market research information for indigenous operators. They note five key dimensions of the tourist experience in the context of Maori cultural tourism offerings and the complexity of relations between indigenous groups and tourists in terms of their varied cultural backgrounds. They note also the lack of knowledge of tourists about Maori culture and the absence of information before they arrive in New Zealand, which affects expectations and behaviour, but indicate that there is considerable potential for further development of indigenous tourism where desired by local groups. The second chapter in this section by Goodwin focuses on one of the major global goals for the millennium, the reduction of poverty and the potential for tourism to assist in achieving this goal. He notes that poverty alleviation is not always the same as economic development and that utilising tourism to reduce poverty among minority indigenous groups presents different problems, in particular ensuring that benefits accrue to those most desperately in need of economic improvement. Goodwin notes the lack of detailed information on the benefits to marginal indigenous populations resulting from tourism development and draws heavily on applied research reports and surveys, particularly from African studies, to elaborate on this problem. He concludes with a review of key strategies needed to ensure that the benefits of tourism make a positive difference to poverty-stricken groups. The final chapter in this section illustrates the other extreme of indigenous tourism development, by exploring reactions of non-indigenous neighbours to two mega-projects in the United States, first nation owned casinos in Connecticut. The spread of commercial gambling on Indian reservations has been one of the major developments in indigenous tourism in the last two decades, and the economic returns have been massive. Such dramatic and rapid large-scale developments have resulted in a range of perceptions held by the surrounding non-indigenous community as Carmichael and Jones illustrate. While few appear to be opposed to the beneficial impacts of the casinos on the indigenous populations, the lack of involvement in their planning and development and concerns over employment patterns are significant concerns to the residents of neighbouring towns. As with all forms of economic development, tourism attracts both positive and negative reactions and can deliver costs and benefits at a wide range of scales.

CHAPTER 6

The market perspective of indigenous tourism: opportunities for business development

Alison J. McIntosh and Chris Ryan

Introduction

Despite the increased focus given to indigenous tourism in public policy and academic literature, tourists' perspectives of indigenous tourism remain under-researched (McIntosh, 2004). Yet, public policy frequently calls for the increased participation of indigenous peoples in the tourism industry, as well as the increased development of indigenous cultural product. In New Zealand, for example, the New Zealand Tourism Strategy 2010 has called for 'increased participation of Maori throughout the (tourism) sector' (p. i), building 'Maori capability', providing 'greater resourcing and support for the sustainable development and management of Maori tourism' (p. 32) and developing 'Maori tourism product' (p. 32). Tourism is viewed as a major source of potential economic growth for Maori communities in New Zealand because in the past: (a) Maori have experienced many of the social and economic problems evidenced by other indigenous communities around the world (Mitchell et al., 1992; Ryan and Crotts, 1997) and (b) have a history of involvement in tourism, particularly the Te Arawa peoples in Rotorua since the mid-nineteenth century. Consequently, market perspectives of indigenous tourism yield important information for the economic development of indigenous communities; notably for indigenous business and product development, especially in relation to the search for new commercial opportunities to attract new audiences and for extending the tourism season. Indeed, the benefits of a consumer-focused approach to tourist attraction management are widely acknowledged (Beeho and Prentice, 1997; McIntosh, 2004). Visitors to indigenous tourism attractions can also gain increased awareness, understanding and appreciation for indigenous cultures and the situations of indigenous peoples on major issues. This benefit can contribute to a more equitable relationship between indigenous and non-indigenous peoples (Sofield, 1991; Pearce, 1995; Butler and Hinch, 1996; McIntosh and Johnson, 2004).

Until recently, the lack of market research available to help Maori tourism businesses in New Zealand adapt, develop and market their products to meet identified demand has been notable. Given this dearth of information, the aims of this chapter are to synthesise and examine the nature of demand for Maori tourism in New Zealand. Previous market research will be referred to demonstrate the importance and interest shown by international tourists for consuming Maori cultural products or attractions, and their perceptions and experiences of those attractions and of Maori culture. Comparisons will also be drawn with market research elsewhere to examine whether the sorts of experiences gained by tourists in New Zealand are similar to those gained from other indigenous cultures or indigenous products. Implications will then be considered in relation to opportunities for indigenous commerce.

The nature of Maori tourism business in New Zealand

It is not the aim of this chapter to describe in detail the nature or scope of Maori tourism in New Zealand; as this has been discussed in other sources (see e.g.,

Ryan, 1997, 1999). However, a discussion of the types of experiences provided for tourists visiting New Zealand provides a context to the conclusions presented in this chapter. Maori involvement in the tourism industry is rapidly increasing, especially compared to non-Maori involvement (Ministry of Tourism, 2004). Generally, Maori involvement in tourism in New Zealand has been categorised as entertainment, arts and crafts, display of *taonga* (see Glossary at end of the chapter for italicised words), cultural interpretation and accommodation operations (Barnett, 2001). Overall, there appears to be reasonable demand for Maori cultural experiences and products in New Zealand (McIntosh et al., 2000; Colmar Brunton, 2004). Maori products are thus an important focus for tourism activity in New Zealand. In 2004, a total of 74,711 international visitors to New Zealand attended an 'organised' Maori event, with 306,470 (or, 29.7% of all international visitors) recorded as attending a Maori cultural performance (Ryan and Higgins, 2006). According to Colmar Brunton (2004), an overnight stay at a *marae* has low participation rates; potentially due to issues such as awareness, perceived lack of comfort and fear of the unknown. However, visiting a *marae*, sites important to Maori history, and Maori cultural performances were activities on which visitors spent more than NZ$ 100. The sorts of experiences of Maori culture gained by international tourists were therefore mainly related to cultural product and performances; arguably, products specifically created for commercial ends (McIntosh, 2004). Official visitor statistics exclude cultural interpretations that add value to tourism experiences, such as Maori perspectives of a guided tour of a region, as well as experiences of the everyday lived nature of Maori culture as *whanau*, *hapu* and *iwi*, including informal chatting or encounters between visitors and Maori. As such, studies such as those by Ingram (2005), McIntosh (2004), McIntosh and Johnson (2004) and Ryan and Higgins (2006), have sought to record qualitative understandings of tourists' experiences of Maori culture.

Most previous market research on Maori tourism has concentrated on demand arising from the international market. It is generally accepted that interest and participation levels in Maori cultural products and experiences among the domestic market are lower than those for international tourists. For example, whilst 32% of international tourists surveyed by Colmar Brunton (2004) had visited a *marae*, only 3% of domestic travellers did the same, and, whilst 45% of international travellers surveyed had attended a Maori cultural performance, only 2% of domestic travellers said they had done likewise. Because of domestic travellers' awareness, perceptions and the relatively short time frame of their vacation, it is argued that there is not the same potential to increase domestic travellers' participation in Maori cultural products as with international tourists (ibid). Ryan (2002) notes that in New Zealand it might be said cultural difference and spatial proximity co-exist in a tourist system determined to a large part by supply for an overseas demand, and thus within New Zealand there is a co-existence of separateness between domestic and international tourism. Nonetheless, any potential to increase the engagement of the domestic market with Maori cultural products and experiences remains an important opportunity, not only for tourism, but also on a wider social stage.

Understanding international tourists' demand for indigenous tourism

Market research into international tourist demand for indigenous tourism remains somewhat piecemeal. Published academic studies tend to have differing agendas, including the views of tourists at specific cultural attractions (Moscardo and Pearce, 1999; McIntosh et al., 2000; Ryan and Huyton, 2000a, b, 2002; Ryan and Higgins, 2006), issues of authenticity (Daniel, 1996; Moscardo and Pearce, 1999; McIntosh and Johnson, 2004), tourist knowledge and perceptions (Dann, 1994; Milne et al., 1998; Notzke, 1999) and tourists' reactions to and satisfaction with indigenous experiences (Husbands, 1994; Milne et al., 1998; Notzke, 1999). In addition, there are consultancy and government research reports that remain unpublished in the scholarly tourism literature (e.g., Finlayson, 1991; Lang Research, 2000; NTTC, 2000; Colmar Brunton, 2004). In New Zealand, it has been argued that the lack of appropriate and recognised Maori tourism definitions has contributed to measurement difficulties and resulted in a paucity of research data on Maori tourism and Maori tourism businesses (Stafford Group et al., 2001; Kanara-Zygadlo et al., 2005). However, previous market research suggests that a high proportion of visitors to indigenous attractions in New Zealand have also experienced indigenous attractions in other countries (Moscardo and Pearce, 1999; McIntosh et al., 2000). Unfortunately, this research has not culminated in a substantive collective body of knowledge that can be used to inform indigenous business and product development, or sustainable indigenous host–tourist relations.

Issues for discussion

The following questions are important for understanding the demand for indigenous tourism among international tourists. To what extent are tourists motivated by indigenous tourism? What levels of interest do tourists hold for certain types of indigenous tourism products? What are the main indigenous tourism activities that tourists engage in? What are the reasons for visiting/not visiting indigenous tourism products? What perceptions do tourists hold of indigenous cultures and of cultural products? In relation to other heritage tourism products, for example, ecotourism attractions, tourists are frequently seen to consume products out of their search for novelty, spectacle and gazing on difference, rather than the search for formal understanding (Urry, 1990; Ryan et al., 2000; Schanzel and McIntosh, 2000). As such, in many instances, tourist demand is seen as superficial, generalist, stereotypical and embedded in the search for the 'exotic' or 'primitive other' (Cohen, 1993; Taylor, 2001). What this means for tourists' consumption of indigenous tourism products and their interaction with indigenous peoples needs careful attention in the pursuit of sustainability.

As mentioned, McIntosh (2004) has advocated an experiential approach to understanding tourists' perspectives of indigenous tourism as tourists interpret the environment and host communities they visit in their own personal ways. Indigenous cultural experiences are subjectively consumed and negotiated in terms of tourists' prior knowledge, interests, expectations, mythologies and personal meaning, rather than by the cultural offerings of the destination (ibid). Indeed, Colmar Brunton (2004) confirm the Maori cultural offerings with which tourists reported most satisfaction are those where there was physical or emotional involvement with the particular activity being experienced, such as being able to talk to or interact with Maori performers. Furthermore, the element of learning or experiencing difference to everyday life was noted as being essential to the visitor's sense of knowing more about the Maori cultural experience. It is important to note, however, that indigenous value and belief systems are difficult for outsiders to understand. The Maori of New Zealand have a spiritual and symbolic bond with the environment; they perceive humankind not as separate from the environment but as part of an indivisible whole. The *mauri* is 'the life that is shared by all objects, animate and inanimate, the state of being, the interconnection between things that exist' (Ryan, 1997, p. 275). Spiritual and cultural values and beliefs are dynamic and may even evolve within indigenous communities themselves (Hollinshead, 2006). As such, focus on the nature of interaction being experienced through indigenous tourism is important for product development and promotion, and opportunities for raising cultural awareness among travellers.

Experiential approaches

It is important from an experiential perspective to understand how tourists experience indigenous cultures in differing contexts; whether in the formal setting of an indigenous tourism attraction, more generalist interaction, chance meeting with indigenous people, as an added-value experience at a 'mainstream' tourism attraction/activity, as added-value interpretation such as in a museum, through the symbolic purchase of authentic indigenous arts and crafts or souvenirs, or, through formal participation in authentic cultural experiences or dance. Many studies only consider visits to specific cultural products (e.g., Colmar Brunton, 2004). Market research generally reports that indigenous culture is not a major motivation for visiting a destination (Lang Research, 2000; NTTC, 2000; Ryan and Huyton, 2000a, 2002; McIntosh, 2004), but instead, constitutes an important part of a visit. Indigenous culture is viewed by tourists as a major 'point of difference' in the total experience of a destination. And indeed, the majority of tourists visiting New Zealand do expect to experience something of New Zealand's Maori culture (Colmar Brunton, 2004). Respondents in McIntosh's (2004) study reported that the activities they most intended to experience included a visit to a Maori 'dance or concert/ performance', 'visiting a *marae* or Maori community', 'buying Maori arts and crafts' or 'sampling Maori food'. Furthermore, Colmar Brunton (2004) similarly found that the majority of potential travellers to New Zealand expressed an interest in visiting a *marae* (56% of all potential travellers), participating in Maori cultural performances (44%), visiting sites important to Maori history (43%) or going to exhibitions of Maori history (39%). Activities preferred by travellers commonly include those that emphasise a point of cultural difference. For the most part, these attractions represent the traditional products or staged experiences of Maori culture. Authors such as Ryan and Huyton (2002) and McKercher and Du Cros (2002) have suggested that this may also result from tourists' search for experiences that are entertaining as opposed to more intellectual forms of experiencing host culture.

In her study of tourists' expectations, motivations, perceptions and experiences of Maori culture in New Zealand, McIntosh (2004) found five central dimensions of experience from which tourists reportedly appreciated Maori culture, namely *gazing, lifestyle, authenticity, personal interaction* and *informal learning*. These dimensions provided information in relation to the types of experiences demanded by tourists and the ways they preferred to experience Maori culture. They were also found to be similar to conclusions drawn in previous research concerning tourists' experiences of other indigenous cultures (e.g., Moscardo and Pearce, 1999; Pitcher, 1999). Of particular note, the study provided evidence to show that the experiences demanded by tourists generally constituted the desire to 'gaze on difference' through the viewing of indigenous culture in a fairly shallow, easy to consume experience; although this conclusion requires validation with respect to different contexts and among different market segments. Furthermore, the study found that tourists sought the opportunity to see how Maori people live in everyday life, for example, by visiting a Maori community or *marae*, or through personal interaction; in other words, by experiencing indigenous culture in a more authentic setting or more genuine 'less commercial' encounter than existing product offerings may currently provide. Craik (1997) has cautioned, however, that although tourists want authenticity, most require some degree of 'negotiated' experience from which they can selectively sample certain experiences to promote enjoyment. Ryan and Higgins (2006) have suggested that the authenticity demanded by tourists is more to do with the sense of staging induced by the environment in which the activity takes place, rather than the nature of the performer or performance itself. In relation to expressed demand for authenticity, tourists also appear to value that the arts and crafts they purchase are Maori made, and to have an interpretation or Maori perspective provided on guided tours presented by a Maori guide; thus placing importance on the authenticity of value-added cultural experiences.

From a review of previous studies, other commonly reported findings yield information to support suggestions that whilst tourists' awareness of indigenous cultures is generally high, many tourists' specific prior knowledge of those cultures is rather low (Dann, 1994; NTTC, 2000; McIntosh, 2004). Often, tourists' awareness of indigenous cultures emanates from sources such as the *Lonely Planet Guide* and film or television. Yet, tourists are very rarely found to search for specific information on an indigenous culture prior to their departure. Tourists' impressions of indigenous cultures prior to their arrival at a destination are generally traditional and somewhat stereotypical (Silver, 1993; Ryan and Huyton, 2002; McIntosh, 2004). In examining tourists' perceptions of Maori culture, McIntosh (2004) found that the most frequently reported words used by tourists to describe their impressions of Maori culture were stereotypical and traditional in nature; including, 'rugby', 'All Blacks', '*haka*', 'painted faces' or 'face tattoos', 'warriors' and 'tribal image', 'mostly black/dark skin colour' and 'concert or dance performance'. Interestingly, most of the tourists interviewed by McIntosh (2004) did not feel their impressions of Maori culture changed after their visit to New Zealand, although slightly more respondents did indicate that they may have received a more contemporary and less stereotypical experience and impression of Maori culture during their visit to New Zealand. It appears likely, therefore, those stereotypical impressions of indigenous people and their culture may to some extent be reinforced by tourists' experiences of those cultures; potentially due to the nature of the existing tourism product and generalist motivations among tourists. Furthermore, the spatial and cultural distance between host and tourist is likely to affect the depth of understanding and appreciation that tourists can gain of an indigenous culture. For example, it is unlikely that tourists will ever be able to fully appreciate the affective and spiritual dimensions of Maori culture, or of tribal differences.

As mentioned, tourists rarely make specific enquiries about how to experience these activities prior to their arrival in New Zealand. Furthermore, with the exception of overnight stays on *marae* and *marae* visits, intention to pre-book and pre-pay for Maori cultural products is generally low. Most information is gained through tour operators, travel guides or brochures and information centres in the host destination (Colmar Brunton, 2004; McIntosh, 2004; Ryan and Higgins, 2006). Yet, intention to experience Maori culture is high amongst international tourists, and a significant proportion of tourists indicate that they would have liked to have experienced other aspects of Maori culture but had not had the opportunity. Reasons why visitors do not experience Maori culture included it had not been 'what they had come for', 'lack of time', 'not aware that it was available', 'didn't know enough about it', that 'not everything was open', or, 'that they felt they had already seen it before' (Colmar Brunton, 2004; McIntosh, 2004). Indigenous tourism experiences may also be perceived as 'one-off experiences' by tourists during a short length of stay (Finlayson, 1991; NTTC, 2000; Ryan and Huyton, 2002; Colmar Brunton, 2004; McIntosh, 2004). There is an opportunity therefore to raise greater awareness of Maori cultural products among travellers during their pre-trip planning so that they know what is possible to see/do with a considerable degree of detail and breadth. For example, the highest participation levels in Maori cultural experiences in New Zealand are in Rotorua and Northland; regions notable for their associations with Maori history, and also the locations of the majority of Maori tourism products available in New Zealand (Colmar Brunton, 2004). Conversely, some local areas that are saturated in Maori history remain unknown as sites of rich cultural experience. Therefore, among tourists, there is perhaps a lack of awareness of the opportunity to experience Maori culture in certain parts of New Zealand. Studies by McIntosh (2004) and Ryan and Higgins (2006) found that tourists reported this to be the case for the South Island of the country.

Variations in the demand for Maori cultural products and experiences among different market segments are also an important consideration. Colmar Brunton (2004) highlighted that international tourists visiting New Zealand from the United Kingdom, Germany and the United States, those who stay longer in New Zealand (more than 6 weeks), and those in the 55–64 years age group tend to be more interested in participating in and/or experiencing Maori cultural products. The New Zealand Ministry of Tourism (2004) similarly found key differences between the characteristics of international tourists who experience Maori cultural activities. Whether these general differences remain apparent among tourists' experiences of Maori culture in a holistic sense remains to be examined.

It is suggested that past research into visitor perceptions of indigenous people's product is divided into two broad categories; that which is located and specific to a product, and that which locates the indigenous product within a wider context of a portfolio of tourism products. Studies of particular products possess an inherent bias in the sample, in that the researchers survey those who have made a conscious decision to make such a visit to a native people's place. Consequently recorded interest levels tend to be high, and visitors may bemoan a lack of contact with indigenous peoples (e.g., Moscardo and Pearce, 1999). On the other hand, research that asks about the attractiveness of, in this instance, Maori product against a portfolio of wider product tends to indicate much lower levels of interest. For example, Nielsen's (2002) study of the 'interactive visitor' showed that while cultural performances were of some importance to visitors, *marae* visits were not, and in both instances satisfaction levels were low. Recent studies (e.g., Ryan and Higgins, 2006) have attempted to combine both scenarios to create a better understanding of tourist motives, and arguably researchers need to be aware of this distinction in the research context – perhaps again an example of where method determines response!

Conclusions

Maori tourism

A market perspective of indigenous tourism is important for identifying pertinent consumer demands for business and product development, and for assessing appreciation of indigenous host culture in the pursuit of tourism that is mutually beneficial for both host and tourist (McIntosh, 2004; McIntosh and Johnson, 2004). Indeed, findings from previous market research have provided some consistent evidence as to what tourists seek from their encounters with indigenous peoples. For example, it has been shown that indigenous culture may not represent the primary motivation for visiting a destination. Instead, demand for indigenous tourism potentially needs to be seen in terms of how it reinforces the nature of 'difference' at the host destination. Consequently, if demand for indigenous tourism is inflated, there are important consequences for indigenous product development and the economic viability of indigenous tourism enterprises. Noting this, Altman and Finlayson (1993) have argued that unrealistic expectations about the potential demand for indigenous tourism ventures can lead to increased dependence on long-term government financial sponsorship that prolongs the welfare dependency of indigenous communities (see also chapter by Schmeichen and Boyle, Editors' Note). Furthermore, the nature of demand, and the experiences gained by tourists appear to be generalist and somewhat superficial, iconic and stereotypical in nature. Indeed, existing product offerings that mainly centre on cultural product and performances and which have been created for commercial ends may have resulted in a limited array of experiences for tourists. As such, tourists consume what they perceive to be identifiable symbols of an indigenous host culture; and limited product offerings potentially inhibit growth for indigenous tourism. Ryan and Higgins (2006) further argue that current tourism products may homogenise Maori culture, and the Maori perspective that to be Maori has sense only within a tribal setting is set aside; tribal differences are thus generally unappreciated by tourists. It is argued, therefore, that indigenous tourism development needs to extend beyond the promotion of traditional imagery and address the contemporary and regional nature of an indigenous culture in product development; indicating difference rather than duplication of existing product (Finlayson, 1991; McIntosh, 2004; Ryan & Higgins, 2006).

Recent consultancy research for Tourism New Zealand and the New Zealand Ministry of Tourism has identified opportunities to better service current demand for Maori cultural products and to create new demand by increasing awareness of Maori cultural products amongst travellers to New Zealand (see Colmar Brunton, 2004), and equally for indigenous tourism in general (e.g., in this book as demonstrated by the chapters by Williams & O'Neill and Schmeichen & Boyle). The recommendations made included providing opportunities for improving the authenticity of Maori cultural performances, ensuring the performances were not overcrowded, providing opportunities for tourists to meet and talk to Maori people and having performances explained/translated to increase understanding so that visitors are engaged and involved. The opportunity for tourists to visit *marae* was found to be a strong driver of overall holiday satisfaction, especially among younger visitors, yet it was recognised that participation and awareness levels are currently low. Furthermore, approximately half of the visitors who did visit a *marae* rated their visit as 'okay' or 'poor'. In particular, less aware tourists found elements of the visit confusing and/or upsetting (such as the challenge in the *haka*), or wanted to participate more fully but could not because of intercultural barriers or lack of understanding. However, a visit to a *marae* provides the opportunity for a more genuine, sincere and educational cultural exchange (Taylor, 2001; McIntosh & Johnson, 2004). As such, there is a need for improvements to *marae* visits, including reducing the overcrowding on *marae*, increasing service quality and providing an authentic, moving experience for visitors as part of a living culture, and having these experiences available at a convenient time (Colmar Brunton, 2004). As visitation levels to *marae* are not as high as visits to cultural performances, there is a greater opportunity to promote this particular cultural product more vigorously to international tourists. There was also a noted opportunity to develop Maori cuisine as a unique and distinct product offering, especially as food and wine trails or local cuisine. Increasing visitor involvement such as learning *waiata* (songs) in Maori cultural performances or during visits to *marae*, and better explanations of protocol and history were also reported as opportunities to enhance the tourist experience.

Indigenous tourism

In the context of Australian Aboriginal research, Ryan and Huyton (2002) argue that cultural perspectives permit indigenous operators to provide difference to more mainstream product, and Ryan (2002) makes a similar observation with reference to Maori. The nub of the argument is two-fold – indigenous peoples should capitalise upon mainstream areas of interest and then create added value or a unique selling proposition through the use of culture. Kaikoura Whale Watch is probably the foremost exponent of this in New Zealand with its nature-based focus. Second, such actions move indigenous people away from a peripheral position in tourism with reference to the marketplace, thereby creating more opportunity for employment and income generation.

Yet it still remains true that much of the recent market research shows that the most meaningful experiences for tourists may occur through informal personal contact with indigenous people, in contrast to experiences of staged cultural events. Again, this contrasts somewhat with the nature of existing Maori tourism product in New Zealand, as well as the current priority of public policy for further Maori product development set out in the New Zealand Tourism Strategy 2010 – situations not unknown in places such as Canada, Australia or Taiwan. Furthermore, inviting tourists into an indigenous community has implications for impact management as staged performances, arguably, have less disruptive impacts on a community and its way of life. Thus, despite tourists' reported preferences for authentic and meaningful interaction with indigenous peoples, the brief, rather superficial nature and generalist context of tourism consumption must be taken into consideration. Indeed, there is growing concern that indigenous tourism is increasingly consumed out of the desire for a 'romanticised' version of the culture and may constitute desirable but not essential 'one-off' experiences (Ryan and Huyton, 2000a, b; Colmar Brunton, 2004; McIntosh, 2004; Ryan and Higgins, 2006). If tourism is to be a major source of economic growth and independence for indigenous peoples, indigenous business development may be best served by offering added-value experiences within a destination to attract a wider visitor market for indigenous tourism. Coupled with this, such businesses need to maintain strategies for the control, authenticity, integrity and cultural acceptability of the experiences they share with visitors (Colmar Brunton, 2004; Kanara-Zygadlo et al., 2005). It is questionable whether indigenous hosts can ever truly deliver authentic experiences in the short-time frame and given the superficial nature of most tourist experiences. Nevertheless, opportunities to use authenticity marks, for example, *toi iho* in New Zealand, can further enhance appeal to international tourists who purchase arts and crafts, and other souvenirs associated with the culture of indigenous peoples. Moreover, there are an increasing number of case studies illustrating ways in which 'native people-centred tourism' can be achieved. These case studies illustrate specific forms of indigenous tourism that incorporate cultural values into tourism development to sustain cultural integrity, and are distinguishable from the general involvement and participation of indigenous peoples in the tourism sector (Hinch et al., 1999; McIntosh et al., 2002; McIntosh et al., 2004; Kanara-Zygadlo et al., 2005). Throughout these developments tensions remain. To address them first, an understanding of market demand is essential in acquiring commercial success, and second, there remains the question of to what degree indigenous peoples wish to engage in tourism, and on what terms (see chapter by Pettersson and Viken, Editors' Note). People have a perfect right not to engage in tourism enterprises, even while National Tourism Organisations may wish to promote sources of destination difference – yet, whatever decision is made, it needs to be recognised that along with potential gains come possible costs in terms of reduced incomes or unmitigated intrusion effects.

Glossary

This chapter uses many Maori terms and tries within the text to indicate their meanings. However, exact translations into English do not always exist, and the following glossary is intended as a guide only.

Haka (a war dance): A general term that covers a range of different dances. Probably the *haka* is best-known outside of New Zealand through its association with the All Blacks Rugby team.

Hapu: The extended family, the sub-tribe.

Iwi: Tribe.

Marae (the meeting place): Each *iwi* will have its own *marae*, and thus they are specific to *iwi* and *hapu*.

Mauri: The life that is shared by all objects, animate and inanimate, the state of being, the interconnection between things that exist.

Taonga (property, treasure): Used more widely to mean culture as well as tangible items.

Waiata (songs): A term that is often associated with the use of songs within protocol – as for the welcoming of people to the *marae*.

Whanau: The people, often with a common ethnic or spiritual relationship.

CHAPTER 7

Indigenous tourism and poverty reduction

Harold Goodwin

Introduction

In this text, indigenous tourism is defined as forms of tourism activity where indigenous people are directly involved either through control or 'by having their culture serve as the essence of the attraction.' As has been argued elsewhere in this volume (see chapter by Hinch and Butler, Editors' Note) it is far rarer for indigenous peoples to have control over the tourism which they experience than for them to be the objects of it. We are concerned here with the contribution which a Pro-Poor Tourism approach may be able to make to developing forms of indigenous tourism which benefit minority groups, or to increase those benefits where some already exist. Thus the focus of this chapter is on what a Pro-Poor Tourism approach has to offer indigenous people who are engaged in tourism or being visited by tourists. Elsewhere in this volume, the issues of authenticity, commodification and other negative social and environmental impacts are considered. In this chapter the major emphasis is on the contribution which tourism can make to poverty reduction for minority indigenous communities.

At the turn of the millennium there was a significant shift of emphasis by international and national agencies as they responded to the adoption of the Millennium Development Goals (MDGs). Since the early 1990s there has been an increasing emphasis on poverty reduction rather than on the broader objective of development in international and national policies. Tourism's traditional emphasis on trickledown and multipliers was developed to assist the industry and tourism policy makers in arguing the case for tourism's contribution to national economic development and growth.

The World Tourism Organization's (WTO's) *Global Code of Ethics* adopted in 1999 referred to the fight against poverty, and the United Nations (UN) Commission on Sustainable Development in the same year called on governments to 'maximize the potential of tourism for eradicating poverty by developing appropriate strategies in cooperation with all major groups, and indigenous and local communities' (UN, 1999, p. 2).

Poverty

Poverty is multi-dimensional. It is not only about a lack of monetary resources. The dimension of exclusion/marginalisation is particularly relevant when considering the position of minority indigenous communities. For example, the Batak in Palawan in the Philippines, like other indigenous minorities on the island, have come under increasing pressure as a consequence of immigration by lowland agriculturalists and now 'literally disappearing' much of what was unique in their traditional culture has been 'irretrievably lost' (Eder, 1977). This is a marginalised community aware of its perilous condition with deaths exceeding births. The community is intermarrying but recognises that the culture is being lost. The Batak are one of the 'cultural attractions' of Palawan and are used to market opportunities to trek in areas where they live; they are objects of tourism with little or no ability to control the intrusion:

> Poverty means a lack of basic capacity to participate effectively in society. It means not having enough to feed and clothe a family, not having a clinic or school to go to, not having the land on which to grow one's food or a job to earn one's living, not having access to credit. It means insecurity, powerlessness and exclusion of individuals, households and communities.
>
> (IMF and IDA, 1999, p. 5)

In the MDGs, a number of targets are set for some of the major dimensions of poverty including hunger, access to drinking water, daily income, maternal mortality, education and a range or other priorities (UN GA, 2000; World Bank, 2005). In considering the ways in which tourism can contribute to poverty reduction, it is important to consider how and to what extent tourism can address the wider poverty agenda by contributing to health, education, welfare and community capacity building.

It is true that because of the multi-dimensional character of poverty, the socio-cultural elements of the definition, and the fact that poverty is a relative concept (Boltvinik, nd), the measurement and reporting of tourism impacts on poverty is difficult. However, there is an increasing realisation of the importance of measuring the impacts of interventions both to assist in identifying approaches and interventions which deliver results and to win the support of funders (Goodwin, 2006).

Tourism and poverty

There is very little data available to demonstrate the impacts of tourism on poverty. Although there have been many interventions (by national, regional and local governments, international development agencies and banks, national and international Non-Government Organization's (NGO's) with poverty reduction and conservation objectives) there are still very few examples where poverty impacts have been reported to funders, let alone publicly (see chapter by Salole, Editors' Note) (PPTP, 2005). Many ecotourism and community-based tourism initiatives have been justified by pointing to benefits for local communities, but there is little or no data on the outcomes. In the marginal areas around national parks in Africa, Asia and South America it is often minority indigenous people who were the intended beneficiaries.

Traditionally, tourism development has focused on macro-economic benefits – the impact of tourism is most frequently measured in numbers of international visitor arrivals, contribution to employment and to the balance of payments in foreign exchange earnings. Tourism satellite accounts and multipliers have been used to identify the economic contribution of the industry in world trade and to support assertions about the importance of the tourism industry to economic development at the national level (Jamieson et al., 2004). Trickledown and multipliers have been used to support the contention that local communities benefit from employment (direct, indirect and induced) and through the local economic development impact of spending in the destination, but there is limited hard evidence to support this view (WTO, 2002).

In the context of the MDGs the challenge is to demonstrate positive impacts on poverty, to demonstrate that tourism can contribute to the eight MDGs and that the impacts can be scaled up to make a significant contribution to the eradication of poverty. Recognising that it is possible to have significant economic development and growth whilst not reducing the number of people continuing to live in absolute poverty, the MDG targets are not defined in terms of economic growth; they relate specifically to poverty, for example to halve the number of people who live on less than one dollar per day by 2015 (UN GA, 2000). In this context international visitor arrivals and spend figures, tourism satellite accounts and multipliers have little utility as they cannot be used to measure the impact of tourism on local economic development in general and poverty reduction in particular (Goodwin, 2006).

It is important to recognise that because there is so little data available on the benefits accruing from different forms of tourism to local communities in general and minority indigenous people in particular, this chapter draws on the research undertaken by the Pro-Poor Tourism Partnership (Caroline Ashley of the Overseas Development Institute, Harold Goodwin of the International Centre for Responsible Tourism and Dilys Roe of the International Institute for Environment and Development – www.pptpartnership.org) and a relatively limited number of published case studies. However, the chapter is also informed by direct experience of implementation projects in Africa and Asia and discussions with practitioners and policy makers. Very few initiatives on tourism and poverty reduction have addressed the mainstream industry and despite the plethora of community-based tourism and ecotourism initiatives since the Integrated Conservation and Development Projects of the 1990s, there is surprisingly little literature on which to draw for evidence of impacts on poverty.

Local communities and indigenous people in particular have often been seen as one of the 'frills' – they provide added exotic flavour, and they are objects of tourism, suitable to be photographed and 'visited'. They are often not seen as stakeholders in tourism. When tourism was discussed within the Rio agenda at CSD7 at the UN in 1999, explicit reference was made to indigenous people. The resolution called on governments to 'maximise the potential of tourism for eradicating poverty by developing appropriate strategies in cooperation with all major groups, and indigenous and local communities' (UN, 1999, §3f). For reasons of geography and history, minority indigenous people often find themselves living in, or adjacent to, areas which have remained marginal and unfarmed. These areas are frequently gazetted as protected areas (Hall, 2000). The creation of protected areas has generally been justified on conservation and environment grounds and for tourism, but this has often disadvantaged indigenous peoples who have lost access to natural resources, which have been a significant part of their livelihood.

Although conflicts may arise wherever the tourism industry impacts on indigenous people, it is in the context of the debates about biodiversity conservation at the Conference of the Parties (COP) to the Convention on Biological Diversity that the issue is most vigorously raised. At COP 7 in February 2004 a group of developing country NGOs argued that the *Guidelines on Biodiversity and Tourism Development* (Secretariat of the Convention on Biological Diversity, 2004) paid 'minimal attention to the rights and expertise on sustainable use of Indigenous Peoples and other local communities' (Joint NGO's Statement on Tourism, 2004, p. 6). They argued that ecotourism and other programmes linking tourism and poverty 'are actually promoting industrial tourism models oriented to economic growth. These forms of so-called "sustainable tourism" are known to be exploitative of both people and land' and that tourism 'is increasingly a pretext for pushing industrial style development into Indigenous ancestral territories' (Joint NGO's Statement on Tourism, 2004, p. 6).

The engagement of the poor and marginalised in the planning and management of tourism is as important as their gaining from it. Exclusion and marginalisation is one of the defining characteristics of the poor and often of minority indigenous peoples. Tourism can provide opportunities for engagement in management and control of an important socio-economic activity; and, empower indigenous communities to negotiate with more powerful economic interests and to exercise a degree of power as well as to secure revenues and economic advantage from it. This is an important dimension of Pro-Poor Tourism.

Pro-Poor Tourism

Pro-Poor Tourism is defined as tourism which generates net benefits for the poor (Ashley et al., 2001; WTO, 2002). It is neither a product nor a sector. Any form of tourism can be pro-poor. Pro-Poor Tourism seeks to unlock economic and other livelihood opportunities for the poor and to enable poor people to secure an income stream or other poverty reducing benefit from tourism, for example potable water, improved road access, school books or a school building.

The Pro-Poor Tourism Partnership identified a broad range of strategies for using tourism to address the issues of poverty, from the primarily economic (employment and business development) to mitigating environmental impacts which adversely impact on the poor and addressing social and cultural impacts. The Pro-Poor Tourism Partnership argues that tourism has a broad range of impacts on the poor, amongst which economic and financial ones are prominent, but other livelihood impacts (human, physical, social, natural capital, access to information); and cultural value, optimism, pride and participation and exposure to risk and exploitation are all aspects which need to be considered (Ashley et al., 2001).

The Pro-Poor Tourism Partnership approach recognises that measuring net impacts is necessary because in some circumstances there are negative impacts on the poor from tourism through, for example, loss of access to a beach or river frontage, conservation of land traditionally used for foraging and/or hunting and consequent exclusion from and even criminalisation of traditional activities, or from competing demands on time or labour resources. These negative impacts should not be ignored; they have to be managed if the poor community is to be sure of a net benefit from engaging in tourism.

Expanding the tourism industry may help achieve poverty reduction, by increasing employment or total spend on goods and services produced by the informal sector, but it is not in itself sufficient. Increasing numbers of visitors to hill tribes in Asia or to townships in South Africa will not necessarily have any positive impacts on the livelihoods of poor people – for poverty to be reduced, poor people need to secure a sufficient increase in their household income to make a significant contribution to poverty reduction (however locally defined) or to remove the household from poverty altogether.

Pro-Poor Tourism is one of a set of broader strategies of pro-poor growth. Pro-poor growth increases demand for the goods and services produced by the economically poor resulting in higher levels of employment and/or opportunities for microenterprises, for example in food, craft, local guiding and performance. Pro-poor growth also reduces the costs paid by the poor to meet their basic needs, for example by reducing costs by improving road access or communications; and it may increase government revenues available for poverty alleviation. Growth is pro-poor if it enables poor people to realise the value of their asset base, which includes their culture. The everyday way of life of indigenous minority groups is a significant asset of the economically poor. Pro-poor growth should decrease the exposure of the poor to variability and risk (Ashley et al., 2001).

The non-economic benefits of tourism for the economically poor include capacity building, training and empowerment in the management of tourism in their communities. However, the realisation of these potential benefits will depend to a large degree on the policy and regulatory framework in which they operate, the support of national and local government, the nature of the engagement with the private sector and critically the social capital of the community. The essence of social capital is the ability to organise and to act collectively to secure the best possible forms of engagement with tourism and significant revenues, household and collective, from that engagement. From a Pro-Poor Tourism perspective, one of the key issues is the extent to which minority indigenous communities are able to engage meaningfully in decision-making processes about tourism in their communities and to maximise sustainable economic benefits from tourism, whilst controlling and minimising any negative social or cultural impacts.

This issue of the management of tourism is particularly acute for minority indigenous communities because of their marginalisation in the decision-making processes of the wider society. Such marginalisation tends to occur because the operators who bring tourists to their communities are unlikely to be of the same ethnicity; and because it is the everyday life, the agricultural practises, religion and rites, the houses and family life of the minority communities which are of interest to the tourists. This interest is necessarily highly intrusive; larger numbers of visitors bring greater economic opportunities but also bring more negative impacts.

The livelihoods approach

In the case of minority indigenous peoples, it is generally the natural and cultural heritage of the area and the living culture of the local people that attract tourists. The negative impacts of tourism on the environment and local communities need to be managed and the adverse impacts mitigated in order to maintain these assets. A tourism monoculture adversely affects the inherent quality of the destination and over-dependence on tourism increases the economic vulnerability of the area to decisions made elsewhere by consumers, government, operators and investors.

Livelihood analysis is a methodology which can be used to assess the contribution that different forms of tourism make to the livelihoods of the economically poor or other groups who are new to tourism. The great advantage of livelihood analysis is that it provides a methodology for look-ing at both the positive and the negative impacts of a particular form of tourism development upon the livelihoods of the economically poor.

The livelihoods framework is an analytical structure for tackling the com-plexity of rural livelihoods where individuals, families and groups have a whole series of ways of securing their living including, conventional earnings and a range of subsistence practises. Livelihood assets, 'the livelihood building blocks' are:

- *Financial capital*: Cash at hand or which can be borrowed.
- *Human capital*: The skills base of particular individuals and of the group.
- *Natural capital*: The resources of the environment available to individuals and the group: water resources, forest, arable land, pasture, rivers and lakes, wildlife.
- *Physical capital*: Buildings, machinery, equipment.
- *Social capital*: The social cohesion of the group and the strength of its networks.

Livelihood assets have to be seen in the context of a particular community's vulnerability to external shocks (e.g., drought, flooding or the consequences of disease or crime on tourism numbers), seasonality (harvesting and planting, tourism arrivals) and trends (particularly climate and market trends). The structures and processes are extant and take time to change, but a livelihoods approach can contribute to the substantial empowerment of the econom-ically poor. Different groups and individuals will adopt different livelihood strategies in seeking to minimise their vulnerability whilst maximising a diverse range of livelihood outcomes including cash and subsistence incomes; increased well-being – for example education and health; improved food security and, more sustainable use of natural resources through non-consumptive tourism (Farrington et al., 1999).

As Ashley and Roe (1998, p. 26) have argued:

Rural households rarely rely on one activity or source of income. In order to diversify risk and exploit available opportunities they combine on-farm and off-farm income sources, . . . The fact that tourism earnings are often unreliable, involve high invest-ment, and a delay before earnings flow, can also conflict with livelihood strategies of poor households to maintain flexibility and minimise risk.

The strength of the livelihoods approach is that it can be used to identify livelihood opportunities for economically poor communities which link to tourism, and provides a framework for analysing with communities what the positive and the negative impacts would be on other elements of their livelihood strategy. This approach has been used by Ashley (2000) in Namibia, Wood (2005) in Peru and Saville (2001) in Nepal. The Nepal case is of particular interest here because it demonstrates the value of engaging local communities through social mobilisation, participatory planning and capacity building in a very remote and poor area. The initiative successfully enabled these economically poor communities along a trekking trail to develop goods and services for use by tourists and trekking agents. By build-ing on existing livelihood strategies they were successful in selling porter-ing, horse and mule services, grazing and vegetables and collecting a trail maintenance tax. This additional community and household income signifi-cantly raised the living standards of the communities along the trail (see chapter by Nepal, Editors' Note).

Pro-Poor Tourism strategies

The Pro-Poor Tourism Partnership (Ashley, 2001) used a livelihoods approach and identified ways in which economically poor people could bene-fit from tourism at community, household and individual levels through employment and micro-enterprise opportunities. Other identified livelihood benefits included infrastructure (roads and water), health and education and empowerment benefits including capacity building and training, engage-ment in planning and partnerships with the private sector. The Pro-Poor Tourism Partnership also pointed to the importance of the economically poor being empowered to manage and mitigate negative social and environ-mental impacts, and the optimism and pride which would result.

The Partnership pointed to the importance of managing risk and avoiding exploitation. The Desk research case studies warned 'strongly against the poor becoming too dependent on tourism because the industry is too volatile' (Ashley et al., (2001), p. 27). The livelihoods methodology is central to the Pro-Poor Tourism Partnership approach because it identifies ways in which com-munities can achieve additional earnings and other benefits from tourism, whilst mitigating negative impacts. This priority was endorsed by the WTO in their report on Tourism and Poverty Alleviation launched at the World Summit on Sustainable Development in Johannesburg in 2002. The WTO pointed to the importance of facilitating community access to the tourism market, maximising linkages to the local economy and minimising leakages, ensuring that tourism projects contribute to local economic development and that they 'build on and complement existing livelihood strategies through employment and small enterprise development' (Goodwin, 1998, p. 4). They added 'policies and practises must also promote the preservation of natural and cultural assets.' And they must minimise and ideally eliminate adverse effects on local communities and socio-cultural systems (WTO, 2002). As has been argued elsewhere in this volume, tourism poses particular risks for minority indigenous groups (see chapters by Hinch and Butler and by Hall, Editors' Note).

O'Grady (1981) suggested that communities should participate in the planning of tours and argued that at least one tour guide should understand local customs and speak the language. Twenty five years later expectations are higher and more operators and tourists want guiding in villages and communities to be conducted by local guides from and of that community. The guide as teacher is an important authority figure and employing local guides who have the support of their community can contribute a great deal to the empowerment of the community and the quality of the tourism experience. In other situations indigenous people may prefer to have no direct contact with tourists. For example Altman and Finlayson (1993) reported that some Aboriginal groups in Australia prefer to receive a proportion of gate fees and/or produce crafts which are then sold by others rather than to have direct contact with tourists.

The WTO (2004) identified seven different ways in which spending associated with tourism can reach the poor:

1 *Employment of the poor in tourism enterprises*
This may be one of the easiest ways for tourism to benefit the poor. However, it raises particular problems for minority indigenous communities who may not want to have 'outsiders' developing accommodation in their community but may not have the resources to develop a facility themselves nor the contacts to market it if they did. On the other hand, a household livelihood strategy where one member of the household secures a cash income from a local enterprise may make a very significant positive contribution to household income without increasing vulnerability at the household level. It may also provide opportunities for the worker to gain experience and contacts useful to the community.

2 *Supply of goods and services to tourism enterprises by the poor or by enterprises employing the poor*
This does not require any direct contact with tourists and does not involve tourists visiting the village. Fruit, vegetables, fish and meat may be sold to tourism establishments; crafts may be sold as soft furnishings for hotels or lodges, or provided for sale through the hotel shop or a cultural performance may be provided at the lodge or hotel.

3 *Direct sales of goods and services to visitors by the poor (informal economy)*
This approach has particular advantages for minority indigenous communities. By accepting day visitors and insisting on local guides and jointly planning the itineraries with tour operators, the community gains the opportunity to present its culture and to benefit economically through crafts, local guiding, the provision of food and performances (Bah and Goodwin, 2003).

4 *Establishment and running of tourism enterprises by the poor small medium or micro-enterprises (SMMEs) or community-based enterprises*
This approach fits well with the direct sales approach. Micro-enterprises owned either by individuals or the community as a whole, potentially with part of the income going to a Community Development Fund, can provide the goods and services to visitors or to tourism enterprises. Partnering with the private sector may ensure market access through the provision of appropriately designed and delivered products and services; secure access to capital information and other resources; and minimise risk (see chapter by Salole, Editors' Note).

5 *Taxes or levies on tourism revenues or profits with proceeds benefiting the poor*
These approaches are currently being tested. Levies or entrance charges are being collected from tourists. Communities are negotiating for a proportion of the gate fees at cultural and natural heritage sights and benefiting from lease fees on communally owned land or are receiving a proportion of turnover or profit as income to community development funds.

6 *Voluntary giving of resources (money, goods, time) by tourists and enterprises in ways which benefit the poor*
In The Gambia 48% of tourists from the UK arrive with some kind of gift (Bah and Goodwin, 2003). There is considerable scope to develop this approach – the community needs to exercise some control over the process to ensure that is equitable and respectful and does not lead to begging. The opportunities and benefits need to be discussed with tour operators and with tourists.

7 *Investment in infrastructure which provides livelihood benefits to the poor*
Minority indigenous communities need to be consulted by anyone making infrastructure investments in the area – private sector, government or donor agency, how the investment can also benefit the community. For example, at Mahenye in Zimbabwe the building of a lodge resulted in the development of the road which brought a bus service and a trading route to Harare in the previously isolated Shangan community. The community also gained a potable water supply piped to the centre of the village, telephones, grinding mills and support in developing a backpackers' lodge in the village (Goodwin et al., 1997).

Conclusion

There is growing interest among visitors for experiencing something of the culture, daily lives and diversity of ways local people have developed as communities in their particular place and environment. The potential for tourism development is therefore considerable. For tourism to be used successfully to reduce poverty amongst minority indigenous communities, active roles must be played by international, national and local tour operators; governments and the tourists themselves.

Tourists can contribute by seeking out high-quality non-invasive opportunities for engaging with minority indigenous cultures on their terms. Guide books provide better and better advice and there are a number of tour operators which, like Tribes in the UK, offer high-quality fairly traded tours including opportunities to visit indigenous communities. Governments can assist by providing resources for local training and assisting communities to develop equitable agreements with the industry which ensure that tourism benefits the community and minimises negative impacts, and then by assisting with enforcement of the agreements. Governments can also assist by ensuring that regulations and certification schemes brought in to ensure quality standards in tourism are not used to exclude indigenous communities and to make market access unnecessarily difficult (Scheyvens, 2002).

In a period when increasing numbers of tourists are seeking an experience of cultural diversity, the market should not be taken for granted. Many community-based tourism projects have failed to be viable because of inadequate volumes of visitors. In thinking about the market it is important to consider both domestic (Ghimire, 2001) and international markets and to avoid projects which involve significant capital expenditure and maintenance (accommodation) or investment in skills which do not exist in the community. The lowest risk, and often the most profitable opportunities, are livelihood diversifications which are an extension of what the community already does – selling vegetables to tourist lodges, crafts to tourists or dance performances in carefully managed environment adjacent to but generally not in the village. There is scope for minority indigenous communities to benefit from tourism but a cautious approach needs to be adopted.

Indigenous owned casinos and perceived local community impacts: Mohegan Sun in South East Connecticut, USA

Barbara Anne Carmichael and Jan Louise Jones

Introduction

While much has been written about the growth of casino gaming in North America in the last two decades (Eadington, 1995; Meyer Arendt and Hartmann, 1998; Perdue et al., 1999), few studies have focused on Indian gaming (Stansfield, 1996; Lew and Van Otten, 1998). Stokowski (2004, p. 406) suggests that Indian gaming 'is of substantial interest, but has received relatively little scholarly attention'. This is despite the fact that it is now almost twenty years since the Indian Gaming Regulatory Act (IGRA) in 1988 in the USA opened the door to Indian Gaming on reservation land. Casino developments have proven to be major catalysts for economic growth, wealth creation and reinforcement of sovereignty for most tribes that have adopted them. However, there are a number of economic, social and environmental impacts that accompany such changes in casino tourism that have affected both indigenous and neighboring communities. Research focus and debate has shifted from whether or not to develop casinos to questions investigating the nuances of casino impacts, not just from the economic perspective but from the wider cultural and sustainability perspective (Carmichael, 2001, Piner and Paradis, 2004).

Large casino developments were identified by McIntosh and co-authors (1994) as a major force in the tourism industry. Large casino resorts, like other forms of mass tourism bring with them benefits and costs which may be perceived differently by local groups. Peck and Lepie (1989, p. 203) suggest that both the rate (magnitude and speed) of development and amount of community involvement and control (power) over change affect the amount and distribution of payoffs and trade offs associated with increased tourism. Rapid changes can be particularly disruptive, and attitudes and social representations are likely to be more polarized in the situation of gaming on American Indian land, where Indian and surrounding communities are further divided on an ethnic basis especially for a controversial attraction like a casino (Carmichael et al., 1996).

Crang (2004, p. 75) states that tourism is 'an active agent in the creative destruction of places in what can be violent, contested, unequal, but sometimes welcomed, transformative and productive process'. He suggests that a destination is fashioned by different combinations of actors. This process is likely to be uniquely based on local conditions and historical relationships. In the case of mega-resort development on Native American land, the actors are the developers (Indians), local community residents (non-indigenous citizens and indigenous sovereign nations), gamblers (tourists and recreational visitors) and migrant workers attracted by casino employment. Such groups are in competition for access to space and resources and are likely to hold different representations of the casino and how it affects their quality tourism experiences and quality of life (Carmichael, 2006). Hence, comprehending residents' perceptions of the effect of tourism development is essential for sustaining mutually beneficial relationships between local residents and tourism businesses (Chen and Hsu, 2001, p. 460).

As a result of their rapid growth in 1990s, the impact of casinos is now an important area of research. As is the case for tourism industry in general, the main types of perceived impacts of casinos are economic, environmental and social and while residents may be concerned about negative social and environmental effects, they usually acknowledge economic benefits (Canaday and Zeiger, 1991). Economic effects are often highlighted as positive (Goodman, 1994; Nickerson, 1996), while social costs and undesirable lag effects may be under-acknowledged (Stokowski, 1993). Personal factors are also important. As Eadington (1995, p. 163) comments, 'one's attitude toward the casino project will depend largely on whether those changes are going to improve or deteriorate one's present quality of life in the community'.

Roehl (1994) proposes the following conclusions about the social impacts of casino tourism: (1) residents are often unprepared for the dramatic changes initiated by casino tourism, stating the number of gamblers is often higher than originally expected; (2) residents are often troubled by the shift from services for them to an emphasis on catering to incoming tourists; and (3) benefits and costs accrue to both the destination and surrounding communities at a rate that is often distributed inequitably. Roehl (1994) concludes that there is considerable ambivalence about casino tourism, noting that associated problems are often recognized, but usually tolerated.

The purpose of this chapter is to introduce readers to issues relating to the development of Native owned casinos and the perceived associated impacts on and attitudes of local residents. It follows the call for research by Hsu in her statement:

It is crucial to understand the impacts of Native American gaming on surrounding non-Native American communities. These communities usually do not have any direct input on gaming policies and operations on reservations; however, the quality of life in those communities could very much be changed because of those gaming operations.

(Hsu, 1999, p. 230)

An overview of the issues related to native owned casinos is provided to set the framework for the discussion of this case study, which examines a rural area in south east Connecticut that has experienced rapid changes as a result of two mega-resort casinos developed on the reservation lands of the Mashantucket Pequot tribe (Foxwoods Resort Casino, opened 1992) and the Mohegan tribe (Mohegan Sun Casino, opened 1996). The casinos are located in close proximity to each other (about 20 miles apart) within a predominantly rural region (Figure 8.1). The differing histories of the two tribes and their changing relationships with the surrounding Connecticut residents provide an interesting example of cultural politics in which rapid economic development is situated within the cultural, social and political relations that surround it. This chapter focuses on the perceptions of local residents and their changing relationships with their Indian neighbors in a small Connecticut town (Montville), based on the results of a survey conducted in 2002. Findings are

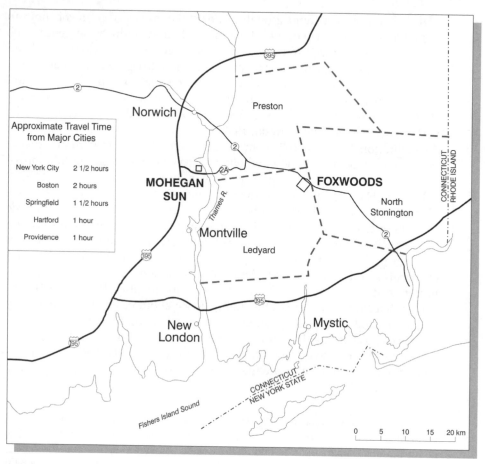

Figure 8.1
Location of Mohegan Sun and Foxwoods Casinos (Southeast Connecticut)

also compared with previous research of one of the authors on the Foxwoods casino that was conducted in 1995. Major themes and implications of the development of indigenous owned casinos from the non-indigenous perspective are highlighted.

Indian gaming in the USA

The key to understanding the rise of Indian gaming is the desire for sovereignty (Ferber and Chon, 1994). Indian Nations on federally recognized reservations are recognized as 'dependent sovereigns' (Stansfield, 1996). Sovereignty according to the American Political Dictionary means 'the supreme power of the state, exercised within its boundaries, free from external interference'. However, without a sound economic base such independence is hard to achieve. Thompson and Dever (1994, p. 5), appear to state the obvious: 'Money allows people to survive.'

Gaming provides a tool for restoring sovereignty for Native American Nations. The IGRA passed by the US Congress in 1988 declared its purpose as being 'to provide a statutory basis for the operation of gaming by Indian tribes as a means of promoting tribal economic development, self sufficiency and strong tribal governments' (cited in Thompson and Dever, 1994, p. 5). At the time the Act was passed, Native Americans living on reservations suffered from high unemployment and lack of capital for investment. Many were dependent on Federal Aid which only allowed for sub-standard living. Land was held in trust by the US Government and thus could not be used as collateral for loans (Ferber and Chon, 1994). Gaming represented a route to economic development and perhaps one of the few possibilities because of the poor quality of the land base of many reservations.

The speed at which casino development has occurred on tribal lands in the USA is evidence of changing mores and relaxed restrictions concerning gambling. Indian gaming, and the sizable profits accumulated have, however, stimulated a fresh round of cultural conflict (Raento and Berry, 1999). The introduction of gaming on tribal lands received a major boost by the successful outcomes of the Oneida Tribe's (Wisconsin 1981) and the Cabazon Band's (California 1987) appeals in federal court that allowed them to have the right to conduct high stakes gaming without state regulation (Long, 1995). Their legal cases rested on the fact that many states already allowed minor charitable gaming and the Federal government could not, therefore, enforce laws stating that gambling on reservation land was illegal. These victories in turn encouraged other Indian tribes to begin operating gaming facilities. In response to this, many states began lobbying the federal government to regulate Indian gaming, citing unfair competition and tax regulation problems (Long, 1995). As a consequence of continued state pressure, the IGRA and the National Gaming Commission were established. Stansfield (1996, p. 129) suggested that the explosive growth of legalized gambling on reservation lands was explained by: the unique legal status of Native Americans; the rapid mainstreaming of gaming from pariah industry to one regulated, sponsored and even promoted by governments; and, the determination of Native Americans to revitalize poverty-ridden tribal communities.

While many Native American gaming establishments are relatively small scale and dependent on 'day trip' trade (Stansfield, 1996), the two casino developments in Connecticut featured in this case study, are mega-resorts and are major tourist attractions. Stansfield (1996) likens the increasing scale and extravagance of Las Vegas Casino developments to a 'Dreadnought' hypothesis where one development tries to out-scale another. The Connecticut Native American casinos function as destination resorts in their own right and have copied this trend, aiming to be bigger and better than some of the Las Vegas facilities. They are certainly more accessible to the east coast market and form an 'intervening opportunity' diverting potential business away from Las Vegas, as well as from Atlantic City.

Indian Gaming in Connecticut

All federal approvals (from the U.S. Department of the Interior, National Gaming Commission and the Bureau of Indian Affairs) for operating a major casino in Southeastern Connecticut were granted in 1995. Connecticut's former Governor, Lowell Weicker, was initially opposed to casino gambling in 1991. However, faced with considerable opposition, he entered into an agreement allowing the Mashantucket Pequot Tribe to develop a full-scale casino, provided the state received a share of its revenues (Hadwiger, 1996). The Pequots, at that time the only federally recognized American Indian tribe in Connecticut, subsequently joined Governor Weicker in supporting a gaming compact with a related tribe, the Mohegans, after the Mohegans gained federal recognition in 1993 (Hadwiger, 1996). The Mohegan Tribe entered into a contract with the State of Connecticut and a joint venture with Trading Cove Associates (TCA). The tribal leadership gave away rights to investors at a time when they were nearly penniless and were relying on lawyers apparently paid by those investors, these included 40% of revenues and exclusive rights to develop and manage a hotel at the casino site on the reservation (http://graphics.boston.com/globe/nation/packages/gaming/congressman_seeking_probe.html, 10/10/2006). The casino opened in 1996 and by 2000 it employed over 5,600 people (The Mohegan Tribe, 2000). In 2000, TCA sold complete control of the resort to the Mohegan Tribe for $430 million but will receive a 5% annual dividend on gross revenue generated by the Mohegan Sun until 2014 (http://en.wikipedia.org/wiki/Mohegan_Sun, 10/10/2006).

Both Foxwoods Resort Casino and the Mohegan Sun agreed to pay the state of Connecticut 25% of slot revenues (in both cases over $ 100 million dollars in the first year of operation). As of 2004, more than $ 32 million per month goes to the state from slot revenues and the enterprises employ about 20,000 people (Green, 2004). This agreement was meant to ensure that the tribes maintain their joint monopoly over casino development in the state. In addition, the Mohegan tribe was required to make a one-time payment of $ 3 million and annual payments of $ 500,000 to the local town of Montville. The Mashantucket Pequot, while not required to compensate local communities have, in fact, acted as benefactors to the region supporting a number of new initiatives including road improvements (Carmichael, 1998).

Profile: Mohegan Sun Casino

Wallheimer (2006) reports that, together, these casinos employ more than 22,000 people and have provided income and jobs to local residents during a time when the traditional local industry of defense manufacturing was on the decline. Many residents praise the casinos for creating a shift in the region's economy from manufacturing to tourism (Wallheimer, 2006).

The Mohegan Sun Casino is located on the Mohegan Tribe's reservation next to Uncasville, Connecticut. Visitors can access the casino directly from

Figure 8.2
Mohegan Sun Casino and Resort Hotel (photographed by Barbara Carmichael, November 2003)

Route 395 and Route 2A with little to no increased traffic through the town of Montville. The Mohegan Sun Casino opened its doors on October 12, 1996 and is argued to be the second largest casino in the country. Figure 8. 2 shows external appearance of the Mohegan Sun casino and skyscraper resort hotel. It includes approximately 300,000 square feet of gaming space in the two casinos (Casino of the Sky and Casino of the Earth). It is reported that the Mohegan Sun Casino has more than 6,200 slot machines and 276 table games (including roulette, baccarat, black jack, and craps). In addition to their gambling facilities, the Mohegan Sun Casino has a luxury hotel with convention space and spa; a 10,000 seat arena; 410-seat lounge; and a 300-seat cabaret (Center for Policy Analysis, 2005).

Profile: Montville, Connecticut and the Mohegan Tribe

Montville is one of the 21 towns in New London County and was incorporated in 1786. The Mohegan Tribe is located near Uncasville, Connecticut and members of the Tribe have lived in the surrounding areas such as Montville and other areas of New London County for hundreds of years. The Tribe was federally recognized in March 1994 (The Mohegan Tribe, 2000). Tribal members originally moved to the area from what is now New York just before the first colonists in the seventeenth century. Historically the Pequots were resistant to the colonists, while on the other hand, the Mohegans, were friendly. Eventually the Mohegans and colonists banded together against the Pequots. The Mohegans were very liberal in giving or selling land to the colonists during this period (Town of Montville, 2006).

The Connecticut Department of Economic and Community Development (2001) and US Census Bureau (2000) collected demographic information about the town of Montville. Respondents were not required to identify their race on the survey, but the data indicated that 86% of the residents of Montville identified themselves as White, 5.5% as African American, 1.5% as American Indian, and 1.9% as Asian. Before the Mohegan Sun Casino opened, the town of Montville had a population of approximately 16,673 and by 2001 the population had grown to approximately 18,712 (Connecticut Department of Economics and Community Development, 2001). The median age of residents in 2000 was 36.5 with those between the ages of 25 and 49 representing the highest proportion of residents (US Census Bureau, 2000). According to the 2000 census, approximately 60% of the population earned more than $ 35,000 per year. Before the casino was built the Town of Montville's Assessors Department identified the major employers as: United Nuclear; Faria Corporation; RAN Whitney/ Stone Container (paper mills); AES Thames (power company); and the Town of Montville (Connecticut Department of Economic and Community Development, 2001). In 1997 after the Mohegan Sun Casino was built, the top major employers in the town of Montville included: Mohegan Sun Casino; State of Connecticut Correctional Facility; Board of Education; Faria Meter Corporation and Beit Brothers Corporation.

Methodology

Qualitative data were gathered as part of a wider study of casino impacts (Jones, 2003). While not all respondents provided answers to the open ended questions, some interesting insights were revealed by those who did. Their answers provide a contextual understanding of their quality of life perceptions with reference to the Native American casino.

The Mohegan Sun data were collected in 2002, six years after the opening of the casino. The research population of the Mohegan Sun study, referred to as local residents, included those residents 18 and over currently registered to vote (8,500) in Montville, Connecticut (total population of 16,750) (US Census Bureau, 2000). For research purposes, permission was granted by the Registrar of Voters to acquire address labels for 2002 registered voters. A systematic random sample of 400 was drawn from the population of 8,500 Montville registered voters, with 218 responding to the survey, giving a response rate of 54.5%. Almost 50% (117) of respondents added a qualitative comment at the end of the survey. A summary of the demographic characteristics of the study sample indicate that the overall sample was representative of the population of resident voters in Montville based on the 2000 census data for age, gender, occupation and income levels.

Analysis

The summaries of qualitative comments were first sorted into two main groups: negative impacts and positive impacts. Comments were then subdivided into smaller more manageable categories within each section. If a person had both a positive and negative comment, their views were included in both sections. Overall, there were 43 positive responses about community impacts in Montville, Connecticut and 124 negative.

Some Montville residents were very enthusiastic about the casino providing statements like 'The casino is the best thing that has happened to our community!' and 'I've seen the Mohegan Sun as a positive influence to our community. It has provided employment opportunities and much needed entertainment/recreation while being supportive to the residents. I am proud to say it is in our town!' Another stated 'I have no problems with Mohegan Sun. They have built a beautiful facility and have had a positive influence on the town of Montville.'

In contrast to these positive statements, other people were adamantly opposed to the existence of the casino and the perceived negative impact that it has had on their lives and community. The following quotes are a sample of some of the negative feelings expressed: 'Casino development has killed the area'; 'get rid of the casino; the casino should be in someone else's backyard'; 'and if people think casinos are so great they should try living with them'.

Discussion of 'hot button' issues

At the time of the survey, the casino resort was in the early stage of rapid product development. Resident comments and reactions may reflect 'social disruption theory' (Perdue et al., 1999) where they are faced with major changes in the quality of their environment and experiences. The 'issue attention cycle' aspect of this theory suggest that when new issues catch media attention and affect resident lifestyles and perceptions, usually in the early stage of an event or threat, such issues may become 'hot button' items. At the time of this survey residents were in the early stage of coping with a mega-resort in their midst and were venting their views. While some of the dialogue addresses immediate issues, some is deep seated and reveals historical relationships with the nearby indigenous community.

Several of the comments that the residents made in the survey were consistent with previous research findings on resident attitudes toward tourism (see for example, Pearce et al., 1996; Ap and Crompton, 1993; Haralambopoulos and Pizam, 1996). These included job creation, employment, recreational opportunities, development and planning issues, crime and traffic issues, environmental issues, and local participation in development decisions. Other concerns included: the casino facilities, the Mohegan Tribe as neighbors, increased diversity in the town, tribal sovereignty and federal recognition, impacts on education, opinions about future developments, the immorality of gambling, some general comments and the idea that gambling is not tourism. There is not space in this chapter to examine all of these perceived impacts in detail so we will concentrate on the 'hot button' issues that seemed to be specific to the setting and of great topical concern to the residents. These impacts are directly related to changing power relations in the region and competition over space. Issues were raised over control of the scale and pace of development over which the surrounding communities had no control. One sensitive issue was resentment against incomers of Asian origin who were attracted to the community as workers or gamblers. Their presence was perceived to have led to traffic problems and overcrowding in schools. In addition, while comments about Foxwoods were not specifically asked in the Mohegan Sun survey, such views and comparisons were volunteered by some residents.

Development and planning issues

It appeared that while respondents may, in general, feel that the Mohegan Tribe respects the issues facing the town, they did not feel that townsfolk have influence on the decisions being made in relation to the casino. Several respondents stated that the tribe worked with the town to ensure that the town's concerns were being met while others argued that the residents of Montville have no say in what happens on tribal land or in relation to casino development. Most agreed that it is important to maintain the traditionally strong working relationship between the Mohegan Tribe and the Town of Montville. Some compared their situation with the nearby Foxwoods scenario, where there was no local consultation. Samples of the positive responses include:

The Mohegan Sun developers did a good job including Montville in their plans and construction. It is a much better environment than Foxwoods. All casinos developed should be responsible for the increased costs for services – it should not be placed on the local taxes. Tribes should be as 'town friendly' as the Mohegan's have been this far.

I grew up and know many Mohegan members and they work hard at making sure the people of Montville are not negatively impacted by casino development. There is some negative impact, but I believe the benefits to the Town outweigh the negative.

I am against the town promoting development (casino). But I am not against them doing it themselves within their 600 acre boundary. As of today the Mohegan Tribe and casino has been very good for our town (unlike across the river).

Two of the more negative responses include:

I don't believe that the community (townspeople) really has any say in the casino development.

The Town leadership has worked hard to have a good relationship with the Mohegan Tribe – I think this is wise. With Native American gaming it seems that local communities have no say in casino development. I worry about the 'pro gambling' culture in Connecticut.

Mohegan Tribe as neighbors

This issue was important because there were several comments made about the Mohegan Tribe in terms of it being a 'good neighbor'. It appeared that the people making these statements felt somewhat lucky to be working with the Mohegan Tribe and appeared to have some sympathy for their counterparts working with the Foxwoods casino. This was interesting since there was no mention of Foxwoods anywhere on the survey; yet respondents still made reference to it in comparison to their own issues. The following statements were made with respect to the Mohegan Tribe as a 'good neighbor':

Montville is fortunate to be dealing with the Mohegan Tribe, who have been very good neighbors. At least to this point, my sympathy is to Foxwoods neighbors.

The Mohegan Sun has not impacted Montville, like Foxwoods has Ledyard. In some ways, due to the Tribe's long-term connection to the Town of Montville and their love for the area, they have actually provided enhancement. However, I do not believe that continuing expansion is healthy for the Town and its residents. If the Mohegans and Mashantuckets are as proud of their heritage as they claim, perhaps they should promote their tribal culture, instead of gambling.

Tribal sovereignty and federal recognition

There were a few comments that demonstrated resentment toward the sovereignty of the Mohegan Sun. However, this resentment emerged as more of an issue in the earlier Foxwoods study (Carmichael and Peppard, 1998). The following are comments, some more extreme than others, made in reference to this topic in the Mohegan Sun data:

It is a scourge; a hoax hiding behind the twisted notion of tribal sovereignty; a racist loophole benefiting only those citizens demonstrating 1/16 Native American heritage (or more); a pandering malignancy, which creates obscene wealth on the backs of citizens with weak wills. The endorsement by the Federal Government of this activity seems blatantly out of step with the USA constitution.

I do not believe there should be any more casinos in the state of Connecticut. I do not believe the Indian nations should have special privileges – we should all be 'ONE' Nation – all Americans.

Ethnic diversity and immigrant workers

There were many comments about the casino's practice of hiring 'foreigners' in the Mohegan Sun data, an issue that was not raised at all in the Foxwoods responses (Carmichael and Peppard, 1998). Many of the comments were directed towards people of Asian descent. Comments ranged from concerns about their negative impacts on housing, education and traffic to complaints about some of the workers' lack of English language skills. Overall, Montville residents seem to feel that they were suffering from an 'Asian invasion' that impinged on their idea of an attractive living space. Some of these comments hint at coping strategies related to boundary maintenance (Dogan, 1989) and withdrawal (Ap and Crompton, 1993). The following positive comment was the exception: 'Our town is much more diversified, racially, now which is good in my opinion.' However, the majority of the comments are more negative:

Our neighborhoods are being inundated with Chinese who do not understand English and are walking our roads at all hours of the day and night because they don't drive and have been recruited by the Casino to work here from Boston and New York.

... Casinos provide mostly low paying jobs, and many of these have gone to 'outsiders' who have combined into groups to price many locals out of the housing market.

Biggest negative – Casinos (Mohegan Sun) hires Asians to work menial jobs – housing and transportation is an issue. It will be little time before a large loss of life and injury – major injury – accident or fire occurs.

The quality of casino employees coming in from literally all over the world is extremely poor. They are rude; they overcrowd nice homes and apartments claiming to be from one family – sleep in shifts with beds and mats on the floor. The tourists have been tolerable so far. The employees who are taking up residence here have brought down our quality of life.

Immigrant impacts on traffic

Some of the issues concerning the Asian influx focus upon the impact on local traffic:

I find it very unsafe for the Asians working there. They do not drive; therefore they walk, with dark clothing late at night to and from the casino. It is very very dangerous ...

The roads right now are terrible because they are widening them because of traffic. Hundreds of Asians have moved to Montville. Very few drive, most walk down Rt. 32 and cause serious traffic problems, prices of houses have gone up and they are building so many new stores and businesses.

Immigrant impacts on education

Concern was raised about the influx of children into the local school systems who were not proficient in English. The impact on the school system was expressed as the need for special education such as a second language (ESL) training and the resources that were required to meet this challenge. There were many comments made in reference to this issue. Some of these comments are as follows:

Even though it provided jobs it is costing the town more as people move in. There is a great influx of Asians with children at school age. More teachers and tutors and interpreters need to be hired and there is starting to be overcrowding in the schools. More crime has surfaced. We were just fine before the casino.

The tremendous impact of school age children has yet to be addressed. The language problems of non-English speaking children in school are just getting attention.

Environment and rural degradation

In the Mohegan Sun survey data, a few comments were made about the actual environmental condition of the town as a result of the casino. Several other comments were made about the change in the community atmosphere of what was once a very quiet rural setting to one that is visited by considerably more people and had several new developments as a result of the casino. A sample of these comments includes:

The air now stinks.

...What about our animal population. The more woods taken, the more we see in our yard. That's not safe either.

Buildings are being built everywhere! We moved here to be out in the country.

These views are consistent with those expressed in the earlier Foxwoods study where changes to the environment were found to be a major issue for surrounding communities (Carmichael, 2000, 2003).

Conclusion

This study was intended to provide insight into the social, cultural, economic and environmental impacts perceived by local residents about indigenous owned casino growth in their communities. When compared with some of the findings from previous studies of Foxwoods Casino (Carmichael and Peppard 1998; Carmichael, 2000) it may be concluded that the attitudes toward native owned casino development vary but some common themes emerge. Some of the variation in the findings may be related to the different historical relationships maintained by the Native American and white communities. Common issues likely result from the similar large scale of casino developments and the subsequent competition for resources. It is clear, however, that 'tourism communities are not static but constantly evolving places in terms of tourism development, resident attitudes toward tourism, resident power relationships and resident control over resources' (Carmichael, 2006) and that the communities surrounding casino developments in Connecticut are no exception.

This qualitative analysis indicated that resident attitudes toward casino development vary but on some 'hot button' issues they tend to be polarized. Residents voice strong concern about future casino developments and expansions in Connecticut. In the case of the Mohegan Sun Casino, residents appeared somewhat complacent about its initial construction but generally felt that they had little access to or control over the decision-making process in relation to future expansions. While there was an overall sense that the Mohegan Sun casino has improved the economic situation in the region, residents were critical of the changes and social impacts associated with its development. These results are consistent with other research on casino impacts and quality of life (Canaday and Zeiger, 1991; Long et al., 1994; Carmichael et al., 1996; Nichols et al., 2002).

Residents perceived, however, that long-term planning would alter the nature and the distribution of the impact associated with casino development. The need to balance the needs of different stakeholders in such planning is reflected in the words of one of the Montville residents in this study who stated, 'I believe with proper planning and much consideration for the environment (i.e., noise, light, traffic congestion) the casino, the community and the tourist can all co-exist and have a positive impact for all parties.' Residents would like more involvement in future planning and felt that the town can resolve and control many of the associated impacts with proper planning. The qualitative responses suggest that the community was kept informed of casino developments by the Mohegans and were generally not surprised by the rapid development that occurred. Furthermore, because Foxwoods was already in operation close by Montville residents were aware of what some of the changes were likely to be, even though they had little control over the decisions. Where residents and businesses are able to adjust to and anticipate the effects of Native American casino gaming on their communities, their reaction to the casino is more likely to be positive.

Respondents in the Mohegan Sun survey were generally more positive to the development than respondents to the earlier Foxwoods casino survey were to that development. Foxwoods area residents were aware of economic benefits to their towns but critical of traffic congestion and of the Native American developers' rights to the land (Carmichael et al., 1996). They were threatened by the possible annexation of land and this proved to be a 'hot button' issue in their responses (Carmichael and Peppard, 1998). Indeed attitudes toward the tribe in the case of Foxwoods area residents was much more negative than those of the Mohegan Sun area residents, reflecting deeper seated resentments related to sovereignty and the more hostile relationships from the past.

For Mohegan Sun area residents, the qualitative data revealed a different and interesting cross-cultural 'hot button'. Cross-cultural studies in tourism include those that consider host/guest relationships and interactions (Reisinger and Turner, 1997), different types of tourists and their behaviors (Kim and Lee, 2000) and different types of residents and their behaviors (Ryan et al., 1998). Previous studies have tended to ignore the interactions of employees attracted to a region and the existing local residents, although some studies have considered employee reactions towards different types of tourists (Kim et al., 2002). Where employment is considered it is within the context of economic rather than social impact. However, an unexpected finding in the qualitative analysis of the Mohegan Sun data was the level of resentment found by the Montville residents that was directed toward the casino's Asian employees.

In the case of the Foxwoods study, resentment was directed more toward the Mashantucket Pequots and, at the time of that survey, immigrant employees were not even mentioned (Carmichael and Peppard, 1998). Together, the two casinos created over 20,000 jobs. In the case of Foxwoods which developed first, many unemployed local workers obtained casino jobs and employees were attracted from a wide region including Connecticut, Massachusetts, and Rhode Island (Carmichael, 1998). After the Mohegan Sun opened, immigrant workers were attracted to the casino development and clustered in Montville. Roehl (1999) suggests that more in depth work is needed on the employment impacts of casinos on the quality of life and the nature of the jobs created. While he was referring to aspects of the jobs themselves, as this chapter reveals, the types of workers attracted to these jobs may impact quality of life for other residents in the region.

As casinos continue to expand and additional tribes are federally recognized, casino development and a more diverse gaming industry will require further investigation as to the perceived impact on different segments of locally affected populations (Jones, 2003). At the time of writing, two other tribes have recently won federal recognition: the Eastern Pequots of North Stonington and the Schaghticokes of Kent. Both are eager to open casinos well financed by private developers (Green, 2004).

In addition, studies about the impacts of tribally run casino developments on the lives of tribal members are an area of investigation that is underdeveloped but starting to emerge (Piner and Paradis, 2004; Foley, 2005). In the case of Foxwoods, historical discourses have been analysed to infer tribal views and representations (D'Hauteserre and Carmichael, 2005). The opinions of different groups within a community would provide a more comprehensive understanding of casino impacts. This chapter has shown that in the situation of Indian gaming in Connecticut, the opinions of three groups need to be studied: non-native local residents, tribal members and in-migrant employees and their families. Indeed, if tourism is to merit its pseudonym of being 'the hospitality industry' it must look beyond its own doors and employees to consider the social and cultural impacts it is having on the host community at large (Murphy, 1985).

Part Three

Indigenous Environment and Tourism

One of the strongest and most enduring features of most indigenous cultures has always been the way in which indigenous peoples have integrated with the land in terms of their livelihoods and identities. While many indigenous people have shifted to urban areas thereby altering this close relationship to the land, in contemporary society there remains a strong presence of indigenous people in peripheral areas. The land and its resources are of far greater importance to most indigenous groups than the basic economic value of these attributes, and it is essential that any tourist development does not damage the land and its resources or the relationship which the indigenous population has with those resources. From the perspective of potential non-indigenous tourists, these peripheral areas are not only attractive in terms of their flora and fauna but also as unique indigenous landscapes. In the fist chapter in this section, Carr explores the way in which indigenous nature tourism operators in New Zealand handle this relationship and how they are able to integrate the intrusion of the non-indigenous world in the form of tourism into their traditional areas. It is clear from their responses that while they take their heritage and cultural responsibilities seriously, they appreciate the need to use conventional management approaches in their operations. Carr's respondents see tourism as something which allows them to maintain their links with their traditional lands and to utilize the traditional resources and indigenous culture. In this sense they see tourism in the forms that they provide as complementary to indigeneity. The second chapter by Suntikul looks at the effects of tourism on indigenous communities in Laos. She examines similar issues to those of Carr and Goodwin, in particular the way that ecotourism can be used to alleviate poverty in poor remote agricultural communities. At the present time tourism is seen as providing supplementary income to those communities who choose to become involved in tourism, and not surprisingly is requiring adjustments and change. Development is still at a small scale and generally effectively integrated into the communities but in the future the scale and type of tourism and tourists may change and if so, the nature of the benefits and costs will also change. The final chapter in this section presents somewhat similar results from a study undertaken in Sarawak. Bratek, Devlin and Simmons discuss the development of ecotourism and cultural tourism in and around a national park in Sarawak and the involvement of local communities. One major issue is the role of tourism in the preservation of the national park, as by providing a supplementary income for the communities, it could reduce the need for hunting and lessen the pressure on protected wildlife. They demonstrate that the relationship between tourism and conservation is complex, and that successful tourism development, even at a small scale, is heavily dependent on suitable links with intermediaries who provide the tourists with information about and access to the indigenous tourism opportunities.

Māori nature tourism businesses: connecting with the land

Anna Carr

Introduction

The past decade has seen increasing numbers of nature or ecotourism operations owned and operated by Māori, the most internationally renowned business being Whale Watch in Kaikoura (Neale, 1998; Curtin, 2003). Nature tourism operations that incorporate a Māori perspective of the environment or landscape are diverse and include those that feature consumptive and non-consumptive activities such as guided hunting and fishing, guided walks, canoeing, rafting and wildlife watching (Warren and Taylor, 1994; Higham et al., 2001; Higham and Carr, 2002a, 2003; Carr, 2006). New Zealand's natural landscape is consequently an important economic resource for Māori tourism operators. Cultural tourism opportunities that enable 'learning about Māori mythology' and 'tours of a region with a Māori guide' were identified as being in demand by 'cultural tourists' in a recent review of 82 reports and studies about cultural tourism in New Zealand (Van Aalst and Daly, 2002). Although other reports suggest there is varying demand for Māori cultural experiences, particularly amongst New Zealand residents (McIntosh et al., 2000; Ateljevic and Doorne, 2002; Ryan, 2002), there is support for the view that international demand is growing and domestic visitors are major target markets for some Māori tourism operations (McIntosh et al., 2000; Warren and Taylor, 2001; Colmar Brunton, 2004). Whilst the reports and the academic literature about the cultural philosophies of Māori tourism ventures, and demand for Māori cultural experiences, are plentiful, there has been limited focus on Māori involvement in the nature tourism sector. This chapter provides an overview of Māori operators' contributions to this sector by presenting findings from a study of nature-based tourism operations that included businesses offering Māori perspectives of the natural environment.

Landscape and identity

The diversification of indigenous tourism products beyond staged cultural tourism attractions (e.g., dance performances) is a trend that has gained momentum as the increasing appeal of adventure tourism and ecotourism encourages visitors to experience natural areas with indigenous guides (Almagor, 1985; Hinch and Colton, 1997; Hinch, 1998). Another trend has been the increased awareness of the economic and social significance of cultural and heritage landscapes as tourism resources (Shackley, 1998, 2001). Such landscapes are often an integral component of individual or group identity. The relationship of indigenous peoples to traditionally inhabited landscapes is typified by characteristics including spiritual values, mythology, resource use, ancestral ties and historical links (Walker, 1990, 1992; Hinch and Colton, 1997; Hinch, 1998, 2001; Atkins et al., 1998; Kearsley et al., 1999). It has been suggested that when indigenous peoples have their own personal and collective identities intertwined with cultural landscapes there may be demand from visiting 'outsiders', especially tourists, to experience such values thus gaining insight into the culture (O'Regan, 1990; Hinch and Colton, 1997; Strang, 1997; Hinch, 1998). The communication of a 'sense of place' by tourism operators or guides, who act as mediators between the visitors and the landscape, is one outcome of the visitor experience that may occur. Upitis (1989) commented that the interpretation of cultural sites was important as it enabled understanding of other cultures – 'their needs, values and aspirations, and understanding how people see their place within the environment. It is a sense of place and its significance that one tries to capture when interpreting a cultural site' (p. 154).

Māori often refer to themselves as *tangata whenua* which translates literally as 'people of the land' (Hakopa, 1998). Many Māori consider the land, water, landscape features and various natural resources as living things that possess *mauri* (life force) and consequently may be *tapu* (sacred) (Matunga, 1995; Williams, 1997). They believe that their *mana* (spiritual well-being) is manifested by their associations with traditional lands and resources. Place names, history and mythology or legends add meaning to features in the landscape and the Māori relationship with the land has a psychological value known as '*turangawaewae*' which signifies the 'right of a person to be counted as a member of an iwi or tribe and thus establishes a person's "sense of belonging" to the land and people that occupy the land' (Hakopa, 1998, np).

At a local level, Māori have distinct relationships with the landscapes based on *whanau* (family) and *iwi* (tribe) attachments, and nationwide there is a sharing of traditional values for landscape common to all Māori (Walker, 1990; Roberts et al., 1995). Regional distinctions amongst *iwi* include specific relationships particular to traditional lands, for example legends or stories about ancestors; visiting areas for traditional purposes such as the gathering of *mahinga* or *moana kai* (food) and resources or attending events, such as *tangi* (funerals) on *marae* (meeting grounds) (Walker, 1990, 1992; Sinclair, 1992a, b). The ability to *whakapapa* (demonstrate awareness of one's family tree and ancestral ties) to an area is a way of asserting the identity of individual Māori whilst illustrating the deep relationship between landscape and people. When formally introducing themselves Māori people will often link their *whakapapa* to their geographic place of origin, by identifying their *maunga* (tribal mountain), their *awa* (tribal river), then their *iwi* (tribe), *hapu* (subtribe) and *tupuna* (tribal ancestor) (Matunga, 1995, p. 8).

Numerous academic studies exploring relationships between Māori and tourism have found a wide range of costs and benefits of tourism related to culture, with concerns focusing on issues such as the need to ensure authenticity and Māori control in the development of tourism based on *taonga* (treasured cultural values) (Te Awekotuku, 1981; Ryan, 1997, 2002; Tahana and Opperman, 1998; McIntosh et al., 2000; Zygadlo et al., 2003; Carr, 2004, 2006). At the same time, tourism is perceived as offering opportunities for the improvement of Māoridom's socio-economic status owing to the marketing appeal of the 'bicultural uniqueness' of Māori culture (Ingram, 1996, 1997).

Māori involvement in New Zealand's tourism industry

The 1990s saw a period of rapid growth of the Māori tourism sector ranging from traditional cultural stage performances at the cultural tourism centre of Rotorua to diverse products spanning all sectors of the tourism industry in numerous locations. By the year 2000, the scale of Māori involvement within the tourism sector was estimated to be over 250 indigenous themed or Māori owned and managed operations nationwide (The Stafford Group, 2001). In 2006 the New Zealand Māori Tourism Council (NZMTC) suggested there were more than 600 Māori tourism businesses employing over 18,000 people (Da Cruz, 2006).

The diversification of the Māori tourism product has been supported by government policy and the existence of organizations that enable Māori to be actively involved in the management of tourism within New Zealand. For example, Tourism New Zealand's (TNZ) 'Three Year Strategic Plan 2003–2006' included one strategic outcome listed as being to 'naturally express through the campaign the values of New Zealand's Māori cultural identity' (TNZ, 2003a, p. 3). At the time of writing (2006), a number of government organizations employ Māori staff at upper management level enhancing Māori tourism interests by providing strategic input into policy and product development, marketing and promotion, education and training. Te Puni Kokiri (TPK), the Ministry of Māori Development, offers mentoring, guidance and support to tourism businesses from a centralized base in Wellington and regional offices around the country. The most notable event of recent years has been the formation, through the hard work of a number of Māori tourism operators themselves, of the NZMTC. This organization works alongside agencies including TPK to develop Māori tourism marketing initiatives and provide networking opportunities for operators whilst concentrating on issues including quality standards and authenticity. The NZMTC has established formal relationships, including advisory roles, with nine national bodies relevant to the tourism industry including the Ministry of Tourism, TNZ, TPK, Tourism Industry Association of New Zealand (TIANZ), Inbound Tour Operators' Council (ITOC), Aviation Travel and Tourism Training Organization (ATTTO), Qualmark and the New Zealand Qualifications Authority (NZQA), the latter being concerned with training and standards within the industry (NZMTC, 2005). Furthermore, since 2001, Māori Regional Tourism Organizations (MRTO) have grown in number from four to eleven including some regional organizations with sizable memberships, for example Te Ara a Maui and the Tai Tokerau Māori Tourism Association (TTMTA). NZMTC, MRTOs and the Poutama Trust (an advisory and consultancy service established in 1988 to assist Māori business owners) work together to ensure that nature tourism operators and others involved in related sectors, such as hospitality, have access to information on the development, management and marketing of Māori tourism products that reflect the objectives of the national organizations, reducing any sense of isolation. Networking to enable the international marketing of Māori tourism operations is gaining momentum through initiatives such as the *Māori Experienz and*

Poutama Trust's Indigenous New Zealand website (http://www.inz.Māori.nz/) which listed 97 tourism products ranging from accommodation and transport to guided walks at the time of writing. The existence of such local, regional and national level organizations ensure Māori have an active role in the formation of government policy and other aspects of tourism management at a national or macro-scale.

Methodology

The discussion presented within this chapter is informed by findings from a qualitative research project *exploring the entrepreneurial characteristics and personal experiences of nature tourism operators*. A database of nature tourism operations was developed after an intensive search of relevant internet websites, including the New Zealand Birding Network, NZMTC, Indigenous New Zealand and TNZ's 100% PURE sites. The database resulted in the identification of 316 nature-based owner/operator tourism businesses of which 37 were owned and operated by Māori. *Clusters of nature tourism operators identified in Northland, Otago/Southland and Canterbury resulted in twenty-five businesses being approached to participate via site visits and semi-structured interviews* conducted between August 2004 and March 2005. Five of the participating interview participants identified as Māori and it is their responses that will now be discussed. The promotional material from company websites and company brochures was compiled and reviewed to identify cultural themes and content. Three additional interviews were conducted when the opportunity arose to meet with nature tourism operators at the 2005 annual New Zealand Tourism Industry Conference. Each interview and site visit lasted from one hour up to half a day depending on the business location and availability of the operator. The site visits, detailed written records and participant observations provided valuable insights into the operations. The interview questions were open-ended and asked operators to describe the historical development of their operations, networking, marketing, business attitudes and aspirations, management issues and relationships to the natural environment. All interviews were taped, transcribed and analyzed using themes based on the question topics to interpret the responses.

Results and discussion

A total of eight interviews, including five site visits, were conducted with respondents who identified as Māori. Six of the interview participants were Māori tourism operators and another was an employee of TPK who regularly worked alongside Māori tourism operators. The eighth participant worked for a Māori tourism association. Six participants were male, two were female and five had university or post-graduate educations. Five tourism operators were primarily involved with offering guided walking or soft adventure activities; four of the businesses providing wildlife watching experiences and one of the operators also provided accommodation as well as nature-based activities. Seasonality was a common feature for all the businesses involved in the study, most of them experiencing limited tourism demand over the winter months. All had been in operation for at least 5 years and thus regarded themselves as being well established. The interview participants all reported a shared perception that there was visitor demand for Māori cultural perspectives of the environment. Such demand was thought to be a driver in the emergence of specialized, indigenous tourism products offering guided interpretation within the eco-, nature and adventure tourism sectors. All of the interview participants voiced the belief that their business success was interwoven with the ability to provide experiences of the landscape from a Māori perspective that was unique to New Zealand. Each operator indicated that their identity as Māori influenced the management of their business to varying degrees, particularly in respect to networking with other operators or as members of organizations including the MRTOs or the NZMTC. Whilst one of the operators, a hunting guide, did not refer to his cultural background during interactions with visitors, his cultural identity was mentioned in his biography and Māori artwork was a dominant design feature on the business website. In contrast, a rafting operator identified strongly with his heritage and felt that he was able to 'provide a genuine glimpse into Māori culture; assisting with the growth of the *marae* financially and the guests in life enrichment'. Four of the operators primarily communicated their Māori identity to visitors through the retelling of myth or tribal history and the focus of three businesses was on the need to conserve indigenous flora and fauna during guided walks. An important aspect of offering cultural perspectives was that it enabled the operators themselves to learn more about personal tribal histories.

Key themes emerging from the interviews associated with cultural identity are summarized as:

- Identity expressed by working on traditional lands;
- Storytelling – myths and legends;
- Relating personal family or tribal history to visitors;
- Identity and environmental causes;
- Traditional physical activity in the landscape;
- Self-improvement through business management;
- Affirmation of identity in marketing.

Connecting with traditional lands through work

That nature-based tourism provided opportunities to gain employment on traditional lands was seen as a positive outcome by three of the interview participants. The literature review and analysis of websites and brochures revealed numerous examples of Māori operators who incorporated references to their sense of belonging within the environment when marketing their products. Historically, the 1840 Treaty of Waitangi is the founding document by which the British Crown and Māori agreed to the settlement of New Zealand by British subjects. Article Two of the Treaty of Waitangi was intended to guarantee Māori their exclusive rights and interests to collective land, resources and *taonga* (Sinclair, 1992a, b). However, by the late nineteenth century a combination of colonization, government legislation, land wars and land confiscations had disenfranchised Māori society, with many individuals and *iwi* losing their lands (Walker, 1990; Sinclair, 1992a, b). The consequence was that the majority of New Zealanders with Māori ancestry live outside their traditional *rohe* (boundaries of tribal homelands) despite Treaty settlements that recognize traditional land rights, including the *kāitiakitanga* (guardianship) of natural resources (O'Regan, 1990; Walker, 1992; Roberts et al., 1995). Since 1987, Māori have been recognized as partners with the government in the bicultural management of New Zealand's natural resources. The rights of the *tangata whenua* to exercise *kāitiakitanga* of natural resources have been acknowledged in government legislation. Employment with Māori government agencies or departments such as Department of Conservation (DOC) and the increased participation by Māori in the provision of nature or ecotourism products has further enhanced Māori involvement in the management of natural areas (Higham and Carr, 2002a, b, 2003; Carr, 2004, 2006).

Kapiti Alive Nature Tours (Kapiti Island) and Ulva's Guided Walks (Stewart Island) are best practice examples of Māori owner–operators whose businesses provide the opportunity to live and work on traditional lands. The promotional material of both operations include statements that (a) they offer experiences of natural places incorporating local perspectives and (b) convey their personal self-identification with their Māori cultural heritage.

Kapiti Alive Nature Tours is a family operated business based on traditional whanau lands at the north end of Kapiti Island (near Wellington). The business not only provides boat transport and accommodation in an ecolodge but the family and employees also manage an interpretation service that informs all visitors arriving on the island about Kapiti Island Nature Reserve. The island is a haven for endangered bird species as a result of a highly successful pest eradication programme in the 1980s. The interpretation narrative of the business interweaves the socio-cultural history of the island within an overarching message of the need to conserve natural habitat for indigenous New Zealand species. Kapiti Island is under the management of the DOC and there are strict regulations governing visitor access, visitor numbers and visitor behaviour whilst on the island. These regulations are observed on the privately owned whanau lands. A strong sense of kāitiakitanga underlies the company's philosophy as the family's identity is intertwined with the land and there is an unspoken assumption that their future generations will continue to live on the land. According to the promotional website:

John and Amo's iwi (tribe) and whaanau (family) have been living on Kapiti Island since the 1820s, and have accumulated an unsurpassed collection of knowledge and experiences on the island's history and growth as a world renowned nature reserve, and willingly share this knowledge with their visitors.

(http://www.kapitiislandalive.co.nz/ThePeople.htm)

This business's brochure, titled 'Kapiti Island: it's a very special place', incorporates a Māori panel design on the front page logo and the inner page background includes an image from a Māori carving. These design features, complemented by the greeting 'Haere Mai: Welcome', set the scene for a nature-based experience with Māori influences.

Ulva Amos is the other operator whose family ties with the landscape within which she works are highlighted in promotional material. The Ulva's Guided Walks website includes an introduction that states how her personal identity is linked with the environment within which she works.

Ulva is named after the Island, is a direct descendant of the first Māori peoples of Stewart Island. She is passionate and very knowledgeable about this special place and would love to share it with you . . . we will provide you with a unique experience, learning about native flora and fauna from a Māori and local Stewart Island perspective.

(http://www.ulva.co.nz/)

Three of the operators, a hunting guide and two guided walks operations, considered the opportunity to operate their businesses on tribal lands as a privilege and birth right. One operator considered his concession to operate on Crown land as a political victory for his family who were from an *iwi* whose land had been confiscated in the nineteenth century. Being able to return to the 'family lands' to operate his business increased not only his sense of attachment to the land but also his political identity as a member of an *iwi* involved in a Treaty claim who were now acknowledged as *tangata whenua* by officialdom. Whilst having to endure the typical challenges facing small businesses in the early years of business start up, all three operators enjoyed being able to personalize the experiences of native wildlife and landscapes by incorporating their ancestral histories and family attachments to the land in visitor interpretation, the focus of the next two themes.

Storytelling: myths and legends

Another recurring theme that was observed during the analysis of promotional literature was reference to mythology and legends about landscape. Figure 9.1 provides examples of written excerpts from websites and brochures that inform visitors of cultural aspects of the businesses. Numerous writers have acknowledged that mythology and legends entwine communities of people to the landscape and that narratives are an important aspect of collective heritage identity and the cultural landscape (O'Regan, 1990; Uzzell, 1996; Kearsley et al., 1999; Pfister, 2000; Shackley, 2001).

Mythology relates, for contemporary Māori, the deeds of their ancestors and explains the traditional view of the formation of the natural world (Walker, 1992). One of the initial marketing campaigns of the TTMTA was inspired by mythology with a brochure inviting visitors to experience the world of the Māori in the Northland region of the country through the tourism products, undertaking 'a journey hearing the stories and legends as

Figure 9.1 Cultural references in eco-cultural tourism promotional material

Operation Name	Region	Summary of brochure/website references
Tall Tale Travel 'n Tours	Kaitaia	Field trips to visit areas of significance, pa sites, marae, bush and sea . . . visit Te Rerenga Wairua Departing Place of the Spirits. . . .
Bay of Islands Heritage Tours	Paihia	Hear myths and legends relevant to the children of Tangaroa and experience a traditional Māori welcome as you board the boat. The whanau has been in the bay for over 900 years!
Te Rawhiti 3B2, Cape Brett Walk	Russell, Cape Brett	Walk the Valleys of our Ancestors. Learn the history. Marvel the beauty (Māori proverb), . . . Learn more about Māori and our attachment to the land, bush and history.
Manaia Hostel and Treks	Kohukohu	Hear the myths and legends from your Māori guides as you cross massive canyons containing fossilized remnants of the pa . . . strong traditions associated with Nukutawhiti, grandson of Kupe.
Kaitoki Bush Camp	Kawakawa	A Māori cultural experience with a Ngatihine family on pristine Northland forest with unpolluted water . . . learn about Māori cultural perspectives, Māori medicines of the forest and the transition to the modern world of Māori as we are today.
Footprints Waipoua	Hokianga	Step into the spiritual environment of the Waipoua Forest and stroll amongst the largest remaining stand of kauri in the world. Let our local guides introduce you to the beautiful natural surroundings while listening to mythological interpretations.

(Continued)

Figure 9.1 (*Continued*)

Operation Name	Region	Summary of brochure/website references
Kaitiaki Adventures	Rotorua	Every river excursion that Kaitiaki undertakes starts with a traditional Maori prayer (karakia) to pay respect to the Ngati Pikiao, the people of the river.
Rotoiti Tours	Rotorua	Situated on the shores of Lake Rotoiti which is the first lake discovered in the district by our revered ancestor Ihenga.
Te Kohu Track	Whakatane	Guided walks through Te Urewera National Park with a Māori guide, special 3 day trip to Maungapohatu sacred mountain.
Whirinaki Escape Walk/Trek Whirinaki	Taupo/Rotorua	An introduction to a world-renowned rainforest and the Tangata Whenua, the original people of the land . . . 'all tours involve local Māori guides, a Marae visit following protocol observed over many centurieis, a hangi meal and an introduction to the legends and myths of a region long inhabited'.
Wairua Hikoi Tours	Jerusalem	Spiritual and cultural journey explaining the history of the Whanganui River' "journey through serene valleys clad in native forest which hold the ancestral stories of both Māori and European".
Mt Taranaki Adventures	Mount Taranaki	Legend of Taranaki – cultural and adventure tour from Kaponga to Dawson Falls on the southern slopes of Mt Taranaki . . . secret locations known to Māori.
Myths and Legends Eco Tours	Marlborough	Sixth generation Kiwi, Peter Beech, and his Maori wife Takutai, take you out into the Marlborough Sounds on an eco-oriented wildlife and cultural cruise, highlighting fascinating stories handed down through their Maori and Pakeha families.

seen through the eyes of Māori' (TTMTA, 1998). The analysis of promotional material typically found comments such as that in the Bay of Islands Heritage Tours brochure which mentioned that visitors are able to hear 'myths and legends relevant to the children of Tangaroa (Māori God of the Sea)'. Five of the operators mentioned that, depending on their visitor audience, they would refer to such common mythology shared by all Māori when guiding people through the landscape.

Relating personal family or tribal history

The interpretation of family history or a locally specific legend provides Māori with an opportunity to reaffirm their sense of place or identity by informing visitors of their historic, ancestral and spiritual ties with culturally significant areas (O'Regan, 1990; Keelan, 1996). Māori businesses throughout New Zealand not only communicate the common myths shared by all *iwi* but also refer to local legends or tribal history within their tourism products, sometimes at the very physical settings where the events occurred (Kearsley et al., 1999; Carr, 2004, 2006). Such references to specific family or tribal knowledge as part of the cultural tourism experience were utilized by all but one of the seven operators (a fishing guide). One operator remarked that he interpreted 'The Ngatimaru history – the specific *hapu* and *iwi* stories – as it relates to this particular area' preferring to focus on local events rather than more general myths common to the wider Māori community. The NZMTC and TNZ have both been proactive with the development and promotion of products that encourage the use of storytelling skills by tourism operators at the same time realizing the need to protect such stories as intellectual property that should only be shared after consent is obtained from Māori. There is also a growing awareness of the potential for specific *iwi* to differentiate their nature tourism ventures by delivering unique *iwi* values or traditions to receptive members of the visiting public (NZMTC, 2005; Carr, 2006).

Identity and environmental causes

Dependence on the environment for their livelihood undoubtedly contributed to all the Māori operators expressing their concern with issues such as habitat loss or the plight of endangered species. Five of the seven Māori operators interviewed for the study felt that environmental mismanagement was of great concern to them as individuals and business owners. Pollution and competition for resources such as water and fisheries were seen as negatively impacting on both cultural values and business (see chapter by Butler and Menzies, Editors' Note). All the operators reported being involved with some form of environmental project. One adventure tourism operator commented that 'as part of our concession to raft the Motu River we are asked to report all our sightings of endangered species, plants and animals as well as any noticeable pest activity'. Another operator was proud of his involvement in DOC initiatives such as a 'kiwi recovery programme and the replanting of native trees, mainly rimu and totara' to compensate any negative impacts from his business. Another operator participated in pest eradication and two operators reported long-term involvement with tree replanting and re-establishing native bird populations in their respective areas. Not only were they nature tourism operators but through their interest in the sustainable management of local habitats they identified as environmentalists or caretakers of the landscape through their activities.

Traditional physical activity in the landscape

The non-consumptive activities mentioned in the previous theme contrasted with interview responses concerning the consumptive use of nature. Three operators considered the ability to partake in traditional food gathering activities (hunting, gathering *kai moana* sea food and fishing) through their business was an essential aspect of how they identified with their Māori culture. The benefits of connecting with cultural landscapes through physical or traditional activities have been acknowledged by previous writers for instance:

An outdoor or resource based experience personal to Māori, which invigorates, refreshes and creates in Māori, the 'new person', which reinforces cohesion within the whanau, promotes self esteem, cultural pride, an understanding of one's history and tradition, and a reinforcing of one's identity as Māori.

(Matunga, 1995, p. 8)

Matunga viewed Māori participation in the outdoors as a means of linking people and place, or tangata whenua with their turangawaewae, exploring the natural environments and cultural traditions of their tupuna, reinforcing basic values of Māori culture and instilling a sense of cultural pride.

(Matunga, 1995, p. 18)

Recognition of the opportunities that outdoor recreation offers Māori in developing self-identity has parallels with Māori involvement in delivering nature tourism – both activities being based in outdoor settings. The management of conflicting environmental values between indigenous hosts and their non-indigenous guests is a sensitive area (Hinch, 1998). Such conflicts may only be understood or resolved on a case specific basis. No potential controversy surrounding consumptive tourism activities within the environment had been encountered by the interview participants who viewed traditional food gathering practices as a privilege to be exercised with the utmost respect of the environment.

Self-improvement through business management

Another common theme that was relevant to the participants' personal identities related to their perceptions of themselves as business owners. Whilst Māori operations may incorporate Māori principles and values within business practice, one operator voiced the concern that 'the reality is Māori operators are working within a non-Māori business environment therefore there is a need for commercial "savvy" to ensure economic success'. The economic health of their businesses was paramount for at least three of the operators. One of the interview participants felt secure with his identity as Māori and whilst offering numerous cultural experiences as a primary tourism product (traditional carving, walking activities and *marae* style accommodation) much of his time was spent on business management and administrative tasks. Indeed many Māori tourism operators have been quick to adapt Western-style corporate management structures whilst working within the broader business environment that is heavily influenced by a traditional European-style democratic government. This was not always perceived as a benefit and six of the operators had concerns with the impact of government regulations on their day-to-day business activities. As one Northland operator commented:

Providing authentic experiences and being true to my culture is of importance but at the end of the day I have to pay taxes and ensure I comply with legislation – compliance and dealing with 'red tape' takes up a substantial amount of my time.

Another operator commented that with her business she was more concerned with the struggles of finding time to complete administration work and learn new skills such as computer technology than cultural issues. She praised the work of the NZMTC as they produced comprehensive information that enabled her to remain familiar with the key issues surrounding debates on the communication of Māori cultural identity – something she did not have time to participate in herself owing to the demands of her workplace. The realities of the broader business environment and compliance requirements meant the Māori operators had no choice but to observe western business practices (e.g., marketing, administration, taxation). No operators expressed the viewpoint that they felt compromised in any way, all being happy to move between both cultural systems as necessary.

Affirmation of identity in marketing

Prior to the 1990s much of New Zealand's off-shore tourism promotional material represented Māori as the exotic 'Other' with media stereotypes of Māori maidens or warriors accentuating the difference between Māoris and international visitors. The images within tourism promotional media were usually of packaged tourism attractions and have been accused of not being representative of contemporary Māori, many of whom live in urban environments and are removed from their traditional landscapes (NZMTC, 2005) (see chapters by Hollinshead and Hall, Editors' Note).

Recent promotional material has attempted to present a more realistic image by featuring Māori in diverse settings. Increasingly attractions and iconic destinations are promoted with images that have accompanying statements about the relationship between Māori and the land, especially when associated with eco- or nature-based tourism. Such promotional references have value in selling the uniqueness of the cultural experience when alerting potential visitors to the range of possibilities now being offered by Māori nature tourism operations. All the Māori operators interviewed expressed pride in their identity as Māori and how Māori tourism was being marketed. Zygadlo et al. (2003, p. 11) regarded self-identification as Māori as a pragmatic way of identifying and distinguishing Māori businesses 'from similar products on offer'. Several of the operators worked in peripheral areas away from the main tourism centres and enjoyed the contact and support resulting from networking as members of their local MRTOs and the NZMTC (even if much contact was electronic via e-mail newsletters). Consequently any sense of isolation resulting from operating in remote areas is being reduced and operators have opportunities to voice their thoughts on the marketing of their culture should they desire. All interview participants were aware of initiatives by the NZMTC and other organizations such as TNZ to ensure the sustainable marketing of Māori cultural tourism especially with the use of images or references to cultural *taonga*. Two of the interview participants were on the committees of their MRTOs or the NZMTC and considered resolving issues surrounding the sustainable marketing of Māori culture to be a significant objective of the organizations.

Conclusions

Tourism products that provide visitor experiences based on Māori cultural heritage dimensions of natural areas are unique experiences that cannot be found outside of New Zealand. A recent 'Mana' magazine article reports George Hickton, CEO of TNZ commenting on the launch of a nature walk at Te Puia (formerly the New Zealand Māori Arts and Craft Institute in Rotorua) that:

[t]he sorts of people Tourism New Zealand is targeting to attract to New Zealand are very interested in Māori culture and are seeking an authentic and genuine exposure to it. Te Puia offers the kind of experience these visitors are looking for.

(Mana, 2005, p. 25)

TNZ has identified the 'ideal' tourist as the 'interactive traveller' who 'seek(s) interaction with local culture, especially Māori culture', in their search for 'new experiences that involve engagement and interaction and demonstrate respect for natural, social and cultural environment' (TNZ, 2003b; Colmar Brunton, 2004). The global nature tourism market is a competitive one and New Zealand faces many marketing challenges when promoting itself as a long haul destination. The existence of quality Māori cultural tourism products is perceived as giving New Zealand a competitive advantage. In the words of Johnny Edmonds (CEO of the NZMTC) such operations are 'providing New Zealand with its unique positioning in the global market place' (NZMTC, 2005, p. 63). Nevertheless, such cultural tourism development requires careful planning and community input to ensure the authenticity and cultural integrity of *taonga* such as mythology is not compromised (O'Regan, 1990; Keelan, 1996; Pfister, 2000). The inclusion of references to cultural values serve not only a strategic marketing purpose but enables Māori to identify their relationships with the natural resources or places visited. At the local level, cultural identity was reported in the interviews as directly affecting the development of the nature tourism product by the individual or *whanau* (family) group. Where development is strategically managed, as this study has shown, the economic benefits of owning and operating a tourism business are enhanced by offering operators' opportunities to nurture personal identity through enabling their connection to ancestral land. Simultaneously, Māori operators embrace western business practices to gain competitive advantages by utilizing indigenous brands or incorporating cultural references within promotional material. Inextricably linked to independent marketing of businesses by owner/operators is the development of collaborative marketing strategies by MRTO's and the NZMTC. These collaborative efforts ensure Māori are at the forefront of cultural tourism strategies and promotion nationally and internationally. Thus local, regional and international marketing of Māori owned and operated nature tourism products will increasingly rely on the ability of operators to deliver the 'unique' message through the inclusion of cultural values for landscape as part of the visitor experience. Finally, the continued involvement of supporting organizations in the mentoring of businesses (to ensure operators develop essential business management skills) and careful planning is required, particularly in isolated locations, to ascertain visitor demand and to avoid an oversupply of such experiences.

Acknowledgements

This research was funded by a University of Otago Research Grant. The valuable time that Māori tourism operators spent away from their business to be interviewed was greatly appreciated. Field assistance from Maria Amo and support from Johnny Edmond and Peter Kitchen (both Tai Tokerau Mori Tourism Association and NZ Māori Tourism Council) and Rosalie Williams (Te Puni Kokiri) is acknowledged.

CHAPTER 10

The effects of tourism development on indigenous populations in Luang Namtha Province, Laos

Wantanee Suntikul

Introduction

This chapter is based largely on research on community-based tourism (CBT) carried out on site in Laos in 2006. With the support of SNV, a Dutch Non-Governmental Organisation (NGO) in Lao, and the Provincial Tourism Office (PTO) in Luang Prabang, the author carried out a field study in the northern province of Luang Namtha. The purpose of this field study was to assess the current state and future aspirations for community-based eco-tourism (CBE) in that area. The author was invited by the CBE national project leader of the Lao National Tourism Administration (LNTA) in Luang Namtha to participate in the organisation's fieldwork, to gain a better understanding of the LNTA's initiatives in CBT. This fieldwork included a trek to the village of Ban Nalan in the Nam Ha National Protected Area (NPA), the site of the first official CBE project in Laos, where the author conducted informal interviews with villagers regarding their perceptions of tourists and potential tourism development in their village.

After completing the research in Ban Nalan, the author conducted interviews in Luang Namtha with an advisor to a private tour operator, Green Discovery Tours, and with the manager of the Nam Ha Ecoguide Service (NHEGS) of Luang Namtha Provincial Tourism Office. Semi-structured interviews were conducted, in order to address key issues in CBT in a systematic way, while allowing the flexibility to react on important themes that arose in the course of the interviews. Following the field study in Luang Namtha, the author returned to Luang Prabang to conduct further interviews, using the same questions, with four tour operators who offer CBE products.

Indigenous populations in Laos

Laos is a landlocked country in Southeast Asia, bordering on Vietnam to the East, Cambodia to the South, Thailand to the Southwest, Myanmar to the northwest and China to the North. Historically an isolated backwater of Southeast Asia, Laos is becoming increasingly integrated into regional transport and economic networks. The population of Laos is around six million, 87% of whom are rural dwellers. Laos has the lowest population density of any Asian country. According to 2003 figures, 51% of Laos' GDP is derived from agriculture, with services and industry accounting for 26% and 23%, respectively (Country Report, 2006). Sixty-eight ethnic groups are native to Laos, with ethnic minorities, many of which are indigenous to the area, making up 40% of the population (Evrard and Goudineau, 2004). Many of these ethnic minorities still pursue some of their traditional ways of life and customs. Among the indigenous people of Laos, the Laotian government distinguishes between the primarily ethnic Lao inhabitants of the country's lowland regions (*Lao Loum*, 55% of the population in 1993) and the predominantly ethnic minority midland (*Lao Theung*, 27%) and upland dwellers (*Lao Soung*, 18%). The Lao Theung and Lao Soung are largely isolated from the more developed, affluent and accessible lowlands of the country (Thomson and Baden, 1993). Many of these indigenous ethnic minorities in the more remote reaches of the country subsist at sub-poverty levels in a non-cash economy. An estimated 280,000 families representing 45% of villages in Laos still rely on slash-and-burn agriculture for their subsistence (Evrard and Goudineau, 2004).

Ecotourism and poverty alleviation in Laos

The tourism industry in Laos has grown to become the country's top source of foreign exchange. Tourist arrivals to Laos increased from 346,460 in 1995 to over one million in 2005, by which time US$ 146 million in revenues in Laos was attributed to tourism (LNTA, 2006). The Laotian tourism sector grew by 11.8% in that year and an estimated 18,000 Laotians were directly employed in the tourism industry. An estimated seventeen times that number were employed in jobs indirectly created by the tourism sector, bringing the total number of direct or indirect tourism jobs to 321,155 (Lao PDR Country Report, 2005). The Laotian government has named 'tourism and service' as one of eight 'national socio-economic priority programs'.

Most of the main tourism attractions in Laos are natural or cultural heritage sites, including three UNESCO World Heritage Sites, 15 national cultural sites and 20 national parks. Approximately 46% of tourism income in Laos is associated with the nature and culture tourism sub-sector.

Tourism development is one of eleven 'flagship programs' in an ADB/GMS (Asian Development Bank/Greater Mekong Subregion) development plan for furthering the subregion's 2015 Millennium Development Goals (MDG) of reducing poverty, increasing gender equity and promoting biodiversity and sustainable development. The number of international non-government organisations (INGOs) working on poverty-reduction-related projects in rural areas of Laos increased from 13 in 1985 to 56 in 2000 (Chithtalath, 2006). Wells-Dang and Buasawan (2006) have commented that, because 93% of Laotians subsisting below that country's poverty line are members of ethnic minorities, poverty eradication in Laos corresponds to ethnic development (see chapters by Goodwin; Sofield and Li; Salole, Editors' Note).

Conservation, tourism and poverty alleviation are closely related in Laotian government policy. In 1993, twenty zones accounting for an eighth of Laos' total area were declared National Biodiversity Conservation Areas (NBCAs), for possible later development into national parks that would be foci for nature-based tourism (Country Report, 2006). Ecotourism has been identified by the Laotian government as a highly promising strategy for development of tourism offerings that cater to this demand. The stated goals of ecotourism in Laos are to bring socio-economic and environmental improvements to rural communities, abetting the conservation of NPAs and expanding the number of tourism products for the international market. Because CBE also keeps tourists under the watch of local authorities, ecotourism is used as a strategy for maintaining control over tourists' movements and monitoring their safety (Interview with Green Discovery, 2006).

Tourism in Luang Namtha province: background

Luang Namtha is a province in the northwest of Laos, bordering on China's Yunnan Province and Myanmar (Burma). Luang Namtha consists of five districts with a total population of 125,000. The provincial capital city is also called Luang Namtha. More than twenty indigenous ethnic groups live in the province, many still living in rustic villages and practicing their traditional lifestyles and customs. It is a mountainous and forested region. Centrally situated in the province is the 222,400 square hectare Nam Ha NPA, which is densely forested and home to a wide range of wildlife, including more than 37 mammal species and 280 types of birds. Twenty-six ethnic villages of the Akha, Khamu, Hmong and Lantaen people are also located within the NPA (Oula, 2005).

Although most tourists tend to concentrate on the country's more established and accessible tourism centres, the more remote areas of Laos have also seen an increase in tourism in recent years. The number of visitors to Luang Namtha Province rose from 4,732 in 1995 to more than 24,700 in 2000. To accommodate these visitors, as of 2000, there were 37 hotels and guesthouses serving tourists in four districts in the vicinity of Nam Ha, ranging in price from US$ 1 to US$ 15 a night (Lyttleton and Allcock, 2002). A survey of international tourists already in the Luang Namtha area found that the two strongest factors that attracted these tourists to the area were ethnic minorities (67.9% of respondents) and nature (66.0%). Cultural attractions (50.4%) and the 'novelty effect' of a new destination (43.5%) also were strong influences (Schipani, nd).

The Nam Ha Ecotourism Project

Poverty alleviation and conservation initiatives are important drivers for tourism development from the perspective of the Laotian government. Since 1999, with funding from the governments of New Zealand and Japan, UNESCO and the LNTA carried out a pioneering project to create a framework for the economically and socially sustainable development of tourism in the Nam Ha NPA. The main collaborations are the Ministry of Agriculture and Forestry, and Ministry of Information and Culture. The project aims to use ecotourism as a catalyst for social and economic empowerment and livelihood improvement for the poor local ethnic minorities as well as formulating guidelines for sustainable ecotourism development that can serve as a model for other areas of Laos. The Nam Ha Ecotourism Project (NHEP) is the very first CBE project in the country and is already serving as a demonstration of ecotourism development principles. In participation with provincial governmental bodies, local people and tour guides in the area, three trekking programs and a river tour have been developed. These programs provide opportunities for visitors to experience the area's most distinctive natural attractions and visit ethnic minority settlements, where lodging is provided for the trekkers, while giving local communities and authorities the opportunity to participate in the planning of tourism in their area and to share in the benefits (Schipani and Marris, (n.d.). The Nam Ha project was given a United Nations Development Program (UNDP) award for its contribution to poverty alleviation in the area (Project Development Facility by GEF, 2005).

A 3-year-long second phase of the NHEP was begun in 2004, to consolidate and build upon the success of the first phase by improving and expanding the CBE model in Luang Namtha, bolstering the local management capacity for CBE, increasing private sector involvement in offering of CBE products and optimising coordination of CBE measures with conservation, natural resources management, rural development and poverty alleviation, with an emphasis on the training of local guides, private sector stakeholders and especially women and members of ethnic minorities to actively participate in the planning and administration of CBE activities (LNTA, 2004).

Tourism and the local economy

The increase in tourism has brought income to locals running tourism businesses and has encouraged a proliferation of tourism related businesses that contribute to the local economy. From 2001 to 2005, NHEGS operated 1,331 tours served 6,801 participants and generated US$ 137,794 in gross revenue. Of this total, US$ 9485 went to village funds (Harrison and Schipani, 2007). A 2005 assessment of Nammat Kao and Nammat Mai, two of the ethnic minority villages participating in the NHEP, concluded that around US$ 10,000 in revenue had been generated in these two villages through the provision of guide services, accommodation, food and handicraft sales to tourists in the period from October, 2001 and December, 2003. However, richer families earned more than poorer families due to their influence in the village and their superior business and financial management skills (Oula, 2005). According to the provisions of the project, income generated by treks within the NHEP is distributed 26% to villagers, 29% to the guides, 22% to businesses providing transport and food and 23% to cover administration costs.

In a 2005 interview, Bill Tuffin, owner of the Boatlanding Guesthouse in Muang Sing acknowledged the role of cultural pride and access to information as motivators for indigenous people in tourism, but said that most villagers in Laos with whom he had spoken see tourism primarily as a way to earn money (Tuffin, 2005). The government-enforced elimination of opium farming and slash-and-burn agriculture, the increasing integration of remote areas of Laos into the national market economy, as well as growing access to retail goods such as manufactured clothing may all be factors motivating this money-oriented thinking. However, a Participatory Poverty Assessment from 2000 found that many rural communities in Laos still defined well-being in terms of food security rather than income, so that economic development in these areas may not necessarily contribute to perceived improvements in well-being (Wells-Dang and Buasawan, 2006).

The area's former dependence on opium farming, and the current government suppression of this practice, are problems with which indigenous communities are struggling (Shum, 2005). Tourism has been referred to as a 'replacement crop' for opium, just as tourism served as a replacement crop for waning sugar production in Cuba in the 1990s (Winson, 2006). Some of the handicrafts for tourists are produced by opium addicts, needing to earn cash to support their habit now that the villages are no longer allowed to grow opium. Tourism entrepreneur Mr. Tuffin observed that the village with the most opium addicts also has the largest selection of handicrafts available for purchase. While not belittling the seriousness of the opium addiction problem, he saw this as a way to give addicts a measure of control over their lives and to reduce the environmental damage caused by the wildlife poaching by which they might otherwise earn their sustenance (Tuffin, 2005).

Money earned from tourism has already had a positive effect on the village of Ban Nalan where US$ 4,000 in tourism revenue was used to give the village a clean water supply. Ban Nalan was the first village in Laos to practice CBT, since October 2000. Villagers here receive training in tourism skills and the money earned from home-stays goes into a village bank from which villagers can borrow. The villagers themselves decide on distribution of funds from this pool (Interview with the national NHEP project manager, 2006). The frequency with which each family is allowed to serve food to tourists and thus earn income is determined by the family's economic standing. The poorest families are allowed seven times, average families five times and more well-off families three times. The village chief reported that life in the village had improved greatly since CBT started (Personal communication, 2006).

Patterns of economic activity in these areas have been influenced by tourism. Akha women bring their handicrafts into towns such as Muang Sing to sell to tourists during the high tourist season, often staying in town for several days. Women in Laos have traditionally produced handicrafts, both for domestic use and for sale to provide supplemental income. Until 1987, the Laotian government encouraged the wearing of traditional clothing, for economic and ideological reasons. Recent relaxation of trade controls has given Laotians access to inexpensive market goods, decreasing demand for traditional clothing and crafts (Thomson and Baden, 1993). While foreign products are finding their way to the more remote areas of Laos, indigenous people in Laos do not have access to far-reaching networks of distribution for their own products. Tourism represents an alternate source of demand for these products, which could help in preventing these crafts from disappearing altogether.

Since the arrival of tourists to the villages, villagers have not had to take their wares to larger markets to sell them. The villages have also benefited from providing the tourists with accommodation and food. One village chief explicitly wished for a road that would bring many big buses full of tourists to his village, adding that he would not welcome tourists that just wanted to pass through the village without staying overnight, because then the village could not profit from them (Neudorfer, 2006).

Indigenous groups in Laos as tourism attraction

Recent tourists to the area seem to be drawn by the image of the local indigenous minorities as a society largely unspoiled by contact with the modern world, (i.e., the exotic other) and express interest in experiencing close contact with this culture during their stay in the area. About a quarter of tourists in a 2005 survey professed interest in a homestay in a village, yet in the same survey many expressed apprehension that the village could become overrun with tourists, compromising the authenticity of their experience (Shum, 2005). Authentic and unspoilt cultural and natural environments are key attractors for tourists coming to Laos. Trekking tours to visit natural sites and ethnic villages are quite popular. A 2002 survey identified 55% of international tourists to Laos as being interested in hikes to remote villages and 38% in river rafting excursions (Country Report, 2006).

'The Akha Experience' is a community-run tourism enterprise providing 3-day tours to experience the life of the Akha minority in Muang Sing. It is operated by eight Akha villages in cooperation with the tour operator Vientiane Tours/Exotissimo and the German non-profit organisation GTZ (*Deutsche Gesellschaft für Technische Zusammenarbeit*). The project seeks to support the preservation of Akha culture whilst bringing income and knowledge into the Akha community (LNTA website). This project is seen as a groundbreaking assistance initiative, in which the government pursues poverty alleviation by investing in a local private sector enterprise. Villagers provide the labour, run the guesthouses, provide the guides and other services and offer handicrafts for sale to tourists. All proceeds are put into a communal fund for the village (Shum, 2005). The government tourism office funds the building of the lodges. Families serve as 'local guides' on a rotating basis, cleaning the lodge and bringing water to the guests. In exchange, the government pays the family 10,000 KIP (about US$ 1) per visit. This unit price per visitor has fallen from 17,000 to 20,000 KIP per visit at the beginning of 2004. Other enterprising villagers sell rice and vegetables, handicrafts and massages to tourists, although there are almost no handicrafts available in the villages with lodges for overnight stays, and villagers are often uncertain as to how to approach tourists to make sales to them (Neudorfer, 2006).

Whilst gaining contact and exposure to Akha culture, the participants in the Akha experience and other such tours are by no means integrated into the day-to-day life of the village. The two villages where participants stay overnight have constructed bamboo lodges for the visitors on their outskirts. Early in the process of ecotourism development in Luang Namtha, villagers were hesitant to agree to allow tourists to stay overnight in their village, fearing that tourists would be put off by their poverty and that they would have nothing to offer that the tourists would want. After doing a trial run with guests staying in locals' houses and those staying separately, it was decided that it would be better to house tourists separately from their hosts (Interview with the national NHEP project manager, 2006).

A participant in the tour wryly quoted the GTZ information brochure that stated 'everything in the lodges is a genuine Akha experience except the solar heated hot water showers, flushing toilet, thick mattresses, mosquito nets, pillows, blankets, filtered water, photovoltaic cells for electricity, electric lights, etc.' (UWIP website). This is an arrangement for contact between tourists and indigenous populations that minimises the concessions that each group must make to the lifestyle of the other.

Guides

The Laotian government is trying to achieve a level of tourism development that maximises biodiversity conservation and poverty alleviation while minimising degradation of the host culture and environment. A list of 'dos and don'ts' for low-impact tourism features prominently in brochures and other information and publicity materials given to tourists, and all trekkers must go with a registered local guide, no more than eight tourists are allowed to visit a village at a time. Villagers will usually refuse to host anyone coming without a guide.

While most of those participating in treks and river tours are independent travellers, an increasing number come with tours organised by outside tour operators. This is allowed as long as the tours are organised through the Nam Ha Ecoguide Service and local guides are used to guarantee sustainable practices. In Luang Namtha Province, trekking can only be done with a registered guide (SNV, 2005). Between 1999 and 2006, one hundred and seventy people were trained to be ecoguides in Luang Namtha (Interview with the national NHEP project manager, 2006). Of the seventy-four guides currently working for the service, 15–20% are women and 46% belong to ethnic minorities (Schipani, 2006a). Lyttleton and Allcock (2002) have pointed out the role of guides as 'buffers' between tourists and the local communities, since most interaction between hosts and guests happens through guides, who serve as interpreters, both in the linguistic and in the cultural sense. For this reason, the training of guides is a very important component of sustainable tourism development. It would likely be the case that guides for tourists of Asian origin would need different types of training than those for predominantly Western tourists.

Besides the general exchange of information and knowledge that can come with intercultural contact between tourists and indigenous populations, those who are trained as guides can attain a formal education that deepens their knowledge of their own culture, provides generally useful practical knowledge and equips them for cultural exchange with tourists. Ecotourism guides in Muang Sing receive training in guiding principles, English, ecotourism, first aid, the history of the area as well as the specific cultures of individual villages. However, remote villages may not even receive information of opportunities for guide training, or the information may only be available in Lao language, which is not spoken by some villagers, especially women. Thus, indigenous ethnic minorities may be effectively excluded from education opportunities as well as from participation in the national market economy (see chapter by Berno, Editors Note).

Indigenous people's impressions of tourism impacts

The development of tourism in Laos in recent years has brought about a great increase in the interaction between Laotians and foreigners, inclusive of the potential for cultural frictions as well as economic and social gains. At present, indigenous ethnic communities in the Luang Namtha area are glad to have visitors to their villages, and there is little evidence of negative impressions of tourism and tourists on the part of the locals. Villagers in Ban Nalan, interviewed by the author, have said that they are excited when tourists come to their village, and bored when there are none. Tourists could be seen as symbolic of an end to isolation as many of these villages have previously been cut off from the world by war and by their geographical remoteness.

Guides interviewed by the author had varying assessments of the relative impact of Asian tourists and Western tourists on the local communities and natural areas they visit in Laos. Some guides noted that Asian tourists have an unspoken basic understanding of other Asian cultures and know better than even well-intentioned Westerners how to behave among Laotians, including ethnic minorities (Interview Tiger Trail, Savanh Banhao Travel, Diethelm Travel, 2006). Westerners are perceived as sometimes independent making them hard to control (Interview Lao Youth Travel, 2006).

However, another operator expressed apprehension at catering to what they saw as Asian tourists' predilection for objectification and consumption of culture through staging, turning ethnic minorities into objects to be looked at rather than cultures to be experienced (Interview Green Discovery, 2006). This suggests that tourism can undermine the very foundations upon which it is built. Already, some aspects of traditional lifestyles are seen to be disappearing and there are fears that if the area becomes overdeveloped or 'urbanised', tourists will no longer be interested in coming, raising the question of the extent to which ethnic groups should be expected to adjust their way of life in exchange for the benefits brought by tourism (Interview Diethelm Travel, 2006).

Tourism also has to compete with other interests for use of land in the province. For example, rubber plantations have replaced forest in some of the areas through which treks pass, causing a loss of shade and a reduction in attractiveness to tourists coming to experience nature. As a result, tours must sometimes be moved or cancelled (Schipani, 2006b). It is claimed that the government allows such developments because it perceives plantations as a quicker, more direct way of generating revenue than tourism (Interview Anonymous, 2006). However, the validity of this assumption has been disputed. In 2005, the total annual income from Luang Namtha's rubber plantations was estimated at around US$ 2.8 million, while the revenues from tourism in the province were US$ 3.1 million (Alton et al., cited in Schipani, 2006b).

Tourists' perceptions of their impacts on indigenous communities

Although more mature, higher-spending tourists have begun to come to Laos in recent years, the 'backpacker' niche of younger, more independent travellers accounts for the majority of the country's visitors and is characterised by the longest average stay. This preponderance is even more pronounced in areas away from the main accessible tourism centres of Luang Prabang and Vientiane.

Current tourists to Luang Namtha are concerned about the effects of tourism on the area. Visitors to Muang Sing village in Luang Namtha expressed concern about the impact that they are having on the area. They worried that an increase in tourism could detrimentally affect the local lifestyle and to impose on the daily lives of their communities. It is important for these tourists that the money they spend on a trek will be used for the good of the indigenous communities (Shum, 2005). A poll of tourists visiting this village revealed mixed perceptions in regard to the perceived effects of tourism on the province; 28% saw tourism as a primarily positive influence on the area while a slightly lower 25% saw tourism's effects as primarily negative. The remainder, nearly half of all those polled, were ambivalent regarding the net effect of tourism. Most of the negative impressions had to do with changes in the villagers' way of life with the introduction of a market economy, including aggressive hawking of handicrafts. It should be noted, however, that the reasons for tourists' negative perceptions may not correspond with a negative impression on the part of the locals (Schipani, 2003). While some tourists may think that tourism is to blame for changes in the villages, such as some villagers eschewing traditional garb for modern clothing; this is just as likely the result of the indigenous Akha people gaining increasing access to a market economy through trade with lowland Laotians.

In some villages, the only locals that approach tourists are children asking for sweets or sick villagers begging for medical help, giving some tourists the impression that tourism is encouraging begging. The practice of poorer people asking wealthier people for assistance is considered proper in Akha society, as any contribution is usually reciprocated with a small gift of thanks (Neudorfer, 2006, p. 10).

Cultural incursions

Foreign tourists have only been allowed to travel freely within Laos since 1994, and the Laotian government is still apprehensive both about the potential detrimental effects of tourism on the Laotian people and culture and about the safety of the tourists themselves (Tuffin, 2005). In some areas, residents have already commented that traditional lifestyles are being affected by the influx of tourism, with some customs disappearing from heavily-touristed areas (Laos expanding eco-tourism niche, 2004).

However, the most immediate current tourism-related threats to the indigenous society in Luang Namtha come not from the foreign tourists that visit the area but from foreign-funded tourism developments and the type of tourists and modes of tourism that they can be expected to attract. Increasing integration of Laos into the regional tourism landscape and growing cross border tourism and tourism development seem set to bring about developments of dubious value to the cultural and natural integrity of the area. For instance, a Chinese/Malaysian joint venture is planning to establish a casino, which promises to bring a different scale and character of development and a different type of tourist to the area in the form of Chinese crossing the border from Yunnan Province where gambling is illegal (see chapter by Carmichael and Jones, Editors' Note). Such developments raise the question of what costs must be borne in order to attract regional tourists to the area, and whether these costs are worth the potential benefits accrued.

Not all foreign cultural incursions into this area are because of tourism. A 2002 provincial policy encouraging Chinese development support has brought higher levels of cross-border trade with China, and an increasing number of Chinese entrepreneurs have opened restaurants and other businesses in Luang Namtha (Wells-Dang and Buasawan, 2006).

There is certainly no consensus among governmental and non-governmental organisations in Laos that tourism development is necessarily, or even potentially, beneficial to the local indigenous population. The Akha Heritage Foundation denounces tourism as by nature exploitative of the Akha minority in Laos, Thailand, Myanmar and China (Akha Heritage Foundation website). NGOs that advocate tourism development for the good of the local population acknowledge the potential threats posed by tourism to indigenous societies, and many are involved in the planning of sustainable tourism development.

Neudorfer (2006) has noted that the ideals of equality, sustainability and ecology on which CBT is based, are rooted in the Western societies of the tourists rather than the society of the host culture. Thus, the government's initiatives of ecotourism and poverty-alleviation can be seen as implicitly imposing external cultural ideals onto indigenous societies, essentially requiring them to adjust to accommodate the needs and expectations of foreigners in order to reap the benefits of tourism. The skills needed for locals to participate in this tourism sector involve understanding and accommodating the needs of these tourists, gaining English-language proficiency and comprehending the philosophy of CBT. This latter criterion was found to be especially problematic in the course of the NHEP, in which staff with over two years experience were still found to lack an understanding of the fundamentals of CBT, thereby interfering with the running and evolution of the project (ibid.).

Resettlement and indigenous populations in Laos

During the US/Vietnam War, the lowland areas were controlled by US-supported royalist troops and the less-accessible uplands and the northeast were controlled by the communist Pathet Lao. However, for several years after the Pathet Lao assumed rule over Laos in 1975, American-trained guerrillas continued to stage attacks in southwest Luang Namtha. In order to better control the people of this area, the government moved all remote villages to the main roads (Evrard and Goudineau, 2004). The Laotian government, like many others in Southeast Asia, continues to use planned resettlement as a strategy in the pursuit of development goals and to exercise control.

In its Resolution No. 7 of 2001, the Lao People's Revolutionary Party declared three main goals for development: an end to slash-and-burn farming, the elimination of opium cultivation by 2005 and the eradication of poverty by 2020. Resettlement of indigenous populations is one means used to achieve these ends (Wells-Dang and Buasawan, 2006). This involves the displacement of ethnic minority villages to more accessible areas, to facilitate better provision of services and government control of these populations and to open up their lands for other types of exploitation such as logging, which is the country's main source of income (Evrard and Goudineau, 2004).

The links and relationships between resettlement and tourism in Laos merit further study. Villages will sometimes be moved to take better advantage of resources and infrastructure, and it is conceivable that the tourism trade could provide a strong enough incentive in the future to justify the displacement of villages to gain better access to tourist flows, especially in the case of villages that do not draw tourists to visit them via organised treks.

At least one case of friction between tourism and resettlement has been noted. Akha tradition considers it unlucky for strangers to visit the village site for a village for ten days during the moving process. Nonetheless, in 2004, the local tourism office arranged a tour group to visit an Akha village that was moving to a site with better access to a road and river, causing an outrage amongst the villagers and the immediate expulsion of the tourist group (Neudorfer, 2006).

Often, these displaced villages find it difficult to adjust their social and agricultural practices to the new conditions in which they find themselves. The uprooting of a group of people can sever links to their 'cultural resources' and sense of community (Wells-Dang and Buasawan, 2006). Though not explicitly stated, it would seem that villages that are able to attract tourists may be more likely to avoid resettlement, as they demonstrate economic independence. The very remoteness of their communities and the perceived 'authenticity' of their way of life are important attractions for tourists interested in ethnic minorities and to resettle these villages would eradicate their attractiveness to tourism.

Conclusions

Indigenous populations in Laos are currently experiencing many dimensions of change in their life-world. 'Progress' is being visited upon these remote villages as they gain their first contacts with national and even international market economies. Tourism is just one facet of this development. However, tourism needs to be seen as more than just another economic sector promising economic gain for outside investors and threatening the exploitation of locals. The national government sees tourism development as a prime tool for assisting in poverty alleviation, and international NGOs stand ready to give support. The development of CBT can provide indigenous communities with a tool for self-determination, self-preservation and evolution within the market economy.

In the coming years, some indigenous communities may be transformed by tourism, for better or worse, while, some may be bypassed by it. The type of tourists who come to this area and the type of tourism that they practice may also change. The contacts between the indigenous population and tourists in Laos are currently at a small scale and of a largely benign character. For Laos' isolated ethnic minorities, these visitors herald an opening up to the world and an opportunity to broaden their knowledge and to capitalise on economic opportunities. Tourists to Laos are still a small and intrepid group, willing to go off the beaten track to come into contact with these indigenous cultures. Because of language and cultural gaps, the interaction between these two groups remains at a largely superficial level, but is nonetheless built on a foundation of respect.

CHAPTER 11

Conservation, wildlife and indigenous tourism: longhouse communities in and adjacent to Batang Ai National Park, Sarawak, Malaysia

Oswald Bratek, Pat Devlin and David Simmons

Introduction

The relationship between tourism and the environment is complex. Much of what has been written carries the risk of naïve assumptions that tourism is a natural ally of nature conservation. This is especially so in the case of tourism and wildlife protection – where visitors are expected to automatically provide an inducement to protect wildlife and their habitat for the visitor gaze. Such propositions, in turn, beg other questions of what forms or volume of tourism might lead to these outcomes; and under what conditions, if any, will indigenous people forgo traditional hunting practices to secure financial gains from wildlife tourism. It is to these questions that the research underpinning this chapter was directed (see chapter by Salole, Editors' Note).

Sarawak is one such place where tourism promotion and packaging is focused on its people and their culture (Hon, 1990), its natural areas and wildlife (WCS & FD, 1996). In terms of people and culture, the Iban communities have been extensively promoted for their unique way of life and organised tours to Iban longhouses have long been a major tourism product (Zeppel, 1993).

While managers increasingly recognise that local communities need to be able to benefit from protected areas if they are to support conservation efforts (Ite, 1996), traditional patterns of resource use by local communities may weaken conservation efforts (Hackel, 1999). This need to change patterns of resource use has prompted successive park managers to support tourism for its potential benefits. Tourism is seen to be compatible with the objectives of conservation in that it can provide benefits to the local communities while reducing their dependence on the harvest of wildlife in protected areas (Horowitz, 1998). It is also generally assumed that tourism would be effective at reducing hunting because it occupies the men's time (Horowitz, 1998). These views, are not borne out by this research.

Study area and research context

Research was conducted in 2003 to investigate the role of tourism in reducing pressure on the local community harvesting of forest resources from Batang Ai National Park (BANP), one of Sarawak, East Malaysia's, 15 national parks (Tisen, 2004). BANP designated in 1991 is well situated for tourist visits, being 275 kilometres from the capital Kuching (Figure 11.1), and is accessible by sealed road to the Batang Ai Dam and reservoir built for hydroelectricity generation purposes in the 1970s. The conservation values of BANP are dependent on the sustainable extraction of natural resources by local communities with harvesting privileges within the park. There are seven traditional longhouses communities (perhaps best equated to a village community) with a total of 448 people holding privileges to hunt, fish and collect natural resources from the park, which has a total area of 240 square kilometres (Ahmad et al., 1999). For some longhouses in Batang Ai, the Agricultural Department has supported conservation by initiating fish farming projects in the hope that fish would provide a source of protein and

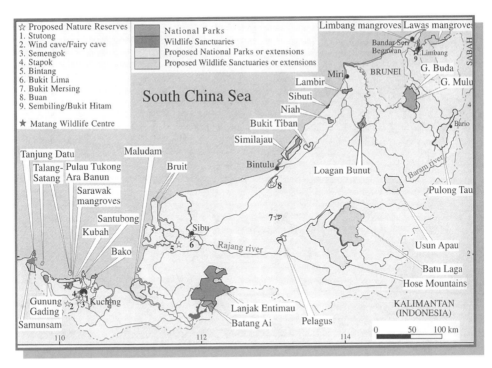

Figure 11.1
Location of Batang Ai National Park among other protected areas of Sarawak (Sarawak Forest Department)

income as a substitute for wild meat. In the regional conservation context, BANP shares a common boundary with Lanjak-Entimau Wildlife Sanctuary in Sarawak to the north and Betung-Kerihun National Park in Indonesia with a combined area of about 1 million hectares. The apparently large total size of protected habitat does little to satisfy the fears of wildlife conservation professionals for the future of orangutan and other species given the potential for shifts in pressures for the utilisation of forest resources.

Visitation by tourists is still relatively limited as it requires boat travel across the Batang Ai reservoir. While lake and river travel provide a novel tourist experience, the resultant visitation patterns are strongly shaped by both distance and the need for organised transport provision. Figure 11.2 demonstrates these patterns, noting most tourist activity occurs in the buffer zone in the front – country of BANP with little visitor penetration into the park proper. While these lands serve as a buffer zone, Sarawak does not have, or use, this description for un-alienated forest lands. All forests between the park boundaries and the dam are either 'State Forest Lands' or 'Native Customary Right Lands'. Few people live between the dam and the park, enhancing the forest's capacity to protect watershed and biodiversity values.

A key motivation for the gazetting of the Batang Ai area centred on protection of orangutan habitat (Meredith, 1993a, b). However the current orangutan population requires a minimum area of 300 square kilometres for continued

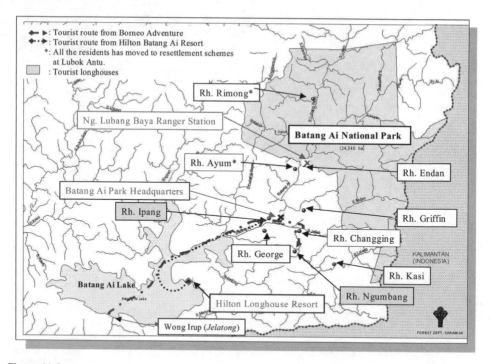

Figure 11.2
Location of longhouses and tourist routes in Ulu Batang Ai (own data over map supplied by Sarawak Forest Department)

survival (Bennett and Shebli, 1999). Furthermore, the number of local people with gazetted rights and privileges to hunt, fish and gather forest produce from the protected area is more than the theoretical capacity of the forest to sustain (Ahmad et al., 1999; Tisen et al., 1999). Wildlife, inclusive of protected species, also ranges beyond the park boundaries into surrounding forest areas where local communities farm, hunt and gather forest products (Meredith, 1993a, b). Thus, the cooperation of local communities is crucial in achieving the conservation objectives of the park (Tisen and Meredith, 2000).

Research on the use of tropical forest shows that one person per square kilometre is considered sustainable if these individuals are dependent solely on wild meat for their protein needs (Robinson and Bennett, 2000). Thus, the protein needs of 448 people with privileges over BANP are clearly not sustainable if they obtain all their protein from wild meat from the park (Ahmad et al., 1999).

Tourists have also been visiting the Batang Ai area for many years but their role in reducing local consumption of forest resources has not been clear. In one study, a longhouse with revenue brought about by tourism '. . . has significantly more non-wild protein in the diet than its nearby non-tourist longhouse . . . [but which] was eaten in addition to, not instead of, the wild protein' (Nyaoi and Bennett, 2002, p. 5). Their research showed that tourism does not necessarily reduce dietary dependency on natural resources.

In the broader regional context several studies on tourism and Iban communities show that tourism generally provides only part-time employment for a few members of local communities (Sagging et al., 2000; Yea and Noweg, 2000; Zeppel, 1996) and that 'men tended to be involved in tourism-related work much more extensively, while the women remained primarily agricultural workers' (Yea and Noweg, 2000, p. 11). Yea and Noweg (2000) found that '. . . during the high tourism season, the women normally had to spend more time in agricultural work to compensate for the lower availability of men to work on the farm' (p. 8). Bennett et al. (2000) have also noted that fish would provide a source of protein and income as a substitute for wild meat, however, women tend the fishponds and sell all the fish for cash while the men continue to hunt.

Cultural and development context

The people of Sarawak can be divided into two major groups, the Bumiputra or indigenous people and the non-Bumiputra or non-indigenous. People of Chinese descent constitute the majority of the non-Bumiputra, followed by Indonesians, Indians and other races. The indigenous people of Sarawak in turn can be further classified into two broad groups; those who live in the coastal areas comprising Malays and Melanau, and those in the interior or Dayak (Hong, 1987). The Dayak is a collective term that refers to ethnic groups inhabiting the Island of Borneo and includes Iban, which is the largest along with 24 other smaller ethnic groups (Hong, 1987).

Until relatively recently, most Dayaks lived in the interior of the island, in places that were often inaccessible except by boat or on foot. They are mainly shifting cultivators, living off the land and forest. '[T]he land, the waters, and the forests have provided [the dayaks with] their livelihood and daily needs ever since they can remember' (Hong, 1987, p. 3).

Most traditional Dayak societies had three key features. These were long-house social organisation, customary land tenure and shifting cultivation (Hong, 1987). The family was the basic social and economic unit, with each family occupying an apartment (*bilik*) within a longhouse. The longhouse was the centre of the social organisation (Hong, 1987). Except for the Kayan, Kenyah and Kelabit ethnic groups who maintained a ranked social order of aristocrats, commoners and slaves, the Dayaks were basically classless with a complex system underlying the principles of reciprocity and cooperation among the families. Each family had rights over their own plots of land, allocated tasks and controlled labour among family members, obtained the fruits of their labour, and exercised rights over its own living conditions within their individual longhouse 'apartment' (Hong, 1987).

A suite of customary beliefs and values known as '*adat*' guided behaviour. The '*adat* was the unwritten body of rules and principles which was extended to all things and all relationships in both [the] physical and supernatural world[,]. . . .include[ing] the living and the dead, the evil and the good, sacred and profane' (Hong, 1987, p. 12). Under the *adat*, it is believed that everything has a soul or life of its own and it is important to conduct oneself in a proper way in order to maintain the balance and harmony of all elements (see chapter by Carr, Editors' Note).

Land provides the Dayaks with their basic needs and holds deep significance in their spiritual life. Under the *adat*, the person who cleared the forest had the 'rights to the use and disposal of the land [which] belong jointly to the family of the original feller' (Hong, 1987, p. 14). The right of ownership reverts to the community if the family abandons the longhouse or when there is no mark of ownership shown. This practice 'enabled each family and community to gain access to the abundant forests, land and water, as well as providing for cleared but unused land (or old forest) to be the property of the community' (Hong, 1987, p. 14). Members of the community also have the rights over the forest surrounding their longhouse.

In traditional Dayak society, shifting cultivation was the most important economic activity. Other economic activities such as hunting, fishing, gathering forest produce, and rearing of pigs and poultry were also pursued to supplement their daily needs. All family members had their own roles; the men hunted and fished to provide meat for their families, and felled and burned forest for farmland. The women were responsible for sowing and weeding crops and gathering jungle produce while harvesting crops was shared by both sexes (Hong, 1987). Fishing, hunting and gathering of jungle produce were important supplementary activities that contributed substantially to a family's daily food requirements. The main jungle products collected were mushrooms, bamboo shoots and fern which comprised the major vegetable component of their diet. Wild meat or fish was often shared with other families in the longhouse, thereby serving '. . . as a kind of "insurance policy" for an individual in lean times as one [could] always expect a share of meat and fish from one's neighbour' (Hong, 1987, p. 29).

Today, most rural Dayak communities still practice shifting cultivation and continue to depend on resources from surrounding forests to supplement their food and income (Sidu, 2000a). They are mainly subsistence farmers, planting hill rice and some cash crops such as rubber, pepper, cocoa and fruit trees to supplement their family income (Sidu, 2000a). The traditional activities of hunting, fishing and gathering wild vegetables for subsistence remain important activities in rural Dayak communities (Sidu, 2000b). In Ulu Batang Ai (originally *'orang ulu'* meant 'up-river people', generally the term still refers to up-river, or remote /backcountry areas) and in areas adjacent to Lanjak-Entimau Wildlife Sanctuary, wild boar is the most popular animal hunted (Sidu, 2000b). Other species that are hunted include sambar deer, barking deer, mouse deer, porcupine, and other small animals, supplemented with occasional fishing.

Among the Dayak communities found in northern Sarawak at Ulu Baram, Miri, 'the dependency on wild resources for food is high with wild meat constituting 83 percent of all meat side dishes and wild vegetables constituting 40 percent of all vegetable side dishes' (Christensen, 2000, p. 367). Certain communally owned forest areas are especially reserved and serve as reservoirs for wild animals, trees, and plants for exclusive use by the community and are not made available for farming.

In summary, the rural Dayak communities '. . . continue to be dependent on the available resources, particularly, the surrounding forest to supplement their food and income, as well as to meet their other basic needs' (Sidu, 2000a, p. 193).

Communities in Ulu Batang Ai

In Ulu Batang Ai, Iban dwell in traditional longhouses comprising 5–30 families. In this region rice farming is very important. Here local people are self-sufficient in terms of food and are able to obtain most of their daily requirements locally, however, they do not have a steady cash income (Yong and Basiuk, 1998, p. 1). Some families obtained cash from growing pepper, rearing of fresh water fish, working in tourism and occasionally selling of wild meat (Nyaoi and Bennett, 2002). Cash is also sourced through the payment of remittances by younger members who work in logging companies, in factories, on offshore oil rigs, or as labourers in coastal towns (Arman, 1997; Nyaoi and Bennett, 2002).

Against this long history of traditional activity, the Iban of Batang Ai have been increasingly subjected to outside influences. In 1980, they were forced to move into resettlement schemes as their existing villages stood in the way of development for a hydroelectric generation scheme (Ayob and Yaakub, 1991). This forced resettlement led to misunderstanding and mistrust of government initiatives in the area and when BANP was proposed, it was seen as another way in which the government might cheat the locals (Horowitz, 1998).

The local Iban communities agreed to the establishment of BANP only after extensive consultation. Conservation education programmes were conducted, some involving the personal attention of the government Minister incharge of National Parks. The Batang Ai communities also experienced socio-economic changes and like the rest of Sarawak they have been influenced by the increasingly pervasive cash economy (WCS & FD, 1996). Local communities have taken advantage of the opportunity to send their children to school, to travel to town centres for medical attention and to purchase goods to enhance their standard of living (Arman, 1997). They are no longer satisfied with subsistence benefits gained from within the park, but want to be able to gain cash benefits from it. This led some residents to disregard both traditional customs (*adapt*), and national park regulations on hunting, fishing and gathering jungle produce (Horowitz, 1998). Tourism is seen as an alternative way in which local people could gain cash benefits thereby reducing their dependence on the harvest of natural resources thus promoting conservation within the park (Nyaoi and Bennett, 2002).

Wildlife, indigenous harvest and sustainability

Ungulates in tropical forests are generally smaller and fewer in number per square kilometre than those in open grassland. The lower overall biomass of mammals in tropical forest affects the amount of meat produced, and the maximum number of animals that can be secured by hunters (Robinson and Bennett, 2000). The carrying capacity of tropical forest in relation to human use refers to '... the maximum number of people depending on meat from wild species who can live in a forest while still conserving adequate populations of these species' (Robinson and Bennett, 2000, p. 23). Assuming that local people depend solely on wild meat for their protein requirements, dividing the maximum sustainable production of wild meat in tropical forests (150 kilogram per square kilometre) by human per capita animal protein needs gives an estimate of the carrying capacity of the forests. Robinson and Bennett (2000) suggest that 65% of a live animal is edible thus a square kilometre of tropical forest will produce 97 kilograms of edible meat per year. The recommended daily amount of meat intake per person per day is 0.25 kilograms which is equivalent to 91 kilograms per year. Thus for tropical forests to be sustainable for people depending exclusively on wild meat, the human carrying capacity can be taken as one person per square kilometre (Robinson and Bennett, 2000).

Christensen (2000, p. 359) recorded among the Kelabit in Ulu Baram, Sarawak, that 'dishes made from wild vegetables and wild meat represent more than half of the total amount of side dishes' eaten. Local residents do not depend solely on wild meat for all their protein requirements. They also consume fish, crab and domestic animals. In this context, the carrying capacity of one person per square kilometre may be an underestimate of sustainability for tropical forest. For the purpose of this chapter, however, this estimate of carrying capacity will be used to indicate sustainability in terms of the study site.

In many Bornean forests, the long-term presence of humans and their ongoing harvest of wildlife indicate that traditional practices were sustainable (Robinson and Bennett, 2000). Today, wildlife remains an important source of protein for people in the tropical forests and its harvest remains widespread (Chin and Bennett, 2000; Robinson and Bennett, 2000). Wildlife has also formed an integral part of the people's culture including the use of animal parts in traditional ceremonies and dances (Caldecott, 1988; WCS & FD, 1996; Chin and Bennett, 2000; Robinson and Bennett, 2000). Often, hunting is a symbol of the achievement of manhood and subsequent standing with tropical forest people (Bennett et al., 2000; Chin and Bennett, 2000; Robinson and Bennett, 2000). Wildlife also plays important roles in indigenous religion, mythology and ceremonies (Cleary and Eaton, 1992). However, given changing hunting practices and land management allocations, the hunting of many species in the tropics is no longer considered sustainable.

In Sarawak, Bennett et al. (2000) estimated that 29% of all meals consumed in the interior included wild meat, rising to 67% in the remote areas. As a group, subsistence hunters and their communities in Sarawak are estimated to consume more than 23,000 tonnes of wild meat per year, which would cost about US$ 75 million to replace with domestic meat in the market place (WCS & FD, 1996; Bennett et al., 2000).

Wildlife is also hunted for economic gain and income from its sale is a significant part of the economy of rural communities in tropical forests (Bennett et al., 2000; FitzGibbon et al., 2000; Noss, 2000; Robinson and Bennett, 2000). Prior to a total ban in (commercial) trade of wildlife in 1998, a significant amount of wild meat was sold in towns and markets (Caldecott, 1988; Cleary and Eaton, 1992; WCS & FD, 1996).

Chin and Bennett consider that there is no clear distinction between hunting for commercial gain or subsistence among forest-dwelling people, 'with patterns ranging from an additional animal hunted for sale on rare occasions when the hunter goes to town, to frequent hunting to supply a regular trader, to full-scale professional hunting' (2000; p. 30). Robinson and Bennett (2000) suggest that the single greatest factor decreasing wildlife sustainability is increased access to tropical forests. New and improved roads mean increased access to many hunting areas and this is accompanied by increased infringement on traditional land rights by outsiders and by concomitant decreases in consumption of animal protein among rural communities, which undermine their well-being (Robinson and Bennett, 2000).

Research objectives and methods

The over-riding goal of the larger study on which this chapter is based was to determine how local longhouse communities in, and adjacent to, BANP perceive conservation and tourism in the area, and whether tourism benefits both local communities and conservation. The primary research objectives were to study the relationships between tourism, subsistence agriculture, hunter/gathering and conservation of a national park. This involved determining local residents' views of tourism as an alternative source of income, its distribution, and the implications of these activities for traditional use of natural resources. Data collection also focused on the amount of time local residents spent in tourism-related activities and the benefits derived from tourism compared with time spent in the traditional activities of farming, and collecting and harvesting natural resources.

Semi-structured interviews with community groups ($n = 11$), key informant interviews ($n = 16$), a questionnaire survey ($n = 152$) and researcher observations were all used to investigate whether or not tourism was seen to benefit local communities and conservation in Ulu Batang Ai. These methods facilitated the collection of data on the amount of time spent in traditional work relative to tourism-related work and the benefits brought about by tourism. Local perceptions about tourism and conservation were also investigated. Questionnaires were used to gather data on the levels of agreement with a variety of statements about tourism and conservation. The questionnaire also requested information on time spent farming, harvesting forest produce, hunting, fishing and other work. Views and opinions of the communities and key informants were obtained to cross check data collected from the questionnaire survey. The multi-methods approach was based on the idea that the strengths and weaknesses of each method complement one another and, therefore increase the validity of the research process (Mathison, 1988).

Findings

A traditional and changing economy

The longhouse communities in Ulu Batang Ai are primarily engaged in traditional 'swidden' (slash and burn) shifting agriculture in areas within an hour's walking distance from their longhouses, and adjacent to the Park. Only the Rumah (longhouse) Rh. Endan residents farm within the boundaries of BANP (refer Figure 11.2). Other communities residing in negotiated resettlement schemes – Rh. Ayum, Rh. Rimong, Rh. Rumpang and Rh. Betok (outside the Ulu Batang Ai area) claim native customary land (NCL) within the boundaries of the Park; however, they no longer farm there as it is too costly to travel to these traditional areas. Generally, farm productivity in Ulu Batang Ai remains the same as it was before tourism. However, members of some longhouses said that it was no longer successful. The main reasons given for their lack of farming success were a shortage of labour as younger people have left to work in town and damage to crops by wildlife. Those in the resettlement schemes practised modern methods of farming including the planting of wet rice on the same plot of land every year and the use of fertilisers and herbicides to increase yield. Farming success in the resettlement schemes was reported as high.

Harvesting forest produce, however, remains an important activity among longhouse communities remaining within Ulu Batang Ai. Forest products, such as mushrooms, fern fronds, 'hearts' of palms, fruits and other produce, were the most commonly harvested. Other forest produce harvested by communities in the Ulu includes building materials (*ramu*), rattan (*we*) and illipe nuts. The yield from harvesting forest produce and the effort required remains the same as before tourism in Ulu Batang Ai. The Rh. Endan and the Rh. Ayum residents were the only communities that collected forest produce within the boundaries of BANP with other longhouses relying on forests next to their longhouse and outside the designated park.

Hunting in Ulu Batang Ai is mainly undertaken by men with dogs, spears and shotguns. The main species hunted are wild pigs, sambar deer (*rusa*), barking deer (*kijang*), mouse deer (*pelanduk*) and civets (*musang*). Generally, hunting success in Ulu Batang Ai remains the same as before the construction of the dam. Only the Rh. Ipang residents reported that hunting is not successful for the reason that they now have to share their hunting ground with the Rh. Changing residents. The Rh. Ayum residents reported that hunting in the Ulu was more successful after BANP was gazetted.

Gill and cast netting were the main methods of fishing. Fishing successes were reported as remaining unchanged in Ulu Batang Ai. The Rh. Endan and Rh. Griffin residents indicated that fishing was no longer as successful. Rh. Endan residents attributed the lack of success to over-fishing by outsiders, while Rh. Griffin attributed it to a lack of fishing equipment. Fishing is no longer an important activity among the communities in the resettlement schemes as their longhouses are sited away from the main rivers and travelling to Ulu Batang Ai is expensive.

The communities in Ulu Batang Ai and the resettlement schemes spent less than one day per week doing 'work other' than the major tasks described above. The residents of Rh. Ngumbang listed work related to tourism in occupations related to transportation, cooking, helping and cultural performances. Those in other longhouses specified 'other work' connected with homecraft activities such as weaving baskets or *pua kumbu*, building or maintaining of boats or houses and making *parang* (knives/machetes). A number of respondents in the resettlement schemes specified 'other work' such as contract work, rubber tapping and small businesses like merchandise retailing.

Little cash was earned before the construction of the dam in Ulu Batang Ai in the 1970s. This lack of cash income was reported as being largely due to transportation constraints as it took some days to travel to the (coastal) markets to sell products. Transport to market became much easier after the construction of the dam, and earning cash was therefore comparatively easier. For the Rh. Endans' residents, the lack of cash crops was reported as the reason for their difficulty in earning cash. After the gazetting of BANP, a number of longhouse communities mentioned the total ban on trade of wildlife (1998) as a reason for their reduced opportunities to earn cash.

Communities in the resettlement schemes agreed that it is much easier to earn cash in the resettlement area compared with their original settlement in Ulu Batang Ai. They attributed this improvement to the presence of more job opportunities and increased road access. The forces pulling people out of Ulu Batang Ai to resettlement schemes and to urban areas are much greater than those keeping them in the Ulu (Arman, 1997). Lack of work opportunities and poor access to medical and educational facilities in the Ulu are significant incentives to move to the resettlement areas (Arman, 1997). Three longhouses in Ulu Batang Ai are now deserted and a number of others are losing their members. However, where work opportunities exist due to tourism, such as in Rh. Ngumbang, the number of occupants has increased. This trend suggests that tourism in rural settings can provide work opportunities and contribute to population retention.

Local communities' beliefs, perceptions and attitudes towards tourism

In Ulu Batang Ai, Rh. Ngumbang received a regular flow of tourists through their cooperation with Borneo Adventure (a specialised tourism operator based in the state capital, Kuching). Rh. Ipang hosted tourists from the Hilton Batang Ai Longhouse Resort. The other longhouses in Ulu Batang Ai received very few tourists. Rh. Endan had tourists visiting their longhouse from 1990 to 1992, brought in by Borneo Adventure. However, they have received few tourists since Borneo Adventure shifted their tours to Rh. Ngumbang. There were no longhouse tourist operators in the resettlement schemes which underscore the significance of natural landscapes as tourist settings.

For the longhouse communities visited by tourists, the aspects of tourism they 'most like' are the financial benefits and the knowledge that they gain from tourists. A majority of the longhouse communities reported that there was very little to dislike about tourism. The 'most disliked' aspect of tourism was associated with tourists' behaviour, such as the attire used when bathing/swimming.

Only the remote Rh. Kasi residents would like to have tourists visiting their longhouse during specified times only. All the other longhouse communities said that tourists could visit at any time, as long as the community benefited. This finding illustrated the locals' preference to work in tourism rather than on farms. A number of individuals in other longhouses also indicated that they preferred tourism over agricultural work because it is seen as clean and engaging work delivering immediate cash benefits. The communities in Ulu Batang Ai did not experience any labour shortages due to workers being involved in tourism. However, communities in the smaller longhouses pointed out that there is a potential shortage if more tourists visit their longhouse, as there are only a few families remaining with adequate working aged members. Residents' views of tourism as source of income and alternative to traditional collecting and harvesting of natural resources reinforced the overall positive assessment of tourism. Most importantly, the communities in Batang Ai believe that tourism in their area has created jobs. A majority (89%) believe that tourism is good for their longhouse and that benefits from tourism are distributed widely throughout the longhouse.

Set against these positive attitude and experiences, the communities in Ulu Batang Ai hold unrealistically high expectations of tourism. They unrealistically expect tourism, if it were to develop at their longhouse, to be the answer to all their problems and that they will all become business operators. A major impediment to the establishment of tourism in Ulu Batang Ai has been that the communities were very poor and it would take considerable effort and time to develop the infrastructure and skills necessary to provide satisfactory services for tourists.

One of the misconceptions of the communities in Ulu Batang Ai was an assumption that tourists simply would come if they built the facilities. A tourist lodge built by Kooperative Serba Guna Ulu Batang Ai adjacent to Rh. Ayum appears to be based on such an assumption. However, the lodge was seldom used as Kooperative Serba Guna Ulu Batang Ai did not have any formal agreements with tour agencies and few independent tourists managed to find their way to the lodge. This was a situation where longhouse tourism failed, primarily because of the absence of an effective link to the market.

In summary, the commitment of a tour operator was crucial in making longhouse tourism work in Ulu Batang Ai. Longhouse tourism in Rh. Ngumbang worked because Borneo Adventures was committed to a win–win situation with the longhouse residents. They worked as partners, and mutual respect and understanding were the governing principles.

Income distribution and traditional resource use

The earnings of respondents from the longhouse communities in Ulu Batang Ai place them within the State's 'hard-core' poor category. Cash income, however, was not a clear indicator of their well-being because of their self-sufficiency in terms of food and daily necessities from materials found locally. A majority (88%) of respondents in the study site were farmers earning less than RM 500 per month. Most of the respondents from longhouses in Ulu Batang Ai earned less than RM 100 per month. In 1997, the poverty line in Malaysia was RM 515 per month, the average income of the 'hard-core' poor was RM 158 per month, and the 'poor' was RM 403 per month (Berma, 2000).

A majority of the respondents from the Rh. Ngumbang longhouse were in the RM 301 to RM 500 income bracket, which is above the average income of the people in Ulu Batang Ai. This marked increase in monthly income can be attributed to the presence of tourism. However, the income is still below the poverty line and although they receive supplemental income through tourism, it is still too little to make a significant difference in their ways of life. Meanwhile, their well-being remains very dependent on the traditional use of resources found locally. Overall tourism was seen only as a marginal contributor to wealth.

Three of the longhouses in Ulu Batang Ai have been abandoned and others have lost members to resettlement schemes or migration to urban centres. Only the Rh. Ngumbang and Rh. Ipang longhouses recorded increases in population. Both of these communities are involved in tourism – the Rh. Ngumbang longhouse received tourists through their cooperation with Borneo Adventure and the Rh. Ipang longhouse benefited from tourists staying in the nearby Hilton Longhouse Resort. This finding supports the earlier conclusion that longhouse tourism, when located and managed well, can bring about stability or an increase in population through an increase in job opportunities.

There was no significant difference in time spent in traditional activities of farming, hunting, fishing and gathering forest produce by longhouses (Rh. Ngumbang and Rh. Ipang) actively involved in tourism in comparison to longhouses not involved in tourism. This lack of difference reflects the fact that tourism in Ulu Batang Ai is a part-time activity, numbers of tourists are relatively small, and participation in tourist activities is rotated among the members of the community.

A majority of the respondents (52%) who had tourists visiting their longhouse reported tourism revenue of less than RM 100 per month. Higher tourist spending was reported in Rh. Ngumbang and Rh. Ipang. All respondents that reported tourists spent more than RM 2,000 per month in their longhouse were from Rh. Ngumbang (estimated at RM 147,000 total in the research year). Rh. Ipang was the only other longhouse where the respondents reported that tourists spent more that RM 500 per month.

Tourism work in Ulu Batang Ai was found to be part-time but not seasonal in nature. The most important tourism-related work was providing transport, followed by accommodation, cultural performances and guiding. A majority of workers received fewer than RM 100 per month (from tourism-related activities). This does not mean that tourism-related work in Ulu Batang Ai is low paying but rather reflects the organisation and allocation of the work, which is rotated among the longhouse residents. For example, each individual might only work for a few days in a month while spending the balance of their time in traditional tasks. Overall, tourism in Ulu Batang Ai has little effect on the traditional ways of life, and community well-being still depends on the traditional activities of farming, hunting, fishing and gathering forest produce.

It is essential for the well-being of the communities in Ulu Batang Ai and for biodiversity conservation in BANP that the forest areas next to the longhouses continue to provide the local people with their daily dietary requirements. In the event that these forests fail to be able to provide them with their daily requirements; their well-being will be at risk. In response, they are likely to turn to the park for their daily requirements by exercising their harvesting rights and privileges which may ultimately undermine the conservation objectives of the park and also its tourist appeal.

Implications for tourism management and planning

Tourism in Ulu Batang Ai is in its infancy, possibly the early stage of involvement in a 'tourist destination life cycle' as proposed by Butler (1980). There are few tourists and the number of tourists at any particular time is much lower than the number of local people. Rh. Ngumbang with the most regular tourist visits received fewer than 1,000 tourists evenly spread throughout the year. The longhouse residents also believed that tourism in Ulu Batang Ai had very little negative effect on the environment or on their culture. Their response to tourism may be considered to be at the stage of 'euphoria' in the 'tourist irritation index' as proposed by Doxey (1975). It has little or no influence on their normative behaviour and they were pleased to see tourism development, perceived tourism positively and welcomed tourists.

The study indicated that tourism-related activities could provide local communities with a source of income, and could occupy their time as in the case of the Rh. Ngumbang residents. Tourist lodges were constructed adjacent to three longhouses: Rh. Endan, Rh. Ayum and Rh. Ngumbang. The longhouse residents, with assistance from Borneo Adventure, constructed the lodges adjacent to Rh. Endan and Rh. Ngumbang. Koperasi Serba Guna Ulu Batang Ai constructed a third lodge adjacent to Rh. Ayum. However, tourism has failed to benefit the residents of some of these longhouses such as Rh. Ayum and Rh. Endan. On the positive side, even though the local people in Ulu Batang Ai have experienced tourism since 1987, they still perceived tourism with enthusiasm despite the failure of some longhouse communities to benefit directly. Tourism success and failure factors in Ulu Batang Ai will now be discussed.

Success factors • • •

Longhouse tourism worked in Rh. Ngumbang, the most visited longhouse, for the following reasons:

(i) A strong collaborative relationship between the longhouse residents and Borneo Adventure. Both parties strive for a win–win situation whereby Borneo Adventure have a strong local partner and have provided the longhouse residents with a fair share of the revenues.

(ii) A robust social fabric among the longhouse residents with strong leadership from the headman and the tourism committee.

(iii) A relatively large longhouse population (209 people) compared with the 1,000 visitors spread evenly throughout the year.

(iv) A pattern of slow but steady development which has enabled the community to adopt realistic expectations about tourists and tourism.

Failure factors • • •

Longhouse tourism failed in Rh. Ayum and Rh. Endan for the following reasons:

(i) A break-down in, or no cooperation with a tour agency resulting in no direct link to, or understanding of the tourism market.

(ii) A weak social fabric and lack of leadership among the residents of Rh. Ayum as indicated by incidents of fighting and drunkenness. Residents of Rh. Endan lost a strong and experienced leader when the late headman, Tuai Rumah Sumbu died in 1991.

(iii) Low populations in Rh. Endan or Rh. Ayum. There are only four families in Rh. Endan and the residents of Rh. Ayum are residing in the resettlement scheme and only live in the longhouse in Ulu Batang Ai when there are visitors.

In summary the key reasons for the failure of some longhouses to develop tourism in Ulu Batang Ai are the lack of association with a tour agency that has links to the markets and lack of skill development for members of the local communities. Ulu Batang Ai is an exciting tourism destination, however, tourism requires infrastructure and human resources, both of which are in their infancy in the park. Infrastructure development may not be enough to enhance tourism in Ulu Batang Ai if the link to tourism markets and human resource development in the area is not improved. Importantly, tourism levels appear to remain below 'carrying capacity' due largely to the remoteness of most longhouses, and the long-term vision of a benevolent tourism operator who, as the sole partner, resists and avoids exceeding capacity. As pressure to increase tourism grows, neither of these factors can be assured, or taken for granted.

Implications for conservation and tourism • • •

Generally, the benefits from tourism in Ulu Batang Ai at this stage are too small to make much difference to the traditional way of life of the local people. Thus, their well-being continues to depend on forest resources adjacent to their longhouses. Local people retain long-term rights and privileges to hunt, fish and gather forest produce within the national park, and may exercise these rights if the forest areas next to their longhouses are depleted, or if these forests are converted to other forms of land use. Aggressive harvesting would undermine conservation goals.

The communities in all the longhouses under study have been affected by the gazettement of BANP. For some, what were once their traditional hunting, fishing and gathering grounds are now a national park. Often, they view BANP as an obstruction to their traditional ways of life. They are constantly defending their rights which often results in an atmosphere of conflict between park managers and local people. Local communities must recognise the benefits from the park if they are to support conservation of the area. Unfortunately, at current visitation levels, tourism has done little to demonstrate such benefits.

Notwithstanding the above, tourism is still seen as a way in which benefits could be channelled to the local people without undermining the conservation efforts of the park. During the time of this survey, benefits from tourism were seen to be more of a 'bonus' for the longhouse residents. Even Rh. Ngumbang, with the highest level of visitation experienced only very minor changes to their traditional way of life. Borneo Adventure pointed out that the maximum number of tourists to Rh. Ngumbang is 1,000 per year spread out evenly to '. . . provide the longhouse people with means of production . . . which is compatible with their day-to-day lifestyle' (Yong and Basiuk, 1998, p. 5). This arrangement provides positive effects for both tourism and conservation – the longhouse residents are still enthusiastic about tourism and have taken initiatives to protect the forest and wildlife that attract the tourists. A key consideration has been the avoidance of overdependency on the benefits from tourism.

The needs of local people with privileges to hunt, fish and gather forest produce from BANP could exceed its carrying capacity if they drew on the Park for all of their daily dietary requirements. Furthermore, if privilege holders harvest forest produce from the park at high rates, the park would lose its natural attraction thereby undermining tourism activity. For BANP to continue to maintain its conservation goals, it is crucial that the forest areas next to the longhouses continue to provide the longhouses with their daily requirements so that they do not have to collect from the park. Findings from this study back management decisions to support the conservation objectives of the park by encouraging sustainable tourism, while protecting buffer areas for multiple use objectives. Thus, for tourism to benefit both local communities and conservation, a commitment is required by all parties – government agencies (e.g., park managers, tourism planners and promoters), the tour operators and the local communities.

Conclusion

The findings indicate that local communities benefit from tourism, albeit at a low level. Local communities believe that tourism can benefit them, and that it is important for them to protect the environment, forest and wildlife in order to attract tourists. However, the lack of opportunity for revenue generation means that the well-being of the local communities continues to depend on the use of natural resources from the forest. Conservation goals would be better achieved if there was sufficient benefit brought about by tourism (or other sources) to allow for reduced dependence by local communities on the harvesting of natural resources from BANP. Alternatively, BANP can continue to meet its conservation objectives if the forest areas outside the boundaries of the park, particularly those next to the longhouses in Ulu Batang Ai, continue to provide the longhouse residents with their forest produce requirements including wild meat. In the event that the carrying capacity of these forest is exceeded, community residents will logically begin exercising their harvesting rights and privileges in the park, which could ultimately defeat the conservation objectives.

It is clear from the research findings that tourism economic benefits for the longhouse communities described, range from a small cash 'top up' to virtually 'nothing'. Reliance on traditional plant and animal foods has remained largely unchanged and these continue to be harvested from the communal forests and from the National Park. Time spent on these traditional activities has likewise remained virtually unchanged.

The relative lack of unacceptable impacts on biodiversity and conservation values is to a large extent serendipitous. Numbers of longhouse people in Ulu Batang Ai with hunting privileges have declined through residential relocation strategies, thus easing pressure on the natural resources. At the same time tourist numbers have stayed below 'carrying capacity limits', thereby avoiding the serious erosion of biodiversity and cultural resources.

Pressures to develop infrastructure and expand opportunities for tourists at destinations like Batang Ai while currently static, remain unknown in the longer term. The challenges will only increase for the longhouse people, protected area managers, the tourism industry and the Sarawak Government. Managers from each of these groups have varying responsibilities for addressing these challenges. Of the few variables over which there is some degree of control, two stand out. These relate to access and the creation of facilities. If these are kept under a 'tight rein' some measure of sustainability for traditional ways of life, tourism and biodiversity remain possible.

There is a need for more research into the changing roles in longhouse tourism. Specific questions that need to be addressed include: how the benefits from tourism are distributed among the communities, and what changes tourism brings to the local communities, particularly with respect to time spent in their traditional ways of life of farming, gathering and hunting in and adjacent to BANP. Additional research topics that should be addressed include those related to: the volume of tourists that can provide benefits to local communities as well as conservation; what exactly is taken from the forest to sustain the people; and how tourism contributes to the decrease or increase in extraction of natural resources. Comparisons with other areas which have longhouse tourism, such as the Skrang area, could provide key insights of the impacts of higher visitation. Finally, longitudinal research incorporating a finer scale for the measure of 'time spent' on traditional activities is especially recommended in order to better understand the sustainability of use of natural resources from BANP.

Part Four

Indigenous Culture and Tourism

Introduction

Indigenous peoples have long been seen as tourist attractions because of their often unique cultures and there has developed great concern among many communities over the preservation of genuine indigenous culture when it becomes the focus of tourism. Commodification and commercialization of culture, and subsequent loss of authenticity have increasingly worried cultural commentators, and critics of tourism have often blamed tourism for causing these problems. The chapters in this section look at examples of tourism attractions that focus on cultural celebration and difference. The first chapter by O'Gorman and Thompson reports on the development of tourism to Mongolia, a relatively new tourist destination, and the role of the major national cultural festival as a focus of attraction for both international tourists and the local Mongolian population. They reveal the different perceptions of the two groups, and not surprisingly, the different levels of satisfaction with attending the festival. The two groups of visitors, while viewing the same event, have significantly different experiences; the international tourists rarely stay for the whole festival but watch only the part to which they might relate, while the domestic tourists view the festival as complete experience rather than a set of disparate events. Maintaining the quality of the two different experiences at the same event, as well as maintaining the cultural heritage is a difficult and common problem in tourism. The second chapter, by Pettersson and Vikin, discusses the role of the Sami of Scandinavia in both providing and being a tourist attraction and their reaction to these roles. They reveal the difficulty faced by indigenous peoples in a modern world in maintaining their culture while working in an activity such as tourism, and the different ways in which Sami in different parts of Scandinavia respond to this challenge. Their respondents also note the problems which they have in dealing with expectations and stereotypes of non-indigenous populations about how Sami should behave and appear, problems common to many indigenous groups in all parts of the world. Where these groups are offering cultural experiences to tourists this problem is compounded, and different communities in different settings respond with different strategies at different stages in development. The final chapter in this section by Ryan, Chang and Huan examines the situation with respect to the 12 indigenous tribes in Taiwan, not a destination generally thought of for indigenous tourism. They note the relatively recent development of indigenous tourism in Taiwan and the way in which information is now available. Ryan, Chang and Huan note the representation of indigenous peoples often involves what they term 'a discourse of silence' in terms of what is and what is not represented of the communities' history and culture by the normally dominant non-indigenous authorities, particularly those promoting tourism. They present two models illustrating indigenous tourism and the presentation of tourism based on indigenous peoples' cultures, and conclude that when appropriately handled, tourism can be a positive factor for the well-being of indigenous groups.

CHAPTER 12

Tourism and culture in Mongolia: the case of the Ulaanbaatar Nadaam

Kevin O'Gorman and
Karen Thompson

Introduction

In 2006 Mongolia celebrated the 800th anniversary of the unification of the Mongol tribes, the foundation of the Great Mongol Empire under Chinggis Khan. At its zenith, this empire covered a 12 million square mile expanse that stretched 7,000 miles from the Pacific Ocean to the Baltic Sea. Historically, Mongolia's isolation and the combination of high-altitude steppes, deserts and mountains produced a small, but hardy population of horse-riding, nomadic herders. The country is entirely landlocked and held to be the nation furthest from the sea. Today Mongolia has a population of fewer than 3 million people, the majority of whom are indigenous, in a country about the combined size of Western Europe. Roughly half the population still pursue a traditional semi-nomadic lifestyle on the steppe, while the rest live in the cities, mainly in the capital Ulaanbaatar.

The country's name is synonymous with remoteness and wilderness and, as Yu and Goulden (2006, p. 1331) note, 'stirs up the nomadic, exotic and mystic images of an international tourism destination'. Perhaps for this reason, it is relatively well positioned in the mind of the potential tourist, for whom the country's lack of infrastructure is part of its attraction. The tangible appeal of Mongolia for the tourist is clearly its natural resources, rather than the few built heritage sites which survive throughout its territory. At the same time, the exotic and alien image of the country creates a substantial cultural tourism market, propagated by the flourishing, semi-nomadic culture of the Mongolian people. Cultural festivals throughout Mongolia celebrate the rich nomadic tradition and the largest, the Ulaanbaatar Nadaam, has become a significant attraction for international, as well as domestic tourism. However, whilst international visitors are attracted by the historical tradition and cultural uniqueness of the events that take place during Nadaam, Mongolians are attracted by indigenous sports and the opportunity to spend time with friends and family and renew old acquaintances. Indeed, the experiences of international visitors may be quite different to that of Mongolians attending the festival, mediated as they are by tour operators and an assortment of special arrangements.

The chapter discusses the different experiences of the two sets of visitors to the Ulaanbaatar Naadam festival, based on a study conducted in 2005, and explores the challenges for this traditional cultural event posed by modern tourism and other forces. It commences with a brief overview of international and domestic tourism in Mongolia. The overview is followed by a review of the origins and history of Nadaam as an indigenous cultural festival. The experiences of modern day visitors to the festival from overseas and from Mongolia are then examined and compared, with reference to similarities and differences between the two groups. Finally, the chapter considers issues and future challenges for the festival as a result of the increasing number of international visitors and their expectations of the festival.

International and domestic tourism in Mongolia

Up until the end of the 1980s, tourists from the Russian Federation, Central and Eastern Europe accounted for the vast majority of international visits to

Mongolia. According to Kokubo and Haraguchi (1991), for example, only 5% of the total 236,540 overseas visitors to Mongolia in 1989 came from beyond the Eastern Bloc countries. All leisure visitors were handled by the state owned tour operator, Juulchin. However, the evolution of democracy at the beginning of the 1990s led to rapid but peaceful change in Mongolia, with the result that, since 1990, the number of international leisure visitors from beyond the Eastern Bloc Countries has grown, on average, by around 20% per year with the main generating markets being Japan, South Korea, France, the United Kingdom (UK) and the United States of America (USA) (Ministry of Road, Transport and Tourism, 2005). Yu and Goulden (2006) note, however, that this rise was offset by a sharp decrease in visitors from the Russian Federation with the result that total numbers fell to a low of 82,000 in 1997, before rising steadily and dramatically after 1998. In 2004, a total of 300,537 leisure tourists visited Mongolia, an increase of 49% over the previous year (Ministry of Road, Transport and Tourism, 2005).

An understanding of the profile of international tourists to Mongolia has been facilitated by a number of recent studies, principally funded by international development organizations. Since 1998, four surveys of international visitors have been undertaken (TACIS, 1998; Saffery and Sugar, 2003; Gansukh, 2005; Weinig, 2006). Although funded and organized by different groups, each of these studies has attempted to build on the previous ones, using similar methodologies and producing data which are comparable. It has thus been possible to build a picture of how international tourism to Mongolia has developed in the period since 1998. Less information is available on domestic tourism within Mongolia, however one study, undertaken in 2003, does shed some light on the profile, behaviour and expenditure of domestic tourists (Gansukh, 2003).

In 2005, 68% of overseas visits to Mongolia were for leisure, recreation and holiday purposes. Sixty percent of leisure visitors to Mongolia originated from the European Union, with visitors from France representing 16%. Visitors from the USA represented 14% of total leisure arrivals with Japan, South Korea and China together accounting for 14% (Weinig, 2006). Since 1998, the number of Asian and American tourists has decreased, while leisure visits from European countries have increased (TACIS, 1998; Saffery and Sugar, 2003; Weinig, 2006). The average age of leisure visitors to Mongolia is falling. Whilst, in 1998, 58% of visitors were aged over 40 years, in 2005 only 42% fell into this category, with 51% being between the ages of 20 and 39 years (Saffery and Sugar, 2003; Weinig, 2006). In 2005, the most important reasons leisure visitors cited for travelling to Mongolia were natural scenery (78%), Mongolian traditional culture (60%) and adventure tours (32%) (Weinig, 2006). In regards to domestic tourism in Mongolia, Gansukh (2003) reports that the most common purpose of travel is visiting friends and relatives (40.5%), followed by leisure (35.2%). The Mongolian countryside is the most popular destination, with 63% of those surveyed indicating that they travel to the countryside one to two times per year. The most popular motivation for travel, as with international visitors, is to enjoy the natural scenery (53.7%). Gansukh (2003) also reports that Mongolian history, culture and nomadic traditions are increasingly attracting domestic tourists to rural areas to enjoy indigenous cuisine and hospitality.

Mongolia's political history and commercial and economic isolation have clearly constrained large-scale tourism development and, consequently, the product which Mongolia offers to overseas tourists is comparatively limited, highly seasonal, resource based and focussed on wilderness and cultural tourism. Attractions include relatively unspoiled natural resources such as the Gobi desert, scenic lakes such as Khuvsgul and the mountains of the Altai. The country is rich in flora and fauna, which attracts both naturalists and sportsmen. It also contains a number of interesting archaeological, geological and palaeontological sites. Yu and Goulden's (2006) survey identified nature as the destination attribute with which international visitors to Mongolia were most satisfied. Although, as related above, Mongolian traditional culture is the second most important reason overseas visitors come to Mongolia, Yu and Goulden (2006) report a lower rate of satisfaction with this aspect of the tourism product. Nonetheless, it is evident that the culture and civilization of the Mongolian people, well preserved by years of isolation, are major attractions for visitors from post-modern societies.

The Department of Tourism Policy and Coordination, located within the Ministry of Road, Transport and Tourism, has responsibility for formulation and coordination of tourism policy and strategy, including product development and promotion. Within the constraints of its limited funding (Gansukh, 2003), the Mongolian Tourism Board promotes a calendar of events to domestic and overseas visitors that celebrate Mongolian culture and tradition. Featured attractions include the Ice Festival at Khuvsgul Lake, festivals of reindeer herding and shamanic art, as well as poetry and art festivals. In 2006, the events calendar was expanded to highlight the celebrations surrounding the 800th anniversary of the Great Mongolian State. Despite this range of attractions, the National Nadaam Festival in Ulaanbaatar in mid-July, organized by a special organizing committee appointed by the Mongolian government, remains the centrepiece of the annual events calendar and was highlighted as the main event of the anniversary celebrations. The Nadaam, therefore, is important both as an element of the cultural tourism product for international visitors and as a celebration of indigenous culture for domestic visitors.

Nadaam: history and traditions

Eriyn Gurvan Nadaam, the Festival of the Three Manly Sports (commonly known as Nadaam) is the biggest festival of the year for Mongolians. Separate festivals are held across the country; the largest, in the capital Ulaanbaatar, takes place from the 11th to 13th of July each year and in 2005 was attended by approximately 50,000 spectators. Official attendance figures are unavailable, however the stadium has a capacity of 35,000 and a further 15,000 are estimated to have attended the festivities outside the stadium and elsewhere in the city. The modern day festival begins with a colourful opening ceremony, followed two days of horse racing, archery and wrestling competitions with a third day generally reserved for eating, drinking and relaxing. Despite still being known as the three manly sports, women now participate in all but the wrestling category.

Nadaam is an enduring celebration of the indigenous majority culture in Mongolia. According to Kabzińska-Stawarz (1987), contemporary Mongolians trace the origins of the festival back to the needs of war, defence and hunting. In Old Mongolia, the festivals celebrated the prowess of the male and were linked to religious rites intended to both celebrate and attract wealth, health and prosperity from the gods of nature and from ancestors. After the advent of Buddhism in Mongolia, monasteries held four or five festivals each year at ritual sites around the country, which occasionally were huge affairs, drawing people from many different provinces. These festivals coincided with sacrificial offerings made in autumn to local spirits or Buddhist gods, to initiate the next stage of the annual cycle. They began with ritual offerings of sheep and dairy products to the gods followed by traditional sports and closed with a distribution of food to the poor. Bulstrode (1920) observes that at the beginning of the twentieth century in Urga (now Ulaanbaatar) there were spectacular festivals lasting up to 2 weeks. These festivals were scheduled to coincide with the oncoming of autumn and contained both Buddhist ceremonies as well as the three traditional sports. Carruthers (1914) notes that wrestling bouts were frequently held between representatives of church and state and were attended by the Bogd Khan (living Buddha), the religious and secular leader.

After 1921, the Nadaam festival became an official celebration of the National Revolution's victory. On 11 June 1921 the revolutionaries mounted a successful attack on Urga, the capital city, and expelled the Chinese military garrison. So the first Nadaam of the 'new Mongolia' was celebrated on the first anniversary of the state's foundation, 11 July 1922, on the south bank of the River Tula – a spot reportedly chosen by a great Mongol hero, Sükhbaatar (Montagu, 1956). During the communist regime, Nadaam was secularized and organized by the local state controlled cooperatives. The differences between the festival during the socialist period and those preceding it were substantial. For example:

in Old Mongolia, a festival lasted until all the competitions had been won; in the socialist period, it was limited to two days. Attendance became compulsory. Mongols had to be seen supporting the [communist] flag or forfeit their wages.

(Pegg, 2001, p. 213)

Dashdondov (2005) observes that each of the individual sporting events within the festival have special cultural and historical significance and contain deeply embedded rituals. To help develop an understanding of the centrality of Nadaam for Mongolians, it is important to gain some understanding of the origins and history of the festival's sporting events.

In Old Mongolia, horse racing was linked to rituals which offered the first milk of the new year to the gods, and the consecration of mares who were then left to run free. With the help of a Shaman or Lama, a spiritually and climatically auspicious time close to the summer solstice was chosen for these offering rituals. The ceremonies were followed by the racing of stallions, with the aim of the contest being to determine the swiftest horse, rather than the best rider. Serruys (1974), noted that, along with racing, contestants and spectators sang praises to the gods. These praises were an amalgam of folk, shamanist and Buddhist beliefs. Offerings of milk were made to gods appropriated from Mongolian folk religion with the winning horse being consecrated to the gods and allowed to run free. Just before the communist era, Andrews (1921) observed a horse race where the Lamas, in dazzling yellow gowns sat on a hillside northeast of Urga (Ulaanbaatar) and opposite them were positioned the judges. Horsemen were dressed in colourful robes, chanting their ritual songs. The winners were given cheese to scatter towards the spectators and ritual sites as an offering to the gods and ancestors. Bulstrode (1920) noted that both boys and girls competed in these races.

Kabzińska-Stawarz (1991) records that, until the early years of the twentieth century, the skills of archery were used by Mongols for both war and hunting. Bows and arrows also symbolized fertility and life force during weddings and funerals and were used as offerings at ritual places to ward off evil spirits (Bawden, 1958). Similarly, in the late nineteenth and early twentieth century, archery contests, featuring cylindrical camel skin targets stacked to the height of a man, were thought to dispel illness (Kabzińska-Stawarz, 1991). In a match observed by Bulstrode (1920), archers positioned themselves in front of tents at the southern end of the arena and shot in pairs; princes and herders alike. Archery exists in Mongolia today primarily as a competitive sport rather than a tool of war or hunting and has declined even as a sport because of restrictions on killing animals under the communist regime (Pegg, 2001). Lattimore (1941) noted that in 1941, it was only the rich that could afford a bow which by then had become an extravagant luxury.

In addition to being a trial of strength, Pegg (2001, p. 217) states that Mongolian wrestling 'is a combined performance of music, ritual and dance that encourages an exchange of powers between the wrestler, community, gods of the universe and spirits of nature'. The Mongols considered the best wrestlers to be incarnations of their epic heroes, personifying the strength, skill and courage of the ideal of man (Kabzińska-Stawarz, 1991). Ritual symbolism is important in wrestling. For example, victorious wrestlers were traditionally given some cheese which they held to their forehead before throwing a portion toward the mountains and sky, eating some, and flinging the remainder toward the spectators (Andrews, 1921). In this way, the wrestler shared his victory with the spirits of nature and with the spectators. This tradition continues to be practiced in the festival's wrestling event.

A further ritual that has survived, albeit in modified form, is that prior to the match, each wrestler's trainer or herald chants the wrestler's praises. In Old Mongolia, the recitation situated the wrestler by referring to the noble or monastery to whom he gave allegiance, the gods, clan, lineage, any titles and achievements; thus introducing the wrestler to the audience, other contestants and his opponent (see chapter by Carr, Editors' Note). Pegg (2001) notes that during the communist era, so as not raise questions of race, history or religion the traditional chants were adapted to fit the new ideology by only providing the name of the sports club to which the contestant belonged. Wrestlers also perform the Garuda Dance (commonly known as the Eagle Dance) during the introductions and before and after each round. In this dance, the wrestler stretches out both arms and flaps them as he leaps into the air. In doing so, the wrestler is 'imitating two birds – the legendary, powerful Khan Garuda of the Buddhist pantheon and the hawk, admired for its bravery and the way it swoops, dives and quickly snatches its prey' (Pegg, 2001, p. 217). These rituals and traditions are still woven into the fabric of modern day Nadaam. Whilst these rites serve to entertain the visitor from overseas, there is often a lack of appreciation among the foreign tourists of their deeper cultural significance.

The historical and cultural significance of Nadaam serve as important attractions for both international and domestic tourism in Mongolia. This festival is by far the most important event of its kind on the Mongolian calendar and represents a fascinating combination of historical tradition, indigenous cultural and sporting competition. The aim of the research reported in this chapter is to explore differences in the visitor experiences of this festival in order to develop an understanding of how the different elements of Nadaam interact to attract and entertain both domestic and international visitors and the challenges for an indigenous event that has recently targeted two distinct audiences. Moreover, the study explores potential differences in the behaviour and experiences of domestic and overseas visitors, and possible conflicts between promotion and development of the festival as an international attraction while retaining its indigenous attributes and heritage. Finally, the investigation highlights positive and negative influences of tour operators and festival organizers on visitor experiences.

Methodology

The study was undertaken by a team of researchers from the University of Strathclyde, UK and Orkhon University, Mongolia. Mixed methods were employed for the research, namely a combination of observational and social survey techniques. Due to an apparent absence of academic literature on the Nadaam festival and the special nature of the festival as a combination of cultural and sport attractions, exploratory techniques were felt to offer the best opportunity to develop an in-depth understanding of the visitor experience. Direct observation requires the researcher to actively participate in the event that is being investigated because in 'observing and talking to people you learn from them their view of reality' (Agar, 1996, p. 157). Observation has the advantage that it allows patterns of behaviour to be observed, which may not be apparent to individual subjects involved (Veal, 1997). The observational research was undertaken during the first two days of the festival, in and around the Nadaam stadium and the other sporting sites used for the festival. The temporal and spatial behaviour of both overseas and domestic visitors was observed and recorded in the form of research notes.

It has been noted that observation should play a role in most strategies, but often needs to be supplemented by other data collection techniques (Veal, 1997; Elliott and Jankel-Elliott, 2003). To this end, and to augment the observational component of the research, a three page self-completed questionnaire was designed to be administered to visitors to the two-day Nadaam festival in Ulaanbaatar, Mongolia on the 11th and 12th July 2005. The main content of the questionnaire consisted of a series of 27 statements regarding motivation for attending Nadaam. These items were drawn from the literature on motivation for attending cultural festivals and events and sports events in the USA and South East Asia (see Lee et al., 2004). Subjects were asked to rate their level of agreement/disagreement with each statement on a Likert-type scale. Further sections of the questionnaire asked about the characteristics of respondents' visits, their levels of satisfaction with certain aspects of the Nadaam festival and the event overall, as well as their likelihood of revisiting. Questions were also included to collect demographic information on respondents.

Some changes were made to the questionnaire as the result of a test for face validity, conducted with tour operators and festival organizers. The questionnaire was translated into Mongolian by a native speaker and, as a further test of validity, a back-translation was conducted by a different native speaker and compared with the original. Some slight differences were necessary between the Mongolian language questionnaire and the questionnaire for international visitors with regard to trip characteristics, as certain questions were only relevant to one cohort.

The survey was undertaken at a number of sites across the festival including inside and outside the main Nadaam stadium, the archery stadium and the horse racing venue. International visitors, with English as their first language, were targeted by researchers, whilst a team of Mongolian speaking researchers collected data from domestic visitors. A total of 539 useable questionnaires were obtained from a convenience sample of those attending the festival. Of these, 34% were completed by international visitors and 66% by Mongolian nationals. A large majority (75%) of Mongolian respondents were from Ulaanbaatar with the remainder coming from throughout Mongolia but also from overseas. The most frequently represented nations among the overseas visitors were Australia, France, UK and USA.

Overseas and domestic tourists experience of contemporary Nadaam

The role of Nadaam as a bridge between the urban and nomadic populations of Mongolia has been commented on by Finer (2002), who observed the uniting of traditional and contemporary lifestyles, but also a blending of the traditional and the commercial. The population of Ulaanbaatar experiences a dramatic increase over the three days of the Nadaam public holiday. The city fills up with nomadic families visiting from the countryside with gers and livestock, so that small animal holdings appear across the suburbs; an interesting sight in a capital city. For some of these families, Nadaam represents a commercial as well as a leisure opportunity. At the same time, overseas visitor numbers experience a peak during the Nadaam period, with accommodation being in short supply. The Director of one incoming tour operator reported that 60% of the overseas visitors handled annually by the company arrive within three days of the Nadaam festival (Wigsten, 2005).

The main part of the festival takes place within the National Nadaam stadium, just south of the commercial centre of Ulaanbaatar. The opening ceremony, on the first day, serves as a useful barometer of how Nadaam has evolved. During the communist period, there was little reference to Mongolian national heroes, such as Chinggis Khan. The opening ceremony contained a marching brass band playing 'The Red Flag', a military parade saluting the Party leaders and various other military-esque behaviour (Dashtseren, 2001). By contrast, the modern opening ceremony is a mix of traditional and modern symbols. It starts at the Parliament building, where the Mongolian national flag is raised, alongside the nine-legged, white standard of Chinggis Khan. A short procession carries the standard to the Nadaam stadium where around 35,000 spectators are packed into fairly basic seating (see Figure 12.1). In 2005, Mongolians paid approximately US$ 2 for their entrance tickets, whereas western travellers paid US$ 25. However, visitors from overseas are automatically allocated seats in the only shaded area of the stadium. This system of dual pricing is commonly employed at visitor attractions and arts venues throughout Mongolia. However, in the case of Nadaam, it has the effect of segregating overseas and domestic visitors.

Most tour groups attend the opening ceremony on the first morning of the festival. They may stay briefly to watch the wrestling or travel out of town to the horse racing, but normally move on to the next item on their tour itinerary by the afternoon of the first day. Independent travellers and local people, on the other hand, are more likely to spend a full day at the stadium, watching the various sports competitions that are taking place as well as eating, drinking, shopping and socializing at stalls which are located outside the stadium. Among the independent overseas travellers who were interviewed, the substantial presence of organized tours, consisting mainly of older Japanese and American tourists, had a negative impact on their satisfaction with the festival. Visitors on these organized tours were more likely to complain of overcrowding and the lack of comfort in the stadium, while independent travellers particularly disliked the behaviour of other international tourists. For independent international travellers, segregation into tourist enclaves appeared to detract from the authentic experience of Nadaam as it limited the possibilities of mingling with local people inside the stadium.

The opening ceremony itself takes the form of a gala-type celebration, complete with an aerial show, a parade of lavish floats, Mongolian traditional and contemporary song and dance and an address by the Mongolian President. Feedback from overseas respondents indicated a level of surprise and slight distaste at the content of the opening ceremony. The presence of motorbikes, cheer leaders and hip-hop dancers apparently did not correspond to the

Figure 12.1
Nadaam stadium

more traditional display of Mongolian culture and customs which these visitors had expected. Nonetheless, levels of satisfaction with the opening ceremony were relatively high, on average 5.36 on a 7-point Likert scale for overseas visitors and 5.63 for Mongolians attending the festival (with 7 being the highest satisfaction score). Corporate sponsorship of the event by national and international companies, such as Dell, Panasonic, Pepsi and Coca-Cola, has become increasingly visible in recent years within the main stadium. This commercialization extended to the opening ceremony, since several of the parade floats were designed to advertise local products such as beer and food. Commercialization and corporate sponsorship were cited by both Mongolian and overseas visitors as negative aspects of the Nadaam festival. The commodification of festivities has previously been criticized by, *inter alia*, Boissevain (1996) and Taylor (2001) for jeopardizing the authenticity of social relations and cultural rituals.

Wrestling is the most important sport of the Nadaam games, and the competition begins immediately after the opening ceremony and finishes at the end of the second day of the festival. It is extremely popular with the

Mongolian spectators. Organized tour groups have an opportunity to observe the initial stages of the competition on the first morning. However, constraints imposed by organized itineraries mean that overseas visitors in tour groups have a limited opportunity to experience this unique competition. Whilst the novelty of the costumes and the 'Eagle Dance' performed by the competitors hold the visitors' interest for a short period, the lack of explanation and interpretation detracts from their experience. For the tourist who is unfamiliar with the rules of the competition and who does not understand the Mongolian commentary, it is difficult to remain absorbed by the contest. There would appear to be considerable opportunity to improve the experience through a better explanation of and education about the sporting events by the tour operator or event organizers. For example, a festival programme for visitors could highlight the cultural significance of the sporting events and the rituals surrounding them. This is arguably more important for independent travellers, who are not accompanied by a guide and were observed to be more likely to spend longer in the stadium. Visitors on organized tours miss the excitement and atmosphere generated in the stadium among local spectators by the wrestling finals, which are held on the second day of the festival. As such, they miss a key cultural highlight of the event.

Such mediation of the visitor experience of Nadaam by tour operators and guides extends to other aspects of the festival. It was observed, for example, that tour groups entering and exiting the stadium were discouraged from exploring other areas of the stadium complex, including the thriving marketplace outside the stadium. This market is an important centre of activity for local people and serves as a site where competitors, traders and spectators mingle. Moreover, at the horse racing venue, a dusty plain about 30 kilometres outside Ulaanbaatar, the few tour groups that did attend this captivating event were accommodated in temporary, tiered seating set up on the finish line of the races. Again, their experience contrasted greatly with that of independent travellers and Mongolians attending the festival, most of whom spectated from within a chaotic and dusty throng of people and horses (Figure 12.2).

In terms of the domestic visitor experience, it is possible to identify a number of key reasons that Mongolians have for attending Nadaam. Spending time with family and friends was observed to be highly important to domestic visitors to Nadaam, since the celebrations present an opportunity for nomadic herders to assemble together, renewing old and making new acquaintances. The Nadaam holiday is the time of year when families traditionally reunite. Clearly there is also a strong sports attraction for Mongolians visiting the festival. Many respondents indicated that they had attended the festival in order to support certain competitors. The wrestling contest in particular attracts a large number of serious fans, in the same way that an important football match would in Europe. Thus, the festival must be regarded not only as a cultural festival, celebrating Mongolian ethnicity and traditions and showcasing them to the international visitor, but also as an important national sporting competition. Indeed, given that the opening

Figure 12.2
Spectators on horseback at Nadaam

ceremony is increasingly being criticized for over commercialization and a subsequent loss of meaning, it is perhaps the sporting events themselves which offer the most authentic cultural experience for both overseas and domestic visitors.

At the same time, questionnaire responses indicated that the festival is perceived as an exciting event with 'seeing new and different things' being rated as the most important reason for Mongolians to attend Nadaam. This finding highlights an interesting phenomenon amongst the domestic market as domestic visitors, on average, indicated that they were unlikely to attend the event in the future. It seems, therefore, that, although 75% of Mongolians attending the festival live in Ulaanbaatar, they do not represent a potential repeat market for the festival. Overseas visitors also declared themselves to be, on average, unlikely to return to the festival, although somewhat more likely than domestic visitors. Thus, attendance at the festival seems to be a 'once in a lifetime' experience for Mongolians, as well as for international visitors.

As an overview of the festival experience, it is useful to summarize the levels of satisfaction experienced by overseas and domestic visitors, with regard to key aspects of the festival. Figure 12.3 illustrates that levels of satisfaction

Festival attribute	Level of satisfaction (7-point Likert scale, 7 = highest level of satisfaction)	
	International	Domestic
Opening ceremony	5.36	5.63
Authenticity of cultural experience	5.37	5.54
Wrestling	5.34	5.98
Horse racing	5.58	6.03
Archery	5.29	5.39
Festival atmosphere	5.53	5.41
Uniqueness of experience	5.78	5.54
Level of sports competition	5.19	5.59
Safety	4.88	4.75
Amenities and facilities	4.48	4.43
Overall satisfaction	5.51	5.33

Figure 12.3
Levels of satisfaction with attributes of the Nadaam Festival

with the festival are relatively high, with the exception of safety and amenities which proved less satisfactory.

Whereas overseas visitors were, on average, most satisfied with the uniqueness of the Nadaam festival, Mongolians particularly enjoyed the two key sporting events; horse racing and wrestling. Perhaps surprisingly, it was domestic visitors to the festival who were least satisfied with the level of safety at the festival and the amenities and facilities. This is also evidenced by the fact that drunkenness, cheating, and a generally chaotic lack of organization were frequently cited by Mongolians as key dislikes about Nadaam. Many Mongolians also felt that the level of rubbish in and around the stadium was unacceptable.

T-tests were run on the satisfaction variables to investigate the presence of statistically significant differences between the groups. For those satisfaction variables on which statistically significant differences were found between overseas and domestic visitors to Nadaam, an eta statistic was calculated as a measure of the degree of association between independent and dependent variable. Results are shown in Figure 12.4.

As demonstrated by Figure 12.4, statistically significant differences of moderate magnitude exist between overseas and domestic festival attendees on satisfaction with wrestling. The significantly lower level of satisfaction among overseas visitors with the wrestling competition can, potentially be related back to issues discussed above, such as lack of interpretation and the fact that the final stages of the competition are experienced by only few visitors from overseas. Differences also exist in terms of satisfaction with the

Satisfaction Variable	Eta^2
Opening ceremony ($t = 2.02$, df $= 112.87$, $p < 0.05$)	0.01
Authenticity of cultural experience ($t = 2.46$, df $= 273$, $p < 0.05$)	0.02
Wrestling ($t = 4.95$, df $= 273$, $p < 0.01$)	0.08
Horse racing ($t = 3.66$, df $= 273$, $p < 0.01$)	0.05
Level of competition ($t = 2.68$, df $= 273$, $p < 0.01$)	0.03

Figure 12.4
Magnitude of between groups differences on satisfaction variables

opening ceremony, authenticity, horse racing and level of competition, but they are small in magnitude. There is, however, no significant relationship between origin of visitors and *overall* level of satisfaction with Nadaam. These quantitative findings are consistent with conclusions drawn from observation and the open-ended answers obtained from attendees.

Conclusions: issues and challenges for the future

It has been shown that international visitors' experiences of and satisfaction with aspects of the Nadaam festival differ significantly from those of local visitors. The opportunity to observe and participate in a culturally and historically unique event clearly appeals to tourists from overseas, but also appears to be a valuable way of reaffirming Mongolian identity and culture for the indigenous audience, some of whom travel great distances to attend. Nonetheless, there is some evidence to suggest that the sporting events are seen as less culturally important than, for example, the opening ceremony by overseas visitors. This is an aspect of the festival which requires further academic investigation. It also highlights the challenge for festival organizers of reconciling the key cultural attractions of the festival for overseas visitors with those of greatest importance to domestic visitors. This reconciliation could potentially be achieved through better interpretation of the sporting events, their history, tradition and conventions. In addition the cultural programme of the opening ceremony could perhaps be better structured to appeal to both groups of attendees. There is also a need to improve the integration of local and overseas attendees during the event in order to increase the authenticity of the experience which traditionally would not have had two such distinct and segregated audiences.

Many of the negative comments on the Nadaam experience made by both international and domestic visitors related to a lack of organization and general feeling of chaos surrounding the events. For example, despite a sizeable police presence at the opening ceremony, there was serious overcrowding in the stadium and possession of a ticket did not appear to guarantee entry. Indeed, the area surrounding the stadium was poorly organized to deal with the number of vehicles and persons in attendance. Tourists who are part of an organized tour tended to expect a greater degree of organization surrounding their visit to the stadium. Clearly tour operators have to work with the confines of the existing organizational structures. A desire to increase international tourist attendance depends, in part, on improved levels of organization. On the other hand, the degree of chaos may be attractive to independent travellers who are more concerned with experiencing an authentic rather than a clinical delivery of the festival. This is an area that merits further research.

Safety and amenities were the two attributes of the Nadaam festival with which respondents were least satisfied. Both the observational research and the questionnaire survey uncovered evidence that tourists had been victims of crime, such as pick-pocketing and bag slashing both inside and outside the stadium. However, the level of chaos discussed above potentially increases the feeling of risk among tourists to the event. With regard to amenities, there is a need to bring facilities such as toilets up to a more acceptable standard, and this should be a priority. At the present time the introduction of any sort of quality standard for vendors and caterers is considered unrealistic.

The research was conducted at an exploratory level, and has produced a relatively detailed account of the experiences of international and domestic visitors to the Nadaam festival. Insight has been gained about the motivations of the two main groups of visitors who attend the festival, as well as their levels of satisfaction and key likes and dislikes. Moreover, behavioural differences between visitor groups have been noted, as have the mediating roles of tour operators on the experience. It has been argued that international visitors fail to fully appreciate the cultural significance of Nadaam's sporting events, which potentially offer the most authentic cultural experience of the festival. Further research is required related to the commercial dimension of the festival as an important motivator for attendance for Mongolians, both in terms of entrepreneurial activities and networking. Future research should also investigate whether expectations of the cultural product offered by the Nadaam festival are similar or different for overseas and domestic visitors. The key challenge for the Nadaam festival will be to maintain its cultural uniqueness, which has been shown to be a key factor in motivating visitors to attend, whilst catering to two distinct audiences, each of which consists of a number of visitor segments.

CHAPTER 13

Sami perspectives on indigenous tourism in northern Europe: commerce or cultural development?

Robert Pettersson and
Arvid Viken

Introduction

Historically, the Sami people in the peripheral parts of northern Europe have been occupied with harvesting nature, reindeer herding, fishery and farming. Today most Sami live modern lives with modern occupations: only about one out of ten adult Sami are reindeer herders; and only a few are occupied in traditional Sami handicraft, hunting and fishing. Reindeer herding, which has a strong symbolic significance in Sami culture, is partly carried out in the traditional husbandry style, and partly as an adaptation to the market economy (Sara, 2001) using motorbikes, snowmobiles, trucks and helicopters, aiming for large-scale food production. Modern, restructured and market oriented, reindeer herding demands vast areas and fewer reindeer herders, and thus, a decreasing number of Sami take part in the industry. Accordingly, many Sami have found new occupations, and tourism is often seen as an option (Pettersson, 2004), although it is not the only alternative. In terms of tourism entrepreneurship, the greatest potential is with the smaller and husbandry based herders whom have a long tourism tradition. However, Sami people outside the reindeer herding also work as tourism entrepreneurs or employees. The modern, 'non-exotic' Sami entrepreneur who wants to develop tourism is tempted to adapt past traditions to increase tourism attractiveness.

As tourism is characterized by cultural encounters, it gives rise to both positive and negative impacts in the destination area (Robinson and Boniface, 1999; Mason, 2003). Therefore, developing tourism in the Sami society is, as often is the case in indigenous areas, an act of balance between commercial efforts and success on the one side, and effects such as over-commercialization and cultural losses on the other. Thus, the Sami see tourism as an opportunity for industrial and cultural development, but they are watching the development with vigilance. These issues will be discussed further in the chapter, based on different accounts of Sami tourism, and interviews with Sami in Norway and Sweden. The chapter starts with a presentation of the Sami and tourism in their home areas. Theoretical approaches to the study of Sami tourism are then outlined and data sources described, followed by sections discussing the nature of Sami tourism, cultural change and commercialization. This is followed by a discussion of the impacts of commercialization.

Sami and Sápmi

Sápmi is the area traditionally inhabited by the Sami in the north of Norway, Sweden, Finland and on the Kola Peninsula in Russia (Figure 13.1). This region, which has no exact borders, is characterized by a peripheral location, large areas with limited infrastructure and a sparse population. In Sápmi, as in other indigenous areas, these characteristics are not simply barriers but may, from a tourist's point of view, be what makes the area attractive. The Sami population is said to be about 70,000, with 40,000 living in Norway, 20,000 in Sweden, 6,000 in Finland and 2,000 in Russia. In only a few municipalities do the Sami constitute a majority, which means that often Sami and non-Sami are living side by

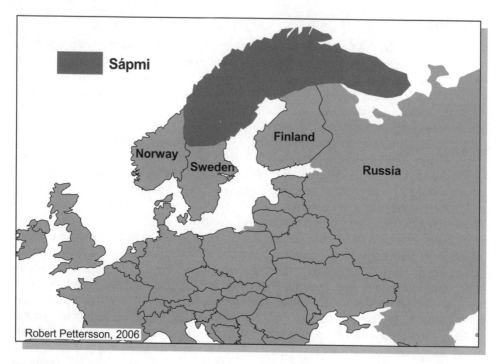

Figure 13.1
Map showing Sápmi in northern Europe

side. Hence, there are today no clear differences between Sami and non-Sami settlements. A large part of the Sami population is found in the cities and the densely populated southern parts of Scandinavia.

The question of who is a Sami is difficult to answer as most people have a mixed ethnic background. One way of determining ethnicity is to make it a question of sentiment and self-ascription; those who feel or claim that they are Sami, are Sami. In Norway one has to be able to document a grandfather or grandmother to be qualified for the Sami Parliament elections, while in Sweden a person should have spoken Sami language at home, or think about themselves as being a Sami.

Most often there is a strong ethnic element in the identity (Viken, 2006). Although the similarities with the surrounding cultures are more significant than the differences, the Sami culture has some genuine distinctive traits. The main characteristics are the Sami languages, some typical Sami symbols including the reindeer, the Sami tent (*lavvu*), the Sami dress, and last but not least, the strong anchorage in traditions (Viken, 2000). The traditional ties are so strong that as Olsen (2006) claims, the Sami often are excluded from the western type of modernity. A study of potential German tourists to Norway some years ago, showed that Germans looked upon themselves as most modern, Norwegian as less modern, and the Sami as partly pre-modern (Viken, 2000).

Tourists to the Sami area tend to regret that the area has been modernized, and judge tourism as one of the causes of the fuzziness of the contemporary indigenous culture (Lyngnes and Viken, 1998; Tuuluntie, 2006), ignoring the fact that the Sami people themselves have fought for modernization and for being regarded as modern.

The Sami society has a stronger political and formal position at the beginning of this new millennium than in the most of the two previous centuries. There is recognition of and a regret for a history of suppression by the Norwegian and Swedish national states. In response, many Sami institutions and support systems have been developed. There are also many signs of a re-ethnification among the Sami, a process that has many similarities with what has been called indigenism (van den Berghe, 1994; van den Berghe and Ochoa, 2000). Signs of this include the creation of a Sami flag, recapturing of Sami traditional names, Sami parliaments, writing place names in Sami language, creation of Sami museums, and the strong emphasize on traditions – many of which are similar to those observed among different Indian tribes (Jamison, 1999; van den Berghe and Ochoa, 2000).

Sami tourism

There are several reasons for the Sami to start tourism enterprises, but most important is the recent decline in reindeer herding and the increased demand from the tourist market for Sami experiences. The number of tourist attractions and offered activities in Sápmi increased during the previous decade. Sami culture is currently accessible to tourists in museums, at cultural events, in outdoor cultural sites, during escorted tours of different kinds, and at places where Sami handicrafts are sold (Müller and Pettersson, 2001).

Tourism development based on the Sami culture has a different history and has had different conditions in the four nation states that comprise Sápmi. Besides national legislation and rules, considerable regional differences regarding, for example, Sami language, traditions, and relations to the non-Sami population affect the preconditions both for reindeer herding and tourism development. Hence, even within each country, the Sami area is rather heterogeneous.

In Finland, many fortune hunters, Sami and non-Sami, have developed controversial tourism ventures that have been harshly criticized as being exploitative in terms of the way Sami themes are employed (Saarinen, 2001). Norway, on the other hand, is often mentioned as having good examples of Sami tourism. Here the Sami themselves have been involved in the process of tourism development (Lyngnes and Viken, 1998), but more on the experience and activity side, and in the simple accommodation sector rather than in the hotel industry. In Sweden, there has been a growth in sustainable Sami tourism and Sami tourism entrepreneurs (Pettersson, 2004). Many of the tourist attractions in Sápmi take place outdoors, or in the 'indigenous habitat' as Smith (1996) called it. In the Sami habitat, reindeer are a natural ingredient, constitute a vital part of the attraction system and are a symbol of Sami tourism.

Limited accessibility is a common constraint for tourism in remote and sparsely populated areas (Lundgren, 1995). However, this depends on how one looks at it. Most parts of Sápmi are accessible within 4–5 hours from the capitals of the Scandinavian countries, combining airplane and car (Fredman et al., 2001). Many visitors also approach Sápmi by cruise ship, a tradition that has been practiced since the 1870s, but many of these tourists only get glimpses of the Sami. Most tourists travel along the highways that run in a south–north direction along the coast or in the interior. Throughout the area there are settlements within a 100 kilometres range, and the infrastructure is relatively good. Thus, the tourism development has mainly evolved around the existing service infrastructure.

Tourism and Indigenous people – blessing or burden?

Tourism has, along with many other institutions, influenced the societal development of indigenous people around the world. It has been a mechanism for modernization, globalization and integration. The accounts of these processes often focus on the negative side, but positive impacts also exist. The dark sides of the story are about exploitation of local resources, loss of local control, commodification, bastardization of culture, and losses of authenticity and identity (e.g., Turner and Ash, 1975; MacCannell, 1976, 1992; Crick, 1989; Dogan, 1989; Sofield, 1991; van den Berghe, 1994; Hinch and Butler, 1996; Johnston, 2000; V. Smith, 2001; M.K. Smith, 2003; Ryan and Aicken, 2005). Many of these accounts are about vanishing cultures and ways of life. The authors often seem to regret the changes from the traditional ways of life to a modern lifestyle, rather normatively, and blame tourism for bringing about these changes. However, as MacCannell (1992) asks, are there really any alternatives? For many indigenous groups, tourism is not something coming from outside, it is as much emerging from the groups themselves, as a means to survive, but also inspired by their own experiences as travellers around the world (Tuuluntie, 2006).

On the positive side there are many examples of tourism being a contributor to cultural and economic development within indigenous communities (e.g., Smith, 2003). Firstly, there are several studies that show that tourism enhances cultural preservation. It is an arena for exposition of the culture. Traditions and heritage displays are also important for the locals, as they remind people of their cultural roots (Grünewald, 2002). Secondly, the fact that tourism presents indigenous cultures in ways that makes them exotic and interesting in the eyes of others, creates pride and self-confidence among those who are the focus of tourism (see chapter by Thompson and O'Gorman, Editors' Note). Thirdly, tourism also constitutes an arena for trying out new expressions of culture. Examples would be soap stone artifacts produced by Inuit in the Canadian Arctic, or Indian knitwear in Ecuadorian Otavalo. Thus, tourism adds to the dynamics of a culture, and links indigenous people to the modern and global world.

The situation of the Sami areas is somewhere in between. Some accounts about the cultural significance of tourism in Sami areas have been produced

(Ruotsala, 1995; Viken, 1997a, b, 2000, 2002; Lyngnes and Viken, 1998; Saarinen, 1999; Pettersson, 2004; Müller and Pettersson, 2005). Even if the impacts generally are small, a series of cultural adaptations to tourism have occurred (Lyngnes and Viken, 1998). Most of these have been accepted, but there are also examples transgressing the line of acceptance. The majority of those are found in Finland, where there are several accounts of relatively vulgar use of the Sami culture (Ruotsala, 1995; Saarinen, 1999). Thus, Sami attitudes towards tourism are both positive and negative; the opportunities within the industry need to be assessed, as do the risks. In this way, the Sami people fit well into the ambivalence that is typical of the post-modern society, according to Bauman (1991). This is a reflexive recognition of a situation where institutions and development tracks are appreciated as having both positive and negative sides, which must be addressed. These challenges will be discussed more thoroughly in the following section.

Sources: accounts and data

The analysis provided in this chapter is based on studies in Sápmi, mainly from the Norwegian and Swedish parts. Although the accounts relate to situations and observations in two different countries, the differences between these countries are of minor importance. Studies conducted in Norway include Lyngnes and Viken's (1998) study of tourists visiting the Sami areas, a study of the innovation potential from 1999 (Viken et al., 1998) and several minor studies (Viken, 2000, 2002, 2006; Olsen, 2003, 2006; Bongo Gaino, 2005). In Sweden there are several studies conducted by Pettersson (2002, 2003, 2004) and Müller and Pettersson (2001, 2005, 2006).

Besides relying on these accounts, this chapter is based also on data collected in 2002 and 2003 within a Nordic project on Sami tourism (Viken and Müller, 2006). The method employed in this project was focus group interviews, following the approach of American sociologist Robert Merton (Merton et al., 1956). Focus group interviews are centred on a specific issue (focus), organized and led by a chairman who seeks to generate primarily qualitative data through the interaction within the group. The collective focus and the communication in the group are vital (Webb and Kevern, 2001). Both Wilkinson (1999) and Jarrett (1993) argue that the focus groups create a situation for data gathering that is less artificial than other ways of data collection, but first and foremost it is a time- and cost-effective way of data collection (Sim, 1998). Research shows that focus group members came up with only 60–70% of the number of ideas that were identified through individual interviews with an equal number of people (Morgan, 1996). The major problem with the method is that it usually is easier to recruit well educated and middle class people, and hence, those who most often constitute the privileged public voice also contribute the most to group discussion.

In this study there were seven groups focusing on Sami culture and Sami tourism. Four of these groups met in Norway (Karasjohka) while three met in Sweden (Jokkmokk). The size of the groups was between three and seven participants who were recruited by local representatives.

Tourism: conserving and contesting culture

In the focus group interviews the first question asked was: 'What does it mean to be a Sami?' It may seem to be a silly question, even provocative, but none-the-less is often posed. As one informant said, 'Being a Sami, I do not know when I act in a particular way because I am a Sami.' But most people answered by pointing at the areas where the Sami deviate from non-Sami Norwegians and Swedes. This is a common way of marking particularity. They talked about a different language, more valued kinship, more respect for elder people, love of nature and nature as a place to harvest, the reindeer, another perspective on time and other traditions. Most important is that Sami feel that they have another way of thinking and communicating. 'When I meet a person, I immediately can sense if the person is Sami', an informant claimed. Many of the focus group members are proud of being Sami, and express a strong self-confidence. This is not how it used to be; the history of the Sami is a history of suppression and feelings of inferiority. 'Twenty years ago, people did not admit to be a Sami, and even changed their names', whereas 'today it is popular to be a Sami, and people change from Swedish to Sami names'. The focus group interviews revealed a rather strong collective identity, a feeling of communality among Sami people. Today, this is also related to autonomy. It was maintained that 'It is we, the Sami who decide how the Sami society develops.' However, there certainly also are threats; the global society being influential in all respects, the authorities that still ignore Sami needs and voices, and limited funding of Sami projects. And of course, media has a strong influence, with only a very small part of the media using the Sami language. Also mentioned was the fact that multicultural identity means that Sami identity gets weaker and less distinct over time.

So what about tourism? Does tourism influence the way the Sami look at their culture? Partly yes. Several informants were flattered by the fact that people come from all over the world to look at them. This created pride. As well as people accepting that Sami culture is exotic and interesting for tourists, Sami hosts realized that tourism was a showcase of their culture, and gave life to discussions about what is a reliable, respectful and authentic representation of their culture, and what is not. Thus tourism is an element in the discourse that constitutes modern Saminess. But at the same time tourism is part of the global society that puts pressure on all minority cultures, and that makes the Sami culture less distinct. Nobody claimed that tourism was particularly central to the changes in the Sami culture. However, during the discussions people revealed both irritation and vigilance (Viken, 2006). They were irritated because tourist operators, both non-Sami and Sami, make many mistakes in their presentations of Sami culture, and vigilant because they do not have confidence in all actors who use their culture for tourism purposes (see chapters by Williams and O'Neill and Hollinshead, Editors' Note). Referring to a new tourist attraction, a young Sami said: 'I paid the attraction a visit, just to check it out.'

A study of the Sami as attractions or tourees (van den Berghe, 1994) shows the same concern (Bongo Gaino, 2005). Tourism is accepted, but it is believed that the use of Sami symbols should be controlled by the Sami, and both the tourism industry and the tourists should act respectfully. Dressed in Sami costumes, people realize that they are obvious objects for the tourist gaze. Yes it was felt that to be photographed by a stranger is to have the private sphere of life invaded. This was also mentioned among the informants in Jokkmokk: 'It is not particularly agreeable to be photographed,' but they felt it more or less inevitable; 'when you turn your back to the tourists they take a picture of you anyhow'. And it is admitted that if one works within tourism, and wears traditional costumes, one lives up to the tourists' expectations of the Exotic Other (Bongo Gaino, 2005; Olsen, 2006; Viken, 2006). The problem is that many elder people wear the costume as their natural clothing – and the tourists do not conceive the distinction. The existence of a viable indigenous culture is so overwhelming that the visitors seem to forget decency and good manners. Therefore, and also for several other reasons, the long-term impact of this instrusion on daily life has been a vanishing tradition – dress. More and more, the traditional costume has become something to wear for special occasions and a uniform for tourist hosts.

When the theme 'identity' was raised, several of the informants in Karasjohka maintained that they had multiple identities. Most generally, they felt they were both Sami and Norwegian. One informant contested the common expression: 'half Sami, half Norwegian' by saying: 'I am completely Norwegian and completely Sami.' Others underlined the importance of their modern identities, identities connected to their roles where the ethnic aspect is of little importance. What is displayed depends on the situation and whom they are with at a given time. 'Identity? You play roles in relation to expectations, situations, contexts . . .,' said one informant. Thus, the interaction with strangers, for instance tourists, is dealt within roles as non-Sami, as modern, or as professional. People from the tourist industry admit that their Sami identity is emphasized, when interacting with tourists. In wearing the traditional costume, they expose the exotic aspects of their culture and themselves, but within a modern role. This is probably one of the paradoxes of the post-modern indigenousness, when it is most strongly exposed it is staged.

Commercial adaptation and commodification

Tourism is an entrepreneurial opportunity. In recent decades many jobs have been created within tourism, but fewer in Norway and Sweden than in Finland. This has to do with the development stage of tourism in these countries. In northern Finland, tourism is an advanced and well organized factory-like industry, whereas in Norway and Sweden Sami tourism is more on the level of a handicraft activity. This means that tourism is a more hands-on activity in these countries compared to Finland, and that Sami tourism in Norway and Sweden is less commercialized than in Finland.

To many Sami entrepreneurs tourism is only a part-time occupation. For example, the combination of tourism and reindeer herding requires only part-time involvement in tourism. A study conducted in the late 1990s, revealed some challenging implications of this business model (Viken et al., 1998). Among other things, the study showed that from the perspective of the reindeer herders, the tourism business should not become too big as it is the reindeer herder activities that make the Sami attractive to tourists. Another challenge that was highlighted was handling the extended family that is involved in a reindeer herding unit (*siida*) including: brothers and sisters, parents and children, and as one informant said, "the drunken cousin and the curious and noisy youngsters". The point was that not all individuals in the reindeer herding unit are suited for tourism roles. A third challenge had to do with the 'good life'. Most people working with reindeer, and Sami people in general, love the wilderness life. Therefore several Sami providers avoid receiving tourists in late July or August, so they may personally enjoy this period for their own mountain activities. Unfortunately, this is also the peak season for tourism. Hence, the 1998 report concluded that there was a mismatch between vital values still alive in the Sami society, and the spirit of capitalism. Tourism was seen as an interesting opportunity, but also as a threat for the good life as a Sami. 'To work as a reindeer herder is a chosen lifestyle', an informant in Jokkmokk claimed, and 'Nature is part of us', said another in explanation of their scepticism towards commercialization.

The interviews in Jokkmokk, concerning a Winter Festival, unveiled a similar struggle between traditional and modern values, and between Sami and other interests. One of the informants was responsible for a reindeer race. There was a need for money to keep up this tradition, but he was not in favour of selling commercials that risked overwhelming the Sami profile of the race. There was also an expressed concern about the event becoming an 'Absolut Festival' (Absolut Vodka was seen as a potential sponsor), as well as towards the danger that sellers of low-quality goods would replace Sami handicraft producers. Some respondents identified a tendency for the municipality and their allies to take the best places in the festival area, leaving the more peripheral spots to the Sami organizations and interests. Thus the Sami do not feel that they are particularly central to the festival, although the festival is known as a Sami festival. A couple of informants expressed the feeling that: 'We are put forward to attract people to the region, but when they come, it is the others that make money.' This not only shows a struggle between values, but also the tendencies for Sami people to be featured in marketing promotions, while being marginalized in business.

The commodifying processes

Most Sami tourism ventures are small, and Sami traditions and Sami narratives are central products. Many of the providers have adapted their traditions to fit the needs of the customers and demands of the tour operators, or simply to make the business profitable. For example, there seems to be internationally standardized prices and willingness to pay for outdoor dinners, day-trips and half-day trips. Thus, to be competitive in this market, or for the sake of customer satisfaction, many providers have adjusted traditional Sami practices for their tourism operations. The clients in a Sami tent do not sit on furs on the ground as per traditional practices, but on benches and chairs. Similarly, river boats used for tours are bigger, safer and more comfortable than traditional craft. Among the losses are a feeling of immediacy with the bone-fire and water that characterize the traditional modes. The list of adaptations is long: knives and cups are more decorative, the reindeer skin is for decoration, reindeer meat is prepared in a French style, the folk music, which has traditionally been a way of communicating to another individual or nature, has become tourism entertainment and a variety of modern souvenirs made of fur and bones have been created (Lyngnes and Viken, 1998). Most people accept the adaptations, but there are some unwritten moral limits that operators are not to transgress. On the questions of where to draw the line, a tourist provider said that he thought of his grandmother and considered what her comment would have been on what he was doing. One of the informants in the focus groups could not accept to use the traditional Sami shaman drum as a motif for information plates as is presented in a Sami Theme Park, in Karsjohka. In his view it would be similar to using the Christian cross for the same purpose. Developing commercial products out of important culturally based spiritual icons was seen to be morally questionable, and it certainly impacted authenticity. To make a profit, souvenir providers tend to sell manufactured copies of traditional handicrafts (knives, cups, tents, cloths). Within the Sami society, one widely used criterion for authentic handicraft is that the artifacts should be produced by hand (e.g., Errington, 1998). Thus, a pair of woollen socks, produced by a machine developed in Sápmi, by a Sami, using local material and design, is not authentic from this point of view. It was recognized, however, that there are few absolute correct answers to the question of manufacture and authenticity. Probably the most important lesson learned from this research is to keep the discussion about these issues alive, as it is in Norway and Sweden.

There are many analyses of these processes, and a variety of labels have been used to describe the impacts of commercial adaptations. One such process is commodification. When cultural and relational expressions are transformed to commodities in a market, the meaning certainly changes. For instance, the Sami folk song, (joik), becomes entertainment. The transformation from relational to transactional roles of cultural expressions can result in loss of content, being assessed on the base of economic values, and, moreover, on the basis of the values of actors external to the culture in question. These processes are not necessarily negative, the act of cultural expressions assuming new values is a common dynamic of culture. For example, the Sami tent is a commercial success, and most Sami seem to be flattered that their culture has provided the modern world with a very convenient leisure item. The most perverting tendencies occur when external investors begin to dominate this commodification process as the sale of these cultural products become profitable (Frow, 1997). There has been a tendency for this to happen in the Sami area, and it was a major source of irritation, in one of the communities where the focus group interviews were done.

Another type of impact is what is called 'essensializing' and 'othering'. Essensializing or reification happens when a particular perception gains status as truth; for instance the belief that a culture has a particular structure and certain characteristics. Tourism contributes to this process through over-exposing the traditional sides of the Sami culture in marketing and public relations. This is very much the case with the Sami. There is pressure on them to dress in traditional costumes and to present expositions showing the traditional way of life in order to live up to the expectations of the tourists. These practices further contribute to an image of the Sami that is far from the contemporary reality. It contributes to the image of the Sami as different, as the exotic Other. This is also known as the process of othering (Fabian, 1983; Viken, 2000; Olsen, 2006). It can be problematic when the Sami feel that they are treated differently because they are Sami. Several of the focus group members touched upon the fact that they were used to being treated as a category. It is always 'a Sami did this, a Sami did that, in the newspaper, not a man or a women', and 'you are never only a human, you are expected to be an encyclopaedia of Sami culture and issues', said a young Sami. But even worse, 'you have to answer for all silly things Sami people do and say'. During the focus group interviews in Karasjohka it was stated that the Sami tended to be treated in a different way when performing in costume, than when in contemporary western clothing. Somehow, the exotic aura of the indigenous makes it difficult for non-indigenous observers to behave normally. This is an aspect with the commercialization processes of which people are more or less aware. It is more a reflexive and discursive awareness, rather than something that occurs in people's daily life.

Conclusions

The story about tourism in the Sami areas of Norway and Sweden is one of both optimism and scepticism. Tourism is accepted and seen as a job opportunity, as an arena for cultural change, but also as an arena for commercialization and potential degradation of the Sami culture. One of the implications of being a society with strong roots in traditions is that values other than those dominating the capitalist economy still exist but are in the process of vanishing. While celebrating its traditions, Sami society is and wants to be modern. Therefore ambivalence to tourism is common. The division of tourism impacts into positive and negative categories is never absolute, but is dependant on the goals and values of the observer. In any case, such categorizations give life to a continued and necessary discussion. One also has to bear in mind that although individuals – both hosts and guests – perceive there to be negative impacts of tourism, they may still have positive attitudes regarding tourism's overall benefits to the host area. This is very much the case in the Sami areas of Norway and Sweden.

Above all, indigenous tourism fosters a debate about the commercialization and changes of indigenous culture. A lot of people support the indigenous peoples in their demands that no one other than themselves should decide how indigenous tourism should be developed. However, the vigilance of indigenous hosts in terms of the practices of tourism and other modern industries is very important. There is no authority regulating the borders between commerce and over-commercialization. Sami people in Norway and Sweden tend to criticize their Sami counterparts in Finland for having crossed this border. At the same time, the development of the tourism industry in Finland has been a success from an economic point of view.

Interesting examples of indigenous experiences, both emerging and existing, can be found at many different places in Sápmi and in other parts of the world. These tourism enterprises are often competing for the same group of visitors, and could benefit greatly by utilizing knowledge from each other's failures and successes. Ultimately both hosts and guests will benefit from the development of well-organized and sustainable indigenous tourism. The key factor for such a success is responsibility and respect for the culture.

CHAPTER 14

The Aboriginal people of Taiwan: discourse and silence

Chris Ryan, Janet Chang and
Tzung-Cheng (T.C.) Huan

Introduction

Ryan and Trauer (2005b) present a modification of Leiper's tourism system model in which the tourism supply and tourism generation zones are replaced by an Indigenous People's Tourism Product (Supply) and a demand comprising inter- and intra-personal needs. The novel component of their model is the addition of the media as an agency that signs the type of product to be offered and the implication of that product for senses of self. This is then applied to the issue of indigenous tourism in that the media develops a cultural veil of indigeneity through which Aboriginal peoples and those seeking indigenous tourism product have to negotiate. In their model, the signing and symbolizing of cultures becomes as important as the actual nature of demand and Aboriginal culture that is being commodified for tourism purposes. This chapter is based upon, but will modify that model with specific reference to the Aboriginal tribes of Taiwan. The chapter will provide an initial description and history of the indigenous people of Taiwan and it will then briefly refer to the 'products' available in Taiwan before widening the context by reference to social, political and environmental issues. This is done in the belief that in the representation of Aboriginal people in tourism there is a discourse of silence. The interpretation on offer is selective and is one that serves a form of tourism where any concept of authenticity is subject to a more important discourse of 'authorization' (Ryan, 2005). The final part of the chapter will make reference to studies of demand undertaken by Chang (2006) before revising the model suggested by Ryan and Trauer (2005b).

The number of Aboriginal tribes recognized by the Indigenous Council of Taiwan is 12, and with a total population of about 420,000 they account for about 2% of the total population. This is akin to the proportion of the Australian population accounted for by Aboriginal peoples in that country. Linguists estimate that there are more than 20 Austronesian linguistic groups in Taiwan, and in New Zealand DNA sampling seems to indicate that the forbears of Maori originated in the area between Japan and Taiwan before undertaking a migration several thousand years ago. Certainly there is evidence of linguistic, cultural and genetic linkages between the Aboriginal peoples of Taiwan and those of the Pacific. Whyte et al. (2005) used mitochondrial DNA samples and present an intriguing scenario that Maori females can be traced back to Taiwan, while Maori males for the most part are traced to Papua New Guinea.

From a cultural perspective, the first author on seeing dance performances by Taiwanese Aboriginal groups, remarked that there seemed to exist obvious nuances echoing dances of Samoan, Tongan and Maori peoples with reference to hand movements, gestures and other aspects of choreography, but such interpretations can only be exercised with care inasmuch as similarities may be incidental and should not silence the differences. On the other hand, there does appear to be evident linguistic roots between Maori and some languages of this area. More concrete evidence exists in the ceramic shards found across Asia, Tonga and Samoa. Dating from 3,500 years ago, the name

'Lapita people' has been bestowed on those thought to have developed the kilns and techniques used to make the pots, plates and other items. Green (1991) and Kirch (1997) develop a thesis fully congruent with the work of Whyte et al. (2005) and together these and similar studies imply that the Aboriginal tribes of Taiwan have important linkages to the expanding and colonizing peoples of over 3,000 years ago that have come to be the Austronesian peoples of today. Thus the evidence for connections between the Lapita people who commenced their travels from the Japan–Taiwanese area and their Polynesian descendants is strong.

A brief history

As a people the indigenous tribes of Taiwan share a history and colonization not too dis-similar to those of other indigenous peoples in the sense that their culture and history were marginalized and subjected to oppression by ruling regimes. For example, even within Aboriginal areas, until the 1980s, they were not permitted to use their own language in schools, but had to use the language of the dominant Han (Tsai, 2006a) – a story that is all too familiar for Maori, Australian Aboriginals, Inuit and North American Indian peoples. It was only in 1995 that a Names Act gave official recognition to Indigenous as distinct from Chinese names and provided a procedure for reclamation of a native name – an act of symbolic importance because of the need for an offi-cially sanctioned name for the paperwork that characterizes modern bureau-cracies (Tsai, 2006b).

While many histories of Taiwan tend to start with the Japanese occupation and subsequent arrival of the Nationalist Chinese Kuomintang (KMT) in 1945 there is, of course, a longer prior history. European discovery commences with the Portuguese who arrived off the coast in 1544 to name the island as Isla Formosa – the Beautiful Island. However it was the Dutch and Spanish who established the first European trading posts of note, until in 1642 a combined Dutch–Aboriginal force drove the Spanish off their base at Fort Santo Domigo near present day Keelung on the north-west coast. Dutch–Aboriginal relation-ships were vexed with different Aboriginal tribes being allies or victims of Dutch oppression and in 1661 a Chinese fleet under Zheng Chenggong landed to start the ousting of the Dutch with the aid of some tribal peoples. A Ming loyalist, he in turn was defeated by followers of the Qing, and the sub-sequent Qing dynasty ruled the island until 1875 as two prefectures of the Mainland. Relationships between the Chinese and Aboriginal peoples were mixed. To some extent the Qing sought to protect Aboriginal culture but ten-sions continued over land claims and taxation. However, by the outbreak of the Sino-Japanese War of 1884–1885 about 45% of Taiwan was ruled as a Chinese administrative region while the lightly populated interior was under Aboriginal dominion. Thus, until that stage, the culture of the Aboriginal peoples remained strong and well defined, although coastal peoples, espe-cially those in the west, were adversely affected in this period. Indeed, as is noted below, of the coastal communities the strongest surviving groups are to be found in the south-east of the island (the Puyuma in Tai Tung County at the southern end of the Hualien-Tai Tung Valley and Kavalan just north of the Puyuma).

The period of greatest oppression of Indigenous peoples and Aboriginal resistance to colonizing forces was arguably from about 1902 to the early 1930s under Japanese occupation of the island. Among the events of this period was Ta-pi-ni incident of 1915 in Tainan County and the Wushu Uprising in 1930. In the latter, the Atayal people head-hunted 150 Japanese officials over disputes about conditions in the camphor extraction industry, only to be subjected to fierce reprisals by the Japanese (with other tribal help) that involved the use of poison gas. In the latter part of Japanese rule a more tolerant pattern emerged and again the peoples of the mountains were left more or less unmolested.

The next significant event was the arrival of the Nationalist Chinese Kuomintang (KMT) in 1945. Compared to the final years of Japanese occupation, the KMT government was oppressive in its attitude to Aboriginal peoples, partly born of fear of having to deal with island resistance even whilst trying to secure an existence independent of a growing communist power in the Cold War era, and, at least initially, nursing hopes of being able to re-establish itself on the Chinese Mainland. On the death of Chiang Kai-shek his successor, his son, Chiang Ching-kuo, continued a growing relaxation and democratization of the island, aided by Taiwan's emergence as one of the new 'tiger economies' of Asia. Upon Chiang's death in 1988 President Lee Teng-hui continued to decentralize government and Aboriginal participation in regional government benefitted with the emergence of stronger local government at the County level. As can be noted from this brief history, a sense of Aboriginal identity and the maintenance of cultural roots remained strong among a number of the tribes of Taiwan, especially those inhabiting the mountainous central region and to a lesser extent the poorer coastal area of the east and south-east coast. Those occupying the coastal plain on the west were subjected to greater impacts from sinicization and economic development and have come to be called the Pingpu Peoples. While they retain some racial and other characteristics they have, to a large degree, lost their own languages and are more assimilated within the majority population.

The Aboriginal peoples of Taiwan

The main groups among the 12 tribal peoples of Taiwan include, with reference to size of population, the Amis (numbering about 140,000, primarily in the Hualien-Taitung valley), the Atayal (numbering 87,000 and found in the central and northern mountains of Taiwan), the Paiwan (about 67,000 centred on the holy mountain of Tawu), the Bunun (with about 40,000 in Nantou County), the Rukai (with about 10,500 being concentrated around Maolin in Kaohsiung County in the mountains, and in Pingtung County) and Puyuma (numbering about 8,700 – again primarily living in Taitung County). The remaining groups have much smaller populations. The Saisaat with a population of about 5,000 are centred upon two areas, Shihtan township and Wufeng township, the Kavalan (about 1,750 living in Hualien County) and the Tsou (numbering about 2,000 living on the side of Mount Yushan, Taiwan's highest mountain). Of the remaining three, the Yami, being the only one of the 12 tribes which did not practice head-hunting, live offshore on the island of Lanyu (Orchard Island) which is about 49 miles off the east coast of Taitung. Indeed the name Yami was used by Japanese anthropologists in the early nineteenth century and the people refer to themselves as the Thao, while the name of Lanyu may be translated as 'the island of the people'. The Thao are thought to number only about 300 and mainly live around Sun Moon Lake – a beautiful area well known within Taiwan. The natural area has long been a magnet for people and was much liked by the Japanese. This group has thus had long contact with non-tribal people, and tends to use a specific Taiwanese Chinese dialect known as Hokkien. For some time they were regarded as a sub-group of the Bunun or Tsou tribes, and inter-marriage between these peoples and the Han Chinese has been high. However, after considerable effort on the part of elders they were accepted by the Taiwanese government and Taiwanese Indigenous Council as representing a distinct group in 2001. Part of that distinctiveness was based not only on degrees of linguistic uniqueness but more importantly upon religious beliefs built upon a spirit life. This belief is symbolized by each household maintaining a *Kung Ma* basket which contains clothes, beads and other jewellery like items handed down by ancestors, thereby perpetuating a sense of identity through lineage, past and present and those yet to come. The last group, the Truku, was formally recognized as the twelfth tribe in Taiwan in 14 January 2004. Despite a different language, the Truku share similar customs with the Atayal. For instance, both tribes must abide by the rules set up by the Gaga (or Gaya) – a fundamental unit rooted from the patrilineal society whereby members share hunting, agricultural labours and even fighting against outsiders.

While there are linkages by reason of being Austronesian peoples, social *mores* and customs have become particularized by reason of relative isolation due to the mountainous terrain that many inhabit, and through a reinforcement of identity created by strife wherein differences are important. These differences are quite marked as to religious practices, social groupings and the gender roles. For example, the Tsou lived a strictly patriarchal and clan-based system, while the Amis traditionally had a matrilineal society where female elders determined family matters although males had specific roles in military and religious affairs. Rank and role was also partly age determined. Paiwan society was based on a class system and inheritance accrued to the eldest child in the case of the Buchur sub-group, regardless of gender. The Rukai also possessed a class system with a recognizable aristocracy or nobility. Clothing and rituals also differed among the tribes. For the Tsou there were elaborate ceremonies associated with the millet harvest, at the end of which *mayasvi* or Council of War was held. This in turn evolved into *kuba* – a period of training for unmarried men – followed by the chopping of sacred trees and the welcoming of the spirit. In one of the best known rituals which are today played out for tourists, the Amis spend several days in dance and song to celebrate the harvest. This celebration is also a period of social reinforcement and includes initiation into age-based groupings. The Rukai also commemorate the harvest, but in this case a main feature is the baking and consumption of millet cake. The Atayal on the other hand have retained only a few traditional songs, but are noted for their weaving, and skill in weaving bestows seniority among the women. The Puyuma possess elaborate commemoration of the dead in annual events of memory which also enable the bereaved to be received back again into the normal life of the community. They also celebrate the New Year and in the Monkey Festival and Grand Hunting Festival focus on hunting skills. There are also differences in architectural and building styles. Some use granite slates while others tend to build using bamboo and wood. In short, even while there are similarities with reference to an agrarian base for the most part, the cultures are diverse in language, dress, ritual and nuances of religious belief – all of which translates into potential product for the tourist.

Tourists and Aboriginal tourism sites

The visitor who possesses an interest in seeing, learning and appreciating the culture of Taiwanese Aboriginal peoples no longer needs to search far for information. The tourism bureaux at both national and county level provide several leaflets that either specifically (or generally for attractions within a destination) make reference to the existence of indigenous culture. For example, with reference to Maolin National Scenic Area the potential tourist can not only pick up information about hot springs, adventure tourism and scenic values but also easily obtain, in English, a suggested circular 'Aborigines Tour' of 118 kilometres from Kaohsiung. Yet the accompanying pictures also show hang gliders and river swimming as well as illustrations of Rukai tribal people. It also has to be said that at times the translations from the original Chinese into English possess a certain idiosyncratic characterization to the point that the first author felt impelled to provide a more fluent text for a local mayor. Certainly, within this area the local authority and tribal people have sought to make aspects of their culture readily available within the village. The road that approaches the Maolin visitor centre climbs through an embankment upon which larger than life murals have been constructed in stone depicting the local Rukai people in traditional dress (see Figure 14.1). At the visitor centre an enquiry will enable the visitor to have a guide who is a member of the local people. Visitors are taken to see a traditional house and are able to wander at will within it. The house contains photographs and traditional bead work – the meanings of which are explained. At the edge of the village the curious visitor will be taken to a site honouring the eagle, and containing a wall within which was placed the heads of decapitated former enemies.

For such visitors, two pre-requisites seem to exist given an interest in this type of tourist attraction. First, the tourist has to be independently mobile,

Figure 14.1
Embankment at Maolin

which primarily requires a car. Most of these sites are in the mountains and while it is possible to use public transport, the latter requires the second prerequisite, some knowledge of Chinese, if only to read transport instructions. In short, for a non-Chinese tourist unaccompanied by a local person, to be able to access the mountains and penetrate if not the 'back stage', then at least to fully take advantage of the front stage provision, requires significant perseverance. Additionally, the distances and transport schedules imply a need for overnight stays. In many ways these circumstances present for the adventurous the potential for memorable experiences, but at the time of writing, few visitors seem willing to adopt this approach. Two alternative means present themselves. First, it is possible to book a tour that includes such visits as a major objective or as part of a more general trip through scenic settings, but currently, for the most part such organized trips are in groups of Chinese speakers only. Second, it is possible for the overseas visitor to hire a car and self-drive to the Aboriginal Village, or Indigenous People's Cultural Park.

This park is located at Majia Township in Pingtung County about 70 minutes drive east from Kaohsiung. It was established in 1987 and covers about 83 hectares. Within the park are representations of each of the tribal peoples of Taiwan and the park is divided into three main sections. Given the area, the park literature recommends a series of alternative tours that can last up to 3 days in duration, and in this last instance it is possible to stay in local homestays. The nature of the park and its visitors are discussed below.

Constructions of discourse

Arenas of silence

In order to analyse the nature of the presentation, reference has to be made to wider contexts to establish areas of silence. Like other groups living in peripheral areas, the Aboriginal peoples have been subject to imposition by the majority. A key example is the debate over the Ma-chia Dam. It was proposed, in 1993, to develop a dam by flooding a valley within the region of the Rukai. This would have meant the flooding of two Aboriginal Villages, those of Kochapogan (Hao-cha) and I-la. A subsequent proposal to build the Meinung Dam has further created coalitions of opposition that involve indigenous peoples and a combination of environmental, academic and indigenous stakeholders which have, thus far, successfully stalled these proposals. The debate highlights the costs of Taiwanese economic development as these dams have been built to provide power for the growing factories, even whilst some of those factories have been the cause of environmental degradation. For example, the Taiwan Sugar Corporation reclaimed over 6,000 hectares from the Linpien River with almost immediate devastating effects on drainage and ground water deposits that, ironically, also caused water shortages for the new sugar cane areas being planted (Meinung People's Association, 2006).

Economic necessities of finding work and income have also had their past impact upon the population composition of Aboriginal villages. People of working age have left the villages to find employment in the Han dominated plains of the west, leaving communities comprising primarily the very young, the old and a gender imbalance where females with child care responsibilities outnumber males. In due course, to retain family ties, in some instances a nuclear family will migrate, thereby breaking the immediate extended family ties based upon close spatial proximity. The Taipei Times of 15 August 2000, provides an example of what this means in the 'Return to Kochapongan Movement' that developed in 1990 (Chi-Ting, 2000). In 1980, 500 Rukai residents of Kochapongan moved their community to Pulhakele in Pingtung County to take advantage of government sponsored housing complete with modern conveniences and a location offering better employment prospects. The migration did not stop there, and the article describes a slow process of Hanization as the young learn Mandarin and Han culture and slowly loose their embedded status within the tribe, even while the older members continue traditional practices and wear traditional clothing. By the mid-1980s the government closed the local primary school, thereby reinforcing this tendency toward Hanization. By the late 1990s a movement to return to their original location grew. One solution posited for their problems was that of tourism – yet this too was perceived as a double-edged sword. On the one hand it was perceived as a source of employment, on the other it was seen as a means of commodification whereby the control of visitor flow would be in the hands of the Han majority (Taipei Times, 2000).

Culture is sometimes expropriated, albeit unintentionally at times, by those not associated with these Aboriginal groups. Wong et al. (1999) provide the example whereby an Ami tribe song, 'Jubilant Drinking Song', sang by Ami singers Difang and Agay was used in a commercial for the 1996 Atlanta Olympics. In this instance, an out of court settlement was reached and it would appear that the mis-use was indeed unintentional, and the motive for the court action was inspired by a wish to make the Ami culture better known. But this instance is not atypical and many Aboriginal groups would be able to cite similar instances of cultural sensitivities not always being honoured through a mainstream society not appreciating a different world perspective.

Being on marginal lands also brings with it other risks. This is perhaps most vividly displayed by the use of Lanyu Island (the home of the Thao or Yami peoples) as a site for nuclear waste disposal.

Another issue is that of tribal designations. The fight for recognition by the Thao has been noted, but what also needs to be noted is that arguably those currently designated as being Atayal are actually three separate groups of peoples – namely the Atayal, Sediq and Taroko. In other words official recognition is not that of self-recognition – and thus the Aboriginal peoples have to work with their own self-designation and then officially through a designation that does not recognize the distinctions that they themselves make. It might therefore be said that while things are considerably better than once was the case, several issues nonetheless persist that hinder Aboriginal development. It also has to be noted that these impediments are not all external. For example, the Alliance of Taiwan Aborigines established in the mid-1990s became a means of perpetuating tribal differences and historic animosities. This phenomenon is, of course, not unique to Taiwan. For example, the Maori of New Zealand also has a history of past inter-tribal warfare, and additional divisions can be attributed to allegiances to various political parties or Christian denominations. The same is true of the Taiwanese Aboriginal peoples, and this lessens their effectiveness as a pressure group. In some ways it might also be argued that representation at the highest level is emasculated. As in New Zealand, there are specific seats set aside for Aboriginal representation in the Legislature – but these are divided along party alliances. Second, the Council of Aboriginal Affairs, established in 1996, is subject to legal regulation to the point where some radicals regard it as being little more than a 'PR exercise'. Nonetheless, as in other countries there is an emergence of a political self-awareness among Aboriginal peoples – but arguably in Taiwan the position is made more complex by Taiwan's status within the international community and the stance of the People's Republic toward it. Thus any claim for independence on the part of Aboriginal peoples is problematic for the People's Republic whose official stance is that Taiwan itself is not an independent Republic.

These incidents and realities are part of contemporary life for the Aboriginal peoples of Taiwan. One resultant question is to what degree are these realities present in the interpretations provided for tourists? The answer is, hardly at all.

Representations of Aboriginal peoples

The two main parks in Taiwan that represent Aboriginal culture are the Taiwanese Indigenous People's Cultural Park that is government run and the private sector Formosan Aboriginal Cultural Village. The latter is located near the popular tourist resort of Sun Moon Lake in Nantou County. Together they attract approximately 1.3 million visitors per year (Chang et al., 2006). The two are very different in that the latter includes an amusement park with 'white knuckle' roller coaster rides and thus a different ethos exists between the two. Therefore, while there is a strong cultural component to the Formosan Aboriginal Village, it can be questioned as to what degree the two complexes are wholly compatible. While Chang, Wall and Chu do compare them, the differences of the parks are not wholly articulated. However, both do have performance areas where traditional dances are displayed to visitors. Nonetheless, it may not be wholly coincidental that overall impressions of the parks do vary with the Formosan Park scoring a satisfaction rating of 3.88 and the Taiwan Indigenous People's Cultural Park scoring 4.08 on a five-point scale (where 5 represented 'strongly satisfied') – although whether this difference is statistically significant is not provided by Chang et al. (2006). For purposes of this chapter, the text will concentrate upon the Taiwan Indigenous People's Cultural Park inasmuch as arguably, at a *prima facie* level, it represents a more 'authentic park' in terms of cultural tourism. However, it can be observed that there is a perceived need to incorporate fun orientated components at the Formosan Park that are more associated with parks like Disney or Six Flags. It should also be noted that this merging of the frivolous and the more serious is not unique within either a Taiwanese or Asian setting. For example, Janfusun FancyWorld, even while primarily an amusement park, also sustains more serious components with reference to an ecological garden setting in one corner of the park. Nevertheless, from the perspective of Aboriginal people the issue arises as to whether an amusement park setting is wholly congruent with an interpretation of their culture, especially given that stays for the most part are of less than 1 hour. (It is here noted that there is also a 'European Park' with palaces in the Formosa Village.)

The Indigenous People's Cultural Park is centred around a representation of the peoples by reference primarily to the arts of those peoples. Entertainment is provided by enactment of dances that are decontextualized spatially and temporally from the origins of the dances (e.g., being harvest time dances) although a commentary is provided as to the original purpose of the dance. As is common in tourism, the culture is packaged to fit into the itinerary of the tourist, and thus dances and rituals that once took several hours become 10-minute performances. Dress and weaving skills are featured. Displays provide tableaux of daily life, but it is the daily life of a rural past. In any representation of an indigenous people there exist at least three tensions.

There is the story telling of a past prior to the coming of the dominant peoples – but the untold text in such stories is a culture frozen often in a pre-technological state, implying therefore a form of backwardness. A contemporary story of life style would be of a people facing many of the same daily problems and engaging in occupations similar to those of the visitor – so the visitor experience that is often based on difference (Dann, 2000) is negated. The third tension is the political and social context described above. As is often the case, the representation of cultures and the stories constructed upon them take place within a public sector financed setting. In politically sensitive places, stories of conflict and tension are silenced for any number of reasons. At a personal level those funded by a government sector are aware that too contentious a story could invite political retribution. At an institutional level there is an awareness of not only the political realities of funding, but also a market orientation whereby it can be asked whether visitors, particularly holidaymakers, really wish to be faced with serious analyses of social conflict. As Chang et al. (2006) found, the main motives for visiting the Aboriginal sites were those of wanting 'a change from routine' followed by 'boredom alleviation'. In another study Chang et al. (2005) found that the emotional advertizing appeal found greater resonance among visitors than appeals to rationality. Thus, even while Chang (2006) found in a third study that a wish to learn about Aboriginal culture was an important motivation for visitation, the finding runs into difficulties as highlighted by Ryan and Higgins (2006) who found that depth or profundity of interest is another issue. One test of seriousness is the degree to which visitors actually wish to spend nights in accommodation with Aboriginal people as hosts – and data from outside Taiwan indicates that many fail this test (Ryan and Higgins, 2006). Similarly Chang (2006) observes that Taiwanese tourists are not likely to stay at a Bed and Breakfast (B&B) accommodation or homestays operated by the Aboriginals except in some well-known tribal areas where B&Bs provide unique living experiences and complementary local guides and cultural interpretations are provided (e.g., Rukai in Wu-tai County). For instance, from participatory observation, the second author and her research assistants (six in total) experienced wearing Rukai traditional outfits voluntarily provided by the hostess in order to participate in the ceremony celebrating Rukai Day (the New Year for Rukai). Additionally, they played hide-and-seek with the host's children outdoors and even had the privilege of using the hosts' bedroom on the Rukai New Year's Eve, when the host family were too busy preparing for the next day's celebration to sleep! However, such experiences are generally unusual, and require preparation on the part of tourists evidenced by mutual respect and cultural understanding of tribal customs that helps to provide entry points to gain some authentic Aboriginal experiences – hard liquors and betel nuts, for example, are popular gifts among tribal areas in Taiwan.

One irony of these sanctioned Indigenous 'Villages' is that they reflect, and by their presence arguably protect, what has been a significant movement that commenced in the 1990s, which is the return to Aboriginal villages by the formerly urban based. For example, there exists the Mihu Reconstruction Society founded in 1990 at Shuangchi Village after the Chichi earthquake (Tsai, 2006a). Village workshops are slowly beginning to flourish where a rediscovery of arts and artefacts is taking place. From these embryonic economic revivals, a social rediscovering is occurring where today 8% of Taiwanese Aboriginal peoples are now pursuing higher education in 2006 compared to 2% in 1996 (Tsai, 2006a). Unemployment has fallen from 14% in 1998 to 5.7% in 2004. In 2003 the Executive Yuan approved draft legislation on autonomous regions for indigenous peoples, and in 2006 the Truku people completed a draft Truku Self-Government Act as a prelude to greater degree of autonomy, although still circumscribed by legislation and financial dependency upon central government. By providing the tourist 'honey pots', the life of the slowly reviving villages is protected from a tourist onslaught that could potentially threaten embryonic social ordering based on cultures very different from the concepts of western-based small entrepreneurial undertakings (Cave, 2005).

Conclusions

As noted at the outset of this chapter, Ryan and Trauer (2005b) present a model of indigenous tourism. Figure 14.2 presents a modification of that diagram by reference to the experience of Taiwanese Aboriginal Peoples.

The stages of the model are as follow.

Tourism Demand (initially the tourism generating zone in Leiper's (1990, 1995) original formulation) comprises two aspects – the intra-personal which is the affective and cognitive perception and evaluation of indigenous tourism product that is internalized within the tourist, and the inter-personal which is the perception and evaluation arrived at by the tourist with reference to external social groups, and thus includes motives pertaining to status, perceived reaction of significant others and similar external points of reference.

Indigenous People's Tourism Product (initially the tourism receiving zone in Leiper's (1990, 1995) original formulation) represents the supply of the tourism product that is embedded within the minority culture. The degree to which it is embedded determines the extent to which the product is 'authorized' by the indigenous peoples, which is, itself, a determinant of 'authenticity' as generally discussed with the tourism literature (e.g., Wang, 1999, 2000), but which in the eyes of Ryan (2005) is actually a secondary consideration subject to 'authorization'.

The 'cultural veil' is both a process and an outcome as it shapes the presentation of product in terms of the interaction between perceived tourist needs (as perceived by both tourists, tourism intermediaries and suppliers of product) and the needs of the host.

Ryan and Trauer (2005b) argue that an important component in this process is the role of the media in that it shapes and symbolizes what each participant believes is important in product design, and shapes the process of the cultural

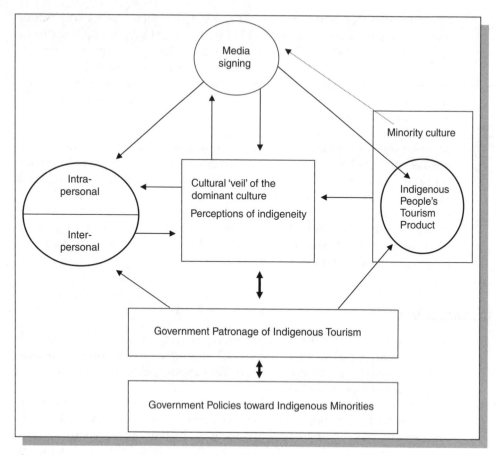

Figure 14.2
The Indigenous Tourism System

veil. The media signs the product as being 'desirable' – shapes the image of product as being appropriate to self-image of the tourist participant, and shapes the image of the purchaser that informs the marketing strategy and product design of the supplier.

To this one can add, in the case of Taiwanese Aboriginal Product, the role of government, its policies and its agencies, and by implication the wider political processes. The 'official' legitimization of Indigenous aspiration by acts of patronage/concession by government, and the direction of government policy helps shape, as has been discussed above, *the modus operandi* of tourism product as to its funding, promotion and financing. Figure 14.3 is taken from Ryan (2005) and illustrates the complexities that surround the presentation of tourism based on the cultures of indigenous peoples.

One such complexity is the omission of a story of oppression and revival that is present in the Aboriginal tribal villages of Taiwan that are built and presented as tourist attractions and which therefore possess both strengths and

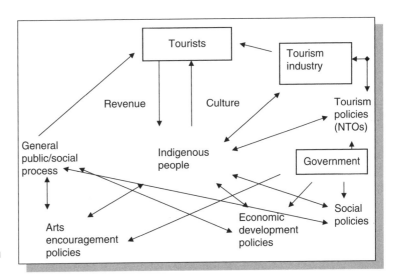

Figure 14.3
Framework of
Indigenous Tourism
(after Ryan, 2005)

weaknesses. The emphasis is upon dance, art, theatre, song and bead work and the tourism literature is replete with the notion that tourism commodifies a culture, decontextualizes it from its origins and presents it as solely a tourist entertainment. The implication is that this is a process that destroys the roots of a culture. But for a reviving culture, the tourist gaze has importance. It is an acknowledgement of the importance of art, it bestows economic value upon performance, and it provides reason for learning traditional skills. The performer engages upon acts of creativity and rediscovery (Daniel, 1996; Tahana and Oppermann, 1998) and many native people seek to not only learn movement and design, but the symbolism and significance of those designs, thereby articulating in both the spoken and printed word the deeper cultural roots that gave rise to the artistic performance. From this rediscovery emerges a subsequent stage, an examination of the role of that culture in contemporary society – a process not necessarily devoid of pain and questioning before a satisfactory dialectic emerges – a dialectic that is often not homogenous but is shaded in a continuum of meanings for separate individuals.

Indigenous peoples need room in which to occupy the worlds of their own culture, the culture of the majority and the transitional world between the two, and a case exists whereby the concentration created by the tourist 'honey pot' is a means by which an indigenous society negotiates room to conduct its own discourse before it is exposed to the wider world. However, one possible disadvantage is that the cocoon that is weaved around the 'honey pot' and the partial interpretation to which it gives rise, shapes the tourist gaze into a lop-sided optic of a people frozen into a hunting–fishing–arable lifestyle more commensurate with the past, rather than a view of a people re-asserting themselves, challenging the implications of past oppression and seeking to establish a unique identity in the twenty-first century. For majority populations, a celebration of the past is continually contextualized within full membership of the technologies and social structures of the twenty-first century: for colonized peoples the authorized version of their 'distant' past becomes decontextual-ized from their 'recent' past and subordination to the majority, and equally separate from their present and potential futures. This framing of time is often at odds with an indigenous perspective of time that is often characterized as a seamless mosaic of inter-generational dialogue.

It is suggested that the history and current development of Taiwanese Aboriginal Tourism illustrated these processes, and the model demonstrates the states of tensions that exist within not only the Taiwanese case, but by extension other instances of indigenous people tourism. While visitors are not arguably 'lay anthropologists', the levels of interest being expressed by both domestic within and international visitors to Taiwan undoubtedly cre-ates opportunities for a growing expression of indigenous sentiment and belief, and provides a means by which income, employment, social and political advancement can occur within a domain perceived as bestowing advantage for many Taiwanese stakeholders. Properly managed, it can be concluded that tourism product, its interpretation and story telling can enhance the position of indigenous peoples within Taiwan.

Part Five

Indigenous Community-Based Tourism

Introduction

One of the most critical issues associated with indigenous tourism is who controls the tourism product and image. In many cases, for both indigenous and non-indigenous communities, *de facto* control over tourism development and management is exerted by external agencies, whether they be in the public or the private sectors. While the call for increased local and community control over tourism is now well established, even where such a situation exists, there is often dependency on external agencies to promote the attractions and to bring tourists to the area involved. The chapters in this section deal with this sensitive area in terms of the transference of control over the operation of tourism enterprises from external to internal agencies. In the first chapter, Salole illustrates a relatively successful example of community-based control in terms of joint tourism ventures in the Torra conservancy of Namibia. Namibia has begun to develop tourism only in recent years but has considerable natural resources suitable for the development of nature-based tourism in particular. The case which Salole examines illustrates well the complicated nature of establishing a truly community-based tourism enterprise in a country facing problems stemming from its political past and recent independence, a lack of familiarity with tourism, and a relatively weak image in terms of international awareness. Key elements in the success of the project have been the commitment of the external partner to a planned community take over of the project and appropriate training of key local personnel, as well as a carefully planned development programme. A similar situation is discussed by Colton, although in a very different geographic and political environment, namely in eastern Canada. Here, a community-based ecotourism development in a Mik'maq settlement in Prince Edward Island, Canada, was developed to improve the economic well-being of the local first nation community. Of key importance in the establishment and appropriate operation of the tourism developments was the education and training in tourism of one of the community members. Local support and involvement within the community and the development of an appropriate range of facilities and opportunities has enabled the community to create a tourism development which is based on the strengths of the community and local resources.

The third chapter in this section, by Nepal, looks at the administration of tourism and resources at the local level in the Himalayas, and the involvement of both the local communities, varying levels of government, and Non-Government Organizations. While problems exist, one of the keys to the overall improvement in the situation has been the active involvement of local residents on a number of committees established to create and oversee the necessary regulation of tourism and associated enterprises. All three chapters in this section stress the necessity of active local involvement and support in order to achieve successful tourism development in their respective communities.

CHAPTER 15

Merging two disparate worlds in rural Namibia: joint venture tourism in Torra conservancy

Mai Salole

Introduction

Community participation

Murphy (1985) put community participation firmly on the tourism agenda. 'The growing emphasis on community responsibility should continue, since the industry [tourism] uses the community as a resource, sells it as a product, and in the process affects the lives of everyone' (p. 165). Yet 'community' is an 'amorphous term' (Mowforth and Munt, 1998, p. 252), and there is a general consensus in the literature that a community is not a homogenous group (Taylor, 1995; Brohman, 1996; Joppe, 1996; Tosun and Jenkins, 1998). It is defined by itself or others upon varying grounds of common locality, environment, and/or common interest.

Stakeholders consider the potential value of community participation from their own perspective. It is encouraged by governments when incorporating sustainable tourism into policies, an important factor since it is difficult to develop sustainable community tourism in a limbo without a framework of enabling regional policies (Middleton, 1997). The private sector's motivation for community participation in tourism development may be derived from the wish to have good and positive neighbours and/or a more marketable product. Despite state and private sector interest, however, the two are often constrained in their effort due to other more urgent priorities. Thomas (1992, p. 117) refers to 'the "third sector", non-state and non-profit organizations' as filling a gap the state and private sector have left open. Non-Government Organizations (NGOs), practiced with community participation from other spheres of experiences, are increasingly involved in tourism. Community-based conservation and tourism ventures are generating employment, income, and funding for ecological projects by marketing basic community resources: the physical and the social environment. According to de Kadt (1990), alternative tourism mirrors alternative development. Unlike the latter, however, alternative tourism is not solely concerned with issues relating to familiar conditions. The major stumbling block in alternative tourism is the crucial involvement of a commercial third party, the client. Tourism may be a totally alien concept to some indigenous communities (see chapter by Berno, Editors' Note). The resources and their management are within cultural reach, but the basic knowledge needed for decision-making and skills to manage and control this highly commercial enterprise are lacking (Middleton, 1998). As a result, communities aspiring to tourism development may be dependent on middlemen. De Kadt (1990, p. 30) mentions the danger of external agents 'appropriating the organs of participation for their own benefit' (cf. Tosun and Jenkins, 1998). Community participation thus has the potential to be a double-edged sword.

The case study

This chapter describes the complicated journey taken by an indigenous community in Namibia's semi-arid North West, following the process of negotiations and product development from inception to its current status as a multiple award winning sustainable tourism destination. The focus is on this community's participation in tourism development, its original human and physical resources, partnerships, and current role in the venture including control of the tourism product. The Torra conservancy, referred to as 'the community' in the case study, constitutes a defined, voluntary membership within a geographical boundary (see chapter by Colton and Harris, Editors' Note).

The research for this study comprised a combination of data extraction from secondary sources, primary research consisting of interviews with key stakeholders, and participant observation in Damaraland Camp. Damaraland Camp and conservancy staff were interviewed in Torra, using semi-standardised, open-ended, in-depth individual interviews. Other interviews, notably with development agencies, government tourism officials, and management of Integrated Rural Development and Nature Conservation (IRDNC) and Wilderness Safaris (WS) were conducted in Windhoek. They were focused (Fielding and Thomas, 2001); individually designed to collect data based on each person's experience and expertise.

Partners

Opportunities in tourism post independence

Namibia is a vast country, with a total land area of 825,418 square kilometres and an average population density of less than one person per 2 square kilometres (Namibia Holiday and Travel, 2003). At the time of independence in 1990, the new government inherited a traditional tourism industry with an asset base renowned for spectacular sand dunes, the world's oldest desert, Africa's oldest petroglyphs, remarkable indigenous fauna and flora, a national park rated among the world's best (Poon, 2000), and unique cultural experiences. Global trends, including a focus on conservation, the greening of consumers, and an increasing interest in regional products from the long haul, affluent originating markets, placed Namibia in a position to develop its tourism sector in line with its new policies.

Namibia was the first country in the world to include protection of the environment and sustainable utilisation of wildlife in its constitution (Poon, 2000). Concerted efforts by government and NGOs led to legislation designed to benefit the previously economically disadvantaged in a concurrent effort to conserve the country's fragile environment. The Nature Conservation Amendment Act was passed in 1996. It gives self-defined groups of farmers on communal lands, subject to certain conditions, the right to apply for conservancy status for the land they occupy in order to manage and derive revenue from its resources (Jacobsohn, 2001). This legislation process caused a number of rural communities to view tourism with high expectations.

Ward 11 (later the Torra conservancy) is one such community, situated in a remote communal area in Kunene province in northwestern Namibia. Settlement is on small scattered farms and in the village of Bergsig with a police station, clinic, primary school, a few government offices, and shops (Nott et al., forthcoming). The relatively small population represent four ethnic groups: the Damara, Riemvasmakers, Ovambos, and Hereros. It is difficult to establish the exact number of residents at independence, but Torra was recorded as having an estimated population of 884 in 2001, with an average population density of one person per 4 square kilometres (Central Bureau of Statistics in Humphrey and Humphrey, 2003). These people live in interspersed clusters, mainly as a result of various forced displacements by colonial governments (Jones, 2001). The Damaras were traditionally hunters and gatherers (Malan, 1995) and had lived in and around the region for centuries. The Riemvasmakers, who had moved away from the area and settled along the Orange River in northern South Africa, had been uprooted and forcibly resettled into the newly established Damara homeland in 1971 (Jacobsohn, 2001). The Ovambos and the Hereros are small minority groups that recently moved into the area as either public servants or small-scale traders (Humphrey and Humphrey, 2003). Some residents were employed in urban centres, but the majority of the population were small stock subsistence farmers (Jacobsohn, 2001).

Namibia's independence induced the optimism of newly acquired rights, and a committee was formed to investigate options for local economic development. Such development was severely challenged by the natural setting of desert and semi-arid savannah (Long, 2002) with 70–100 millimetres yearly rainfall (Humphrey and Humphrey, 2003) and the isolation from urban centres. The very challenges to livelihoods – the isolation, wildlife, and rugged, barren landscapes – had attracted visitors to the region for years, and when the new government declared tourism to be a potentially important contributor to the national economy with wildlife as its main asset base, it became evident to the community that this was a sector worth investigating. The original initiative was to build a campsite for self-drive tourists. Lack of know-how was a major obstacle and thus gave impetus to the possibility of involving an experienced operator. The natural course of action was to consult with IRDNC, an NGO with an office bordering on Ward 11. They had already assisted the committee with the training of game guards to reduce the poaching of wildlife in the area, and personal relationships between the members of the community and the development committee were well established.

The founder of IRDNC had extensive experience in co-operating with numerous indigenous groups in the region to promote and generate conservation efforts, funded by revenue generated through safari operations (Jones, 2001). IRDNC's mission statement includes the democratisation of legislation and practices related to nature conservation and tourism policies as well as the promotion of skills, capacity, and vision to enable communities to actively take part in wildlife conservation and ecotourism (IRDNC, 2002). The NGO had also been a key player in the development of the Nature Conservation Act. During that process, the IRDNC were part of a team that conducted a socio-ecological survey to establish the parameters of a future partnership with rural residents on conservation of wildlife (Jones, 2001).

As is the case in many communities, the residents of Ward 11 were divided on the issue of conservation. Despite the intrinsic traditional value of wildlife, particularly as appreciated by the older generation who wanted cultural continuity, an increase in wildlife population would create a marked conflict of interest due to the competition for grazing between livestock and wildlife. Conservation would also suppress the customary control over wildlife numbers exercised by local and external poachers. The physical threat of elephants and predators to both humans and livestock did little to kindle enthusiasm. In addition to physical danger, elephants were constantly attracted to water points, often with detrimental results to water and precious gardens, leaving people and livestock temporarily without these essential resources. Conservation would, therefore, require a major compromise, which, in the event, was reached due to the ongoing quest for economic development and recognition of the potential benefits of tourism. The final consensus was thus a will to participate in conservation efforts if wildlife could generate direct benefits for the community in the form of meat and income (cf. Honey, 1999; Simpson and Wall, 1999; Sindiga, 1999).

When approached for advice by the development committee of Ward 11, the IRDNC offered the community financing for a liaison officer position to work with them on tourism development. Due to the upcoming change in legislation, the NGO was interested in a new model of a joint venture involving a community and a private operator.

WS, a Southern African photographic safari company founded by guides who gradually evolved their business from a no-frills bird tour in Botswana to safari tourism (Szuchman, 2001), were expanding into the Namibian tourism market in 1994. They were planning a tented camp and identified an area in Ward 11. It offered spectacular landscapes, low population density, the endangered desert-dwelling elephant around the ephemeral Huab River, and a rich variety of other wildlife species. There was no local competition, and the only constraint was the required permission to occupy (PTO) before any legal operations could take place. At that time, PTO was negotiated with government, but the trends indicated that rights to communal lands would soon be devolved to communities. The WS representative knew the area and the people of the village of de Riet in Ward 11 from earlier safari operations. He was introduced to the chairman of the development committee and directed to IRDNC. The NGO, familiar with WS in this relatively small environment of ecotourism, could recommend the company as a conservation-oriented operator.

Negotiations

During the first series of meetings the negotiating parties, were on 'completely different wavelengths', and it took time for them to understand each other well enough to find the confidence and trust needed for fruitful negotiations. IRDNC played a vital role in the negotiations, supplying practical support such as vehicles and funding. Concurrently, the NGO was the conduit for communications between the world visions of small stock farmers and the tour operator, as it possessed some insight into both. In addition, they commanded the resources to draw on external experts for advice. When necessary, the latter provided invaluable experience to guide the development committee through the bureaucratic corridors of government institutions. This was particularly important when the development committee needed to become a legal entity with formal rights. Upon seeking legal assistance with the help of IRDNC, they were advised to form a Residents' Trust. This required defining community membership, agreeing on a constitution, and setting broad objectives for the voluntary association.

IRDNC facilitated this lengthy bureaucratic process, and WS patiently awaited its finalisation. It was essential for the company to deal with individuals who had an unequivocal community and legal mandate in order to secure a positive community-wide future working environment and a solid legal basis for operations. Furthermore, there was a clear vision within WS of its final goal, the company had a philosophy which was not exclusively profit oriented, and there was no imminent deadline for the building of the camp.

Once the Residents' Trust had been registered, the negotiations continued. This stage warranted some knowledge of the tourism industry for all parties concerned. WS sought to shed light on the realities of the hospitality business. The committee needed to understand the basic financial projections as they had to explain the final agreement to the community and guarantee that they had negotiated the best possible terms (cf. Middleton, 1998 on the difficulty of finding someone who is informed about tourism to speak for the community, in this case achieved through the concerted effort of all stakeholders). It was necessary to create awareness about projections and actual occupancy rates, and the trade offs between the fixed percentage of community benefit versus the size of the investment and length of contract. IRDNC brought in economic advisers to help in this process and to help determine fair compensation to the community for their contribution to the venture, a complicated task due to the pioneering nature of the proposed enterprise.

The Residents' Trust was accountable to the community, and although the latter was not large, members were dispersed over a vast area and relied on traditional transportation. Disseminating information and convening meetings was a time consuming, logistical challenge. In addition, farmers had more pressing short-term priorities, and were reluctant to spend time away from home. Meetings were thus infrequent (Ashley and Jones, 2001) (cf. Tosun (2000) on basic livelihood struggles and the unaffordable luxury of spending valuable time on potential future improvements). The Residents' Trust was, however, bound to inform the community of all propositions made by WS. There were numerous hurdles to their acquiescence. Among these hurdles was an undercurrent of disquiet at the thought of giving up important elements of livelihood to an unknown entity, and a certain association with the recent past when outsiders had depleted resources through poaching. Additionally, older people were very hesitant to 'give land away' as they were concerned with grazing and trespassing rights, exemplified by the fact that WS's first choice of location was denied due to its excellent grazing potential. It was also imperative for residents to have the right to collect veldfoods for sustenance and medication throughout the area. Finally, residents were fearful of losing their food security, as local poaching (illegal killing of animals for subsistence and commercial use) had traditionally been undertaken within acceptable limits.

The Residents' Trust, with the help of community opinion, IRDNC advice, and a budding understanding for the hospitality trade, developed their terms while negotiating. The time frame for the venture was a significant issue as a major form of risk management. There was general consensus about the uncertainty of entering into partnership with an unknown entity in an equally unknown business. It was therefore necessary to ensure that the length of the contract was as short as possible in order to allow the community the possibility to review their commitments once some experience had been established. Other substantial areas of negotiation included the access to land for grazing, the option of entering into trophy hunting outside the WS use area, the importance of skills training and the sustainability of resources in order for existing livelihoods to continue unchanged. The economic factor was certainly a key issue, but the transfer of ownership and training at all levels, particularly for management posts, took priority over negotiations for percentage points of community income (Ashley and Jones, 2001).

WS had to take all these requests into consideration when finally drawing up the contract. An area around the camp was secured as a no trespassing zone for residents and livestock, and a much larger area was designated for mixed use. The dwellings in the latter were few and far between and would not deter significantly from the image of pristine Africa. The community's plans to develop trophy-hunting schemes were more of a stumbling block to WS, whose image is one of conservation. Hunting was, however, considered to be a major future resource for the community, and WS agreed to the plan with the condition that it was never to interfere with the product offered by the camp. The issue of local employment was a mutual advantage. Training local residents was in line with WS policy although management training was more of a challenge. The latter was, however, made acceptable as there was no time factor for its completion. Financial terms were discussed at length. The final contract included the following provisions:

- local recruitment of all staff;
- procurement of available services from the community;
- a set yearly rental fee for the site of the lodge;
- 10% of net total revenue to be paid to the community including a minimum performance clause for failure to achieve estimated revenues by the middle of the second year;
- clauses on audits and financial transparency;
- an option for the community to purchase the assets and continue alone after 10 years or alternatively to renew the contract for a further 5 years acquiring 20% of the fixed assets every year;
- rules for establishing a joint management committee responsible for selected staff issues, development of lodge, and wider area;

- exclusive use of the lodge area (i.e., no livestock in the immediate vicinity) and tourist access to a much larger mixed use area;
- community commitments including environmental management, respect for security and safety of clients, and business needs of the lodge.

Adapted from Koch and Massyn (2001)

An environmental impact assessment was sent to the Ministry of Environment and Tourism in the name of the Residents' Trust with the application for the PTO. The latter was awarded 2 years after the first meeting in the church hall. When the amendment to Namibia's conservancy legislation was gazetted during that year, the Ward 11 Residents' Trust was in a favourable position to apply for conservancy formation as many of the prerequisites had already been met during the establishment of the former. As a consequence, Torra was among the first conservancies to be registered in 1998.

Damaraland Camp

The product

Damaraland Camp was initially built on a tight budget with big dome tents, basic showers, no running water, and chemical toilets. The camp was a commercial success, achieving a 40% occupancy rate during the first year (Ashely and Jones, 2001). Concurrently, WS experienced an unprecedented growth period, which led to a strategic change as the company expanded into the high-cost, low-volume market. As a result Damaraland Camp was upgraded twice in 2 years, an airstrip was added to the infrastructure, and the resulting niche market allowed for a 425% increase in rack rate.

The revamped camp had eight walk-in accommodation tents built on concrete floors that covered the basalt rock. At the time of writing there are two additional tents as part of the constant upgrading and maintenance process. En suite bathrooms within the tents are fixed structures with stone walls. The main living area, situated in the centre of the camp, combines a dining room, lounge/library, bar, an office, a curio shop, and toilet in a horseshoe-shaped, semi-stone-walled, canvas covered building, designed with an open-air front to maximise the views over the valley and adjacent mountain ranges. An outdoor sitting area around a campfire is located in front of the structure, and a swimming pool is to be found close to one of the side walls. The kitchen is behind the main complex and, situated at a moderate distance, are covered parking, a maintenance workshop and stone walled houses for management. There are 14 staff accommodation units in the form of small prefabricated houses located out of sight of the main camp.

The energy use at the camp is a blend of sound environmental practices and functionality. Diesel generators pump water from a neighbouring farm 6 kilometres away. These generators also power the workshop. Gas canisters are used for stoves, fridges, and freezers. Showers are heated by solar power for individual units that are located outside each tent. All batteries for lights are recharged by solar power. Firewood is brought into the area and used sparingly. Food waste becomes local pig fodder, paper is recycled on site and later burned, and plastics and metals are transported to Windhoek for recycling. Each tent has a septic tank with an organic treatment system which is high maintenance and requires careful attention. Water consumption and its effect on the source are closely monitored by management. All materials and systems have been carefully considered to comply with environmental practices wherever possible as conservation is a prime concern.

The product was redesigned to appeal to the affluent segment of the market. As a result, the majority of arrivals fly in and are generally part of a WS circuit tour paying all-inclusive rates. The 2006 rack rate (WS, 2006), including all meals and full day excursions, is approximately N$ 2900 (June 2006 conversion rate US$ 420). Walk-ins are rare due to the cost and remoteness of destination.

Guests at the camp enjoy breakfast at dawn, a morning safari between sunrise and lunch and a late afternoon sun-downer walk or drive. The latter may occasionally include a visit to a nearby farm. Alternatively there is the possibility for a full day rhino-tracking tour or an excursion to nearby attractions. The campfire is lit at dusk, guides and management serve and partake in drinks, snacks, and dinner, provide company and the occasional musical performance and are present until guests return to their rooms for the night. The product is strongly influenced by the joint venture. Animal-tracking tours through mixed areas add an interesting dimension to 'pristine Africa'. It gives guests the benefit of experiencing wildlife in its natural habitat, that is, among humans as opposed to the protected areas of national parks. It offers the unique experience of seeing a farmer in his donkey cart traversing an area at high speed where herds of springbuck continue grazing (unlike staged authenticity, cf. Cohen, 1995). These types of experiences are only possible as part of a safari product due to the extremely low population density – in Torra three houses are defined as a village.

Service delivery is an integral part of the product and variation in approach is one of the distinguishing factors between WS destinations. Adhering to the minimum standards' manual for WS is required but distinguishing site-specific features are strongly encouraged due to the circuit clientele. This takes the form of the personal touch offered by management and staff. The important value added benefit at Damaraland Camp is the fact that it is almost entirely staffed by local people striving to adapt their cultural background to an alien world of demands with perseverance, humour and, most importantly, the pride of ownership. The guestbook abounds with superlatives. Direct contact with locals, in this case does not, as Krippendorf (1990, p. 60) suggests is the norm, take place 'under the protection of the tourist guide'. At Damaraland Camp the local *is* the tourist guide.

Training

Initially two managers were employed from the national WS pool. Their new local staff had been through a long and rigorous recruitment process, including joint management committee vetting based on degree of household hardship. WS had assessed applicants for social skills and compatibility for the applicable job. A good standard of English, second or third language to the candidates, was a prerequisite for staff who needed to be in direct contact with guests (Front of House). All employees had at least 1 year of high school education, but the majority had never had a formal job, and came to the camp from their daily routines on farms (see chapter by Berno, Editors' Note).

Training was conducted in house and at other WS camps. Recruitment of senior staff was, and continues to be, difficult due to the limited size of the local labour pool and the skills required. Good English and 12th grade education are prerequisites for management posts and guiding, a driving licence strengthens the application for the latter. Community members with these skills are often drawn to the cities, and not necessarily willing to interact with foreigners with unknown demands and/or wild animals with predatory intentions. Additionally, guides and management are expected to be socially adept in a foreign culture, finding topics of conversation and ways of entertaining – expectations which narrow the field of acceptable candidates even further. The point here is that it really *is* a problem to find topics of conversation due to the lack of common ground, rather than simply being good conversationalists. And yet, by 2002, in line with the joint venture contract, the manager and one assistant manager, both women, had been trained in all the necessary administrative systems for daily operations at the camp. One final position is still filled from the non-local WS pool as the skills required for the post of maintenance manager have as yet not been found in the community.

Camp management

Damaraland Camp, for the duration of the contract with WS, is a link in a chain of destinations managed collectively by the Windhoek office. Strategic planning, product development, marketing, booking, budgets, procurement, and quality control are the domain of headquarters. The local responsibilities are thus limited to daily operations.

Camp management includes the following tasks:

- *Communications with headquarters*: Radio contact three times a day, verify guest arrivals and flight landing times, special guest requests, VIP information, food and spare part orders, personnel issues, and conservancy issues. Data concerning stocktaking, guest register, and petty cash control, are sent to Windhoek together with customer satisfaction forms on a monthly basis.
- *Guest relations*: Plan for pick up, meet and greet, check in, physical presence in living/office area at all times when guests are in camp, attend meals and social functions, check out, payment for drinks and curio shop purchases (all-inclusive circuit touring guests are otherwise pre-paid), and payment from occasional walk-ins.
- *Staff supervision*: Quality control, attendance registry, training plan, leave schedule, salary payments, and staff meetings for information or conflict

resolution. This occasionally has its complicated moments due to the difficulty of imposing authority on one's peers in a small environment.

- *Maintenance*: Vehicles, water systems, toilets, swimming pool, supervision of building and repair projects, and helping community with occasional problem animals within the use area.

The General Manager's (GM's) monthly visits are used to address recurring guest complaints when necessary, and for solving staff conflicts which prove too much of a challenge to the on-site camp management. These visits are also an occasion to meet with the joint management committee, which is not involved in the daily management of the camp, but is a forum for discussing change and a tool for resolving conflicts between WS and staff which require cultural mediation. The manager, despite being a fellow community member, represents the company, and her convictions are at times regarded as biased by her staff. The GM is also in continuous contact with the conservancy on issues relating to employment, maintenance of structures such as water points, threats to the community from wildlife, and clarification of hospitality issues when necessary. In addition, the MD and the GM have a yearly meeting with the conservancy committee.

Promotion and distribution

WS has developed rapidly since its first negotiations with Ward 11, managing 49 properties in seven countries (WS, 2006). In addition to its core tour operator business, the company owns a charter flight company and a tour and safari travel agency specialising in co-ordinating travel arrangements for their overseas agents and operators. Most guests are fully independent travellers in search of a customised safari, 80% of business is circuit travel from one WS camp to another. The agents, international trade fairs, media coverage, brochures, and the website are estimated to reach 10 million potential guests and the total cost of marketing is 30% of gross revenue.

Both the Torra community and WS have benefited from the international recognition given to Damaraland Camp through intangible benefits such as empowerment and pride and the more tangible benefits seen as a result of marketing advantage. Damaraland Camp received the 1997 Silver Otter Award in recognition of conservation and work with the local community, the 2004 United Nations Development Program (UNDP) Equator Prize for poverty alleviation through sustainable use conservation of biodiversity rich equatorial belt, and the 2005 WTTC Tourism for Tomorrow Conservation Award (WS, 2006) (see chapter by Goodwin, Editors' Note). In this context, the Torra community is a highly visible part of the camp's image. In addition, WS have received numerous other awards, some for specific properties, others for its work with conservation and communities. WS is described as developing partnerships with local communities 'out of self-enlightenment' (Jones, 2001, p. 172). This practice has also been a powerful marketing tool.

Conclusion

Tourism development in Torra represents the restoration of rights to the local population and is seen by the community as a 'foundation for development' (Koch and Massyn, 2001, p. 28). The negotiations with WS were the impetus for institution building and social cohesion (Ashley and Jones, 2001). Joint venture negotiations and subsequent management function of the joint management committee have empowered the community through increased cooperation, enhanced planning skills, and knowledge of rights and opportunities (cf. Scheyvens, 1999, on empowerment). The conservancy membership, 80% of eligible inhabitants of Torra in 2002, elects a seven representative management committee for a period of 2 years (Long, 2002), thus adding a new stratum of power to the traditional and regional authorities (cf. Harrison, 1992). All major decisions have to be brought to the plenary which takes place annually barring extraordinary assemblies. This governance structure controls the future of Damaraland Camp.

The conservancy formation was driven by NGO assistance and was not a consequence of tourism development, despite the fact that this applied to the Residents' Trust application process which preceded and facilitated it. Economic benefits from tourism, however, are funding the conservancy, and thus current social, economic, and environmental impacts of the conservancy can be regarded as consequences of tourism development. The impacts of Damaraland Camp are multiple and complex, Krippendorf (1990, p. 55) refers to tourism being 'like fog; it penetrates everywhere'. A detailed analysis (Salole, 2003) falls outside the scope of this chapter but the following summary highlights the impacts which affect all voting members and thus have direct implications on the issue of control.

Communal income for Torra conservancy has surpassed all expectations as Damaraland Camp has yielded many fold the original estimates. Moreover, due to the policy of a district sale and trophy quota based on game census, the conservancy has a substantial additional income, the latter exceeding lodge revenue (excluding salaries) by 8.5% in 2005. The total income from lodge (including salaries), sale of game, and trophy hunting for 2005 was N$ 1,343,062 (approximately US$ 210,840, January 2006 conversion rate) (NACSO, 2006). Torra was the first conservancy in Namibia to cover its own financial commitments (Humphrey and Humphrey, 2003). The conservancy covers the costs of an office, its staff including game guards and vehicles.

Due to the employment factor, economic benefit has not been evenly distributed as individuals employed in the conservancy and WS have inevitably reaped more financial and empowering rewards than others (cf. Weaver and Opperman, 2000 on employment as main economic contributor to local communities in tourism). It is difficult to estimate the number of Torra residents, including a large proportion of women (cf. Koch and Massyn, 2001 on the challenges of finding employment when local *and* female), who have had full-time jobs since 1996, as many Damaraland Camp staff have moved on to different WS properties thus creating new vacancies for fellow community members.

The value of salaries to Torra residents working in other WS camps in 2004 was N$ 517,231 (US$ 89,953 January 2005 conversion rate) compared to the value of salaries in Damaraland Camp for the same year, N$ 614,788 (US$ 106,919 January 2005 conversion rate) (NACSO, 2006). Despite this substantial income, and the fact that one wage earner on average supports a family of seven (Humphrey and Humphrey, 2003), numerous conservancy members have been excluded from these direct benefits due to the limited number of jobs and their lack of qualification. This fact has caused some community dissent.

Torra did not have a benefit distribution plan in place when the conservancy was formed. This was not a problem initially, but as several years passed and the bank account reached seven figures (N$ 1,000,000 approx. US$ 91,000, January 2002 conversion rate), the occasional meat distribution from hunts, annual presents for the elderly, and support for the school, did not match expectations. The conservancy members were acutely aware of the financial success of the camp, and the price of conservation in the form of damage from wildlife to gardens and water points, grazing pressures between livestock and wildlife, and the loss of stock to predators. Community cooperation and conservancy efforts had improved environmental conditions, and wildlife was notably more prevalent. A survey by Jones (1999 in Long, 2002) indicates that 61% of households had suffered loss of livestock to predatory wildlife during the previous year, 25% had suffered damage by elephants, and one person had been killed. The conservancy had established a system for compensation of livestock, but farmers demanded more tangible rewards (cf. Scheyvens, 1999; Victurine, 2000, on the need to channel income from wildlife to those who carry the daily cost of its proximity).

The constant need for referral to the membership for decision has delayed progress. When a benefit distribution plan was proposed by the committee in 2001, the same obstacles occurred which had originally prolonged the negotiations with WS. The combination of a democratic constitution, practical challenges around gathering enough members, and a lack of consensus due to the heterogeneity of the group, delayed ratification for 2 years. It was finally approved in 2003.

Crossroads

In 2006, the conservancy will vote on the short-term future of Damaraland Camp. The joint venture contract stipulates that Torra has the option to purchase the assets and continue alone after 10 years. Alternatively, they have the possibility to renew the contract for a further 5 years, acquiring 20% of fixed assets each year and then take on full ownership at the end of the 15-year period (Koch and Massyn, 2001).

The community has been divided on this choice. Total control appeals to a number of members, as they believe that WS is currently generating high revenues on the basis of community assets. It was apparent to this author, however, that the more the interviewees knew about Damaraland Camp, the less they believed in imminent independence (Salole, 2003). Marketing was perceived as the main obstacle with direct conservancy involvement in management as a second issue. Half way into the 15-year period, many viewed a 5-year extension as the best option. A vague notion that more community members may train for managerial positions during that time was expressed by some although at the time of writing, the conservancy has still not implemented any plans for formal hospitality training.

WS has invested time and money in the venture which is now maturing and providing good returns. Concurrently they are sceptical of Damaraland Camp's potential success as a stand-alone destination as it has no significant unique marketable feature. This factor was exacerbated in 2005 when WS built a lodge in a joint venture with the neighbouring conservancy, which due to the conservancy ownership and geographical proximity, has access to identical marketable assets.

To what extent does Torra conservancy thus have control over their tourism product 12 years after the initial negotiations in de Riet? Conservancy members have the skills for daily management, but as it was developed for WS, the higher-level control rests with WS. In order to be maintained at the current level of standard and income potential, the camp is dependent on the support structures the company has to offer.

The conservancy has the power to decide its immediate and long-term future. Tosun and Jenkins (1998) are concerned with the variability of local preparedness for decision-making exemplified by limited schooling and awareness. 'If decentralisation gives authority and responsibility to local people, the local people may not use this power efficiently and effectively, particularly people who have no experience of tourism' (p. 110). Informed decision-making will, however, reflect a situation where the conservancy has limited options if it is to sustain current financial benefits. Firstly, Torra would have to buy the camp assets from WS at the 10-year renegotiation point, making this an expensive choice. In terms of management skills, it may be possible to reduce the standard of the camp, aiming for a different niche market, but that market is currently regarded as saturated. Another option would be to outsource current WS input to a contracted operating company, but due to the new neighbouring lodge, WS would become as formidable a competitor as it has been a partner.

Murphy (1985) stresses the importance of developing and planning in a way that is compatible with local aspirations and capacities. In this case, however, market forces reigned and caused a transformation of the initially intended low key tourism venture. Consequently the community's control over the product has decreased due to developments beyond the community's short-term management potential. Paradoxically, however, the high maintenance, exclusive, niche product that prohibits the community from full control of Damaraland Camp, has become part of the launch pad for empowerment as the community takes control over other aspects of the conservancy, including other tourism products.

The community has been empowered to create jobs, play an invaluable part in conservation, and assist its members in various ways, including meat distribution from game hunting, a soup kitchen for the elderly who are collecting pensions, and an ambulance service. The conservancy also gives financial and logistical support to the school, farmers association, youth groups, soccer team, and HIV AIDS groups. Some community members with Damaraland Camp experience are planning to start less complex ventures which they, to the extent it is possible in the tourism sector, now have the capacity to control. In the long term, the market may sustain two independent comparable lodges in close proximity, and, in the long term, the community certainly has the opportunity to develop the essential formal skills required within their membership if they choose to aim for full control of the lodge.

Middleton (1998) encourages partnerships in tourism planning and development and Torra provides an excellent example of cooperation. Unlike De Kadt's (1990, p. 30) fear of 'external agents appropriating the organs of participation for their own benefit', the Damaraland partnership has collectively strengthened the community. The authorities had the political will to create a positive framework for poverty alleviation. Within the latter, IRDNC and WS supported Torra in their quest for improved livelihood strategies while concurrently promoting their own agendas of, respectively, conservation and business. They assisted Torra in establishing a democratic community voice and gaining some knowledge about the tourism industry. Concurrently, they empowered Torra by developing a good business plan while incorporating the community's needs. The process was driven by dedicated individuals from all stakeholder groups. Torra's involvement in this complex tourism venture is, however, an ongoing, developing process, and some issues of control and management naturally still remain a challenge to a wider voting body consisting mainly of small stock subsistence farmers.

CHAPTER 16

Indigenous ecotourism's role in community development: the case of the Lennox Island First Nation

John Colton and Scott Harris

Introduction

Economic development in and of itself cannot change Aboriginal peoples' history. It cannot erase, for example, a past of oppression, in some cases genocide, policies of assimilation, forced internment, and residential schools. Creating jobs does not fix such things nor does it, in most cases, offer opportunities to address the challenges that many Aboriginal people face on a day-to-day basis as they collectively heal. Yet, governments have worked diligently to bring economic development strategies to remote Aboriginal communities. In Canada, the Department of Indian and Northern Affairs (DIAND) worked tirelessly to bring economic prosperity to Aboriginal communities with, in many cases, very little long-lasting impact. Increasing positive impacts has proven difficult but the resiliency of Aboriginal people in the face of overwhelming challenges has been clearly demonstrated as can be seen by the creation of autonomous territories (e.g., Nunavut), the development of Aboriginal owned and controlled enterprises, and the coupling of cultural renewal with these accomplishments. Rather than narrowly focused economic development strategies, Aboriginal communities are instead, implementing broader community development strategies that work to improve the socio-cultural and environment as well as the economic dimensions of their community. Significant research exists that explores the multitude of Aboriginal community development methods and strategies by which this is occurring but largely missing from these discussions is the role of tourism. The purpose of this chapter is to examine how a community-based ecotourism project has impacted overall community development of the Lennox Island First Nation, located on Prince Edward Island, Canada (Figure 16.1).

Given the elusive nature of community development and in particular Aboriginal community development, this chapter draws on the work of Bell (1999a, b, 2000) who has worked in northern Aboriginal communities for over 20 years and has conceived Aboriginal community development as consisting of the Four C's; *community economic development, community empowerment, community wellness*, and *community learning*. Figure 16.2 provides an overview of Bell's typology and also includes additional insights from scholars in tourism and Aboriginal studies. Generally, the Four C's of Aboriginal community development and those concepts that support this perspective are as follows:

- *Community Economic Development* has been subject to extensive review, particularly relating to tourism development (Cornell and Kalt, 1990; Parker, 1993; Butler and Hinch, 1996; Bell, 1999a; Telfer, 2002). As seen in Elias (1991, 1997), the federal government has promoted economic initiatives as the key to successful Aboriginal community development. Cornell and Kalt's (1998) research states that the 'jobs and income' approach which looks at only the economic side of the equation of community development, seldom produces lasting economic prosperity.
- *Community Empowerment* is discussed in both the tourism (Zeppel, 1998; Notzke, 1999) and Aboriginal community development literature (Cornell

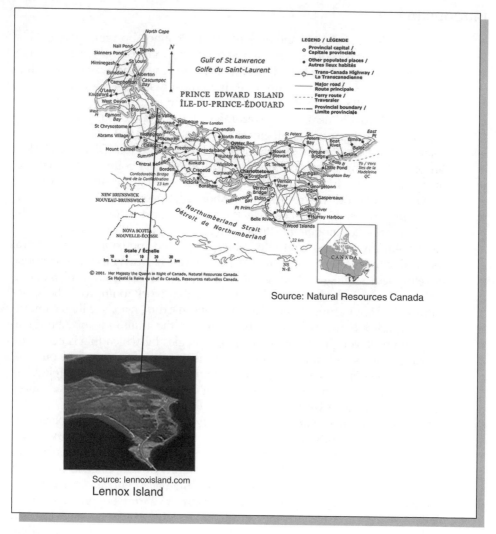

Source: Natural Resources Canada

Source: lennoxisland.com
Lennox Island

Figure 16.1
Lennox Island

and Kalt, 1990, 1998; Elias, 1991, 1997; Bell, 1999a). Community empowerment describes the fundamental steps needed for indigenous people to obtain control over specific development projects and control of their own destiny.

- *Community Learning* refers to acquisition of knowledge and its relationship to building capacity in the communities (Long and Dickason, 1996; Eade, 2000; Warry, 2000; Colton and Francis, 2003). *Knowledge* can come from many different sources including traditional knowledge, which is passed down from generation to generation (MacGregor, 1993; Harris and Wearing, 1999) or from more formal institutional models (see chapters by Butler and Menzies, and Berno, Editors' Note).

Community empowerment

- Governance
- Community control
- Organizational structures
- Representation
- Programs and services
- Resources
- Policy frameworks
- Links with other organizations
  (Bell, 1999a)

- Sovereignty, appropriate institutions, self-determination (Cornell and Kalt, 1998, 1990)
- Vision and planning for comprehensive development (Elias, 1997, 1991)
- Control of mixed economies (Zeppel, 1998; Notzke, 1999)

Community economic development

- Jobs and job development
- Businesses
- Investments
- Community economic development strategies
- Models, partnerships, support mechanisms
  (Bell, 1999a)

- Appropriate institutions where Aboriginal government is at arms length (Cornell and Kalt, 1998)
- Culturally oriented business people (Parker, 1993)
- Economic independence, equitable relationships (Butler and Hinch, 1996; Telfer, 2002)

Community wellness

- Physical, mental, social and spiritual health
- Relationship with the land
- Self-identity through traditional culture
- Healing
- Prevention
- Supportive relationships
- Links between personal and family needs, health care services
- Strong families
  (Bell, 1999a)

- Legitimize traditional lifestyle (Hanson, 1985)
- Appropriate institutions (Cornell and Kalt, 1990, 1998) where healing and wellness occur
- Balance of physical, mental, emotional and spiritual elements (Long and Dickason, 1996; Wyrostok and Paulson, 2000; Poonwassie and Charter, 2001)
- Healthy land base, language, extended family, faith, vision and ethical behaviour (Ayre and Clough, 1999; Voyle and Simmons, 1999; Simpson and Driben, 2000)
- Internal creation (Warry, 2000), self-sufficiency and personal empowerment (Hassin and Young, 1999)

Community learning

- Community as classroom
- Land as a classroom
- Acquiring wisdom from Elders
- Schooling
- Individual and group learning
- Literacy and adult basic education
- Skill development and training
  (Bell, 1999a)

- Being ready to take on knowledge (Gegeo and Watson-Gegeo, 2002) and the abilities and aspirations of communities (Milne et al., 1995)
- Appropriate institutions (Cornell and Kalt, 1998) where community learning takes place
- Experiential education (Harris and Wearing, 1999)
- Collective and individual capacity building (Long and Dickason, 1996; Colton, 2000, 2003; Eade, 2000; Warry, 2000; Simpson et al., 2003; Simpson, 2005)
- Traditional knowledge (MacGregor, 1993)

Figure 16.2
Four C's of Aboriginal community development

- *Community Wellness* refers to a healthy, balanced relationship between oneself and others, and between people and the land (Long and Dickason, 1996; Bell, 1999a, b; Simpson and Driben, 2000; Wyrostok and Paulson, 2000; Poonwassie and Charter, 2001).

Tourism typologies seemingly most sympathetic to Aboriginal community development are ecotourism and indigenous tourism. From theoretical perspectives both concepts suppose an element of community control and a type of tourism synonymous with a community's cultural and environmental assets and the need to protect and sustain these assets. Although ecotourism has its limitations and may not be completely sustainable (Cater, 1994), its premise purports to address issues of community poverty and environmental degradation (Boo, 1990). Communities around the world are embracing ecotourism as a solution to many economic, social, environmental, cultural and political problems and include developments in the Galapagos Islands (Honey, 1999), the wet tropics of Queensland (Sofield, 2002), the rainforest ecotourism projects in South and Central America (Zeppel, 1998), and game parks in Africa (Eagles, 1997). While, ecotourism is not an 'instant fix' that will solve all of a community's economic problems it can be used to diversify its economy (King and Stewart, 1996; Ross and Wall, 1999; Simpson, 2001). Ross and Wall (1999) state:

Communities should not be encouraged to become solely dependent upon ecotourism: rather, ecotourism ideally should complement other activities and help to diversify an economy. Tourism of any type should not be viewed in isolation and its development should be considered as part of a broader plan for the use of resources. (p. 129)

Ecotourism's ability to complement existing opportunities and community assets and its ability to diversify the local economy make it a good fit with Aboriginal development. Many Aboriginal communities are located close to or in natural areas; some of them of global significance. It is also natural for many of these Aboriginal communities to be interested in capitalizing on their unique locations and in many respects, their culture, in order to draw tourists to their communities. Thus, motivations for tourism development continue to be largely economic with objectives such as increasing employment opportunities, diversifying the economic base, and building business investment opportunities. Rejuvenation of culture (Parker, 1993; Hinch and Butler, 1996; Colton, 2000; Hiwasaki, 2000), showcasing one's cultural traditions (Medina, 2003), gaining greater control and self-reliance (Milne et al., 1991; Burlo, 1996; Brown, 1999; Colton, 2005), and pursuing political recognition (Hiwasaki, 2000) are additional factors motivating Aboriginal communities to pursue tourism development. But the most important consideration, identified by researchers of Aboriginal tourism (e.g., Britton, 1982; Keller, 1987; Hall, 1994; Mowforth and Munt, 1998; Fennell, 2002; Zeppel, 1998) is the amount of control and/or ownership a community has over its traditional resources and the degree to which Aboriginal people control the development of Aboriginal tourism experiences. Aboriginal community development literature resonates with calls for sovereignty and self-determination (e.g., Cornell and Kalt, 1990, 1998; Elias,

1991, 1997; Bell, 1999a). At the core of this literature is the argument that self-determination is the foundation for sustained community development. The Lennox Island First Nation pursued ecotourism development as a broad community development initiative with hopes that it was pursuing a development opportunity that reflected its connection to the land, its culture, and its aspirations for controlling and sustaining economic development.

The Lennox Island First Nation

Surrounded by the waters of Malpeque Bay, Prince Edward Island, Canada, Lennox Island is the home of the Lennox Island First Nation, a Mi'kmaq reserve community. The Lennox Island First Nation, like most Aboriginal communities across Canada, experienced dramatic change in a relatively short period of time. This rapid change significantly eroded their culture and affected their ability to develop a healthy community characterized by sustainable economic growth. European settlement brought disease, loss of control of traditional fishing, hunting and trapping grounds, and conversion to Christianity. Collectively, these institutional changes dramatically impacted the every day life of Aboriginal people and severely impacted their ability to develop and maintain traditional social institutions and a traditional way of life. Concerned about the plight of Aboriginal people in Canada and devoted to assisting Aboriginal peoples, the Aborigines Protection Society based in London, purchased Lennox Island in 1870 for £400 (Lennox Island Aboriginal Ecotourism, 2004), so that it could be set aside for the Mi'kmaq of the area. Lennox Island was designated a special reserve after Prince Edward Island joined the Confederation of Canada but it did not receive official *Indian Act* reserve status until 1970 (Lennox Island Aboriginal Ecotourism, 2004).

The *Indian Act* of 1876 effectively took control over the lives of Aboriginal people in Canada. Through this Act, the government assumed responsibility over the welfare of Aboriginal people, determined land use, and controlled the process of education through federally funded but primarily church operated residential schools. Many of the associated government policies were largely executed through the federally supported residential schools. Having lost control of the process of education, Aboriginal communities in essence, also lost the ability to control their own future (Ing, 1990). The Lennox Island First Nation did not escape the introduction of these institutions and on several occasions individuals who participated in this study lamented about their experiences in these schools.

The *White Paper* developed by the Government of Canada in 1968 was an attempt to address many concerns voiced by Aboriginal people across Canada (Elias, 1991). Rather than convincing Aboriginal people that the government actually understood their unique positions and was willing to work with Aboriginal people to address their growing concerns and frustrations, the *White Paper* denied the cultural uniqueness of Aboriginal people and their rights to traditional lands. The negative reaction to this report 'galvanized' Aboriginal individuals and communities and encouraged the development of Aboriginal organizations that fought for collective Aboriginal rights across Canada. Paralleling and complementing the drive for greater autonomy and self-determination, Aboriginal communities have sought to develop community-based economic development opportunities through Aboriginal owned and operated forestry, mining, arts and crafts cooperatives, and tourism initiatives.

Indigenous ecotourism: the case of the Lennox Island First Nation

Lennox Island is a community of approximately 400 inhabitants (Lennox Island Aboriginal Ecotourism, 2004) and before the causeway connected Lennox Island to Prince Edward Island in 1974, economic opportunities were scarce. With access to fishing rights guaranteed under the Canada Supreme Court Marshall Decision, members of the Lennox Island First Nation were able to participate in the lucrative fishery. In addition to a small lobster fishery, other economic opportunities have included a peat moss factory, blueberry and oyster harvesting, a bakery, basket making, small-scale forestry operations, and more recently tourism.

The community was inspired to develop ecotourism after one of its members returned from university with an understanding and awareness of the potential positive impacts that ecotourism development could have on the community given its proximity to the sea, the abundance of wildlife and unique bird watching opportunities, and the strength and the attraction of the Mi'kmaq culture. Partnering with faculty and graduate students from Guelph University, extensive community consultation occurred which led to the development in 1999 of a 10-year Lennox Island Ecotourism Strategy based upon and guided by community and cultural values. Key principles of this strategy included (MacHattie and Wolfe-Keddie, 2000):

- protecting and strengthening ecological and cultural integrity;
- strengthening community and personal self-worth and pride in heritage;
- contributing to economic development by maximizing and spreading employment;
- transferring management, planning, business development skills to community members via capacity building initiatives.

Band members, the chief and council made it clear through community discussions that if ecotourism development was to proceed it must be:

- *Realistic*: The project needed to build on the strengths of the community.
- *Practical*: The project needed to proceed at a pace and scale consistent with the people and resources available in the community.
- *Tangible*: The project needed to produce results such as jobs and other benefits early on to demonstrate to the community what was possible.

(MacHattie and Wolfe-Keddie, 2000)

As the Lennox Island First Nation initially lacked the capacity to implement and administer the ecotourism project, a manager was seconded from Parks Canada to fulfil these roles. The ecotourism manager, a non-Aboriginal from Prince Edward Island quickly built the trust and respect required to work with the Lennox Island First Nation with one of the first projects being the development of a cultural centre. This centre quickly became a focal point for activity in the community. Its development involved the collection of cultural artifacts, recording traditional stories, and community decisions on how best to represent these artifacts and stories through programming and exhibition.

Soon after the development of the cultural centre, cross-cultural workshops were offered with clients such as the Royal Canadian Mounted Police (RCMP), the Department of Fisheries and Oceans (DFO), and local school groups. Along with the construction of the cultural centre was the development of the 10 kilometre interpretive trail called *Path of Our Forefathers* and the ecotourism centre. Sea kayaking and boat charter businesses were also initiated and slowly evolved into successful seasonal businesses. Lennox Island First Nation was 3 years into their ecotourism strategy when study visits to Lennox Island were initiated to explore the broader impacts of ecotourism development on the community. Using Bell's (1999a) conception of Aboriginal community development (i.e., community economic development, community empowerment, community learning and community wellness), the way that ecotourism development impacted broader dimensions of Aboriginal community development was examined (Figure 16.3).

Community economic development

Like many Aboriginal communities in Canada, the Lennox Island First Nation is characterized by high unemployment, few jobs in the community and a lack of economic diversification. Ecotourism development was viewed as an opportunity to address these problems. High hopes were pinned on the ecotourism development initiative and while some economic benefits have been experienced, the project has not yet met the community's high expectations. This is due, in part, to its slow evolution in terms of the gradual development of the ecotourism centre and its related amenities. Also, during this period, the Maritime Provinces as a whole experienced a significant decline in tourism visitation.

Approximately 3 years ago, 20–25 seasonal tourism related jobs existed. Today that number has climbed to 40–45 tourism related jobs although many are still part-time. In terms of overall number of job opportunities provided through tourism, it rivals the largest employer (the Band Council) in the community. Despite the part-time nature of many of the tourism jobs and their low pay, these jobs do serve an important purpose in the community. Individuals, in particular youth, have the opportunity to develop skills related to administration, hospitality, wilderness guiding, cooking native foods and interpretation. Also, many of the youth have the opportunity to work and learn from community Elders. Given that many of these skills are learned in a cultural context, especially those related to guiding, about the preparation of native foods,

Community empowerment	Community economic development
• Fair and open decision-making process • Community control over the ecotourism development • Working towards independence by creating economically viable community development projects • Federal government still has major influence and control over community regarding funding • Little control over own destiny • Strong leadership with open communication with membership	• Increased employment • Build capacity for business and investment on reserve • Mixture of public and private jobs • Public jobs are low paying and seasonal • Training jobs • Bringing in 'new money' from outside sources (tourists) • Building on community strengths • Founded on sound economic principles • Ecotourism has a significant role to play in the success of economy
Community Wellness	**Community Learning**
• Building stronger community relationships through programmes and activities for community members • Developing a sense of pride while presenting culture to tourists • Developing pride because being appreciated by outsiders (tourists) • Enforcing cultural rules related to drugs and alcohol • Increasing the number of cultural performance groups in the community • Becoming more physically active from use of the trail by community members • Hosting events which encourage outdoor physical activity	• Re-learning the culture • Learning traditions from other Aboriginal communities • Involving knowledgeable Elders • Elders passing on knowledge to the youth • Learning protocol • Individual empowerment through acquiring appropriate knowledge and skills • Cross-cultural learning for tourists and neighbours • Cultural awareness activities for outside groups

Figure 16.3
Impact of Lennox Island ecotourism on community development

and cultural interpretation, greater capacity is developed among the youth leading to increased feelings of self-worth as local indigenous people learn more about their own culture through ecotourism employment opportunities.

Ecotourism development has also stimulated entrepreneurial activity including the development of a native foods café, a sea kayaking tour company, a fishing charter boat operation, a drumming group and a bakery. Collectively, these activities represent a type of economic development consistent with the assets and strengths of the community. However, there is local concern that Lennox Island is placing too much emphasis on ecotourism development rather than a more diversified approach to community economic development. As one community member commented, 'it's like putting too many eggs in one basket . . . there is too much money being put into this project and not into other needed things'. While this sentiment was not consistent with the majority of people involved in this study, it nevertheless points to an important point that sustained community economic growth needs to rely on more than one economic activity in order to be resilient to the fluctuations of local, regional and national economies. To this end, the Lennox Island First Nation invests in other projects as well such as blueberry harvesting, the fishery and small-scale forestry operations.

Community empowerment

Community empowerment concerns governance, the level of control the community has over projects, and community-based sovereignty. On Lennox Island, control was a major component of the ecotourism development project (see chapter by Salole, Editors' Note). In fact the issue of who controls the development of the project was addressed from the outset as the ecotourism strategy specifically stated that, 'the pace and scale [of the ecotourism development] should be such that the community would retain control' (MacHattie and Wolfe-Keddie, 2000, p. 8). Yet, while the community proposed how and what was to be developed, funding for the project came primarily from the federal government. Thus, as the project moved forward and the community became more enthused and involved, its success depended on the government's continued willingness to provide funding. Lennox Island, like many Aboriginal communities in Canada lacked financial capital to invest in such major economic development initiatives and also lacked the ability to seek capital from private lending institutions. So while *control* over the pace and scale of what was to be developed rested with the Lennox Island First Nation, the federal government controlled whether or not these plans could be implemented. This frustrated many community members and also served to galvanize their aspirations and hopes for greater sovereignty through economic independence, which the ecotourism project would someday help achieve.

As the project evolved there was considerable discussion over whom would benefit from the ecotourism development and to what extent politics would be involved. There was speculation that perhaps the chief and council would make decisions behind closed doors which, if it had occurred, would be a considerable setback to the spirit of the project as originally conceived and designed. This decision process was put to the test early on when two business development proposals for the ecotourism centre came from individuals related to people on the band council. To avoid conflict and to have a transparent decision-making process, the chief and council asked community members to select seven individuals to serve on an adjudicating committee. The members of this group developed a scoring system and then made recommendations back to chief and council. So what could have been a divisive situation and perhaps a setback to the entire process was instead an exercise in collective community growth as it was the first time a process such as this had been implemented. With strong leadership among the Lennox Island First Nation and the introduction of an open and transparent communication and decision-making process, it became apparent that the ecotourism initiative was paying more than economic dividends.

Community learning

Erosion of Aboriginal traditional knowledge and culture is symptomatic of past government policies of assimilation and the church's suppression of Aboriginal beliefs and practices. The Lennox Island First Nation, like many other Aboriginal communities in Canada, experienced dramatic change after the arrival of the Europeans and the establishment of government institutions dominated by the European newcomers. Gradually, however, communities like Lennox Island have begun to regain their culture with projects like the ecotourism strategy helping to facilitate this transformation.

Ecotourism development on Lennox Island is contributing to the (re)-learning of cultural knowledge and promoting traditional ways of learning. Elders are transferring traditional knowledge to youth through ecotourism programming in which young employees assist the Elders on guided tours. From this experience, the youth are able to observe and listen and soon share this indigenous knowledge with visitors themselves. This experiential style of learning (Harris and Wearing, 1999) is a culturally appropriate method of transferring knowledge and is an important avenue for Lennox Island youth to learn about their culture and traditional practices (see chapter by Butler and Menzies, Editors' Note). Lennox Island community members also control which aspects of their culture are shared and not shared with tourists. This sharing is accomplished through cross-cultural workshops, interpretive displays and other programming.

Cross-cultural workshops and specific programming at the ecotourism centre have been instrumental in breaking down stereotypes and alleviating long standing tensions that have existed between Lennox Island and some of its non-Aboriginal neighbours (See chapter by Carmichael and Jones, Editors' Note). The native foods café in the ecotourism centre which originally catered solely to community members and visitors now attracts local fishermen and people from the neighbouring towns. A drumming group and women's singing group, created during the development of the ecotourism strategy perform for visitors and the community on a regular basis. Interviews with community members indicate that the ecotourism strategy was partially responsible for the development of these groups and members of these two groups believe that they are more connected to their culture as a result of their involvement. Several individuals employed by the ecotourism project have credited this experience with their decisions to enrol in university programs. In fact, one of these individuals has returned to Lennox Island and begun a community planning and mapping exercise which draws on the skills she learned at university.

Community wellness

The Lennox Island ecotourism project has impacted people on many levels, including the physical and spiritual dimensions of their lives. Infrastructure developed such as the *Path of Our Forefathers* is directly impacting community members' wellness. The construction of a well-designed quality trail has encouraged community members and school groups to become more physically active. Since the trail also has interpretive panels that tell stories of the lives of community members who lived on the land, community members can learn more about their past and its relationship to the present on their walks. The trail is also used by the Lennox Island Health Center in their program development related to building healthy community relations. These programs are intergenerational in nature and promote strong bonds between youth, Elders, and other community members. Thus, although the trail was funded and developed to provide ecotourism type activities for visitors, it has become a key component of the community's physical activity and wellness opportunities.

Ecotourism development has also contributed directly to community wellness through building what Warry (2000) describes as cultural esteem, pride and a cultural identity. One community member remarked that, 'since there has been drumming, dancing and more [cultural] knowledge, I think there is a lot more pride of who we are as Mi'kmaq people' (Personal communication, August 26, 2004). Lee (1992) illustrates the importance of communities becoming a source of pride for individuals and how the 'traditional cultural underpinnings must be re-established' (p. 216) to effectively regain Aboriginal identity. Ecotourism has impacted community wellness on Lennox Island by contributing to the re-establishment of a cultural identity among individuals as a result of the promotion of cultural performances and the pride shown by individuals who participate. Many people believe that ecotourism was the catalyst for the emergence of these groups who perform for visitors and community members. As more people participate in these groups, alcohol and drug abuse among youth may be reduced due to the cultural requirement that participants must abstain from drugs and alcohol. One youth commented on how the desire to join these groups had led some of his friends to change their behaviour as it relates to drug and alcohol use.

Youth and other community members working as guides and interpreters have also experienced a re-connection to culture and, in addition, the employment opportunities created by the ecotourism project have led to a strengthened sense of purpose for some individuals. An individual in band administration remarked that since the development of the ecotourism project, there appears to be a greater sense of community; that the Lennox Island First Nation is collectively and proudly sharing its home and history with visitors. The sense of collective community action has created an atmosphere that is positive and supportive. While linking tourism development to community wellness is difficult at best, it is apparent that people on Lennox Island are experiencing broad health and wellness benefits due, in part, to the emergence of the ecotourism strategy.

Discussion

There is little doubt that tourism can and does play a significant role in the economic development aspirations of a community. These benefits range from generating revenue and providing jobs to developing community capacity (Parker, 1993; Milne et al., 1995; Colton, 2005). According to Hinch and Butler (1996), 'Western-based economic rationale underlies much of the argument to use tourism as a mechanism for finding solutions to the challenges facing indigenous people' (p. 5) and this has been the case on Lennox Island. But sustaining economic development in Aboriginal communities requires a *nation-building* approach rather than a *jobs and income* approach (Cornell and Kalt, 1990, 1998). Cornell and Kalt (1998) caution that, the 'nation-building' approach does not ensure the community of economic success but 'it vastly improves the chances that economic development will take root and be sustainable' (p. 193). While the Lennox Island ecotourism strategy is providing jobs and income for some of its members, the approach outlined in the strategy (i.e., the need to build capacity, self-worth and pride in heritage) reflects a commitment to building and sustaining community as a whole.

Rather than being forced on them, tourism development is occurring under the direction of the Lennox Island First Nation. Clear goals were articulated in the ecotourism strategy that included capacity building, the strengthening of community and the development of pride and self-worth among people in the community. Transparent decision-making processes were used to make crucial decisions and to avoid conflict of interest issues. Collectively, these actions supported the development of ecotourism experiences consistent with the Mi'kmaq culture and the relationship of the people to the land. Yet, despite an approach to tourism development that supported broader community development, people in the community sometimes felt powerless and that they ultimately lacked the control necessary to determine their own future. While the Lennox Island First Nation largely had control over their resources, they lacked the ability to consistently influence the scale and pace of development due to their dependence on funding from the federal government. Outright sovereignty may be one of the goals of Aboriginal community development (Cornell and Kalt, 1998) yet there is a belief that sovereignty is an ideal and change will most likely occur incrementally through devolution and legislated adjustments (Elias, 1991). Although empowered in part by the ecotourism strategy and its outcomes, the Lennox Island First Nation still lacks the ultimate ability, to determine their future. Development projects like this one, however, serve to enhance the community's move toward greater sovereignty through greater economic independence (Colton, 2005).

While there may be some debate regarding the degree to which the Lennox Island First Nation is empowered by the ecotourism project, there is little doubt that increased community, regional and visitor learning and acquisition of knowledge is occurring as a result of the project. Tourism development has the potential to preserve, revitalize or even allow some Aboriginal people to re-learn aspects of their culture. Despite the potential negative impacts of having this revitalization occur through the commoditizing of Aboriginal culture (Burlo, 1996; King, 1996; Snow and Wheeler, 2000; Medina, 2003), the culture of the Lennox Island First Nation can be reinvigorated (King, 1996; Hiwasaki, 2000). The fact is that youth in the community are learning from their Elders through a culturally appropriate experiential style made possible through the ecotourism operations (Harris and Wearing, 1999).

Aboriginal community development cannot occur without community learning (Bell, 1999a). This learning should occur at a pace with which the community is comfortable (Gegeo and Watson-Gegeo, 2002). The Lennox Island Ecotourism Strategy was designed to progress at such a pace. This strategy was reflected by the decisions to develop the culture centre first followed by the *Path of Our Forefathers*. Building capacity, pride and enhancing self-worth as people re-connected to their culture and to each other were instrumental tenets of the ecotourism strategy and were essential in ensuring the success and sustainability of the project as a whole.

Categorically linking the impacts of ecotourism and community wellness is difficult, but research has demonstrated that tourism development can positively impact Aboriginal identity and pride (Parker, 1993; Medina, 2003). Fennel (2002) has also articulated the potential psychological and sociological benefits of ecotourism. Ecotourism development can also contribute directly to community wellness through building what Warry (2000) describes as cultural esteem or a cultural identity. The development of cultural performing groups and the promotion of cultural performances in the Lennox Island community became a source of pride for both performers and observers. As Lee (1992) notes, these initiatives can serve, in part, to effectively regain Aboriginal identity. The *Path of Our Forefathers*, not only promoted physical fitness, it also served to reconnect people's historical relationship to the land through the inclusion of creative interpretive displays.

Conclusion

Conceptualizing Aboriginal community development through the use of the modified Four C's (Figure 16.2) has provided insight into how ecotourism contributes to a wider range of factors other than those typically found in Aboriginal tourism related research. By examining the dimensions of community development in this light, communities can begin to explore how tourism might intentionally or unintentionally impact them both positively and negatively. Proactively planning for tourism in this manner can alleviate the growing pains often experienced by small community-based tourism projects.

The intent of this chapter was to provide a glimpse of a community that has embraced ecotourism and to examine just how this initiative impacted on the broader aspects of community development. The Four C's of Aboriginal community development provide a useful framework to accomplish this task but there are other perspectives that have the potential to do this as well. What is important is to recognize, and wherever possible reward, communities that have worked diligently to build the capacity of their people and community. Their efforts support the success and longevity of their tourism development aspirations. The Lennox Island First Nation members have positioned themselves for success and this success promises to build the capacity of the community to address future challenges that it may face.

CHAPTER 17

Local level institutions in tourism management in Nepal's Annapurna region

Sanjay K. Nepal

Introduction

Conflicting opinions exist about whether the development of indigenous tourism is an effective strategy for self-determination, or a process to assimilate indigenous societies into the mainstream culture. Those in favor of indigenous involvement in tourism argue that through the provision of economic stability and the reinstatement of traditional cultural practices, indigenous people can achieve self-determination and self-reliance. It is believed that tourism could provide indigenous peoples opportunities to assert their rights and autonomy through economic empowerment (Pfister, 2000; Smith and Ward, 2000). However, critics have argued that indigenous tourism is yet another form of cultural imperialism (Nash, 1989), and an example of Westernized attempts to assimilate indigenous peoples into mainstream societies (Francis, 1992; MacCannell, 1999; and also chapter by Butler and Menzies, Editors' Note). Tourism has often proved to be disastrous to indigenous communities, resulting in their displacement, conflict, and violence within the community, and disruptions of social and cultural practices (Colchester, 2004). When external agents introduce tourism to local communities as a mechanism to support conservation, it could be seen as a threat to the traditional rights of local residents. To alleviate this threat, steps need to be taken to strengthen indigenous peoples' involvement in tourism and their control of the planning and decision-making processes. This requires the building of equitable partnerships with tourism management authorities (Scheyvens, 1999; Sofield, 2003). Such initiatives are particularly important in situations where indigenous communities are financially unable to make major tourism investments and also lack the necessary skills and knowledge about tourism-related operations (see chapters by Berno and Goodwin, Editors' Note).

Using the Annapurna region as an example, this chapter examines the involvement of indigenous peoples in local level institutions established to manage tourism. The objectives of this chapter are to: (1) provide an account of various types of local level institutions created to promote sustainable tourism, (2) examine the processes of institution building, and (3) determine the strengths and weaknesses of local involvement in institutional development.

Tourism in the Annapurna region

Located in the western region of Nepal, and north of Pokhara, the second largest city in the hill regions of Nepal, the Annapurna region is the largest conservation area in Nepal with a land area of $7,629 \text{ km}^2$, covering five administrative districts.

The region is inhabited by various ethnic groups with a total population estimated at 118,000. The *Gurung* constitute the main ethnic groups. They mostly inhabit the middle hills with the Ghandruk and Sikles villages representing the main clusters. The *Magar* tend to occupy the lower reaches of Kali Gandaki valley while the *Thakali* are their northern neighbors. The

Loba or the Mustang *Bhotia* occupy the higher altitudes in the arid regions of Mustang while the Manangba (Manang Bhotia) mostly occupy the Manang District. In the peripheral areas are inhabitants with a mix of several ethnic groups including *Brahmin*, *Chetri*, *Newar*, and *Kami*. While the Loba and Manangba practice Tibetan Buddhism, the other ethnic groups now practice a mix of both Buddhism and Hinduism. The region has a very long settlement history. The Thakali were skilled traders and innkeepers who controlled a significant part of the historic salt trade along the Kali Gandaki corridor (Fürer-Haimendorf, 1989), while the majority of the *Gurung* and *Magar* males served in the Indian and British Gurkha army. The *Manangba* were also noted as efficient traders who ventured far and wide in the Indian subcontinent (Snellgrove, 1981). Similarly, the Loba in Mustang controlled the border trade with Tibet until it declined, due to political changes in Tibet. Declining trade and deteriorating agricultural productivity in the central hills of Nepal contributed to an exodus of people to the lowlands of Nepal (Gurung, 1980). However, the growth and development of tourism in the Annapurna region in the early 1980s encouraged many local people to return to their original home lands (Heide, 1988) (Figure 17.1).

Tourism in the region started with mountaineering expeditions in the early 1950s. However, it was not until the late 1970s after some basic tourism infrastructure was established, that trekking tourism finally started to flourish. The first lodge in Ghandruk was opened in 1976. In 1977, Manang and Mustang (the southern part) were opened for tourism, which made the Annapurna Circuit Trek feasible. There was a dramatic increase in the number of foreign visitors at that time from 14,332 in 1980 to 35,800 in 1990 and a high of 67,000 visitors in 1999 (HMG, 2000). Similarly, the number of lodges in the area almost quadrupled between 1980 and 1990, and by 2000 there were 518 (Jampen, 2000). During the last 7 years, 300 new lodges have been constructed. The total accommodation capacity in these lodges is over 6,000 beds per night. Tourism has become a major economic activity in the region with over 50,000 persons employed by the industry during peak tourist seasons.

With the proliferation of tourism over the past two decades, the Annapurna region has faced various environmental and economic problems. Localized deforestation caused by heavy demand for fuelwood and timber for the construction of over 500 lodges and teashops have altered wildlife habitats. While higher income from tourism has made it possible for the local community to afford new energy-efficient technologies, the majority of the lodges in the Annapurna region continue to use fuelwood as their main energy source (Jampen, 2000). The seasonality and concentration of trekkers in the three main areas – the Annapurna Sanctuary, the base of the Thorong Pass, and Ghorepani village (a major trail intersection) – pose critical environmental and social problems. Inadequate sanitation practices and extensive non-biodegradable litter such as plastics, tins, and bottles used mainly by the tourists are primarily responsible for polluting the villages and local streams (Gurung and de Coursey, 1994). Tourism has flourished at the expense of agriculture and livestock herding. Kraijo (1997) reported that many villagers

Figure 17.1
Location of the Annapurna region in Nepal

have left their land fallow or converted it into tree-plantation areas as they pursue tourism opportunities.

To address the problems caused by tourism in the region, the Annapurna Conservation Area Project (ACAP) was launched in 1986. The Project is an undertaking of the King Mahendra Trust for Nature Conservation (KMTNC), a national level non-governmental organization established in 1982. From a pilot project launched in the village of Ghandruk, covering an area of 200 km², ACAP today oversees tourism and environmental management activities throughout the entire Annapurna Conservation Area. ACAP has thus become a regional institution that supports tourism and environmental activities undertaken by local communities through various local level institutions.

Over the years, ACAP has acquired considerable autonomy from the KMTNC. It has adopted a bottom-up approach, and its activities related to environmental conservation and community development draw heavily on local participation (Hough and Sherpa, 1989). ACAP has been authorized by special legislation both to charge fees to visitors and to retain the revenues to finance health and sanitation, education, environmental protection, and tourism projects. It has been instrumental in launching various participatory environmental conservation and community development activities throughout the region. Establishing tree nurseries and fuel-wood plantations, introducing fuel-efficient technology, developing micro-hydropower, providing conservation education, improving sanitation conditions, and repairing trails and bridges are some of its most common projects.

Indigenous peoples and local institutions

Historically, many rural ethnic communities in Nepal were governed through traditional institutions. Examples of traditional institutions include the *bhakriti* system, which was headed by seven hereditary *mukhiya* (village chiefs) who controlled and regulated the harvesting of forest products, and designated forest boundaries. Village affairs, prior to the 1950s, were managed by similar traditional social institutions such as *Talukdar*, *Mukhiya*, *Riti-thiti* (in southern region), and *Pekhyung* governed by *Ghampa*, *Chikyab*, and *Mukhiya* (in the northern region). Although tourism is a relatively modern affair, following the communal foundations of indigenous management systems, ACAP adapted traditional management systems to reflect changing times and circumstances (Thakali, 1997).

Various management committees have been established to engage local people in conservation and community development. These committees include Conservation and Development Committee, Lodge Management Committee, Kerosene Depot Management Committee, Electricity Management Committee, Health Center Management Committee, and Drinking Water Management Committee. Women's groups were created in many villages with members actively engaged in various income and awareness generating activities including fund-raising, trail repairs, clean-up campaigns, and observation tours. Committee members are nominated or elected by the local people themselves. Thus, ACAP has encouraged local participation in resource management, helped villagers maintain control over their resources, and has enabled locals to identify their immediate needs and priorities. This is very different from other protected areas in Nepal where resource management and protection are directed by the central government with almost no local involvement.

Ensuring sustainability of projects undertaken, placing local people at the center of development efforts and initiatives, identifying local needs and priorities, and unleashing the local potential for development alternatives have been the rationale for establishing local institutions. A brief description of selected institutions is provided below.

Conservation Area Management Committees

The Conservation Area Management Committee (CAMC) is the main institutional unit at the Village Development Committee (VDC) level. While the VDC is concerned mostly with administrative and political affairs, the CAMC is concerned with the protection and management of forests and other natural resources. A CAMC is typically composed of 15 members, elected from each of nine wards (lowest administrative or political unit). Women, socially disadvantaged groups, and social workers are each represented by one member. The elected members nominate the Chairman and Vice-Chairman from among themselves; all members including the Chairman are elected for a period of 5 years. Most CAMCs meet once a month to discuss activities related to fixing royalties and issuing permits for various forest products; identifying and protecting community plantation sites; enforcing user regulations; allocating timber/tree quotas for lodge and household use; enforcing hunting and fishing regulations, enforcing special policies such as prohibition of fuelwood in certain areas; and monitoring observation of rules and regulations. The CAMCs are also supported by a number of sub-CAMCs, which are formed based on geographical distribution of the villages. The jurisdiction of a sub-CAMC is limited to traditional forest ownership and boundaries respected by neighboring communities. The latter is prevalent among Gurung communities.

Mothers' Groups

Women represent a little more than half of the total population in the region, and are the primary users of forest resources. Since its inception, ACAP has encouraged involvement of women in the planning and decision-making processes, and thus facilitated the establishment of Mothers' Groups (MGs) in the region. The concept of MG was not new, as similar organizations (*Mahila Sangathan* or *Mahila Samuha*) had already existed in the region. However, ACAP introduced formal structures, thereby strengthening organizational capability. Typically, all women of the community automatically become general members of the MG. Each group elects 11 to 15 members to the executive committee which is led by a chairperson, a vice-chairperson, a secretary, and a treasurer for up to 3 years. Meetings are usually held once a month. Such groups have been engaged in various activities including path and trail repair, village clean-up campaigns, community development activities like supporting drinking water projects and reforestation, and managing day care centers. The MGs may also mediate family conflicts, discourage excessive gambling and drinking by men, and organize cultural events for tourists and the community in order to generate funds. Collecting donations are part of village traditions, for example, at birth, marriage, or the return of a soldier. The MGs not only capitalized on these traditions but have also added a tourism dimension by performing cultural dance performances. In the past, money collected from such events was spent on village meals; today, it is spent on community welfare programs. For example, between 1995 and 1997, the MG in Chomrong, a village located close to ACAP head-quarters, had performed 52 cultural dances generating well over Nepali Rupees (NR) 110,000, a significant amount of money by village standards (Nepal et al., 2002). More than 68% of the money was collected from tourists (44 performances). The total cash assets of the group are between 200,000 NR and 300,000 NR, which represents the major source of investment for this group. Investments made in the village also generate local employment opportunities, for example, in construction projects. Some MGs also lend money to local households.

Overall, the MGs in Annapurna have made remarkable contributions to the society and the environment. They have also become economically signifi-cant institutions owing to their roles as money lenders and employers. Women's roles and responsibilities in village development have to some extent also been recognized by the men, many of whom are involved in pro-viding guidance, thereby strengthening the organization. ACAP has played the role of a catalyst throughout the entire process of initiating, structuring, and consolidating the position of women in the villages. Even if they do not benefit directly in economic returns, the majority of women take pride in the contribution they have made to their communities.

Lodge Management Committees

The lodge and tea-shop owners comprise a group directly involved in tourism that has been a priority target group since the inception of ACAP. They were trained, organized, and encouraged to form groups not only to pro-tect tourism resources but also to encourage tourism operators to be more responsible in meeting the social needs of the region. All lodge and tea-shop owners in a village are required to be general members of a Lodge Management Committee (LMC). These members elect seven to ten people to the Executive Committee for a fixed term of up to 3 years. A nominal mem-bership fee is charged annually ranging from NR 50 to 250, depending on the size and type of establishment. Lodge owners also pay a separate fee of NR 500 to VDCs through the local LMC.

Typical activities of an LMC include the organization of village and path clean-up campaigns, standardized pricing and menu presentation, handling tourist complaints, supporting cultural programs, organizing training and inter-village visits, monitoring sanitary conditions, collecting taxes and dona-tions, and calling general meetings to discuss relevant issues and settle dis-putes. The LMCs keep 25% of revenue collected for their own fund, 25% goes to the VDC fund, and the rest is utilized for local projects including trail repairs, toilet and rubbish pit constructions, and erecting sign posts for tourist information.

Institution building processes

Institution building is a long-term process involving various development stages. In the Annapurna region, local level institution building has typically comprised the following stages:

1 *Initial contact*: To establish initial contact and build rapport with local people, the ACAP staff make home visits. General meetings and special events with audio/visual programs are organized to breakdown the barrier between the project staff and local communities.

2 *Investigation and consultation*: This step includes a participatory-based rapid appraisal to assess local socio-cultural, economic, and environmental conditions. Formal and informal meetings with various interest groups (village leaders, farmers, women, herders, school teachers, lodge and teashop owners, students) are frequently organized to disseminate and share information and experiences. The ACAP staff also prepares base line data for monitoring and evaluation, paying close attention to identification of key players, existing social institutions, and other relevant matters.

3 *Building understanding*: Based on information collected through steps one and two, a public meeting (like an open house) is organized in the presence of local leaders and VDC officials. Each household is encouraged to send a representative. The ACAP uses these meetings to inform the community of the importance of CAMC, MG, and LMC, and the associated project programs and policies. Generally, these meetings last for 5–6 hours. Local issues are discussed and the formulation of a consensus is attempted. Villagers are requested to have their own meetings to resolve these issues. Decisions are then reported back to ACAP which might be in the form of agreement or disagreement on key issues. This process goes back and forth between ACAP and local community as long as it takes (it may take 2 years if the issue is a significant one, such as those related to forest boundaries).

4 *Committee formation*: When community consensus is reached, another public meeting is called. Ward officials elect their representatives for the meeting and elected officials appoint a chair, vice-chair, treasurer, secretary, and other executive members.

5 *Orientation*: Elected members receive an orientation (lasting for about a day or two) from the ACAP staff. Orientation topics may include sustainable tourism, natural resources protection, environmental management, and community development.

6 *Consolidation*: Committees are authorized to work independently as per the understanding between them and the ACAP. Support is provided to empower the committees and establish their legitimacy and authority.

7 *Monitoring*: All committee members send the minutes of their meetings to the ACAP office for review and reference. If a controversial decision has been made, ACAP holds a meeting with the committee to resolve issues.

ACAP remains in touch with the committees through frequent consultations and any project identified and requested by a committee is discussed thoroughly until a final agreement (nature and type of local contributions to an identified project) is reached.

8 *Implementation*: The committees then implement projects with funding support from ACAP and matching contributions from villages where project sites are identified.

Factors contributing to the success of local institutions

A primary factor in the success of local institutions is the remoteness of many villages. The indigenous system of protection and management of natural resources remains intact due to the lack of contacts with local government administration. With the exception of Jomsom in Mustang and Chame in Manang, there were no governmental offices in the region. Villagers therefore deal with local problems and as a result they function as self-governing communities. Therefore, when ACAP came in as a facilitator to establish rules and regulations decided by village level consensus, and not externally imposed, these rules and regulations were accepted and enforced willingly by the entire community. The inclusion of women and socially disadvantaged groups also helped to give traditional institutions a democratic face.

Technical and financial support from ACAP has also been a positive feature of the various local institutions discussed above. For example, ACAP has well-qualified experts in diverse disciplines (e.g., forestry, agriculture, civil engineering, tourism) who are able to help local communities with the identification, preparation, and implementation of community initiatives such as micro-hydro projects, alternative energy sources, and fuel-efficient technologies. To help with these activities, ACAP has established five regional headquarters in Ghandruk, Sikles, Bhujung, Manang and Jomsom, and two sub-regional headquarters in Lo-Manthang (in the Upper Mustang Region) and Lawang.

ACAP has received funds from several international non-governmental organizations to finance development and conservation efforts of local committees in the region. The funds are neither provided in a lump sum nor as gratuitous handouts. Local communities must be able to provide matching funds although not necessarily in cash, and they must be committed to identifying, planning, implementing, and sustaining the proposed project. Where cash is involved, various subsidy policies are implemented, for example, for micro-hydro schemes 70% of the total cost is given as grants if the power generated is used for lighting and cooking purposes, and if it is only used for lighting only 50% of the cost is given as grants.

Exposure visits are organized annually for committee members to tour various national parks, conservation sites, and tourism destinations. This allows the participants to learn from outside and apply the lessons at home. Training programs in forestry, silviculture techniques, drinking water management, lodge and tourism management, micro-enterprise development, and conservation education are provided so that local entrepreneurs can initiate projects on their own.

Through ACAP, local institutions also have the opportunity to network with other government and non-governmental organizations. For example, the World Wildlife Fund-USA, the Netherlands Development Organization (SNV), the Canadian International Development Agency (CIDA), the United States Agency for International Development (USAID), have supported various local level projects identified and implemented by local institutions. The KMTNC is one of the largest Non-Government Organizations (NGOs) which has supported conservation and tourism management in the Annapurna region through its involvement in the ACAP. This agency has been authorized to raise funds in the country and abroad to complement governmental efforts. These features have made the KMTNC one of the most influential, resourceful, and credible NGOs in the country.

Unresolved issues

ACAP has done a commendable job in raising local awareness about environmental conservation, sustainable tourism management, and the importance of including women, minorities, and socially disadvantaged people in the planning and decision-making processes in Nepal. However, several issues remain unresolved and are discussed briefly below.

The heterogeneous community and pronounced social and economic stratification at household levels have made local committees somewhat unrepresentative of the village's demographic and socio-economic conditions. For example, it has been suggested that the CAMCs are mainly represented by lodge owners, saw mill operators, and timber concessionaires (Thakali, 1997). Villagers view the CAMC members as elite groups, who make self-serving decisions that exploit community resources (e.g., fuelwood and timber). In the past, some CAMC members have, through secretive decisions, obtained substantial volumes of timber for their businesses, and as a result conflicts have occurred between members and non-members of the committees. The CAMCs in Lete and Kobang had to be dissolved due to such practices. Similarly, power differences between women from elite ethnic groups (e.g., Gurung) and low-caste and landless people also make institutional structures more hierarchical and coercive than pluralistic. For example, the Chair and Vice-Chair of MG in Chomrong hold enormous influences due to their social and economic status in the village. While they may be capable leaders, their priorities as privileged members of the community are vastly different from the priorities of poor families. Some MG members in Chomrong complained that a share of funds generated by the group should be redistributed among the members so that they could derive direct benefit for the extra time they spend performing dances and discussing development issues at general meetings (Nepal et al., 2002). Similarly, the MGs want to discourage men's excessive gambling and drinking habits, yet the women from poor families tend to be the ones who brew *rakshi* (home made liquor) to support their families. Thus, the issue is not only about inequality in power but is also about divergent economic strategies and livelihood priorities among members from various ethnic and economic backgrounds. Significant differences also exist between those who are directly involved in tourism and receive conservation benefits and those who are not involved in tourism and do not receive benefits. The latter groups often do not see the need to comply with rules and regulations that benefit mostly tourism entrepreneurs.

The poor representation of young people in the CAMCs also has been lamented by the elders. In Gurung and Magar communities elders are highly respected, and this discourages younger people from openly contesting cases where controversial decisions have been made. Compounding this reluctance is the fact that many youth in Annapurna have migrated elsewhere aspiring to join the army (British, Indian, or Nepalese) or live in the cities (mainly Pokhara and Kathmandu). Elders have complained that the young generation in the village neither has the interests nor the capacity to carry on with village traditions. Also there is some reluctance among the older generation to accept leadership of the younger generation.

Creating local level institutions is an important step in encouraging local people to participate in conservation and development activities. The KMTNC through ACAP has provided various levels of financial and technical support, networking opportunities, and administrative consultations for local institutions. While these supports are very critical during the initial and consolidation phases of the institutions, without long-term plans for their independence from external agencies, the sustainability of local institutions could be problematic. Even after more than a decade of experience, proven capacity, and success in generating substantial funds, local institutions in Ghandruk still depend on ACAP for planning and executing community projects. Thus, ACAP's continued support to local institutions appears to have created an unhealthy dependence.

There are also problems of coordination between the various types of local institutions outlined in this chapter. From the perspective of empowerment and control of a diverse community, the idea of creating diverse local institutions is a good one; however, this also creates conflicts between the institutions. While each institution has specific roles and responsibilities (e.g., CAMCs generate their funds from sale of permits for forest products, MGs raise funds from cultural performances, and LMCs raise revenue from fees, fines, and voluntary contributions from lodge owners), these groups often compete with one another for revenue generating activities. Because of the highly specific interests of each institution, disagreements also exist for pooling resources for the greater good of the community. While MGs are interested in supporting religious activities (like building a temple or a monastery), LMCs are interested in trail maintenance. Projects that provide benefits to the whole community (like drinking water or irrigation schemes) often get low priority due to lack of coordination between the institutions.

One of the critiques of local participation in the Annapurna region is the limited final decision-making power vested in local communities. It could be argued that local participation has been more symbolic than a true sharing of power. The ACAP project has been heralded as a 'model' for community-based conservation and tourism management, yet it could be argued that the model emanated from the minds and representations of its outside planners rather than from local communities (see chapter by Colton and Harris, Editors' Note).

Conclusions

Indigenous control and ownership of tourism are important issues in the present context of the highly politicized and globalized nature of the tourism industry. Typically, indigenous communities have been marginalized from tourism planning and decision-making processes. Governments throughout the world are generally aware that the participation of indigenous and local communities is one of the key parameters of a sustainable tourism industry. This chapter has examined how non-governmental organizations have played an important role in creating and nurturing local institutions, and in empowering local communities to plan and manage capacity to ensure tourism's sustainability.

The Annapurna Conservation Project has become a catalyst for reviving traditional resource management structures in the highly heterogeneous community of the Annapurna region. Where once informal indigenous institutions existed, formal institutions with a defined structure and specific goals and objectives, have been created. These institutions have adopted egalitarian approaches unlike the hierarchical and often coercive approaches of the past which continue to exist in other parts of the country. The grassroots institutions have specific interests and goals; however, collectively they address a diverse range of local issues in support of a balanced approach to conservation and development.

Despite the success of grassroots institutions in solving environmental, social, and economic problems, there are several problems which need to be addressed to make these institutions more effective. Imbalanced power relations between the village elite and poorer segments of the community, a widening gap created by tourism between richer and poorer households, dependency on external agencies, and weak coordination between various grassroots institutions are some of these problems, the resolution of which may require a fundamental transformation of village level politico-economy.

A more recent problem has been the political turmoil in the country, which has affected the Annapurna region too. The rise in Mao insurgency in the region, and the recent bombing of ACAP headquarters in Ghandruk have seriously undermined the capacity of local level institutions in all aspects of conservation and tourism management. Given the current cease fire in armed conflict between the Nepalese army and Mao insurgents, and the willingness of the insurgency leaders to break away from the current cycle of violence and compete for power through democratic elections, it is likely that a more radical transformation in village politics, power, and institutional developments will occur. Thus, the growth, development, and consolidation of new and extant institutional structures under a new governance system, and their effects on conservation and tourism management in the Annapurna region would be interesting aspects of a future research agenda.

Part Six

Indigenous Tourism: Policies and Politics

In this final section attention is focused again on control, this time through not only the political system but also by those agencies promoting tourism and establishing policies in this connection. This last grouping of chapters explores some of the macro issues related to power and empowerment, land ownership and claims and relations with governments at various levels. The first chapter, by O'Gorman, McLellan and Baum examines tourism in a country which at the present time, is rarely thought of as a tourist destination, Iran. They show that, perhaps contrary to current perceptions, Iran has a long history and tradition of accommodating visitors and travellers, as well as having a great number of minority cultures within its borders, reflecting its geographic location astride some of the major trade routes in the Middle East. Despite what could be seen as great advantages in the competition for tourism, the present powers in Iran have downplayed the potential role of indigenous groups in tourism, just as they have downplayed the role that tourism could have in the country at large. By exercising strong central and religious power and control and putting forward a strong national image, Iran has discouraged tourism development among its indigenous communities. The dominant centralised power structure of the country is in sharp contrast to that in Nepal for example, described in the previous section, and community-based tourism is hard to find, although there are examples of good individual operations, normally at a small scale. Iran symbolises, perhaps, the dominance of a central uniform control over tourism compared to a local indigenous variety of developments. Sofield and Li, in examining indigenous tourism in China, illustrate a different approach to the subject by another government which practices strong central control. They present a rebuttal to the argument that indigenous tourism is a form of neo-colonialism, and argue that development of tourism in indigenous communities in rural China is in line with central government policy of developing rural areas to raise living standards and improve their economic situation. There is no doubt that central control through such development policies is maintained, and they note the change in perception of the role and significance of tourism in China now, compared to the period when Chairman Mao was in control and visitors who were non-Communists were not welcomed because of potential negative influences on the population. Tourism is now seen as an appropriate form of development and indigenous communities should benefit and contribute to its expansion. The third chapter in this section, by Hollinshead, returns to the themes which he developed in the earlier volume relating to the way in which indigenous groups are portrayed and promoted, using Australia as an example. He covers the complex topics of disidentification and authenticity and the way that tourism can both empower and weaken indigenous communities. He notes the relative absence of strong Aboriginal voices in tourism promotion and development in contrast to the situation in the arts and other areas of culture, where Aboriginal groups have become empowered through their own representations, and argues for the need for the same process to occur in tourism. His chapter provides a detailed discussion of the changes which have occurred in these areas over the past decade and their conceptual implications for indigenous tourism. In the final chapter of this section, Hall discusses the relationships between politics, power and tourism, and illustrates his arguments with examples from Canada and Australia in particular. He begins by presenting the concept of power and different aspects of the decision-making process. He notes the way in which indigenous groups have had to rely on judicial decisions to begin to become empowered, and the implications of such developments for tourism. Hall presents a critique of the political dimension of indigenous tourism, and the fact, that as Hollinshead argues, the way in which indigenous groups are represented and presented is an important aspect of power and control. He concludes with a discussion of the fundamental challenges, and argues that there is a clear opportunity found in indigenous tourism to support the empowerment of indigenous groups and allow the indigenous voices to be heard.

CHAPTER 18

Tourism in Iran: central control and indigeneity

Kevin O'Gorman, L.R. McLellan and Tom Baum

Tourism in Iran: the context

Contemporary Iran is a country shrouded in political, religious, cultural, social and economic controversy. It is a country that courts extreme emotional and ideological debate and faces challenges as a tourism destination both because of this controversial context and as a result of its association with conflicts in neighbouring countries like Afghanistan and Iraq.

Consideration of the indigeneity of tourism in Iran is complicated by its position at a cultural crossroads, the time-span over which invasions and migrations have taken place and the present day situation where a large population of recent refugees exist from wars and political unrest in neighbouring countries. Iran has enormous cultural diversity on the one hand and a homogeneous religious authority on the other but it is the latter that currently dominates. Add to this a government which protects and promotes its own brand of Islamic indigenous culture and heritage with a fierce pride and an international image epitomised by US President Bush's reference to the 'axis-of-evil' and you have a situation where indigenous tourism in the normal sense of the phrase is suppressed.

Even when used in a conventional sense, the term indigenous tourism is much contested but certain key concerns and debates emerge from the literature (Butler and Hinch, 1996; Notzke, 2004). These include: multifaceted host, guest and intermediary relationships; lack of industry knowledge and incorporation of local cultures; lack of local awareness of tourism and ownership of tourism related businesses; and a need for carefully considered policies to avoid degradation of culture and ensure development is sustainable.

Many of these concerns are relevant in Iran to some extent although it is argued in this chapter that indigenous tourism has been suppressed in Iran. Nevertheless, there are indications that a unique form of local tourism infused with indigenous character has begun to emerge. This local variation of indigenous tourism is taking shape despite the striking homogeneous national image portrayed in the international mass media. The early stage in the tourism development life cycle means that tourism is generally considered as a national phenomenon, at a national scale rather than local. Growing links between tourism and the protection of Iran's national cultural heritage were reinforced in 2005 with the merger of Iran Touring and Tourism Organisation (ITTO) and Iran Cultural Heritage Organisation (ICHO) to form the Iran Cultural Heritage and Tourism Organisation (ICHTO). Although the strong influence of the central government is clear with direct authority for the new organisation resting with the Vice President of the Islamic Republic of Iran (WTO, 2006), the link between cultural heritage and tourism allows vestiges of indigenous tourism to survive but not flourish.

Historic development of the tourism industry

Iran is a country that is rich in diversity in cultural and historic terms, representing a recorded human history that stretches back some 10,000 years. The people who inhabit this country have a long history of involvement in tourism. There is considerable evidence for hostels that dates back to at least 2000 BC. These hostels supplied drinks, sex and accommodation for travellers. Drinks included date palm wine and barley beer, and there were strict regulations against diluting them. Driver and Miles (1952) in the translation of the law code of time (the Laws of Hammurabi) show that the punishment for watering beer was death by drowning, and other interesting laws include one under which any woman who had retired from the priesthood and was caught entering an inn, was to be burned alive. The assumption being that she was going there for sex. There was also a requirement that a tavern keeper, on pain of death, had to report all customers who were felons. Oppenheim (1967) observes that at least some of the roadside government hostels in Mesopotamia welcomed casual non-official travellers, whilst Jacobsen (1970) notes that travellers would be accommodated in the local hostels. Amongst many hardships facing travellers, there was also the danger of being robbed or worse, as one contemporary writer noted 'Men sit in the bushes until the benighted traveller comes in order to plunder his load' (Gardiner, 1961, p. 109). This danger was so widespread that Hammurabi's law code excused a trader from repaying a loan if his goods had been stolen. Local authorities were also required to compensate any victim of highway robbery in their territories.

The application of strict Islamic law and a consequent political ambivalence to international tourism is not universal in predominantly Muslim countries. Indeed, Din (1989) focuses on aspects of Islamic hospitality that stress the obligation to guests and strangers that are at the heart of the religion's teachings. Hospitality is frequently mentioned in Islamic traditions known as *hadīths*, one such tradition notes that if the guest stays longer than the '3 days' it becomes charity, and it is forbidden for a guest to stay when he becomes a burden to his host (ibn Anas, 1999). Establishing hostels for travellers is often reflected among the traditions and cited in writings. For example, the historian al-Tabarī (c 830 AD) records the governor of Samarqand (now called Samarkand, Uzbekistan) in 719 AD was ordered to:

establish inns in your lands so that whenever a Muslim passes by, you will put him up for a day, and a night and take care of his animals; if he is sick, provide him with hospitality for 2 days and 2 nights; and if he has used up all of his provisions and is unable to continue, supply him with whatever he needs to reach his hometown.

(al-Tabarī, 838/1989, p. 94)

Samarqand was located along the Great Silk Road, one of the most important trading routes in the region, and no doubt had a regular supply of traders and travellers. There is further evidence from the seventh and eighth centuries, as another writer ibn Abd al-Hakam (1040/1922) who died in 860 AD makes mention of guest houses built by the governor of Egypt, al-Muqaddasī (946/1877) and gives anecdotal evidence from 710 AD that the ruler of Damascus was roundly criticised for funding the construction of a Mosque rather than maintaining the roads and building inns for travellers. In the ninth and tenth centuries there was a well established record of hospitable works for travellers in Bukhara, Uzbekistan (al-Narshakhī, 959/1954) and in the eleventh century a governor in Western Iran had 'built in his territories three thousand Mosques and inns for travellers' (ibn Abd al-Hakam, 1014/1922, p. 133).

Henderson (2003) notes that academic interest in the relationship between Islam and tourism has been relatively limited but that this is an emerging field of study. Unlike the seminal works of Ritter (1975), Din (1989) and Kessler (1992) which all review tourism and leisure within a broad framework of Islam, Henderson's study is a contextualisation of Islam within a single country case study and, in this, has similarities to the earlier contributions of Ap et al. (1991), Baum and Conlin (1997) and Sharpley (2002). This country case study of tourism, while not solely located within a discussion of links between this economic activity and religion at regional or local scale, draws strongly on the Islamic context which dominates all facets of life in contemporary Iran. It is an unavoidable relationship which impacts on all aspects of tourism in the country – operations, marketing, management and, ultimately, economic viability.

Today, Iran's heritage draws both on indigenous histories and cultures as well as the impact of waves of invaders, notably the Greeks of Alexander the Great, the Arabs who introduced Islam to the country, the Mongols from the east and in the twentieth century, the influence of the oil hungry west (Britain, France and the US). Iran's tangible cultural assets include seven ancient locations recognised by United Nations Educational, Scientific and Cultural Organization (UNESCO) as World Heritage Sites as well as a range of renowned Islamic shrines and cultural sites. Iran's natural heritage is also diverse, including desert, mountains and coasts across climatic zones from temperate to sub-tropical.

What has generated particular interest in Iran as a host country for domestic and international tourism is the effect of religious interpretation by the country's brand of contemporary Islam on the political, religious, cultural, social and economic environment and the everyday lives of citizens and visitors alike. Iran adheres to strict standards of observance and the application of stringent penalties for non-compliance with respect to social and cultural behaviour impacting upon personal association, dress and the consumption of alcohol and other recreational drugs. Undoubtedly, these rules impact upon Iran's image, market potential as a destination for international tourism and the role of indigenous people in tourism.

Iran's tourism, geography, product and performance

We have already indicated that Iran has an abundant wealth of natural and cultural assets, most of which are largely under exploited from a tourism perspective. Major landscape features include the Alborz, Zagros and Sabalan mountain ranges, the Dasht-e-Kavir and Dasht-e-Lut deserts, the Caspian Sea and Persian Gulf coasts and the valleys and plateaus of Western Iran. The potential to develop tourism products for international markets (diving, winter sports, hiking) exists in terms of resources but is inhibited by cultural and political barriers as well as a lack of investment in facilities and transport infrastructure. Indigenous communities have little awareness of tourism and little control over much potential development or access to tourism markets.

Iran is located at an intersection between major Asian, Middle Eastern and European cultures. The country bears witness to the manner in which its culture and heritage have been influenced by many of these and, in turn, has influenced their own development. In the contemporary world, this crossroads location creates real challenges as the country adjoins highly sensitive political and religious neighbours, including Iraq, Afghanistan, Pakistan, Armenia and Turkey. As a result, there is evident reluctance on the part of international markets to visit Iran to experience the unique cultural and heritage opportunities that the country has to offer.

Cultural assets range from the era of the great Persian empires, extending back some 10,000 years. Particularly notable is the renowned site of Darius' Persepolis and a wealth of complementary sites within a small radius of this attraction. While the major heritage and cultural attractions are efficiently managed by the ICHTO there is a wealth of archaeological resources in the area, many of which are unexplored and unrecorded. Visitors can, therefore, wander unfettered over large areas of the countryside and experience 'living archaeology' in an unmanaged environment. Iran is also home to the Zoroastrian religion and sites in Cham Chak, Isfahan and Yazd provide unique insights into this ancient but living religion. The Arab invasions of Iran some 1,400 years ago brought Islam to the country and there is a wealth of sites of historic and religious significance throughout the country, representing the influence of both internal ruling dynasties and external invasion.

Iran's turbulent trading history is represented in a number of important trading routes that criss-cross the country. These routes leave a legacy of sites and historic and contemporary cultural experiences that link Iran to countries to both the east and west. The Silk Road is, perhaps, the best known of these routes, running from Xian in northern China through Iran to Istanbul. Others include the Spice Caravan Route, the Great Northern Caravan Route, the Ancient Royal Road and the maritime trading routes through the Persian Gulf and the Oman Sea. Complementing these international routes is a series of domestic caravan routes across the country.

Religious and pilgrimage tourism is very important to Iran. Zoroastrian religious sites attract international visitors to the country, from India and elsewhere. The highest profile form of pilgrimage tourism in Islam is the Haj to Saudi Arabia but far more important in this context is domestic and regional pilgrimage tourism to holy shrines and sites in cities such as Qom and Mashhad. Iran receives a large pilgrimage market based on these Shiite shrines, as well as pilgrims travelling through Iran on their way to and from Mecca in Saudi Arabia and Karbala in Iraq. This major component of Iranian domestic and regional tourism is highly resistant to conflict, as evidenced by continuing visitation to Karbala at the height of the civil strife in that region. No formal quantification of the total extent of this form of tourism was found.

The only contemporary large-scale tourism development in Iran is Kish Island, which is secular in its focus. Kish is located in the Persian Gulf and was developed as a destination for leisure and retail travellers, aiming to compete in the domestic and international marketplace with Dubai and similar destinations. The development as a resort had little to do with the indigenous people or culture having been initiated by the last Shah in the 1970s as a playground for the rich international market and his privileged guests. Tourism in Kish went into decline after the revolution.

Political–economic constraints

The economic and business structure of Iran is likewise complex and, at times, contradictory. As such, it constrains tourism in general and indigenous tourism in particular. About 80% of the country's exports are generated through oil and gas revenues and this has a major distorting impact on attempts to develop other sectors in the economy, including tourism. At present, a one dollar rise in the price of crude oil is worth more to the national exchequer than the sum total of international tourism receipts. As a result, sectors such as agriculture, tourism and manufacturing that operate outside the oil economy are inefficient, internationally uncompetitive and neglected in political and organisational terms. A lack of strategic economic planning, reflecting extended conflict during the 1980s with Iraq and subsequent and on-going threats to national security, perceived and real, has severely hampered the development of the economy.

The economy consists of four distinct elements. Key strategic industries such as oil and gas are state monopolies although foreign joint venture elements are also present in this sector. Similarly, banking and finance are nationally owned and operated. The second economic group consists of quasi-state organisations, frequently in the form of conglomerates operating as trusts under the auspices of religious or welfare agencies. The largest of these is Bonyad, which has interests across the economy from oil and gas to manufacturing. Bonyad also operates the largest group of hotels in the country (Parsian) as well as a major travel and tour operating company. Business organisations, including a civil airline (Iran Air, owned by the state), run by branches of the military also fall within this category. State and quasi-state organisations do not operate under commercial criteria like profitability and are subject to poor and inconsistent management and high levels of political interference.

The third sector of the economy is an extensive private sector, predominantly consisting of small and micro-businesses across the manufacturing and service economy mostly owned by native Iranians. The private sector is particular visible in retail, travel and hospitality and includes a range of innovative and efficiently operated concerns. An example of this would be Caravanserai Zeineldin, which is owned by the ICHTO, and, until recently, was neglected and derelict. Four years ago it was secured on a 12-year lease by three brothers with an agreement to renovate the site as a hotel designed in a style sympathetic to its original caravanserai origins (see Figures 18.1 and 18.2). Three

Figure 18.1
Caravanserai 'Zeineldin': exterior view

Figure 18.2
Caravanserai
'Zeineldin': interior
view

brothers contributed respectively finance, design skills and links into the European travel trade, particularly in Spain, where one of them operates a major travel business. They now employ a professional Iranian hotelier to manage the project and operate the caravanserai. It attracts international visitors, mainly from Spain but also elsewhere in Europe, as well as domestic tourists. Meals are also provided for passing international tour groups. There are also some larger private businesses such as the airline Mahan but they are very much the minority. The final sector of the Iran economy consists of subsistence agricultural concerns across the country.

A key characteristic of Iranian commerce is the almost total absence of foreign investment and management, although changes to the law in recent years could alter this situation. Iran is not a signatory to General Agreement on Tariffs and Trade (GATT) or a member of the World Trade Organization with the result that international patent, trademark and copyright law are not enforced and participation in today's global economy beyond the oil and gas sector is limited. In tourism, the only international investment is in the case of a small number of businesses, generally hotels, that are part or wholly-owned by expatriate Iranian investors and operate independently without international brand affiliation. This absence of international investment in tourism, is a reflection of a number of factors: (1) the generally precarious state of tourism in the country as a result of on-going political and regional security issues; (2) the religio-ideological opposition to collaboration with major international ownership, franchise, management or alliance ventures in the tourism sector, in part because these frequently have substantial American involvement; and (3) the parochial perception of politicians and others that, in a 'simple' sector such as tourism, Iran does not require the engagement with the global economy. As a result, attempts to engage collaboration of major, non-American partners (Canadian, French) in the hotel sector have floundered on political rocks in recent years.

Plans to involve regional foreign capital in the refurbishment of Tehran's flagship political and convention hotel, the Esteglal, were vetoed at the national government level because, firstly, the hotel would have been externally managed and, secondly, a perception that the work could be undertaken with local expertise. As a result, the project remains uncompleted, is of mediocre standard and has cost far more than it would have with foreign engagement. In the transport sector, Iran Air operates apart from any of the main airline alliances and does not offer its passengers the benefits of interlining or through ticketing in a manner that is cost effective to Iran's main tourist market, that of expatriate visiting friends and relatives (VFR) travellers from the US. Therefore, this lucrative business is siphoned effectively through Amsterdam, Frankfurt, London, Milan and Paris by major European airlines who are able to offer through prices to the US that compare with those of Iran Air to its European destinations.

Thus, it is evident that this focus on the creation of a wholly independent national tourism sector has significant operational and marketing consequences for tourism in Iran. While many of these consequences can be viewed as negative, the lack of foreign investment does provide an opportunity for local, small-scale indigenous tourism. Ownership isolationism, in small peripheral tourism locations, can have benefits to a tourism economy (Baum, 1996, 1999). Yet, this opportunity for indigenous tourism tends to be overshadowed by other barriers. Fundamentally, tourism in Iran operates as it does today because either core markets have no option but to avail themselves of its products and services (business, government, VFR) or the pull of key historic and cultural attractions is such that visitors are willing to compromise on aspects of quality and, in the case of transport, safety, in order to access these sites.

Marketing of tourism in Iran at national and regional/provincial level is primarily product oriented with little input from, or recognition of Iran's indigenous people as an attraction or assets for tourism. Tourism orthodoxy in terms of the dominant religion impacts on availability of crafts and cultural artefacts and tends to marginalise those indigenous groups that do not conform to the mainstream.

Tourism performance

The performance of indigenous tourism is often judged in relation to that of mainstream tourism but the lack of data on indigenous tourism in Iran makes direct comparisons impossible. Nevertheless, the performance struggles of mainstream tourism suggest a similar situation for indigenous tourism. In 1999, it was estimated that Iran's international and domestic transportation system and related tourist facilities and services handled the requirements of 1.3 million international visitors and 32.5 million domestic tourists and international tourism generated receipts of US$ 773 million (ITTO, 2002). By 2004, the numbers of inbound international visitors had grown to over 1.6 million as indicated in Figure 18.3 (UNWTO, 2006). The trend points to significant growth in international visitors up to 1999 but it must be remembered that the early part of this decade was dominated by the aftermath of war between Iran and Iraq. Indeed, from a longer-term perspective the number of international tourists fell from 680,000 in 1978 to 9,300 in 1990 (ITTO, 2002). Overall, Iran's international tourist market is primarily regional, mainly by land from neighbouring countries, accounting for around 80% of arrivals. Much of this traffic generates relatively low gross yields in per capita expenditure terms.

Iran's international tourist market comprises a number of distinct segments. The most important is the business sector, representing about 30% of total travellers. Iran caters for relatively small meetings, incentives, convention and events segment and a small summer and winter vacation market from the Middle East, representing 4% of total visitors. The pilgrimage market based on its Shiite shrines, as well as pilgrims transiting through Iran overland to and from Mecca in Saudi Arabia and Karbala in Iraq accounts for about 30% of total visitation. VFR travellers are also a relatively large segment with the combination of both regional and long-haul travellers representing about 26% of the total. Finally, Iran receives a relatively small sightseeing segment, mainly from long-haul originating countries, accounting for about 10%

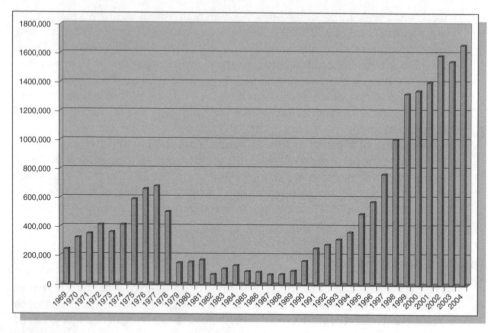

Figure 18.3
Inbound tourism of Iran (*Source*: UNWTO Compendium of Tourism Statistics, 2006)

of the total market. There is great potential demand here in particular for cultural and indigenous attractions. This visitor market is currently small but is growing and tends to be resilient to lack of facilities and local inconveniences. Iran's additional travel restrictions, poor travel infrastructure and image may be holding back this potential demand.

There is a lack of data on the characteristics and volume of domestic tourism (Alipour and Heydari, 2004). Most domestic tourism is generated in the urban areas such as Teheran, travels in family groups and visits the coastal regions, Caspian or Gulf (Kish Island), and the cultural or pilgrimage heritage cities such as Mashhad, Esfahan, Shiraz and Kerman with the main purpose being vacation (39%), VFR (21%) and visiting a shrine (30%) (Alipour and Heydari, 2004).

Issues and problems in Iranian tourism

Economically and politically, tourism is always likely to be a minor industry relative to the oil and other sectors with the result that politicians have little interest in it. This lack of interest is even greater in relation to niches such as indigenous tourism. A counter argument to this reality, which does not receive widespread attention in Iran, is the employment creation potential of tourism. Oil and gas, notwithstanding their value to the country, generate relatively few benefits in employment terms. At the same time, the country's major social and economic challenge is unemployment and under-employment among the youth. The under 25s constitute 75% of the total population and in some urban areas up to 50% of these young people do not have gainful employment. Tourism, despite its labour intense characteristics and geographical dispersion, is overlooked as a sector that can provide opportunity to this group.

Tourism in Iran is characterised by huge opportunity in terms of natural and cultural assets. At the same time, such opportunity is countered by what can be described as political ambivalence at best and antipathy at worst. Encouraging tourism in Iran is a highly contested issue between two main factions in the government, one that views tourism as means to achieve economic benefits and modernise, the other that sees tourism as leading to globalisation and thus threatening Islamic values and norms. The current political orthodoxy is highly suspicious of foreign, non-faith influences and this situation acts contrary to interests seeking to develop tourism as a respectable and respected sector of the economy, particularly in rural and remote areas where indigenous tourism is likely to emerge. Rather than protect and support locally based tourism, the prevailing national ideology stifles local businesses from benefiting from cultural assets. The current environment is not, however, as overtly hostile to tourism as that which existed in the immediate post-revolutionary era. During the period of the Khomeini led government, the state destroyed some historical monuments in the manner of the Taliban in Afghanistan but, more recently, a degree of restraint has prevailed. However, the image of Iran in the international tourist market is almost unique in terms of negative media attention over a sustained period. Only Libya and perhaps Cuba have suffered similar long periods of extremely negative western media coverage. As an outcome, the core perception of Iran in the eyes of the world and in particular, in the eyes of potential tourists from North America and Europe has been of a troubled, strife torn country that should be avoided.

The Government in Iran does not help counter this image as tourism still tends to be subjugated to the 'big project' of promoting a religious – political agenda. For example, the August 2004 public execution of a 16-year old girl in the main street of a Caspian seaside resort, during the height of the tourist season received widespread national and international press coverage and blighted local tourism. Throughout the 1990s negative international media exposure was tempered by the hope that tourism development would be encouraged as part of an attempt to create an image of greater openness under President Khatami. But a constant barrage of damaging news items in the western media reinforced the old negative image. After encouraging foreign tourists to watch the solar eclipse in Iran in 1999, a relatively isolated incident led to the usual western headlines: 'Tourists kidnapped in Iran'. 'Three Spaniards and one Italian were abducted by an armed gang' (BBC, 1999a) and 'Official inquiry into Iran eclipse harassment' as a result of foreign tourists visiting to view the eclipse, particularly women, being subjected to hostile slogans and harassment by Islamic hardliners (BBC, 1999b). The George Bush 'axis-of-evil' speech in 2002 led to a BBC feature on 'my holidays in the axis-of-evil' (BBC, 2003) where a journalist ventured into the six countries mentioned, with the intent of showing the non-threatening character of day-to-day life in these areas. While this seemed to be the case in five of the countries (Iraq, North Korea, Cuba, Syria and Libya), in Iran the journalist was 'detained and intimidated' as the cameras, tapes and tourist visa were viewed as the instruments of spies. This type of behaviour towards visitors by Iranian authorities undermines the work done by official tourism organisations like ITTO and ICHTO. The latest example of this indifference to or ineptness in public relations is the announcement by President Ahmadinejad in October 2006 that all nuclear facilities were to be opened to foreign tourists to prove the nation's disputed atomic programme is peaceful (BBC, 2006a; Sunday Times, 2006).

The lack of foreign investment in tourism can also be seen as a major mainstream tourism challenge, especially in the hotel sector, in that both product and service are woefully inadequate for the contemporary international leisure and business market. Service standards in the major state and quasi-state hospitality businesses are among the poorest in the world, contrasting with the warmth and natural hospitality of service in small, private, indigenous businesses throughout the country. Part of the problem lies in the widespread system of political and religious patronage and favour that operates in the allocation of senior government and quasi-government positions. This means that the leadership of public sector tourism, both in promotional and operational roles, is rarely professional or long term. Alongside this managerial failing, is the absence of effective and co-ordinated human resource development in support of the tourism sector, both in terms of pre-entry training and in relation to the in-service, life-long development of existing tourism employees.

There are also major infrastructure issues with respect to accommodation and, in particular with respect to transport. The country suffers badly from the US embargo in the area of air transport, what might be described as the 'Tupolov blight' (BBC, 2006b). In organisational and facilitation terms, there is a lack of credit card facilities necessary for modern tourism, also as a result of the embargo, and poor or out-of-date systems are generally in place. Such transportation problems constrain tourism development in the periphery where indigenous attractions are concentrated.

In marketing terms, international tourism to Iran is severely challenged by problems with respect to national image, relating to regional political concerns and also national social and cultural matters, notably the hijab requirement for women and the ban on alcohol. For example, there is evidence that some Chinese tour operators are unwilling to promote Iran because of the hijab requirement. Wider concerns about human rights issues are also a barrier to visitation and are further complicated by the challenges facing minority indigenous groups in Iran.

Contested indigeneity

At the core of Iran's representation in the world, in terms of mass media and the minds of potential visitors, is the tension between its national Islamic identity and the myriad of local cultural characteristics. The power and uniqueness of the imagery and centralised control have combined to suppress regional identities and create homogeneous national icons, at least in the eyes of the inexperienced. Somewhat ironically, it can even be argued that the national has become the indigenous at least from the perspective of the international market.

The Islamic Republic of Iran was declared after the revolution of 1979 overthrew the regime of the last Shah. The previously secular, westward looking economy and society, with strong business and military ties to the US, was replaced by a virulently anti-American regime; a theocracy seeking national unity under the umbrella of common religious values. In reality, Iran is by no means a homogeneous society. Contrary to popular belief, it is not mono-cultural, mono-linguistic or mono-faith.

The country is diverse in its peoples, cultures, languages and, to some extent, its religious groupings. The country recognises seven minority communities and tribes and five languages. These are predominately located close to national boundaries and include Arabs, Kurds, Turkmens, Azaris and other groups. In terms of religions, the Iranian constitution recognises the political and worshipping rights of Zoroastrians, Jews, Armenian Christians and Sunni Muslims within a majority Shia Muslim population. This diversity provides richness to the cultural tableaux of the country and has significant, if under exploited, potential in terms of indigenous tourism.

The living culture is seen especially in the towns, villages and rural areas where the indigenous people and the art, crafts, costumes, cuisine, music and traditions of diverse ethnic communities remain unadulterated by tourism development. However, the same factors that preserve their culture mean they are remote and inaccessible to all but the hardiest independent traveller. Basic information, transportation and tourism facilities are absent. The root cause seems to lie in the unenthusiastic government attitude to tourism where urban-based tourism is allowed but more remote, conservative (Islamic) areas are screened from 'infection' by western, modern visitors.

Another factor is the centralised control of tourism that discourages, or at least does not actively encourage, local initiatives. It is noted by Alipour and Heydari (2004) that Iran's tourism development is far from locally initiated and developed. The controlling influence remains predominantly at the centre and apart from pilgrimages, the bulk of tourism activities are confined to Teheran and a few traditional tourist magnets such as Esfahan and Shiraz. Some progress is evident in planning tourism developments such as at Kish Island or in historic cities like Qazvin where a rich cultural and built heritage is being restored for potential tourism in the future. However, even here there is evidence of tension in developing indigenous tourism with top down direction from central ministries overriding local needs, and local suspicion of visitors who do not conform to their brand of conservative religious norms. Minor exceptions include itineraries where tourists stay with nomadic tribes such as the 'Nomads of Iran' tour (http://www.irantrip.com/iran-travel-itineraries/Iran-nomads-Tour.htm). There are estimated to be around 1.2 million nomadic pastoralists in Iran organised in over 500 tribes but there has been little development of the associated indigenous tourism product potential. There is currently insufficient demand and the management, organisation and distribution of tours are centralised through government agencies.

Conclusion

Despite the constraints to indigenous tourism in Iran that have been outlined in this chapter, a range of indigenous projects driven by private sector investment in the form of hotels, caravanserai, restaurants and craft projects have begun to emerge. The majority of these are small-scale local enterprises that are poorly promoted at a national level. Iran is a country with considerable raw potential for indigenous tourism development. However, the political will to address this opportunity is currently absent and this reality will continue to impair the development of the tourism sector in general and the indigenous sub-sector in particular in the foreseeable future.

Thus Iran falls into the category of protecting and promoting 'whole country', national indigenous culture with a fundamentalist Islamic fervour. This strategy is followed at the expense of the diverse range of regional and local communities and their potential for development through locally based indigenous tourism. Nevertheless, the central tourism authorities in Iran (ICHTO) are happy to appropriate the imagery of indigenous cultures for brochures and touring packages, all largely with strict direction from the core. From a market perspective, over 25 years of demonisation in the international media has ensured that Iran has an exotic, 'other' quality that accentuates a homogeneous image of the culture. The combination of central control and lack of demand means there has been little motivation for local communities to exploit or develop tourism in the periphery. In the event of growing interest and visitor numbers seeking authentic indigenous cultural products, the deep routed enterprising bazaar culture, where market exchange has been refined over centuries, would provide a strong base for indigenous offerings. Lack of experience with and awareness of tourism's potential to benefit their communities means that many issues arising in relation to indigenous tourism elsewhere in the world have yet to emerge in Iran.

Indigenous minorities of China and effects of tourism

Trevor Sofield and F.M. Sarah Li

Introduction

'The People's Republic of China [PRC] is a united multi-ethnic state founded jointly by the people of all its ethnic groups. There are 56 ethnic groups identified and confirmed by the Central Government, and as the majority of the population belongs to the Han ethnic group, China's other 55 ethnic groups are customarily referred to as the national minorities [*Shaoshu Minzu*]'. So begins the Chinese Government's White Paper on *Regional Autonomy for Ethnic Minorities in China* which was issued by the Information Office of the State Council on February 28, 2005 (p. 1). As such, it is the most recent in a long series of Government policies on its ethnic minorities and updates the previous White Paper issued in September 1999 titled *'National Minorities Policy and its Practice in China.'* According to the fifth national census, conducted in 2000, the population of all the 55 ethnic minority groups totaled 104.49 million, accounting for 8.41% of the total population of China. The magnitude of China's ethnic minorities situation is far greater than that of any other country: indeed, the total population of its minorities exceeds the individual populations of 208 of the world's 218 countries. They occupy almost 70% of the land mass of China, with many of the minorities inhabiting sensitive territories along China's external boundaries (Xinjiang with Kazakhstan, Kyrgyzstan, Tajikistan and Russia; Tibet with India; Yunnan with Myanmar; Guangxi with Vietnam), so the minorities enjoy a strategic importance well beyond their numbers (Mackerras et al., 1994). Policy formulation towards the minorities is therefore bound up in foreign affairs, defense and national security, as well as economic development, education, health and social welfare. In this chapter, only policy concerning the cultural heritage of the minorities and its concomitant relationship to tourism are considered in detail.

In the past 15 years in the context of tourism being promoted as one of four 'pillar industries' for 'modernization construction' of the national economy, (Zhang and Lew, 2003) China has embarked on a vigorous approach to utilize ethnic cultures as a valuable touristic resource and where some minorities were previously marginalized, many have now been drawn into the forefront of development efforts. When we consider the issue of ethnic tourism in China involving its minorities there is not unexpectedly a wide range of views. At one end of the spectrum some observers allege cultural genocide (e.g., Free Tibet Movement), others suggest there is systemic exploitation and suppression, yet others allege various forms of colonialism (e.g., Oakes, 1993, 1999; Goodman, 2004); and at the other end of the spectrum there are those who laud China's 'enlightened polices' and success in promoting minorities' welfare (IOSC, 2005). Some observers suggest there is forced assimilation (Becquelin, 2004), others suggest there is cooperative integration, and one recent study described as 'path-breaking' provides evidence of the rise of a middle class among China's ethnic minorities (Mackerras, 2006). Our own views are based on more than 20 field trips to China over a 12-year period between 1994 and 2006, including visits to conduct specific research studies among the 25 minorities of Yunnan Province (including the Naxi of Lijiang in northern Yunnan, the Dai of

Xishuangbanna, the Tibetans of Deqin), the Kazakh and Tuwa (Mongolian) minorities of Xinjiang (2005), the Tibetans of the Autonomous Region of Tibet (2002, 2006); the Zhang and Tibetans of Jiuzhaigou in Aba Autonomous Prefecture of Sichuan Province, and the Bai In Hunan.

Before exploring the varying interpretations placed upon the effects of tourism on China's *Shaoshu Minzu,* the chapter begins with a brief overview of China as a multi-ethnic state extending over 2000 years. It then outlines the current policy environment towards ethnic minorities before focusing more narrowly on tourism-specific issues. Several of the orthodox models of analysis are challenged including the labeling of autonomous ethnic regions as examples of internal colonialism, and the alleged waning of place/people/cultures in the face of increasing contact, hybridity and multivocality (Bhaba, 1994; Gupta and Ferguson, 1992, 1997).

Historical continuity over 2000 years

In 221 BC, the Emperor Qin Shi Huang unified the seven Warring States and established the first centralized entity. The subsequent Han Dynasty (206 BC to 220 AD) further consolidated the country's unification. Administrative areas known as *jun* (prefecture) and *xian* (county) were established across the country, and uniform systems of law, language, calendar, carriage, currency, and weights and measures were adopted. These developments laid the foundations for the political, economic and cultural framework of China as a unified multi-ethnic state over the next 2000 years. Over the centuries since, its borders have expanded and decreased (e.g., from the third century BC until the tenth century AD, northern Vietnam was part of China; Tibet was first incorporated into China in the eighth century) but in essence for 2200 years the central government has been following a continuous policy of integration of its many regions and ethnicities to maintain national unity. Throughout these millennia there were two periods of rule by minorities, the Mongols who overthrew the Han Emperor Jin and ruled from AD 1279–1368 (the Yuan dynasty), and then the Manchus, who established the Qing dynasty in 1644 and ruled until 1911 when Dr Sun Yat Sen heralded in the Republic of China. What is important about these two dynasties is that they were – and are – regarded as Chinese first and foremost: they were not foreign oppressors. They considered themselves as 'orthodox reigns' of China and pursued the same objective of maintaining a united multi-ethnic state (IOSC, 2005). In other words China was not colonised by the Mongols or by the Manchu. In the Chinese perspective of its continuous civilization, they were simply different Chinese factions able to exercise their power and authority at certain historical periods. This emic (insider) perspective is important when one considers the application of different constructs to analyze the processes at work in China with reference to its ethnic minorities, and it is our suggestion that at times insufficient weight has been accorded to Chinese understandings of their own histories.

This is not to say that there were not outbreaks of hostilities, war and strife between various ethnicities themselves and between the ruling dynasties and their subjects. But the long-standing existence of a united, multi-ethnic state in Chinese history has contributed to political, economic and cultural exchanges among different ethnic groups and promoted allegiance to the concept of one China. The very length of time over which this process has taken place has led to its acceptance by many, some elements of Tibetan and Uyghur society being significant exceptions in recent decades. It is a process which predates western notions of imperialism and colonialism by many centuries and this in our view makes it somewhat problematic to unquestioningly apply western concepts such as 'internal colonialism' to contemporary situations concerning China's ethnic minorities. This statement is not designed to foreground 'the true nature' of China's dealings with its ethnic minorities as being valid only when derived from Chinese interpretations but neither it is to argue in a reductive way that European notions are really what the analysis of ethnic minorities are about. Rather, the statement highlights that there are alternative histories, in the spirit of James Cahill's (1988) innovative approach to the interpretation of Chinese art (*Three Alternative Histories of Chinese Painting*). Cahill suggests that China's 'art history can validly be written in a diversity of ways or modes, depending upon which aspects of art and its circumstances we choose as the focus of concentration' (1988, p. 9). In this context, it is important to note that for hundreds of years Chinese bureaucrats have been meticulous in recording past events mainly of concern to monarchy and officialdom. In short, there is a wealth of material on the ethnic minorities and their place in China as 'a unified multi-ethnic state' upon which to draw when considering contemporary developments. This historical record is fundamental in examining whether contemporary Chinese policies towards the ethnic minorities, and the utilization of tourism in particular for promoting their economic development and modernization, is simply a continuation of a centuries long approach to integration or is something more sinister and constitutes 'internal colonialism'. We shall return to this argument later.

Minorities policy under Mao Zedong

Peoples who are the object of indigenous tourism tend to be subordinated to varying degrees to the national majority (e.g., the Balinese in Indonesia, the Maori of New Zealand, the Inuit of Canada). In China, with the advent of communism following the victory of the Chinese Communist Party (CCP) under Mao Zedong, the many different minorities were absorbed into an ideologically driven Marxist view that evolution of societies to a pure communist state was a unilinear path, with the Han majority positioned at the top of the scale and the minorities, as backward and undeveloped peoples, cast down near the bottom. It was the task of the Communist state to 'uplift' its minorities from their backward state and assimilate them into the modern socialist state of China. As Swain (1993, p. 37) noted, *shaoshu minzu* 'are expected to ultimately evolve into assimilated members of the majority patriarchal socialist society'. Under Mao, the ethnic minorities were held to be at different stages on the evolutionary road to communism. Some were classified as 'early' into the journey and some as 'advanced' and the thrust of economic, ethnological, linguistic and other endeavor was to 'uplift' them and bring them out of their state of relative backwardness and into the 'progressive' socialist fold as quickly as possible. The *shaoshu minzu* were thus often incorporated in the political campaigns carried out in post-revolution China, including collectivization and the Cultural Revolution (Sofield and Li, 1998). However, under Mao, tourism *per se* was not an accepted form of economic development and so ethnic tourism played no role in those attempts to assimilate the minorities into the broader economy.

Ethnicity, heritage and the social sciences in China under Mao

In considering the place and role of ethnicity in tourism in China it is necessary to trace the control exercised by the CCP over its definition of 'legitimate knowledge'. In October 1950, the PRC Ministry of Education issued a manifesto which categorised academic disciplines as either revolutionary or counterrevolutionary. For a discipline to be worthy of retention it had to be seen to be serving Marxist dogma: a discipline's role was to provide direction for policy to advance society through its various stages to the ultimate perfection of communism. The linkage between socialist culture and education was comprehensive and complete (Li and Sofield, 1994). Redness (political correctness, with commitment to ideology being a major determinant for appointments, promotion and prescriptions for development) was in the ascendancy over 'expertness' and the social sciences became almost defunct in the general repression of the intelligentsia and academia. From 1969 to 1986, for example, humanities students comprised on average only 6% of the total tertiary student population (Hao, 1987).

This began to change after the death of Mao in 1976 with the 'Open Door' policies of 1978 enunciated by Deng Xiaoping in recognition of the need to modernize using all resources available. Until then tourism had not been regarded as a 'correct' avenue for development. Under Mao it was utilized as a tool for propaganda. Both domestic and international tourism were almost non-existent (Chow, 1988; Hudman and Hawkins, 1989). Foreign entry was strictly controlled, and from 1954 to 1978 the China International Travel Service (set up to arrange visits by 'foreign friends') played host to only 125,000 visitors (Richter, 1989). Tourism activity was held tightly in the hands of the state machinery (see chapter by O'Gorman, McLellan and Baum, Editors' Note) and reflected the pattern common to other communist states. The limited foreign visitation which existed was sanctioned on the grounds that the successes of communism could be paraded before a selected international audience (Sofield and Li, 1998).

Given the explicit ideological basis of the political system, all economic and other reforms (which included the Minorities as well) required substantial modifications of the ideological framework (Mackerras et al., 1994) and so Deng had to redefine politics in China. While this change of direction undercut some of the Maoist principles it was, nevertheless, essential to reaffirm the primacy of socialism to justify the legitimacy and right of the CCP to govern. Thus changes had to be rationalized in the context of their capacity to serve socialism. In this way, Deng was able to rehabilitate China's heritage as a valuable resource which was needed to assist in the tasks of:

(i) restoring national unity after the dissension and trauma of the Cultural Revolution;
(ii) revitalising the economy, in this case by making tourism an acceptable form of development (Sofield and Li, 1998).

Ethnic (indigenous) tourism

As part of attaining these objectives, the State began to move cautiously to include ethnic minorities culture as an acceptable component of tourism. This approach gained more purpose when the State launched its poverty alleviation drive in an organized and programmed way in the mid 1980s. Among the 331 impoverished counties designated as key recipients of state aid in 1986, 141 were in ethnic autonomous areas (Mackerras, 2003). In 1994, the State began implementing a Seven-Year Program for 'Delivering 80 Million People out of Poverty', and among the 592 impoverished counties designated as key recipients of state aid, some 257 were in ethnic autonomous areas. This was followed by the, 'Outline Program for Poverty Alleviation and Development in the Rural Areas of China' in 2001, and ten extra ethnic minority areas (a total of 267) were identified as key targets for assistance (Mackerras, 2003). Tibet has been managed as a special case and while it was excluded from the 2001 program, every province in China has been encouraged to undertake its own assistance program by developing 'sister relationships' with towns or villages and providing them with technical assistance and capital grants. Other projects targeting the Minorities have included the 1990 'Food and Clothing Fund for Impoverished Ethnic Minority Areas'; the 1992 'Fund for Ethnic Minorities Development', which is mainly used to deal with special difficulties encountered in the development of ethnic autonomous areas, and the 2000 'More Prosperous Frontiers and Better-off People Action', project that was designed to assist the 22 ethnic minority groups with a population of less than 100,000. A range of benefits are also extended to the ethnic minorities: *Shaoshu Minzu* status confers certain rights and privileges not shared by or available to the majority Han Chinese – certain religious freedoms, cultural freedoms, non-compliance with the one-child policy, access to development funds, and in the past three years the provision of 2,500 scholarships per annum for postgraduate studies (masters and doctoral degrees).

In 2000, the Chinese Government launched the Western Development Project or 'Open up the West', a large-scale exercise aimed at narrowing the gap between the more highly developed eastern coastal provinces and the western interior of the country. China's 'west' is generally defined as the poorer parts of China far away from the prosperous eastern seaboard and the rationale behind the project covers five separate agendas: 'a quest for equality in the context of alarming growth in disparities between east and west, foreign investment, infrastructure investment, ethnic issues, and sustainable development' (Holbig, 2005, p. 21). Since most of the provinces involved have significant minority populations (in some cases they are the provincial majority, such as in Yunnan, Xinjiang and Tibet), the program deals directly with the issue of underdevelopment in ethnic areas. In terms of tourism, the most ambitious is the 'Greater Shangri-la Tourism Investment and Development Project' which covers all of the ethnic Tibetan areas from northern Yunnan to Southwestern Sichuan and west into the Autonomous Region of Tibet.

During the five years since the launching of the strategy of development of the western part of the country, the construction of 60 important projects has begun, with a total investment of 850 billion yuan (US\$ 106 billion). The Chinese Government provides a detailed list of infrastructure and other projects which it considers have 'played an important role in promoting the economic and social development of the ethnic autonomous areas' (IOSC, 2005, p. 4). These include more than 250,000 kilometers of highways, major railway lines linking different ethnic regions, power stations and west–east gas pipelines. The most recent project to attract western interest (and criticism) was the opening of the Qinghai-Lhasa railway to Tibet in August 2006. During the period of the Tenth Five-Year Plan (2001–2005), the central government claims to have invested 31.2 billion yuan (US\$ 4 billion) in 117 projects in Tibet alone (excluding the new railway line) (IOSC, 2005, p. 5).

The 'Open up the West' campaign has been controversial in Western countries for a range of reasons, including skepticism about its intent and likely impact on ethnic minorities because a component is the encouragement of Han migration. In a sense, it is a case China cannot win: if it did not spend the dollars it would be accused of neglecting its minorities and keeping them in a deliberate state of impoverished subjugation; but in spending billions of dollars – several times the size of many western nations' international aid programs to their former colonies – it is accused of 'internal colonialism' and of destroying their culture.

Internal colonialism?

In this context, we question Oakes' analysis of Guizhou as a case of 'internal colonialism' (Oakes, 1999). As noted by Hicks (2004) in his comprehensive survey of the application of the term to more than 60 countries around the world, the concept of internal colonialism has been utilized by social scientists in many different formulations with a range of different emphases – and for a number of different purposes – but with no agreed-upon methodology. Hicks' survey revealed that, beginning in the 1960s, several broad conceptions of the term internal colonialism emerged of which two are the most widely used:

1 internal colonialism as a domestic analogy to forms of economic and social domination in classical colonialism;
2 internal colonialism as intra-national exploitation of distinct cultural groups.

One of the pivotal publications on the subject is Michael Hechter's *'Internal Colonialism'* (1975) in which he adduced English exploitation of Wales and Scotland according to Hick's second category. This text, while influential at the time, has since been criticized for being historically inaccurate, (Page, 1978; Wimmer, 1997).

However, in examining the situation of Guizhou, we find that millions of dollars have been expended in that province on a wide range of nationally important strategic and defense facilities and mining, not because of some grand design to alienate the minorities but because of Mao's *san xian* ('Third Front') defense industrial relocation policy. This policy, as Oakes (1999, p. 34) himself notes, was based on a perception of China being girded by 'a hostile geopolitical environment that ... encouraged the massive relocation of China's defense industry away from the coast to the *san xian* provinces of the interior: namely, Guizhou, Yunnan, Sichuan, Shaanxi, Gansu, and parts of Henan, Hubei, and Hunan.' Oakes (1999, p. 36) stated that 'some 29,000 state enterprises were built during this period, mobilizing a work force of sixteen million' and cites Naughton (1988) who estimated that at its peak in the late 1960s and early 1970s, two-thirds of China's industrial budget was going to *san xian* investments. Guizhou itself was the recipient of 217 such major enterprises between 1963 and 1970 (note that the Cultural Revolution was unleashed in 1966, yet despite the national turmoil, Guizhou was still a major beneficiary of State investment). According to Leung and Chan (1986, cited in Oakes 1999) projects were especially costly due to their remote mountainous locations and almost non-existent infrastructure. The cost of laying railroad track in Guizhou, for example, was between four and five times higher than normal for other parts of China. Utilizing Guizhou's large mineral resources (the province ranks 5th in the country in coal reserves, 2nd in aluminum resources, and 3rd in manganese reserves – Guizhou Yearbook, 1996, p. 379), the central government made the province a center of extraction for fueling rapid industrial development and integration throughout southwest China. This situation continued after Mao and well into the 1990s (Liang, 1993). Because there was little articulation between the rural populations (mainly ethnic minorities) and the mining, defense science and technology industries (which require much higher levels of education than are generally available among members of the ethnic minorities populations), and because the agricultural sector was largely ignored, Goodman and subsequently Oakes interpreted this situation as one of exploitation of the region and its minorities to serve 'outside' interests. They thus drew the conclusion that it constituted an example of 'internal colonialism'.

But just because the modern economic development of Guizhou happened to coincide or overlap in part with ethnic (linguistic, cultural, religious, racial) distinctions cannot be adjudged as a raison d'etre for inferring internal colonialism. Guizhou became a recipient of a particular type of modernization program under Mao which has continued subsequently because of its geographical location (based on a strategic needs assessment of the vulnerability of coastal installations), comparative advantage and factor endowment (strategic mineral resources), and not because of any intent to subject the local minorities to alienation or subjugation as implied in the description of the situation as one of internal colonialism. Oakes (1999, p. 42) himself acknowledges that the 'pillar industries' of the province are coal mining, hydroelectricity, mineral processing, defense industry *and agriculture*. There may be little articulation between these other sectors and the ethnic rural populations but that does not gainsay the fact that the province has benefited from a communications network (roads, railways, airfields, telecommunications) that is totally integrated into national strategic and defense needs. There is nothing in this situation that cannot be explained by 'normal' economic market forces operating in a 'normal' way. It is in essence no different from any country developing some regions in a way that is distinct from others, such as similar industrial concentrations in the Ruhr Valley in Germany, Pittsburgh in the United States, or Kwinana in Western Australia, that would make it a distinct case. To isolate the continued poverty of Guizhou's rural population which coincidentally includes the majority of the ethnic minorities (but also incorporates millions of Han peasants), from overall economic processes within the province and argue that this is neglect that constitutes internal colonialism, is to miss the point that the rural sector throughout China, consisting of more than 600 million Han Chinese peasants, is impoverished. A logical extension of the argument would be to conclude therefore that China is practicing internal colonialism against its entire rural sector, which is patently absurd.

Satzewich and Wotherspoon (1993) have summarized the strengths and the weaknesses of the internal colonial model as it has been applied to Aboriginal peoples in Canada. They conclude that it 'tends to assume that Aboriginal and white are homogenous groups', and thus reifies the two categories and ignores class interests. It assumes that: '. . . all whites have similar interests in relation to the maintenance of an internal colonial relationship with Aboriginal peoples, and that all Aboriginal peoples have a singular set of economic, social and political interests that revolve around resistance to internal colonial domination' (1993, p. 10). On this point Oakes provides several very detailed paragraphs on the role, activities and interests of the minorities elite in 'enthusiastically embracing' objectives elsewhere identified as the prerogative of Han urban dwellers and State officials (1999, p. 47). Rather than drawing the conclusion, however, that this represents a class division as Satzewich and Wotherspoon (1993) would infer, Oakes suggests that: 'The idea of modernization based on preserving *minzu* tradition, an idea now enthusiastically embraced by local leaders throughout Guizhou, may in fact be resulting in a new form of internal colonialism.' However, to paraphrase Hicks (2004) when discussing the Inuit of Canada, the substantial difference between the respective magnitudes of Han and non-Han incomes in Guizhou, and the different levels of income generation between the urban industrial sector and the rural agricultural sector in Guizhou may perhaps be better described in terms of an uneven, incomplete and dynamic process of the incorporation of a minorities people into the national economy of China. Simply invoking the concept of internal colonialism overlooks the possibility of careful theorization of the intersections of class with ethnicity which may occur as a result of the combined and uneven development of China's embrace of a socialist market economy, a path which Mackerras (2006) has followed in examining whether one can identify the rise of a middle class in China's ethnic minorities. In a carefully argued thesis, Mackerras (2006) concludes that there are emerging middle classes among some of the ethnic minorities, especially the Uyghurs and the Koreans, that there are centers of entrepreneurship among these minorities promoting development and modernization (although there are also growing inequalities), and that the positive discriminatory education policies of China towards the minorities are a contributing factor because the emergence of a middle class is dependent upon higher education levels.

Minorities, tourism and modernization

We consider Oakes is on much stronger conceptual ground when he describes tourism as a major factor in the modernisation of Guizhou's ethnic minorities and his analysis in this field has relevance for many of China's ethnic minorities and for tourism development in general. Tourism was identified as a 'vanguard industry' for Guizhou in 1991 and, as with other provinces where ethnic tourism was also added to the constellation of tools for development:

Ethnic minority culture became a fundamental feature of Guizhou's promotional activities, both in terms of using exotic cultural representations as enticements for potential investments, and as a feature of market socialism's potential for rural development in minority regions. Indeed, tourism itself was thought to be ideally suited for these regions by taking advantage of the conditions which made them so poor: harsh but scenic mountainous environments and socio-cultural distance from modern Chinese economies and lifestyles. The representations of minority culture, which became ubiquitous features of promoting the province, would not only make Guizhou more interesting to outsiders, but were meant to establish a model for the 'cultural development' of minority groups themselves, conditioning them to articulate symbolic cultural practices with commercial projects. Tourism was thus seen not simply as a propaganda and marketing tool for Guizhou, but also as a process of development and integration encouraging minority regions to become more modern.

(Oakes, 1999, p. 43)

This is the model which has been followed with ethnic minorities all over China. Yunnan at the government level has moved probably further than most provinces in China in pursuing minorities culture, probably because out of its 46 million population, some 27 million are *shaoshu minzu* representing 25 officially designated ethnic minorities. It has been particularly active in promoting ethnic tourism, taking advantage of this diversity and produced a comprehensive Ethnic Cultures policy paper in 1999 (Yunnan Province Government, 1999) which outlined a wide range of initiatives including the establishment of an academy of cultural studies to ensure that older generations passed on cultural skills to their young people. Yunnan was 'uniquely able to chart this course because of the diversity, vitality and strength of its 26 minority Nationalities, more than any other Province in China. It was an exceptional cornucopia of cultures, ... a living museum of ethnic cultures' (Yunnan Province Government, 1999, p. 4). In a detailed outline of ways in which Yunnan would approach its task, the policy paper noted that tourism would be an important engine for achieving the goal of conserving Yunnan's ethnic diversity and demonstrating its cultural richness to the world: 'major cultural projects would highlight the distinctive local features of different ethnic cultural areas' (Yunnan Province Government, 1999, p. 7). Within the context of tourism as one of the 'four pillars' or engines to drive development and to power modernization, the PRC has formulated a number of policies to promote and market the ethnicity of its minorities for tourism (domestic and international), leading to the extension of commodity relationships into new areas of social life. The Chinese Government's institutionalization of ethnic identities will determine those aspects of culture which are deemed 'safe' for tourism (i.e., will not challenge national unity) so arts, crafts, cuisine, architecture, dance, some festivals and ceremonies, will form the main touristic diet. Celebrations of past victories over Han Chinese, ethnic military prowess and other such manifestations of independence are generally not permitted. Interestingly, however, the Chinese Government has resurrected its 'Ethnic Mini-Games' which include contests in a whole range of cultural areas including traditional forms of warfare such as archery and feats of horse riding. China's Ethnic Minorities Mini-Games were first staged under Mao in 1953, subsequently considered to be anti-socialist, and abandoned. Resurrected in 1982, and held in 1986, 1991, 1995, 1999, 2003 and 2006 the Games feature a major display of the 56 ethnic minorities' cultural heritage in dance, song, traditional arts, crafts and activities. Competitions are held in archery, different forms of traditional wrestling, horse and camel riding, and other sports (see chapter by Thompson and O'Gorman, Editors' Note). The eighth Ethnic Minorities Games were held in Yunnan in June 2006, attracted daily audiences of about 50,000, about 10% of whom were overseas visitors. The official opening speech proclaimed that the Games demonstrated to the world the harmony of the ethnic minorities as part of the one big, happy Chinese family where 'ethnic cultures bloom' (Television Beijing Central Broadcasting, daily news report, June 16, 2006). Some *shaoshu minzu* communities have astutely utilized their Government-sponsored, Government-supported status to obtain advantage over other adjacent non-*shaoshu minzu* communities, or by 'proving' their greater adherence to the 'traditional model way of life' over rival *shaoshu minzu* communities in terms of seeking accreditation for tourism ventures (e.g., as a 'living village museum'). Oakes (1993) has some fascinating insights into this aspect of *shaoshu minzu* and tourism with his early 1990s studies of the Dong and Miao communities in Guizhou.

In some countries, tourism has reinforced a narrow demarcation of 'culture for consumption', limiting it to arts and crafts, and cuisine; but in China perhaps because of its classification system of whole ethnic societies and its need to identify distinguishing features that separate/distance them from Han culture, the broader anthropological view of culture as a group's 'whole way of life' is accepted and often (though not always) promoted for tourism. In this context, there have been several interesting studies of the Naxi Mosuo minority from Lake Lugu, Yunnan, whose social system is one in which females dominate households and economic activity and choose a continuous series of 'temporary husbands' with whom to cohabit (Walsh, 2001). When the Mosuo established home stay facilities, this led to a rush of 'unhealthy' tourism by Chinese males hoping for sexual adventure. The Chinese Government has found itself in something of a quandary since its definition of the Mosuo as a distinct sub-branch of the Naxi minority is dependent upon those very characteristics which set its society apart; and yet the morality of the socialist state frowns upon hedonistic tourism.

Goodman (2004) noted that with reference to Qinghai 'every minority nationality has seen a marked cultural and economic revival since 1999, though necessarily reactions have been far from uniform' (p. 80). He considered that the 'Open up the West' campaign could have a negative impact on traditional cultures, as is often a by-product of development and change. Becquelin (2004), quoting an article by Li Dezhu (2000), the Korean head of the Government's Nationalities Commission, went much further than Goodman and suggested that there had been a 'paradigmatic shift' in the doctrine on ethnic minorities (2004, p. 58). Becquelin interpreted Li's article to 'signal closure: as the long-sought objective of seamless integration of minority nationalities into the "Chinese nation" draws near, history has entered an end-game, and there is no necessity to proceed with caution and coded double-speak any more' (2004, p. 60). This 'no-longer-secret attempt to crush ethnic cultures in Xinjiang' would result in 'increased sinicization and increased ethno-national unrest in the future' (2004, p. 64). However, Mackerras (2006), commenting in turn on Becquelin, countered that Li Dezhu's article, which is about ethnic minorities and the 'Open up the West' campaign in general, not Xinjiang in particular, suggested a change in emphasis rather than a paradigmatic shift. The main point of Li's article was the need for development, which the campaign can provide, and its continued support for integration of ethnic cultures and consciousness among ethnic cadres in opposition to separatism are quite standard, and have been for a long time. Mackerras believed it was an overstatement to interpret the 'Open up the West' campaign as heralding an historical end-game.

Our own experience in Lhasa bears out the 'subversive effects of hybridization' (Rankin 2006) where a number of Han Chinese businesses have adopted Tibetan apparel and other accoutrements of Tibetan culture (Tibetan language, the playing of Tibetan musical instruments, Tibetan handicraft skills) as a 'backstage' front for their souvenir shops on the basis of a very common-sensical notion that tourists do not travel all the way to Lhasa to see Han Chinese. While Chinese visitors are not taken in by this deception for more than a minute when they engage in conversation with the shopkeepers, it is nevertheless a manifestation of acculturation where the dominant culture has taken on aspects of the minority culture. The shopkeepers may not have done so out of respect for the intrinsic values of Tibetan culture, but the outcome is the same: rather than the destruction of Tibetan culture there are Han Chinese business people who actively support some aspects of its material culture. On the other side of the coin we found numerous Tibetans wearing suits, ties and polished shoes who when queried told us that they wanted to be modern, they did not want to wear traditional old-fashioned scratchy clothes! Bhabha's hybridity and multivocality is a two way street.

Gupta and Ferguson (1992, 1997) had also earlier challenged the ethnographer's formerly comfortable world of place/people/culture by the complexity of our growing understanding that virtually no place/people/culture had been so isolated that they had no connection with others; and our understanding that identity has always been based not on tightly drawn boundaries and exclusive recognition of self but on drawing differences with 'others', through external reference points. Connectivities did exist: Malinowski's Trobriand Islanders of Papua New Guinea were part of the socio-economic fabric of wider eastern Melanesia, the Ma'asai were encompassed within and across Tanzania and Kenya where colonial boundaries were largely irrelevant in a cultural context, and even for the extremely isolated Pitjantjara Aborigines of the central Australian desert there was always an 'outside' with which links, however tenuous, were maintained.

Psychologically for the inside people, there was always an 'external world' even if only dimly comprehended; and 'primitive' was a label imposed by outsiders, not part of their vision or understanding of themselves. This connectivity has also been true of China where the different ethnicities have been intermingling for centuries even as they kept many aspects of their cultures distinct and different. The concept of interconnectivity has been married to the concept of mobilities and the way in which through globalization and tourism we now have far greater movement of peoples in and out of their own cultures, in and out of and across the boundaries of their 'own' places and spaces so that it is increasingly difficult to argue that places are homogenous and peoples within places are homogenous. This 'natural' identity between people and place is presented as 'culture' for the tourist, for example in visiting the Dong and Maio in Guizhou, the Naxi in Lijiang, the Kazaks and Tuwa in the Altai Mountains of Xinjiang or the Tibetans in Lhasa. The common school atlas reinforces the notion of place/people/culture with its clear demarcation of the boundaries of the world's countries which are all neatly colored with yellow, green, pink and blue. There are no fuzzy boundaries or vaguely defined unclaimed spaces. The history of national principle is reinforced and simplified for all to understand (Gellner, 1983). Malkki (1996, p. 55) has demonstrated that it is difficult to challenge the notion of community and culture as natural and unproblematic because of what she calls 'the metaphysics of sedentarism', where the *roots* of peoples and cultures in their own territories are taken for granted. Terms such as 'the motherland' imbue this concept with 'naturalness' and reinforce the idea of 'belonging'.

China's map is now demarcated with 155 autonomous minorities regions and the marketing and promotion activities of the China National Tourism

Administration (CNTA) reflect this ethnically territorialized country. Such representations of ethnicity are characteristic of many reconstructions of image for tourism: the authentic and original exist in such an environment: everything else is contrasted as fabricated, false, substitution or modernistic replication. Gupta and Ferguson (1997, p. 78) talk about the 'waning of place as a container of experience' and this may be so for the intellectual stance currently being pursued by anthropologists as they tease out the detail of the disengagement and deconstruction of people/place/culture. From the point of view of the business of ethnic tourism in China, however, its tourism marketing is aimed at the opposite – of producing and projecting place as *the* container of experience. As with many other governments, the Chinese Government is not a neutral agent but the power broker in determining 'the consumptive representation of some people and the consumptive containment of others' (Hollinshead, 1998b, p. 59) and it plays a major role in the 'imaging' of 'national cultures' and ethnicity to objectify symbols and markers to meet political and policy objectives (Graburn, 1997, p. 210) (see chapter by Hollinshead, Editors' Note). The language of tourism, as Dann (1996) argues, has powerfully captured the imagining of peoples, cultures and destinations for presentation as commoditised objects for sale in the global capitalist economy and in China the exotic 'Otherness' of its ethnic minorities can be both an avenue for reconstructing identities in an approved way, and also for establishing identities and assisting them to emerge from under a single sinicized image: only in recent years as China has begun to aggressively market its ethnic tourism has the world realized that in fact China does have an extraordinary richness of ethnic minorities culture. It is what Lanfant (1995, pp. 3–6) has referred to as the way in which tourism can assist 'marginalized ethno-regional movements/groups' to gain recognition on the international stage. In short ethnic tourism is not inherently destructive.

Efforts to interpret cultural and related differences are necessarily problematic because they incorporate an evaluation of Otherness – and in so doing in the overwhelming mass of tourism literature there is little examination of self in determining that 'otherness', so that we have an unthinking, derived, western, metropolitan, colonialist domination of the imagery and production of culture for tourism (Hollinshead, 2002b). If a group of Tibetan musicians play their instruments in the courtyard of a monastery in Lhasa, it will be described as 'religious'; if a version of their performance is enacted at the opening of the Olympic Games in Beijing, or the theater in West End in London, it will be described as 'cultural, artistic'; and if a performance is staged in the China Folk Culture Village in Shenzhen, it will be labeled as 'commoditized for tourism'. For the Tibetan musicians, however, there may be no such distinctions: each performance is reaching out into their spiritual world. As Bruner (1995) noted in his example of Balinese dance, these distinctions between religion, art and tourism are western categories not indigenous realities. Far too often the models used to analyze tourism in host communities are (perhaps unconsciously) locked into etic value systems where the wide range of responses by the host communities to tourism are not permitted by the nature of the research approach to become visible. As Cohen noted (1988), tourism researchers need to engage in more emic and comparative analysis to distinguish between socially constructive/reconstructive processes in order to avoid the pitfalls of (often unconscious) predetermined western evaluation/assessment of touristic phenomena.

Li (2006) provides an example of how this 'Otherness' needs to be approached with caution. For more than 25 years the Tibetan residents of Jiuzhaigou have been posing to have their photographs taken in traditional clothing against a backdrop of the scenic beauty of lakes and mountains, an apparent open-and-shut case of objectification of the exotic Other. However, the roles have reversed in the past ten years, so that now the tourists pay for the hire of the traditional clothes (wedding costumes are a favorite), dress up in them, and the Tibetan hawkers take photographs of the costumed tourists with their own cameras. The tourists have 'Othered' themselves and objectified themselves! According to Li, the tensions that might otherwise come from Tibetan culture being turned into an exotic object for the tourist gaze by outside forces are absent. Rather, the exchange is seen as a form of empowerment socially, culturally, and psychologically as well as economically (Scheyvens, 2003; Sofield, 2003) and it is a matter of pride to the Tibetan hawkers that the Han Chinese value their culture to the point where they pay to dress up as Tibetans. It is an example of what Picard (who has carried out longitudinal tourism research in Bali over the past-30 years) has termed 'touristic culture', where tourism has become an integral component of culture and interaction with tourists is central to their own definition of ethnic identity and authenticity (1993).

Conclusions

In concluding this brief overview of ethnic tourism in China, there are two key areas for further research:

(i) sociological/anthropological;
(ii) the role of the state (political science/government studies).

By its nature, tourism both elicits and illuminates new forms of ethnicity and processes of cultural identity. We can look at the boundary(ies) that defines an ethnic group as well as the cultural 'material' that makes up the group enclosed by the boundary(ies), and the role of tourism in demarcating both the boundary and the cultural material inside. Tourism plays a role in demarcating ethnic boundaries because of its marketing of the 'exotic other' and the cultural 'material' through its commoditization of aspects of that ethnicity. It needs to define and differentiate one 'product' from another in competition with others. By objectifying and externalizing ethnic culture in this way, tourism makes it more visible – and one could argue more subject to discussion, debate and contestation. The community which is the object of this 'tourist gaze' (Urry, 1990) will itself be a vigorous participant in this 'labelling' process, this resignification, this reconstruction, this continuous re-defining of the manifestations of identity and being. Both labels and definitions in these processes will be contested by the different actors for their own purposes – the community itself for pride, dignity, worth (which may lead to economic gain, employment of youth, reinforcement of specific roles, heightened awareness of tradition, respect for elders and other custodians of aspects of culture, and gender issues); the tourism industry for competitive advantage; the tourists wanting to attest to the 'authenticity' of their experience; and the state for political objectives associated with national unity. The nation-state and tourism have a shared affinity in presenting a place as distinct and unique. Where that uniqueness is derived in part from ethnic minorities, there may be tensions between the desire of tourism to promote that distinctiveness and the need of the state to ensure that communalism does not undermine unity. Paradoxically, tourism may thus assist in the assimilation of an ethnic minority into the economy of a country, and work against assimilation culturally as affected communities exercise a range of responses to tourism. The paradox of ethnic tourism remains because of inherent contradictions between conservation and change. Viable cultures are not static but dynamic and tourism accelerates socio-economic change which often affects continuation of tradition in all its forms (often referred to as 'undermining the authenticity of ethnic tourism' as MacCannell (1994) notes). Yet *minzu* tourism in China is focused on maintaining the images if not the substance of tradition and ethnic difference. Cultural pluralism is an important asset in ethnic tourism, but the over-arching aim of Chinese socialism remains to integrate the minorities into the majority Han society, and political and economic institutions tend to act as a strong 'push' factor in this context. How to reconcile the centripetal and centrifugal forces operating on *minzu* tourism in China is a fundamental issue in the sustainability of the country's ethnic tourism. Ethnic tourism in China is not divorced from these processes.

Indigenous Australia in the bittersweet world: the power of tourism in the projection of 'old' and 'fresh' visions of Aboriginality

Keith Hollinshead

Introduction

In the decade since the first version of Butler and Hinch (1996) was published, *the indigenous imaginal* in Australia – that is, the way indigeneity (or Aboriginal being) is seen, felt, experienced, and projected – has changed immensely. There have been some profound movements in 'the discourse' of indigenous affairs (Cowlishaw et al., 2006). It is important to note at the outset four of the most significant changes which have been occurring over the last 20 years, but which have accelerated over the last decade:

- Firstly, while general interest in visitation to Aboriginal Australia continues to be reported at very high levels, particular interest in the indigenous art of (for some) a relic culture and (for others) a vibrant and unique continuing culture reaches stratospheric levels of popularity as incorporated community-based organisations like Tiwi Designs, Ernabella Arts, and Papunya Tula Artists promote their 'traditional' work and adapt Western silk-screening, pottery, batik, and acrylic watercolour painting styles (Horton, 1994).
- Secondly, all sorts of new indigenous bodies and interest groups – not all of them community based (Burchett, 1993a) – have become engaged in tourism enterprise initiatives to such an extent that The Lonely Planet Company was able to publish a four hundred and fifty page handbook on visitation to 'indigenous Australia' (Singh et al., 2001) for the international marketplace in travel (see Hollinshead, In prep.(a)).
- Thirdly, certain Aboriginal groups have become heavily engaged in new media production in terms of the arts, music, and cultural expression, such as has occurred in electronic communication at Yuendumu (Hinkson, 2005), and (in tourism, itself) at, for instance, the Tjapukai Aboriginal Cultural Centre in the Cairns area of North Queensland, and at the Dreamtime Cultural Centre (for the Darumbal people) at Rockhampton in Central Queensland (Kauffman, 2000).
- Fourthly, there is evidence that so-called 'white Australia' is developing a will for reconciliation with Aboriginal Australians, as evidenced by the national Sorry Day that occurred in May 1998 when more than one million white Australians recorded their apologies (nominally for having 'stolen' Aboriginal children from their parents), and when the former Governor-General of Australia, former Prime Ministers, state Governors, and others, took part in 'atonement' marches (Knightley, 2001).

Moreover, there is evidence that significant numbers of 'white Australians' are lately responding in new non-European and less-material spiritual ways to the rugged landscape of Australia (and therein, many of these non-Aboriginal people ARE gradually and increasingly respecting the mythic bonds of those landscapes to the indigenous people of Australia) (Tacey, 1995): in such ways, the place of indigeneity is meditatively rising within the vigour and vitality of the broad Australian nation (Gelder and Jacobs, 1998; Hollinshead, 2002a).

Thus, considerable changes have been afoot in Australia over the last decade, or so, in terms of the ways in which the indigenous imaginal is perceived and understood and misunderstood, and in terms of the fashions and the kinetic technologies through which it is signified and made/de-made/re-made (see chapter by Schmiechen and Boyle, Editors' Note). This chapter seeks to describe some of these changing currents of awareness and interpretation which surround the representation of Australia at a time when increasing numbers of indigenous Australians wish to share their culture with visitors (Ferraro, 2006), yet at a moment in history when a new indigenous critical space is opening up where many new indigenous intellectuals are generating whole new ways of seeing and projecting indigenous Australian history, culture, identity, and knowledge (Grossman, 2005) – viz., ways which are relatively free of 'whitefella narratives' (Muecke, 2004), and which are pointedly more sympathetic towards and relevant to Aboriginal communal experience (Squires, 2005).

In order to convey much of what is going on within these new developments and dynamisms, this chapter seeks to:

- explain the appeal of indigenous Australia to interested tourists – particularly to travellers from overseas;
- describe some of the key philosophical outlooks which are routinely employed behind the selection of policies and practices which govern the promotion and development of Aboriginal people in tourism;
- outline some of the emergent responses to the appearance of tourism which might regulate the degree of engagement which indigenous groups and communities may wish to have with the industry;
- account for some of the other leading imperatives which might direct the performance of Aboriginal interest bodies and groups in today's tourism marketplace; and,
- present 12 precepts of indigenous tourism research and scholarship.

In covering the above material, this 2006 rewrite of this author's chapter in *Tourism and Indigenous Peoples* (Butler and Hinch, 1996) is composed on the premise that as a discipline (or more properly, as a 'field' or 'domain') tourism studies in Australia – like tourism studies elsewhere (Crang, 1999; Meethan, 2001) – has been insufficiently attentive both to the turning identificatory and ideational conditions of the postcolonial moment at the general/worldwide level (Hall and Tucker, 2004) and to the changing psychic and political climate specific-to-Australia under which contests of 'native title' and 'indigenous otherness' are being played out (Edmond, 2004). Hopefully, this new chapter can broaden understanding within tourism studies not only about the responsiveness (and the power and reach) of 'tourism' vis-à-vis such significant cultural warrants, but also about the relevance and the quality of the degree and other educational programmes which Tourism Studies students are given in order to enable them to make informed/intelligent/fitting decisions about such critical and shifting culturo-political matters.

The conceptual market for indigenous Australia

No comprehensive study appears to have yet been carried out to map the parameters of the appeal to tourists of traditional 'First Australian' society and its mysticism as a cultural, adventure, or experiential drawcard across the world. It seems, thereby, that while the tourism industry is working upon assumed knowledge, indigenous groups and communities in many locales are themselves largely working upon next to no knowledge about the shape and character of the visitation that gazes or seeks to gaze upon them (Office of Northern Development, 1993).

In the absence of such a platform analysis of the attractivity of indigenous Australian culture to non-Aboriginals, a conceptual scheme of conceivable push and pull factors is offered for the consideration of readers of this chapter. It is presented in Figure 20.1 in terms of four foundational experiential drives of metropolitan/industrial populations, and is based upon the landmark insight of Yankelovich (1974) into cultural and subcultural change in North America as originally uncovered by work of the Yankelovich, Skelly, and White Monitor Service.

This monitor service was and is a research programme set up to track changes in social trends and cultural values, that is, to measure the changes that occur in the beliefs and the values that North American/Western people consider are worth striving for. According to Assael (1987), surprisingly few marketing researchers ever use such cultural values as descriptors of consumer preference, even though cultural values can conceivably influence consumer behaviour just as substantively as do the commonly utilised factors of lifestyle, personality, and social class. The Yankelovich, Skelly, and White Monitor Service is thus an important historic but still pertinent effort (within general consumer research in marketing) to gauge the rise and fall of the kinds of manifest norms and customs that are likely to influence broad purchasing patterns. That stated, the specific application of a particular/tailored 'monitor service' which just focusses upon the relative appeal of various styles of ethnic/cultural/adventure tourism vis-à-vis other forms of tourism, is long overdue in research of and into the industry, not just for indigenous tourism.

Figure 20.1 constitutes an attempt to show how the old but important Yankelovich work could be fruitfully applied to an unfolding research agenda on the popularity (in the urban-industrial West) of various attractor factors behind indigenous tourism. Yankelovich identified four significant trends in cultural values that conceivably have a significant bearing upon the appeal of indigenous culture in general, and therefore would have for Aboriginal mysticism in particular. They are:

- the increasing focus of certain urban-industrial people on *the self* (in contrast to larger social units such as the family, the neighbourhood, and the nation);
- the increasing drive of such individuals to enhance *the quality of their personal life* (by continually finding stimulation, enjoyment, awe, and diversity from within and across the world in which they find themselves);

The following four major contemporary experiential and adventure-travel trends were uncovered by the Yankelovich, Skelly, and White Monitor Service. They have been translated here for the contextualised appeal of visitation to the lands and cultures of the Indigenous peoples of Australia for tourists from urban settings overseas. Such visions and travel aspirations tend to draw international visitors to Australia to what they see as outback settings, and are not so readily of any desire to see or experience Aboriginal people in 'urban' or supposedly 'non-traditional' settings.

1. An increasing focus on *the self* vis-à-vis the family, the local community or one's own country:

● Incumbent goals   . . . personal enhancement; personal fulfilment; self-realisation:

* Medium in tourism
- . . social/cultural expression
- . . conspicuous consumption
- . . personal creativity
- . . hedonism

e.g. 'I've conversed with "real" Aboriginal people';
e.g. 'Last summer I went to the Australian outback once again';
e.g. 'Can I show you some Aboriginal string figures I've learnt to make?'
e.g. 'While we were there in the Top End of the Northern Territory, we indulged in everything: the wildlife tours in 'The Green', the different foods, the traditional music!'

2. A drive to enrich one's own *personal environment*:

● Incumbent goals   . . . excitement; pleasure; mystery; variety:

* Medium in tourism
- . . mysticism
- . . novelty and change
- . . return to nature
- . . concern about the environment

e.g. 'I found the stories of the ancient Dreaming to be enthralling';
e.g. 'We must get away from this cosmopolitan hell in Boston and the north-east of 'The States', if only temporarily';
e.g. 'I rediscovered my-old-self out there again in the open and free spaces of the desert';
e.g. 'I'm going to the Australian bush to fight for the saving of untouched nature. It is the most precious place on earth'.

3. A drive to help create *an easier world-order*.

● Incumbent goals   . . . a less threatening life-space:

* Medium in tourism
- . . simplification

e.g. 'I want to live back-in-nature, even if only for a month';

(*Continued*)

Figure 20.1
Changes in cultural values in the Western world: related to engagement with other populations through tourism

. . . anti-bigness	e.g. 'I crave the peace of little old Alice Springs, not bustle of the Big Apple, here!';
. . . anti-hypocrisy	e.g. 'I'll see a real and longstanding culture out there in the ancient bush of Australia, in all of its blessed simplicities, and I'll be rid of this media-driven false consciousness we endure here in North America';
. . . new cynicism	e.g. 'We ought to escape from the incessant controls of Big Brother – "it" surrounds us everywhere here – if only for a month'.

4. An increasing focus on *a less-structured lifestyle*

✿ Incumbent goals	. . . looser and more flexible living:	
* Medium in tourism	. . . antimaterialism	e.g. 'I want to go "downunder" for a year or so, to experience the red desert we saw in that film "Rabbit Proof Fence", in lieu of investing my salary';
	. . . away from possessions	e.g. 'I must experience unaccommodated life at Uluru, or somewhere undeveloped in the bush: it is more important to me than having that new car';
	. . . living for today	e.g. 'I will buy these special offer Qantas tickets: We can go "roo hunting, and camel racing", pronto!! We can even stay in luxury hotels in the Kimberleys if we want to. Who cares about the cost?!!'
	. . . tolerance for disorder	e.g. 'Our lives are too mundane here: let's do the Crocodile Dundee thing for a while, let us "go walkabout" and see just where we end up! Let us just escape!'

Source: Adapted from Yankelovich (1974).

Figure 20.1
(*Continued*)

- the increasing desire on the part of those people to construct *more manageable living spaces* for themselves (in which they can more comfortably cope and creatively flourish), or otherwise the increasing desire to merely locate and witness such lifestyles amongst others; and,
- the increasing quest by such individuals to secure a less complex, *more adaptable mix of lived principles* by which modern society can sustain itself everywhere (and by which they, as enabled individuals, can thrive spontaneously and self-determinately).

In so distinguishing these sorts of aspirations in North America (and by extension, in the broader Western world), Yankelovich drew attention to some highly significant changes in the value priorities of urban-industrial people as travellers. He suggests that they conceivably explain not only why certain large segments of consumers from metropolitan or urban-industrial locales are more and more pulled by the general call to gaze upon different climes and upon different/distant social orders, but that they also reveal why such consumers are growingly drawn towards seeing, and knowing, and involving themselves in that targeted other, specifically in what may appear to them to be alien, primal, or virginal cultural and mystical settings. Thirty years later, the data on which Yankelovich worked is undoubtedly dated, and it is now opportune for other market researchers (in Australia and beyond) who work with indigenous populations to refreshingly probe at depth the kinds of changes in cultural norms, beliefs, and predispositions that reveal themselves in both manifest and in latent forms of tourism. Such diagnosis could undoubtedly help indigenous populations (or aid those who work in the marketplace on their behalf or with them) to more discernedly pinpoint 'appropriate tourists' by their existing psychographic mindset. Such found intelligence may provide travel-industry copywriters who produce pre-visit publicity or on-site narratives for indigenous sites with a more relevant set of cultural-value inventories by which they can then market, demarket, or remarket precious storylines. And that is, potentially, a mutual gain of native host populations and curious Other-seeking/cultural-experience-craving visitors alike.

The presentation/representation of Aboriginal Australia

Before comment is provided as to the survival strategies and/or the developmental practices which are newly available for indigenous Australians (and to individuals and agencies working on their behalf and with them) to counteract the dense and commonplace ethnocentrisms and other flourishing cultural predispositions which are embedded in the contemporary tourist gaze (Urry, 1990), the reflective ethnographic logic by which this particular chapter is offered ought to be more firmly clarified. As Figure 20.2 reveals, the *Conservative-Humanitarian* viewpoint is one of the three primary philosophical vistas or applied practices which are commonly adopted to project support for indigenous peoples in any field of endeavour – the other two being the

The primitive-environmentalist outlook

- Basic premise — Tribal cultures are a superior adaptation. We must stop economic developments that threaten them.
- Main objective — To permit the persistence of tribal cultures as a viable alternative.
- Main strategies — The promotion of cultural/environmental sanctuaries. The advocation of conservation. The opposition to specific development projects.
- Routine outlook on tourism — Tourism and travel projects are powerful and corrosive agents of Western/non-indigenous/external infiltration. As lead forces of endogenous rationalities, they should be rejected under almost all circumstances.

The liberal-political outlook

- Basic premise — Indigenous people are economically exploited and politically oppressed. We must help them defend their rights at every opportunity, particularly against unthought assistance in the form of carelessly delivered or poorly designed 'interference'/'aid'/'help'.
- Main objective — To advance the liberation, the self-determination, and the decolonisation of indigenous peoples.
- Main strategies — The promotion of political mobilisation and consciousness-raising amongst indigenous groups and communities. The advocation of the human rights and psychic condition of such populations. The opposition to oppressive policies.
- Routine outlook on tourism — Externally developed and managed tourism and travel ventures are hard to control and monitor. Encouragement should only be given (after extremely careful scrutiny) to tourism projects which have substantial local community involvement and particular rights of veto.

The conservative-humanitarian outlook

- Basic premise — Progress is inevitable. We must help indigenous groups and communities to make the most of the available new/adaptive/transitional possibilities available to them.
- Main objective — To eventually integrate indigenous populations in with (not into!!) the larger national/mainstream system (in ways that are faithful to the found wishes of that Indigenous group or community) thereby helping sustain the 'original'/'preferred-adapted' spiritual beliefs, ethnic identity, and cultural practices of that group/community.
- Main strategies — The promotion of humanitarian assistance programmes. The advocation of the continued use of native language and the sustained development of collective cultural and community pride.

(*Continued*)

Figure 20.2
Principal perspectives in applied anthropology upon traditional/primal peoples

| ❋ Routine outlook on tourism | The tourism industry is potentially a disruptive and impact-laden one, but it also can yield many rewards. There is sense in courting it with or on behalf of indigenous populations (after careful scrutiny) where it is seen to provide material, symbolic, rhetorical, or other sought advances. |

Source: Adapted from Bodley, 1982, p. 192.

Figure 20.2
(*Continued*)

Primitive-Environmentalist and the *Liberal-Political* outlooks (Bodley, 1982). These three action-orientated perspectives each have different goals and different rhetorics, though their discourse and practices are not always mutually exclusive. They each are exercised outlooks, or rather, are forms of administrative advocacy which respectively claim (in their own light) to work towards the broad aim of self-determination for indigenous people, but they each work to ensure that local empowerment in quite distinctive ways.

Primitive-Environmentalist advocacy

- *Expressed aims*: Primitive-Environmentalists are high idealists, and set out to defend the particular ways of life of early/primary cultures on the understanding that those societies are superior human adaptations to the physical world. Primitive-Environmentalists seek to establish permanent protected zones (i.e., protected anthropological areas (Dasmann, 1973)) where natural ecosystems and the people indigenous to them would not be harrassed or suffer interference.
- *Supposed weakness*: Opponents condemn Primitive-Environmentalist approaches for being, variously, 'dehumanising' (viz., where they do not respect the views of those members of society who may want change), 'objectifying' (viz., where the practices and material elements of the culture become more important than the people), and 'discriminatory' (viz., where they are viewed as racist in many quarters of social science).

Liberal-Political advocacy

- *Expressed aims*: Liberal-Political adherents are perhaps not so austere as Primitive-Environmentalists, but they still set out to work with indigenous people to force a complete break with existing communication, trade, and industrial practices. Liberal-Political actors endeavour to end all externally created 'imperial' oppressions and all internally derived 'colonial' subjugations mainly by taking critical positions against prevailing government policies and against company undertakings. The Liberal-Political approach thereby seeks self-determination for traditional peoples/indigenous populations so that those communities, themselves, can hopefully determine their own degree of integration with or within so-called mainstream society.

- *Supposed weakness*: Advocates of Liberal-Political thought are condemned for underestimating the size of the gulf which exists between local and cosmopolitan rationalities, and therefore for being insufficiently realist, and they are also criticised for generally having impractical expectations as to how indigenous peoples can indeed organise themselves to lead their own liberation.

Conservative-Humanitarian advocacy

- *Expressed aims*: Conservative-Humanitarianists are inclined towards what they see as 'realism', and tend to recognise that resource development cannot be stopped; they concentrate, instead, upon ameliorating the effect of endogamous development upon traditional/indigenous societies. In accepting the inevitability of 'progress' – or, rather, of accelerated global change – conservative-humanitarians are inclined to be operationally empiricist, and politically realist. Like the Liberal-Political approach, the conservative-humanitarian standpoint is prone towards the advocation of self-determination, but its relatively straightforward integration policies tend to have greater resonance with established governments and with private corporations.
- *Supposed weakness*: The outlook of conservative-humanitarians is rebutted by diehard protectionists, and by some cultural romanticists, for insufficiently shielding original indigenous hopes and supposedly authentic indigenous causes, and for being, itself, something of a very conduit for the added industro-metropolitan exploitation of local, native populations.

Hence, none of the three views on the above continuum are roundly accepted anywhere. The conservative-humanitarian is the one, however, which in the opinion of Bodley (1982), is least coloured by the possibility of false sentimentalities amongst what one would call mainstream populations about the life of indigenous populations. While the conservative-humanitarian stance is not an outlook which this author would necessarily support in all indigenous/non-indigenous encounters, it will be adopted in this chapter to provide possible guidance for those non-Aboriginal advisers who work closely with Aboriginal groups and communities in tourism in Australia.

Under the conservative-humanitarian approach, marketing practices of the travel trade are not outlawed outright as they routinely would be under primitive-environmentalism, or as they possibly would be under liberal-political action. In Australia, conservative-humanitarians broadly aim for compatibility within marketing practice between the normal interests of the trade and the found or assumed interests of indigenous populations. Interestingly, in Australia as recently as the early 1990s, a major government study yielded the serious judgement that the exigences of the tourism industry and the capacity of Aboriginal people to provide tourism and travel services are 'largely incompatible' (Altman and Finlayson, 1991, p. 23). While many observers have wholly supported the Altman and Finlayson judgement, other commentators might see a touch of racist discourse – or at least, the hint of an unimaginative or disempowering tone of condemnation in it. The supporters of The Altman–Finlayson view tend to believe that it merely reflects the difficult cross-cultural assessment that in reality there is a pervasive lack of harmony between the demands of the trade in tourism and the operational competencies and other abiding interests of indigenous people. Such apparently realist assessments maintain that (in the early 1990s) the mismatch of expectancies lay at the operational level of service delivery in the industry and was not a philosophical level judgement about what potentially indigenous groups and communities could humanly attain or jointly aspire towards. Accordingly, the statement of Altman and Finlayson need not be taken as a logical and permanent rebuttal of conservative-humanitarianism, per se, but as a statement on economic probity of its time, a candid disclosure from what nowadays (just 15 years later) might be seen to be a very large age away, such have been the indigenous dynamisms of creative indigenous thought and pioneering Aboriginal marketplace action since the mid-1990s.

An important requisite of the conservative-humanitarian approach in tourism is for Aboriginal people to be actively schooled over time (where groups and communities are new to the industry), and to eventually school themselves in the realtime and realworld workings of the trade (as many indigenous bodies have indeed sought to do during the late 1990s/early 2000s) (see chapter by Berno, Editors' Note).

In recent years, a number of Australia-wide promotional agencies have sprung up whose mission is to make tourists aware of the sorts of 'heritage' and 'adventure' sites now available for tourist visitation. While Crawshaw (2005) provides an alternative to the aforesaid Lonely Planet Guide, detailing over 200 'Aboriginal-owned' and/or 'culturally–appropriate' ventures, the following websites tend to be favoured by indigenous operators at time of writing:

- www.aboriginaltourism.com.au – run by Aboriginal Tourism Australia;
- www.diversetravel.com – run by Diverse Travel Australia, an operation that is not just concerned with indigenous ventures.

The broad conservative-humanitarian stance is adopted in this chapter because it is rather more responsive to the recent paradigm shift that has seemingly occurred (is seemingly still occurring) in wider areas of indigenous affairs across Australia away from the recent orthodoxies of pure self-determination. At this time, the supreme goal of securing what is culturally appropriate – that is, something that many have argued more naturally sits with liberal-political advocacy and with primitive-environmental advocacy – is no longer as magisterial in applied anthropological circles as it once was, and is increasingly condemned for not so much generating 'better practice' but 'inferior adaptation' (Cowlishaw et al., 2006, pp. 9, 10, 13). Consonantly, conservative-humanitarian stances tend to be automatically dismissed on account of their inherent assimilationist bent because the great evil of assimilation, ipso facto, is no longer so commonly and immediately dismissed: 'the tide which swept us all [mainstream Australians and indigenous "Australians"] into a condition of modernity and into ever more global processes is not a tide which indigenous people want to avoid at all costs' (Cowlishaw et al., 2006, p. 3). Taking this on board, this discussion therefore proceeds via conservative-humanitarian thoughtlines on the grounds that such advocacy best deals with the complex realities which indigenous populations face in their intercultural and intracultural encounters today, and with the involved everyday relationships they have while engaged with non-Aboriginals and with the surrounding mainstream economy. Thus, the chapter is predicated on the view that the attention of some of those who work in tourism studies within indigenous settings in and across Australia need to (perhaps) redirect their attention away from servicing Aboriginal Australia as a sort of adrift or hived-off indigenous sphere (where rather fixed notions of culture are the ruling consideration) towards realms of interaction and influence (where notions of culturally productive possibility – a quite different idea – is the operant outlook) (after Venn, 2006). Tourism can then thereby be seen to be, and can become, a vehicle which can more readily open up new grounds for imagining alternative worlds for indigenous groups and communities. It can more readily open up critical spaces for new narratives of becoming and acts of emancipation where those indigenous populations express the need for such forms of help/guidance/support. In this sense, tourism can be seen as a means through which, overtime, indigenous populations are able to develop new plural lifeworlds today as they forge new relationships between their present and their past.

The power of everyday discourse in the projection (and making of) indigenous realities

We learn from Jaworski and Pritchard (2005) that the images and identities of peoples and places are not constant and immutable entities, but are rather flexible and alterable things very much defined through discourse, and naturalised through repeated-cum-collaborative performance. In the current setting, therefore, the held discourse and practice of the 'national' and 'international' tourism industry not only reflects cultural, social, and environmental reality, it also shapes those things. Thus, it is important that, over the coming decades, Aboriginal interest groups active in tourism become comfortable deciphering how the dominant images and projections of the industry they engage in collaboratively and performatively pre-construct the exhibited and promoted indigenous world (after Kirshenblatt-Gimblett, 1998). Aboriginal groups and communities have to learn – if they do not automatically already recognise it – how the collective multi-agency tourism industry works with shared but mainstream visions of reality, and how it regularly/repeatedly broadcasts genre (and frequently poorly dimensioned) representations of exoticised and weakly authenticated forms of indigenous Being. Here the work of Pêcheux (1982) on discursive agency is highly relevant. It will, over time, be considerably demanding of interdisciplinary skill and discursive effort. It will eventually demand the cross-fertilisation of marketing sensitivities with 'emic' (i.e., local and home community) sensibilities interface between indigenous communities and the enveloping travel industry.

In order to comprehend what Pêcheux (1982) means by disidentification, it is helpful to view the output of the overall tourism development and marketing effort as a form of discourse put out within, by, and through the ongoing and everyday discursive practices of the industry, that is within the 'talk' and the 'deeds' of the travel trade. These mundane but often evocative communications, and these routine but often evocative practices, are inevitably ideological, and they are characteristically contradictory, uneven, and over-determined, as all discursive formations tend to be (Jaworski and Pritchard, 2005). Theorists of discourse like Pêcheux suggest that the forms and the occasions of cultural representation (in this case, the forms are the storylines and images of supposedly 'native culture' and the occasions are the promotional mechanisms and packaged tours through which they are projected) may themselves be seen as power-laden notions, even as, after a while, in situ entities which can act or which can have effects in and of themselves, without the need for human agency. Thus, if Pêcheux's thinking on the micro-politics of such industrious and inventive 'things' (within cultural representation) is translated to the indigenous context in question in tourism/travel, the marketing communication channels through which images of indigenous Australia are conveyed may be seen to be networks of power relations (see chapter by Ryan et al., Editors' Note). These networks produce widely broadcast accounts of what is understood to be accessible in terms of viewable Aboriginality, and accordingly define and magnify in quite particular ways what the essence of that very Aboriginality is. The point is echoed by Ryan (1988, pp. 560–561; emphasis added):

Rather than being expressive representations of a substance taken to be prior, cultural signs become instead *active agents* in themselves, creating new substances, new social forms, new ways of acting and thinking, new attitudes, reshuffling the cards of 'fate' and 'nature' and 'social reality'. It is on this margin that culture, seemingly entirely autonomous and detached, turns around and becomes a social and material force, a power of signification, and this discrediting applies to political institutions, moral norms, social practices and economic structures [of various sorts].

In Spivak's (1987) view, such sorts of commonplace discourse and such cumulative instances of cultural representation are all-too-frequently ethnocentric, and may be deemed to constitute new forms of colonialism. It is the repeatable imbalance of power within the networks and the channels of the marketing efforts of lead corporations, companies, and governments in global tourism that readily produces an additive violence on or against forms of Aboriginality in all sorts on indigenous settings across the world, and which can silence, close off the possibilities, or much reduce the opportunities of indigenous groups being able to present themselves in significantly self-determinate fashions through tourism marketing and travel promotion.

When applied directly to tourism and travel, what Pêcheux evidences is not a mere matter of the need for remedial or re-punctuated storytelling, where the isolated/removed/emergent indigenous community or local/peripheral population is able to satisfy itself by gaining legitimate inclusion (or recognition) within the dominant forms and structures of the gazing industry's discourse. He notes three modalities.

The first such fabricating modality is that of *identification*, where phenomena are routinely and unquestioningly seen to live or exist entirely within the parameters of the given/the dominant/the mainstream discourse. The second modality is that of *counteridentification*, and amounts to that mode of representation as engaged in by the distant or poorly positioned but doubting and challenging 'trouble-making' group or community, which revolts against this mainstream discourse and which reverses the terms of that conventional/orthodox understanding, but yet which stays predominately captive to the structure of those predominant/mainstream ideas and orientations. The final modality, that of *disidentification*, per se, constitutes the attempts of the poorly-positioned or subjugated population to resist the dominant thinking even more strongly, and to overthrow those cultural warrants or institutional doxa by working within pointedly new/different/raw ideological structures which are resolutely oppositional and even antagonistic in force (Pêcheux, 1982). In this sense, disidentification is a form of reasoning and a field of expression which seeks to combat the subjective appropriation of local (in this case, indigenous) knowledge by mainstream discourse. The call to disidentify forms of cultural representation in the international travel marketplace and in tourism development spheres constitutes a recognition that there is never any 'pure' subject out there, waiting there neutrally, ready to be cleanly/clearly/straightforwardly communicated to tourists. Hence, Pêcheux's thesis as applied would legitimate the view that that there is no pure 'traditional' or 'original' Aboriginal culture – that is, no absolute or disengaged object of Aboriginality – lying latent, available for any such non-aligned or uniform non-ideological representation. Implicitly, Pêcheux's thinking on disidentification suggests all portrayals of Aboriginality have their particular interest group biases and their distinct open or closed windows of understanding on cultural reality, historical truth, and group aspiration.

Given these three mechanisms of representation or edifices of reason in discourse, Pêcheux's concept of disidentification may be used to draw attention to the under-recognised 'political' processes of narrativisation (or emplotted storytelling) in tourism, by and through which 'different' and 'Other' subjects, and even ordinary objects and supposedly usual/accepted/customary deeds and events are conceivably 'constructed' in the marketplace. Pêcheux's conceptualisation of the need for agile, assiduous, and vehemently oppositional reasoning is a powerful one: his construct of disidentification teaches marginal groups, and instructs those working with or on behalf of peripheral/different/Other populations in the gazing industry, to be vigilant to the rhetoric of community making and site moulding which they inescapably participate in, and to the privileged representations of culture and significations of tradition which they may be captive within. His concept of disidentification comprises a call for such everyday decision-takers, thereby, to question whether they are complicitly only identifying or counteridentifying when they produce their narratives, and thereby to determine whether they are accordingly serving unconsciously/consciously to bolster exclusively mainstream systems of representation and image mongering which continue to act quietly yet summatively against their own or Other interests, whatever they may be. In this regard, then, disidentification from etic perspectives in the tourism industry beckons the rise of a whole new pungent and emphatic discourse of indigenous outsiderdom (for instance, where in Aboriginal contexts, the whole temporal, spatial, and operational style of management gradually – or even, immediately – becomes reconceived and significantly reconstructed in terms of the Aboriginal sense of being and with respect to the particular indigenous affiliative outlooks wherever they lie on the traditionality/transitionality continuum for the given group or community). For the indigenous community's own point of view, of course, Pêcheux's thoughtlines herald a whole new pungent and emphatic discourse of insiderdom.

The call for much more concertedly disidentified engagement on the part of indigenous groups and communities across the world is, of course, no cry out in the wilderness. The last two decades of the twentieth century and the opening decade of the twenty-first have already produced a wealth of imaginative and heartfelt 'resistance literature' in indigenous settlements and circles around the globe (Harlow, 1987). In Australia, the volume and velocity of such critical indigenous articulation – in the general literature of life and society – was impossible to conceive of a generation ago (Grossman, 2005). Aboriginal Australia already has an emerging, and steadily disidentified literature of demur and rebuff in other domains of culture and aspiration outside of tourism. A so-called Aboriginal Renaissance of the late 1980s (Morrissey, 2005b) has indeed been recognised over a wide range of matters of identity and affiliation, where a new multitude of indigenous voices have confidently arisen to aggressively condemn the institutionally-sanctioned discourses of 'Aboriginality' of yesteryear. But such articulative individuals and institutions do not yet appear to be numerous in such forms of opposition and challenge within the sphere of tourism. As the authors of recent 'Blacklines . . .' text on contemporary indigenous critical writing (Grossman et al., 2005) have made clear, the 1990s has given rise to a new litany of active indigenous agents who are nowadays confidently and (in the positive sense of the term) impatiently reconceptualising the history and culture of Aboriginal and Torres Strait Islander people across Australia (Dodson, 2005). Thus the 1990s and 2000s have indeed seen a fresh critical community of 'indigenous Australians' emerge who have spoken up unerringly to bemoan the manner in which concepts of Aboriginality have been totalised under the absolutist and inflexible institutional terms of yesterrule. Yet the important rider remains to be asked in Australia: where are the Aboriginal intellectuals – or rather, the critically-minded disidentified indigenous vindicators and champions – who articulate their vital messages through tourism? Do they yet exist, genuinely? Dodson has prominently called upon his fellow indigenous people to exercise their rights to define and create themselves and their lives – that is, 'to write and sing and paint and tell ourselves' (Dodson, 2005) – but the cultural politics of tourism is arguably still hegemonically etic, operationally externally industrialised, and therefore rhetorically 'mainstream'. Hopefully, the late 2000s and the 2010s will witness the rise at tourism-settings and in tourism-heritage presentations of the kinds of newly and proudly disidentified voices which have already arisen in other other domains such as music and theatre, where they have notably 'spoken out and up' with force against the received heavy-determinisms and grossly-exoticised external visions of Aboriginality. Hopefully, such new/emergent indigenous voices in tourism across Australia can pointedly and loudly speak out and up to correct, to announce, and to declare transformatively via the new relationalities (Moreton-Robinson, 2006) and the new compossibilities (Venn, 2006) offered by tourism, what is important today under the contemporary Aboriginal brother and sisterhood, as much as each local group or community is ever spiritually safe and culturally comfortable in revealing about themselves, of course.

The realities of indigenous tourism

The late 1980s and the early 1990s have seen a relative explosion of interest in research into the social and economics base of tourism in and amongst Aboriginal societies, with Sullivan (1984), Altman (1989), Coombs et al. (1989), Ross (1991), Simons (2000), Whitford et al. (2001), and Mercer (2005) each yielding particularly noteworthy insights. Yet, as Hollinshead (1988) pointed out, so much of the changing dynamics of indigenous society/tourist society interface have gone unexplored in terms of coordinated research-agenda investigation. In that light, Figure 20.3 lists a number of broad research precepts which are now conceived to channel immediate and high priority enquiry into the character of the involvement of Aboriginal groups and communities in tourism development and into related spheres of 'cultural' and 'heritage' interpretation. The precepts given in Figure 20.3 are part of an ongoing monitoring of matters of policy and practice in regarding indigenous tourism in Australia being conducted by the author. Slowly, and conceivably, and advanced on a case-by-case basis across the world, a more responsible and sensitively informed transdisciplinary tourism studies scholarship can emerge which can help indigenous peoples recover their respective humanity and safeguard their lands and spiritual inheritances through tourism.

A version of ten of these dozen precepts first appeared in Butler and Hinch (1996), but they have been updated here to take account of the changing social, political, and psychic milieu in which contemporary Aboriginal people are located – and to respect recent mobilities of indigenous production and performance in what one could regard as the parallel field of projection (to tourism) like 'the arts', 'film production', and 'television broadcasting'. Although the 12 precepts of Figure 20.3 take much of their original force and pertinence from the first 25 working papers from the 1985–1988 East Kimberley Impact Assessment Project in Western Australia (Coombs et al., 1989, pp. 149–151)), they have been rejuvenated over the last decade through the author's dialogue with representatives of Aboriginal groups and communities in Queensland, the Northern Territory, and Western Australia. That said, they serve as propositions to guide future case study, ethnographic, phenomenological, interpretive, and/or other forms of enquiry into Aboriginal contexts and indigenous communal settings in other locales around Australia and on different continents. Fundamentally, the 12 precepts suggest THAT administrators/managers/developers of tourism operations to indigenous locales:

- Ought not assume that removed and isolated indigenous populations decently comprehend what tourism is and is not, vis-à-vis its Western/urban-industrial meanings [precept 1].
- Ought to take considerable, but respectful, pains to find out why the members of a given Aboriginal population in any social or geographic setting do or do not wish to accommodate tourism development or to otherwise advance tourism visitation – paying particular respect to the non-economic hopes and aspirations of that community/group [precept 2].
- Ought to become sensitive to the given indigenous group's depth of feelings towards its revered tracts and inherited territories, and alert to the reality that no Aboriginal involvement can meaningfully occur until that host indigenous population itself senses that its own held or carried 'country' is secure [precept 3].
- Ought to become sensible to the facts that considerable passage of time is often required to permit the given indigenous group to take a deliberate or decelerated decision about any particular tourism development or other matter, whereby all intragroup viewpoints can seemingly be heard, and by such processes, that this given group may not in fact have designated leaders who are ever able to be readily accessible, willing, and able to speak immediately on behalf of any 'knowable' or 'authorised' deliverable Aboriginal view [precept 4].
- Ought to recognise that *tjukurpa/jukurrpa* (the term for the Dreaming) amongst certain peoples of Central Australia is a vital point of spiritual and communal inspiration, but also a fragile 'psychic state' and 'mystical place'. It is that heightened communal reference point in the timeless visionary geography that constitutes the held reality of that population where and when financial or economic 'profit' may only be welcomed if it is gained through actions which promote ongoing reverence for the present in terms of that inherited and immutable past [precept 5].

1. The nature of the product:

Many Aboriginal people involved in the tourism industry are likely to be poorly informed about the range, type, and fickleness of motivations which bring tourists into their midst.

2. The dominance of non-financial objectives

Many Aboriginal groups which seek to become involved in tourism ventures are likely to value indigenous considerations of identity, community, and the inherited responsibility for 'property' above the direct specific and desire to engage in tourism itself.

3. The need for land base

In the development of tourism on or in proximity to traditional lands, schemes which facilitate the freedom of Aboriginal people to live upon or gain access to these specific and inherited tracts of precious/fortifying 'country' are likely to attract predominant collective indigenous support.

4. The criticality of congenial, respectful, and unhurried decision-making

In the quest for community decisions from Aboriginal people who continue to live in 'traditional' fashions, mechanisms which seek to facilitate the gradual resolution of interference-free indigenous opinion are likely to out-serve those other rather alien sorts of 'induced' or 'template' administrative approaches which rely upon decisions sought via rather impersonal/dissociative/expeditious methods.

5. The tension between longstanding community interests and industry-relevant marketing mission

In the engagement in tourism (and in the servicing of tourists), as in all indigenous community affairs, traditional Aboriginal groups tend to value intrinsic and/or community bequeathed responsibilities of care concerning tjukurpa (Dreaming), above extrinsic notions of economic profitability.

6. Regional public scrutiny: local non-aboriginal outlooks

In areas of Australia where traditional or semi-traditional Aboriginal groups inhabit or frequently visit, the level of cognition about the indigenous cultural practices, environmental and religious beliefs is often not likely to be high amongst non-Aboriginals who live in that immediate/surrounding area.

7. Affinitive duties and non-market obligations

In the negotiations over the conditions which pertain to a given tourism development venture – and to the possibilities of declaring/interpreting/projecting 'culture', 'belief', and/or 'way-of-life' therein, many Aboriginal people living in traditional or semi-traditional settings will tend to be activated more concertedly by affiliative allegiances and kinship-spiritual fealties motivations than by the potential for 'individual' personal advancement or for personal material reward.

(*Continued*)

Figure 20.3

Precepts to guide future research and management of indigenous tourism in Australia

8. The uncertainty of abiding internal support

Non-Aboriginal executives working with indigenous groups will frequently find the local and immediate community levels of human support and in situ participation in/engagement upon given indigenous community ventures in tourism will be predisposed to being 'fluid' and 'uncertain' even in-the-short-run rather than being 'constant' and 'predictable', overtime.

9. Prior worker responsibilities

In traditional/semi-traditional settings, individual Aboriginal people deployed in management positions in tourism will tend to rate opportunities for communal observances or for the due carrying-out of a in-folk care in the community above personal opportunities for self-promotion as an executive officer, management employee, or an administrative worker.

10. Limited and one-dimensional counselling upon tourism: the preponderance of aleatory/pre-judgemental advice

Many government personnel who work in ongoing advisory positions with indigenous communities in Australia in welfare/social security/community service positions are predisposed to regarding the development of tourism to/across/within communities under their charge as a 'negative' and 'unacceptable intrusion' rather than as a 'positive' and an 'enabling' phenomenon in almost any respect.

11. Dominant archetype of real aboriginality

Across Australia, the notion perdures (amongst many non-Aboriginals) that 'true Aboriginals' are bush group/remote settlement people who maintain 'children of nature' forms of ancestral worship and lifestyle: accordingly, 'Aboriginal' people who live in urban locales or who do not ostensibly act 'traditionally' tend *not* to be regarded (externally) as 'real' or 'proper' Aboriginal people.

12. Varied and uncertain constructions of identity

Commonly in Australia – where indigenous populations have been removed from or are no longer associated with their traditional lands – resultant community groups (and individual Aboriginal people) often develop an unsettled (i.e., a sometimes-different-to-mainstream/sometimes-assimilated-with-mainstream) outlook towards received, ancestral notions of Aboriginality: in many country – towns and other transitional places, the Aboriginal groups/individuals living there often do not live under one single notion of indigenous selfhood (which is unified on and across one common/communal mind).

Figure 20.3
(*Continued*)

- Ought to observe how all manner of hurt continues to be metered out to indigenous 'Australian' communities by non-Aboriginal locals (i.e., many of those who live in close proximity to them) who all-too-commonly are oblivious to the distortions which they themselves tend to uphold when regarding or when encountering the 'indigenous'/'primal'/'traditional' populations in their midst [precept 6]. For many 'local' non-Aboriginal people, communication with (and thereby understanding of) Aboriginal populations has regularly been a difficult thing: '[For many such

non-Aboriginal locals] talking to "them" is confusing [and] disorienting
. . . It is [just] too hard' (Langton, 2005b, p. 122).

- Ought to understand that Aboriginal people – particularly those in traditional settings – are inclined to see themselves as a members of a tribal
collective or sodality first, before they ever see themselves as individuals,
and that their revered principles of good community citizenship within
that tribal collective do not encourage the fast gain or the steady accumulation of rewards and/or possessions for the benefit of themselves as single persons [precept 7].
- Ought to comprehend that for each given community encounter with
tourism or travel, there may never be any consistently uniform or fixed
indigenous group or community view over time: although the given
group/community may at first impression appear to be hidebound by
what seems to be longstanding tradition and hostile to change. Aboriginal
life has always been experienced in a context of change of varying degrees
of intensity and a given group/community (whose opinion is being
sought) may itself not easily be defined, since there is frequently much
interchange and fluidity between neighbouring indigenous communities
[precept 8]. In each age, it is something created from received history and
is modified through 'black and white in dialogue' (Langton, 2005b, p. 118).
- Ought to acknowledge the commonality that within so-called 'traditional'
Aboriginal groups, each individual's identity tends to be built upon symbolic and multiple connections to particular lands and to the particular
group that has the received responsibility to look after that given 'estate'
in perpetuity. Consequently, in 'traditional settings', Aboriginal individuals generally cannot readily advance substantively in terms of any identity
reflective of his or her own bounded ego drives or his/her own management competencies as metropolitan Westerners are relatively free so to do.
Indeed, in almost everything he or she does, a 'traditional' Aboriginal person must uphold the network of mutual rights and reciprocal obligations
which have been established within and (in some senses) out beyond his
or her kinship group [precept 9].
- Ought to affirm that many of those non-Aboriginal individuals who coun-
sel indigenous communities on tourism may consistently work from
primitive-environmentalist, liberal-political, or like outlooks, and may
thereby be generally unseasoned in their capacity to envision how an
industrialised endeavour like tourism might help renew *tjukurpa*
(the Dreaming) either in the context of broader Australian society, or with
regard to wider intercontinental streams of understanding which come
with the enhanced media mobilisations of globalisation cum glocalisation
(Meethan, 2001) [precept 10].
- Ought to be aware that across Australia many different mediated versions
of Aboriginality exist, some of which originate as 'Aboriginal' constructions of self, but others of which are conceived/built-up/invented by non-
Aboriginals. Both those sorts of conceptualisms – however 'real' or 'faux' in
their origin – can have significant reality-making consequences (Beckett,

1994) [precept 11]. Over the coming decades, it will be an increasing responsibility of tourism to inform/educate visitors to Aboriginal settings and sites in Australia (and to other indigenous scenarios across the world) that the explanations of being and meaning they come across are always someone's account of cultural identity, of held spirituality, and of communal aspiration. Travellers to indigenous 'outback'/'bush'/'desert' environments will need to be reminded that each and every interpretation of culture given and received is just that – an interpretation. Each and every representation is always some sort of fictionalisation: it is unavoidably always borne as a discursive entity from an act of creative authority (Hall, 1997, p. 49). It will be an increasingly important role of those who work in tourism in the twenty-first century to clarify who is behind which interpretive claim. Inescapably, there is a micro-physics of power even within the ordinary/everyday narratives of tourism (Hall, 1997, p. 50): all tourism presentations and performances are caught up in the sometimes special/sometimes mundane games of legitimation.

- Ought not expect each and every Aboriginal group, or these days, each and every mix of Aboriginal individuals, to be able to offer clean and clear representations of their own being and identity. Many significations of 'communal selfhood' and (these days) individual selfhood will indeed be inchoate [precept 12]. Moreover, some relatively stable indigenous communities may in fact work within double expressions of identity, where, firstly, *a private ethnicity* is carried out in the run of everyday community-centred life, while secondly, *a public ethnicity* is made manifest when that group/those individuals is/are engaged in 'outside'/'beyond community'/'political' demesnes (see Jacobs in Beckett, 1994, p. 34). Indeed, in Langton's view, as Aboriginal communities have been increasingly called upon to explain their narratives to outsiders and to render their stories/legends/'designs' accessibly to non-Aboriginal people, these two fields of identity have emerged: "the *inner* and the *outer*: the *inside* and the *outside*, the secret-sacred and the non-secret-sacred, although these are not entirely absolute and distinct" (Langton, 2005b, pp. 110–111; emphasis added). Langton continues: 'Today, anybody in the world with a mind to can walk into a gallery and see at first hand an Aboriginal design depicting the outside knowledge. They will not, however, see the "brilliance" . . . of restricted inside traditional knowledge'.

The need for vigilance

It is the premise of this chapter that if Aboriginal groups and communities do wish to protect their culture, their lifestyles, and their revered homelands they will need to track the play of powerful, antagonistic, and ideologies which do and will conceivably exist amongst the images and the storylines by which they have been and will be represented within the gaze of tourism. They will need to stay alert to the fashions by which the invented truths and the manufactured storylines produced in the marketplace become entrenched and proliferating accounts. In short, they will need to be ever vigilant over the forms of representation and over the instruments of creative invention which day-by-day allow both selective communication and selective non-communication to privilege some storylines and identities, and which day-by-day silence or subjugate other storylines and identities. Indigenous 'Australians' may be arriving in the tourism industry in numbers and with zeal as the impressive panoply of new sites in Kaufman's *Travelling Indigenous Australia* and Lonely Planet's . . . Guide to Indigenous Australia may both indicate.

While much of this call to voice and articulation may seem fundamentally obvious to some, it is no easy matter to engage in such thorough and sustained industry communications/media communications/human communications activities in an industry so splintered and multi-sited as the tourism industry (Meethan, 2001). Yet, very tightly conceived and carefully conducted research into the role and function of tourism vis-à-vis 'the problematics of cultural hybridity and group identification will be required by and for many of the indigenous and the transitioning populations of the world. The complexities involved in cultural representation which need to be plumbed are indeed intricate. How, exactly, do ideologies run through the everyday play of tourism development and marketing' (after Touraine, 1990)? Precisely which worldviews are being repeatedly privileged through the mundane drama, text, and deed of travel and heritage promotion (after Shohat and Stam, 1994)?

Researchers and practitioners in tourism must learn how slender their narrations of the past and the present are, how their dramatisations can easily miss so many silent but vibrant Others, and how the very processes of identification are always conflictual yet productive 'spaces' (Swain, 2004). Although this mix of established and emergent indigenous intellectuals (viz., the assemblage who write in Grossman et al. (2005) and who are introduced in Taylor et al. (2005)) operate from a variety of positions, perspectives, and places, few (none?) of these patrons of Being and Knowing – are grounded in tourism, per se. Just as there is (or might be) no single non-Aboriginal view of Being, so there will be (or ought not be) one single Aboriginal view of what is decently/truly/properly 'indigenous' (Anderson, 2005, p. 22).

Conclusion

This chapter has started from the premise that tourism is potentially (if not already) a principle means by and through which particular peoples and places can be, not just understood, but re-imagined. Tourism will increasingly play a prominent role in not just the construction of culture, but in the re-appraisal of peoples, places, and pasts – that is, in the disidentification of culture, and constructions of culture are never neutral (Wallerstein, 1990, p. 39). Tourism has a crucial role to play not so much in any revolutionary act of 'kicking down the door', for 'it can [thereby] destroy the very building which is seen as an obstruction on the road to somewhere else' (Touraine, 1990, p. 135), but in finding 'the most certain middle way possible between submission to reason and the creation of an open society which recognises both social conditions and the links that unite the past to the future' (Touraine, 1990, p. 140). Development through tourism (as through any industry) will always be a combination of certain universalisms of reason (which propel that industry) and participation in it of that specific local culture/heritage/history (after Touraine, 1990, p. 139). While many theorists have detailed the essentialising and the normalising/naturalising effects of tourism as it variously represents, mis-represents, and de-represents things, this chapter is arguing that the inventive and collaborative power of tourism to make and remake the world can also gradually be harnessed creatively and positively to communicate particular insights about peoples and places. But judging by what has occurred for indigenous people in – for them – other bittersweet realms (of art, film, television, and music), many of the indigenous groups and communities which will embrace bittersweet tourism over the coming decades will want to work/speak/'fight' continually to subvert the external hegemony that is held over the received, the current, and the vogue representations of Aboriginality (Anderson, 2005, p. 24).

While many have condemned tourism as inherently yet another lead vehicle in the ongoing trivialisation and commodification of supposedly questionable 'authentic' objects and events and for the fast external contamination of particular local cultural and natural heritages, this chapter endeavours to work for something of *a humanitarian-conservative stance* on the part of those non-Aboriginals who work with Aboriginal groups and communities. This is a stance which endeavours to harness some of the so-called *worldmaking* (peoplemaking/placemaking/pastmaking) communicative reach of tourism (Hollinshead, In prep.(b)) and to work with it sensitively in order to develop enhanced understanding about indigenous peoples and their lives. Implicitly, therefore, the chapter argues for enlarged critical inspection of the representational agency and authority of tourism in terms of its interface with indigenous populations in order to help minimise the unthinking/unfeeling/exploitative tendencies which come hand-in-glove with the modernist influences of tourism (Meethan, 2001). Yet, for the indigenous people of Australia there is much potential in targeting the representative/significatory agency and power of tourism for its functional value in:

- communicating a little more about the aesthetic and spiritual values of Aboriginal people – to help them in their constant struggles against external control and influence (Huggins, 2005, p. 61);
- engendering greater internal (Aboriginal) pride in the projection of received ancestral parables about life, nature, and survival – and thereby in the repossession of ourselves (Langton, 2005a, p. 81).
- inculcating shared Aboriginal – non-Aboriginal respect for the symbolic and life-enriching power of particular 'places' and 'spaces' across 'country' (in Aboriginal senses)/across the 'nation'/across the 'continent' of

Australia . . . as indigenous groups and communities counteridentify and disidentify their storylines through tourism in the effort to reclaim their history and their places in their own terms (Huggins, 2005, p. 60).

Whole new latent realms of possibility exists for Aboriginal groups/communities/enterprises in and through tourism during the coming decades, but the naturalising and normalising power and multi-fronted character of tourism renders it yet another activity with *a bittersweet potential* (after Cowlishaw et al., 2006). What will count considerably is the cultural and temporal responsiveness of each and every petty decision-making organisation as it works on these various old sense/heavily-prescriptivist and new sense/only-percipient tourism programmes. When we write the brochure, label the object, or talk at the event, each of us helps make (or debilitate) the people in small but significant cumulative ways. And tourism will be disidentified during the coming indigenous decades, as Featherstone (1991) has forecast. The adaptable culture of Aboriginal people has much greater resilience than many outside commentators (in the business of tourism) and external politicians have ever imagined.

CHAPTER 21

Politics, power and indigenous tourism

Michael Hall

Despite its common consumer association with pleasure and leisure, perhaps as far away from politics as one can get in the popular mind, tourism does not occur in a political vacuum. In fact few subjects better illustrate the political dimensions of tourism than the issues associated with indigenous tourism. Whether it be decisions as to where tourism development occurs or more humanistic concerns associated with commodification and representation of heritage and identity, tourism is political. For example, given that heritage is a symbol of the values and ideology of states, societies, communities and cultures the development of heritage interpretation and associated tourism is not the result of a value-free process. Decisions affecting the location and character of tourism development and the recognition of what actually constitutes heritage grow out of a political process. Politics is about power, who gets what, where, how and why (Lasswell, 1936). Decisions affecting all aspects of indigenous tourism: the nature of government involvement in indigenous tourism; the structure of public agencies responsible for indigenous tourism development, management, marketing and promotion; the type of tourism development; participation in policy formulation and implementation; and the identification and representation of indigenous tourism resources and attractions, such as heritage, within indigenous communities all emerge from a political process. This process involves the values of actors (individuals, interest groups and public and private organisations) in a struggle for power.

This chapter discusses the relationships between indigenous tourism and political issues within the explanatory context of power. It first examines concepts of power then uses Lukes' (1974) concept of three dimensions of power to illustrate power relations with respect to different examples of indigenous tourism. The chapter concludes with comments about the notion of indigenous tourism is itself problematic and embedded within certain knowledge and power relationships.

The concept of power

Power is always present in relationships between individual and institutional actors. Power is exercised every time a group or individual is dependent upon someone else for carrying out a role or task. Political leaders and followers, managers and employees, bureaucrats and clients, tour guides and parties all exercise power through the forms of cooperation and conflict they enact. This relational view of power is a key element of understanding its exercise and nature. Giddens (1979, p. 93) noted that power is always a two-way process 'even if the power of one actor is minimal compared to another'. Such a relational understanding of power is inherent to Lukes' (1974) seminal work on power in which power was conceptualised as 'all forms of successful control by A over B – that is, of A securing B's compliance' (Lukes, 1974, p. 17). However, the very notion of 'power', one of the cornerstones of political analysis, is an 'essentially contested' concept (Gallie, 1955–56) by which there is no universal agreement as to exactly how the concept should be understood and therefore analysed. Indeed, Lukes (1974, 2005) has stressed that the use of the concept of power is inextricably linked to a given set of value assumptions held by researchers which pre-determine the range of its empirical application. Guzzini (2001) for example, notes that any neutral definition of 'power', such as that proposed by Oppenheim (1981), seems elusive, exactly because power is used as an explanatory variable and there is no neutral concept of power for the dependence of theory, empirical and conceptual analyses, on meta-theoretical commitments. Similarly, Gray (1983, p. 94) compared individualist (voluntarist) and structuralist (determinist) positions and concluded that 'since judgements about power and structure are theory-dependent operations, actionists and structuralists will approach their common subject matter – what goes on in society – using divergent paradigms in such a fashion that incompatible explanations (and descriptions) will be produced'.

Given the issues involved in its application the question may be asked as to why it is important to study power, especially within the context of tourism studies where it has only drawn extremely limited attention. According to Morriss (1987) it is because of the practical, moral and evaluative contexts. First, we are interested in power because we want to know how things are brought about, second, because through the assessment of power, moral responsibility for the use of power can be attributed, and third, because people are not just interested in the judgement of individuals but in the evaluation of society. All of these issues emerge in studying indigenous tourism, while the connection between the ideas of power and responsibility that arise in the value dependence of the analysis of power arguably highlights the importance of understanding the morality of power and the political and ethical space of what we study:

When we see the conceptual connection between the idea of power and the idea of responsibility we can see more clearly why those who exercise power are not eager to acknowledge the fact, while those who take a critical perspective of existing social relationships are eager to attribute power to those in privileged positions. For to acknowledge power over others is to implicate oneself in responsibility for certain events and to put oneself in a position where justification for the limits placed on others is expected. To attribute power to another, then, is not simply to describe his role in some perfectly neutral sense, but is more like accusing him of something, which is then to be denied or justified.

(Connolly, 1974, p. 97)

For Connolly the notion of power therefore implies counterfactuals, that is, it could be done differently. Indeed, Lukes (1974) indicated that Bachrach and Baratz's (1962, 1970) conceptualisation of power with respect to the importance of non-decision-making (confining the scope of decision-making so as to deliberately exclude other decision options) served to redefine what counts as a political issue in the sense that what is not done is as important as what is done, and often more so. To be 'political' therefore means to be potentially changeable (Hoffmann, 1988). For Guzzini (2000, 2001) this provides a constructivist dimension to the analysis of power as concept formation is part of the social construction of knowledge; and the defining and assigning of power is therefore a power or 'political' exercise in itself and hence part of the social construction of reality. Therefore, the study of power, in and of itself, runs counter to those who seek to 'depoliticise' policy fields and present them as 'rational' exercises in decision-making. Such a perspective may also be applied to discussion in much of tourism studies about the inherent value of collaboration, partnership and networks without there being any consideration of the power dimensions of such social relationships.

In his review of the concept of power Lukes (1974, 2005) identified three different approaches, or dimensions, in the analysis of power, each focusing on different aspects of the decision-making process:

- a one-dimensional view emphasising observable, overt behaviour, conflict and decision-making;
- a two-dimensional view which recognises decisions and non-decisions, observable (overt or covert) conflict, and which represents a qualified critique of the behavioural stance of the one-dimensional view especially with respect to recognition of values and institutional practices in political systems that favour the interests of some actors over others;
- a three-dimensional view which focuses on decision-making and control over the political agenda (not necessarily through decisions), and which recognises observable (overt or covert) and latent conflict.

Each of the three dimensions arises out of, and operates within, a particular political perspective as the concept of power is value dependent (Lukes, 1974, 2005). For example, a pluralist conception of the tourism policy-making process, such as that which underlies the notion of community-based tourism planning, including its more recent applications in terms of ecotourism and pro-poor tourism, will focus on different aspects of the decision-making process, than structuralist conceptions of politics which highlight social relations within the consumption of tourist services (see chapter by Goodwin, Editors' Note). These distinctions are extremely significant for the understanding of tourism. However, given the need to understand the dominant interests and ideologies operating within the political and administrative system which surrounds indigenous tourism, it seems reasonable to assume that the use of a wide conception of power, capable of identifying decisions, non-decisions and community political structure, will provide the most benefit in the analysis of the political dimensions of tourism (Hall, 2006).

One-dimensional views of community decision-making

Much of the writing in tourism that discusses issues of collaboration, participation and decision-making often fails to recognise the role of power relations between actors. Where this occurs it may well reflect a rather naïve perspective on tourism development that holds that everyone has equal access to power and representation. To an extent this has been one of the driving elements behind utilising the community approach as an appropriate conceptual framework for tourism planning as there appears to be an inherent assumption that it is somehow 'closer to the people'. However, public participation in tourism planning has long been recognised as imperfect (Hall, 2000b). Nevertheless, a one-dimensional view of power in communities suggests that even though imperfect, the community decision-making process is at least observable as it operates through the overt action of pluralist interests (Dahl, 1961; Debnam, 1984). In addition political issues are regarded as coming into existence when they command 'the attention of a significant segment of the political stratum' (Dahl, 1961, p. 92). This concept of power has the advantage that it can be relatively easily operationalised. As Lukes (1986, p. 2) observes, when B seeks to resist the power of A it is 'relevant in the sense that, if it is actualised, it provides the test by which one can measure relative power, where parties conflict over an issue'. The latter observation being significant in that power relations shift according to the issue (Lukes, 1986, p. 8).

Yet power is not evenly distributed within a community and some groups and individuals have the ability to exert greater influence over the tourism development and planning process than others through the access to financial resources, expertise, public relations, media, knowledge and time to put into contested situations (Hall and Jenkins, 1995). Indigenous groups often do not have the same financial and technical capacities to engage in policy debate and lobbying as non-indigenous business interests. For example, Pforr's (2006) analysis of tourism administration and decision-making in the Northern Territory highlighted the extent to which Aboriginal groups had only limited influence on the use of Aboriginal images and representations while simultaneously being encouraged to use tourism as a mechanism of economic development for the Territory as a whole. Indeed, the indigenous groups of Australia, as with those of many other developed countries, have not had the capacity to control tourism development. As Langton and Palmer (2003) noted, 'while there has been Indigenous participation in the tourism industry in Australia since at least the 1900s . . . it was usually non-indigenous people who dictated the way in which Aboriginal people participated in the industry' (see chapter by Hollinshead, Editors' Note).

In the Australian case, the capacities of Aboriginal groups to influence tourism decision-making only began to change markedly at the Commonwealth and State government level in the 1990s when indigenous tourism strategies began to be developed as a result of Aboriginal development being placed on the political agenda (see chapter by Smeichen and Boyle, Editors' Note). However, arguably this itself was a result of the 'Mabo' court case in the High Court of Australia. The Mabo case refers to Eddie Koiko Mabo, a Torres Strait Islander born on the island of Mer, one of the Murray Islands, who was the plaintiff in litigation against the State of Queensland with respect to recognition of Aboriginal title. On the 3 June 1992 the High Court ruled that the land title of Australia's indigenous peoples, the Aborigines and Torres Strait Islanders, is recognised at common law and that indigenous land title, or native title, stems from the continuation within common law of their rights over lands and inshore waters that pre-date European colonisation of Australia. Although the case did not apply to private lands, it did apply to crown lands, national parks, and leased crown lands which recognised Aboriginal use. Control of land is clearly an important factor in tourism development. As Liam Myer, executive officer of the Djabiluka Aboriginal Association in the Kakadu region stated with respect to the establishment of joint ventures between Aboriginal and non-Aboriginal groups: 'The power that the Aboriginal traditional owners have is access to the land, access to the site' (quoted in Langton and Palmer, 2003, np).

The precedence of Mabo has more recently been reinforced by the 20 September 2006 findings on the Noongar people's claim for native title over metropolitan Perth. Federal Court Justice Wilcox found that native title existed over the Perth region by the continued observance of traditional customs despite British Settlement in 1829. Although the findings have no implications for private land, there still have been concerns raised by some politicians and white Australians about access to recreational resources such as beaches and parks (Barrass and Laurie, 2006).

Ownership of land, as well as a set of institutional arrangements that recognise indigenous rights under law, is therefore a vital element in providing Aboriginal groups with a degree of control or, at least, influence in the tourism development process. Without such a set of institutional arrangements, the level of indigenous involvement in tourism planning will often take the form of 'tokenism' in which decisions or the direction of decisions has already been prescribed by government by virtue of other policies and decisions before indigenous participation actually occurs. Without such arrangements indigenous communities will rarely have the political and legal capacity to say 'no' in the longer term.

Two-dimensional views of decision-making: the two faces of power

Bachrach and Baratz (1970) identified two major weaknesses in the pluralist approach to power. First, it did not provide for the fact that power may be exercised by confining the scope of political decision-making. Second, they argued that the pluralist model provided no criteria for determining what were the significant issues. Therefore, two-dimensional views of community decision-making focus on decision-making and non-decision-making and observable (overt and covert) conflict (Bachrach and Baratz, 1962, 1970). Bachrach and Baratz (1970, p. 44) defined a non-decision as 'a decision that results in suppression or thwarting of a latent or manifest challenge to the values or interests of the decision-maker'. A non-decision is a means by which demands for change in the existing allocation of benefits and privileges in the community can be suffocated before they are even voiced; or kept covert, or killed before they gain access to the relevant decision-making arena; or, failing all these things, maimed or destroyed in the implementation stage of the policy process (Lukes, 1974). Non-decision-making exists 'to the extent that a person or group – consciously or unconsciously – creates or reinforces barriers to the public airing of political conflicts, that person or group has power' (Bachrach and Baratz, 1970, p. 8). The role of non-decision-making is now widely acknowledged in the political literature given that political actors, and organisations 'can leave selected topics undiscussed for what they consider their own advantage' (Holmes, 1988, p. 22).

With respect to problems of the one-dimensional version of power in identifying key issues, Bachrach and Baratz (1970, p. 11) also stress the importance of an analysis of the 'mobilisation of bias' which is 'the dominant values and the political myths, rituals and institutional practices which tend to favour the vested interests of one or more groups, relative to others'. Non-decision-making is also the 'primary method for sustaining a given mobilisation of bias' (Bachrach and Baratz, 1970, pp. 43–44). Examples of two-dimensional views of power abound with respect to indigen-ous peoples in developed countries. At the macro-political level indigenous groups may not be able to exercise the same rights of citizenship as the non-indigenous majority. For example, it was not until 1967 that Australians voted to change the national constitution so as to allow the federal government to make laws for Aborigines and to include them in the census, an amendment which provided Aborigines with full voting rights. Similar issues with respect to citizenship and rights have impacted indigenous tourism development in British Columbia (BC), Canada. In 2002 the province's Liberal Government initiated a referendum on Native land claims based on the argument that it was required to secure a new public mandate for a new set of negotiating principles. In an analysis of the referendum Rossiter and Wood (2005) argued that the government and its supporters employed a discourse centred on a private property ethic/neo-liberal logic in order to justify the exercise. Given the community and collective property ethic attached to Native land ownership such a shift in the treaty process therefore needed to be understood as a contest over the terms of citizenship and not simply as a conflict over land resources (Rossiter and Wood, 2005), and tourism was deeply embedded in such processes as a result of both recreation and parks being explicitly mentioned in the referenda as well as tourism being noted as an area of Aboriginal economic development.

Under the 2002 referendum initiated by the Campbell Liberal Government ballots were mailed to the British Columbian electorate, asking voters to indicate their support for the following statements with a simple 'yes' or 'no':

1 Private property should not be expropriated for treaty settlements.
2 The terms and conditions of leases and licences should be respected; fair compensation for unavoidable disruption of commercial interests should be ensured.
3 Hunting, fishing and recreational opportunities on Crown land should be ensured for all British Columbians.
4 Parks and protected areas should be maintained for the use and benefit of all British Columbians.

5 Province-wide standards of resource management and environmental protection should continue to apply.

6 Aboriginal self-government should have the characteristics of a local government, with powers delegated from Canada and BC.

7 Treaties should include mechanisms for harmonising land-use planning between Aboriginal governments and neighbouring local governments.

8 The existing tax exemptions for Aboriginal people should be phased out (Elections BC, 2002).

The limiting of options in referenda, for example, is a classic example of non-decision-making when electors are given a number of options with respect to development or other proposals. In the case of the 2002 BC referendum on Native land claims, the wording of the referendum was described as 'amateurish' by the Angus Reid polling company, 'but the basic message was that it was unjust to put the rights of a minority group to the vote of a majority and that the questions being asked were designed to garner a "yes" vote' (Rossiter and Wood, 2005, p. 360). Indeed, a yes vote was the result with voters responding 'yes' to the various questions with a range of 84.52% (Question 1) to 94.50% (Question 4), with over 20,000 votes not being considered as they did not meet the requirements of the Treaty Negotiations Referendum Regulation (Elections BC, 2002). Such 'spoiled' ballots were likely to be protest votes as a result of a campaign by the Union of BC Indian Chiefs. Elections BC also received letters and written comments that 'expressed concern that there was no mechanism to cast a "protest vote", or to have a means of influencing the outcome of the referendum other than to vote Yes or No . . . Similar concerns that there is not a "none of the above" option on election ballots have also been expressed by voters' (2002, pp. 7, 8). However, just as importantly only 35.8% of registered voters actually returned ballots.

A variation of non-decision-making is the concept of non-implementation in which although policy is developed or regulation enacted it is not actually enforced (Mokken and Stokman, 1976). For example, in New Zealand successive governments since the early 1980s developed tourism policies that aimed to integrate Maori into tourism policy making as well as assist in the development of Maori tourism product. However, it was not until the creation of a coalition agreement between the National Party and New Zealand First in 1996 that the New Zealand Tourism Board had to formally consult with the Maori Ministry over Maori tourism issues. Indeed, institutional arrangements are a critical element in tourism development and policy making yet in many of the governance structures in developed countries indigenous groups only have very limited influence except usually at the most local of scales simply because they are in the minority. To put it crudely, they usually do not have sufficient votes or campaign finances to influence policies at the national and, in some cases state or provincial levels.

Within the political studies literature the role of institutional arrangements has been long recognised as important although studies in a tourism context are extremely limited. As (Schattsneider, 1960, p. 71) commented, 'All forms of political organisation have a bias in favour of the exploitation of some kinds of conflict, and the suppression of others, because organisation is the mobilisation of bias. Some issues are organised into politics while some others are organised out'. Those who benefit from tourism may well be placed in a preferred position to defend and promote their interests through the structures and institutions by which communities are managed. Significantly, the influential models of community tourism promoted by Murphy (1985) clearly fail to address issues of the distribution of power and representation in a community-based approach. Indeed, there is a wider tendency in tourism studies to romanticise the collective capacity of local communities to undertake participative decision-making. 'Communities are not the embodiment of innocence; on the contrary, they are complex and self-serving entities, as much driven by grievances, prejudices, inequalities and struggles for power as they are united by kinship, reciprocity and interdependence. Decision-making at the local level can be extraordinarily vicious, personal, and not always bound by legal constraints' (Millar and Aiken, 1995, p. 629). And in many 'communities' in the developed world, indigenous peoples only have a very limited voice.

Bachrach and Baratz's (1970) method for empirical application of the concept of non-decision-making consists of three stages. First, the study of the actual decision-making process within the political arena and the resultant outcomes. Second, the determination of the remaining overt and covert grievances of the apparently disfavoured group. Finally, the determination of 'why and by what means some or all of the potential demands for change have been denied an airing' (Bachrach and Baratz, 1970, p. 49). For example, to refer again to the situation in BC, Rossiter and Wood (2005) argue that the Provincial government sought to develop a set of indigenous policies that seek to avoid overt protest but which remain committed to private economic development with respect to First Nations. For example, the Provincial government has been promoting the benefits of the 2010 Winter Olympic Games for First Nations peoples including a programme to boost 'Aboriginal tourism'.

As we invest in First Nations by creating new opportunities, one of our priorities is to ensure that we are matching skills training with areas of greatest need in our economy – clearly tourism is one of those. There are enormous openings emerging in Aboriginal tourism as we prepare for the Olympics and we are working to support these. This new programme will help build management and administrative skills for First Nations and enhance the entrepreneurial spirit that every successful industry needs.

(Ministry of Advanced Education and
Treaty Negotiations Office, 2004)

At the same time that the Provincial government promotes its investment in Aboriginal tourism:

The Province is building a New Relationship with First Nations founded on the principles of mutual respect, recognition and reconciliation of Aboriginal rights. The goal is to ensure Aboriginal people share in the economic and social development of BC, in line with government's five great goals for a golden decade.

(Office of the Premier, 2006)

The Province has also simultaneously denied 'the complexity that lies behind First Nations' assertions of land title and rights to self-government' and instead indicated a desire to attract investment 'within the logic of neo-liberalism. As is demonstrated by the "Aboriginal tourism" program' (Rossiter and Wood, 2005, p. 365).

Three-dimensional views of power

The three-dimensional view of power (Lukes, 1974) incorporates the first dimension of observable power in decision-making and Bachrach and Baratz's (1962, 1970) power through non-decision-making, but adds to these the dimension of institutional bias and the manipulation of preferences. The three-dimensional view of power 'allows for consideration of the many ways in which potential issues are kept out of politics, whether through the oper-ation of social forces and institutional practises or through individuals' deci-sions' (Lukes, 1974, p. 240). Lukes (1974, p. 22) argues that Bachrach and Baratz (1970) do not recognise that the phenomenon of collective action is not necessarily 'attributable to particular individual decisions or behaviour, nor that the mobilisation of bias results from the form of *organisation*, due to "systemic" or organisational effects'. He then goes on to emphasise the role that power has in shaping human preferences in arguing, 'to assume that the absence of grievances equals genuine consensus is simply to rule out the possibility of false or manipulated consensus by definitional fiat' (Lukes, 1974, p. 24): 'A may exercise power over B . . . by influencing, shaping or determining his very wants' (Lukes, 1974, p. 23). To Lukes (1974, p. 23), such an approach is 'the most effective and insidious use of power'.

At first glance examination of a three-dimensional view of power in tourism decision-making may appear to be quite problematic. After all, 'how can one study, let alone explain, what does not happen?' (Lukes, 1974, p. 38). Nevertheless, the way 'things do not happen' is as important as what does: 'the proper object of investigation is not political activity but political inactivity' (Crenson, 1971, p. vii). Indeed, Lukes (1974) argued that third-dimensional power may be recognised when it is not in accordance with an individual or group's 'real interests'. Lukes (1974, pp. 24–25) therefore recognises a '*latent con-flict*, which consists in a contradiction between the interests of those exercising power and the *real interests* of those they exclude'. This means that we can arrive at a slightly broader definition of power based on notions of interest in which 'A exercises power over B when A affects B in a manner contrary to B's interests' (Lukes, 1974, 27). Lukes (2005) argues that what counts as 'real inter-ests' are a function of explanatory purpose, framework and methods, 'which in turn have to be justified' (2005, p. 148). The notion of interests can therefore be argued from a number of perspectives including material, rational choice and environmental well-being approaches as well as understood as a way of identifying 'basic' capabilities which existing arrangements preclude. In the case of the latter, Lukes (2005) cites the work of Nussbaum on Indian women's collectives, who argued that the seclusion of women in the north of India, who 'just peep out of their houses and don't take any action in the world' is 'incompatible with fully human functioning' (Nussbaum, 2000, p. 43).

Non-decisions and latent conflicts provide evidence for the existence of the third dimension of power. The third dimension of power is also related to the analysis of structural dominance in the restriction of human agency. However, some critics (e.g., Giddens, 1979; Hyland, 1995) argue that such structural domination is beyond the scope of any focus on intentionally exerted power of individual actors. Perhaps more significantly, Luke's third dimension also intersects with Foucault's (1972, 1980) power/knowledge framework which also acknowledged the relational nature of power: 'in reality power means relations, a more-or-less organised, hierarchical, co-ordinated cluster of relations' (Foucault, 1980, p. 198). To Foucault, knowledge and power are inseparable. Power can be assessed through knowledge, because knowledge itself has a function of power. 'Once knowledge can be analysed in terms of region, domain, implantation, displacement, transposition, one is able to capture the process by which knowledge functions as a form of power and disseminates the effects of power' (Foucault, 1980, p. 69). In this power–knowledge relationship, power in turn impacts the formation of knowledge. According to Foucault (1980, pp. 51, 59), 'the exercise of power itself creates and causes to emerge new objects of knowledge and accumulates new bodies of information . . . Far from preventing knowledge, power produces it'.

In seeking to operationalise the concept of power we therefore arrive at the importance of locating issues of power within particular issue and locational contexts, even though we must also acknowledge that such loci of power relations will be connected to the myriad of other issues and sets of interests. Indeed, the value of a Lukesian approach to power is highlighted in the multi-layering of observations of power occurring in the three dimensions in that it provides an empirical strength often missing in Foucaultian analyses which, while acknowledging the role of structural dominance, often fail to record the actions of individual actors in relation to specific issues and interests. An example of this in tourism studies is the article by Cheong and Miller (2000) that presents a poorly articulated and single dimensional account of power with little empirical grounding. Indeed, arguably there is a substantial amount of such writing in tourism where authors have exhorted the notion of a tourist gaze without interrogation of the concepts of power and knowledge on which it is grounded and have given little thought to the role that individual actors play with respect to power relations from a decision and non-decision-making perspective. Nevertheless, such criticisms aside, tourism provides a number of good examples that illustrate the third dimensional notion of power with respect to knowledge and interests.

Heritage provides a useful setting in which to investigate the third dimension of power. Institutional representations and reconstructions of heritage are often not fully inclusive. Some historical actors are included while others are left out. The roles and actions of even these actors are also represented in certain ways. Particular ideologies represent themselves to the tourist through museums, historic houses, historic monuments and markers, guided tours, public spaces, heritage precincts and landscapes in a manner that may act to legitimate current social and political structures. As Norkunas (1993, p. 5) recognised, 'The public would accept as "true" history that is written, exhibited, or otherwise publicly sanctioned. What is often less obvious to the public is that the writing or the exhibition itself is reflective of a particular ideology'. For example, in the case of Tasmania there is a paucity of official information at national parks and museums with respect to the removal of Aboriginal Tasmanians from their lands and the reasons for their population decline. Arguably the same could be said in some parts of the Australian mainland as well. Indeed, in many 'new world' nations the presentation of indigenous history in museums often seems to finish when the colonists arrive. Pre-European history is fine to represent, exhibiting post-colonial settlement means having to deal with issues of conflict and land rights and not many politicians and domestic visitors are willing to come to terms with the implications of such a realist view of history that serves to expose the range of interests involved.

Within the third dimension of power, concepts of otherness and indigenous itself as a category also become increasingly problematic. For example, the notion of being Maori (or any indigenous group for that matter) is defined in terms of being 'other'. Being *Pakeha* (non-Maori and particularly European) stands in opposition to being Maori. However, for the international tourists to New Zealand, the Maori are just one of a potential range of others with which the visitor comes into contact. Nevertheless, for many Maori being other is vitally important in terms of notions of identity and belonging. But being other contains many paradoxes and problems in relation to the tourist experience. For many contemporary Maori being perceived as other by tourists typically only occurs within identified tourist spaces where otherness is on display and is a deliberately commoditised experience. Tourism promotion of New Zealand typically utilises representations of Maori otherness in a bid to display a 'unique' dimension of New Zealand culture in the international marketplace, yet such representations are often at odds with everyday Maori life in which the wearing of grass skirts, for example, would be seen as most unusual. Overt cultural display of otherness for the benefit of tourists therefore, while providing the possibilities for generating greater income and economic self-determination for Maori, also has the potential to reinforce stereotypical representations of Maori and certain types of knowledge (see chapters by Carr and by Ryan and McIntosh, Editors' Note).

The use of Maori images as a component of international tourism promotion and the development of 'Maori tourism' has become a major source of conflict in terms of the representation, interpretation and control of the cultural and natural resources which serve as the foundation for the development of New Zealand's tourist industry. The stereotyping of the Maori by *Pakeha* for domestic and international tourist consumption has increasingly come under criticism (Barnett, 2000). The image of the attractive *wahine* (Maori maiden) in traditional dress kneeling beside the pool of boiling mud or participating in a *poi* (traditional dance) often as part of a concert party is seen by some Maori as being degrading and racist (Keelan, 1996). Nevertheless, it is somewhat ironic that the national tourism promotion body Tourism New Zealand still retains many of these stereotypes in its promotional material. Even its recent campaign '100% Pure New Zealand' promotional package initially released at the 1999 New Zealand Tourism Industry Conference featured a Maori in traditional costume on the front cover (it should also be noted that, contrary to Maori protocol, the package featured a climber leaping on top of a mountain while a pull out tab was positioned on the ear of the Maori on the front of the package, both inappropriate images in terms of Maori traditional values). Maori authors such as Keelan (1996) have argued that New Zealand government tourism agencies perhaps only perceive Maori tourism as a commodity to sell rather than as cultural activity with enormous personal and spiritual significance. Indeed, an analysis of Tourism New Zealand promotion and advertising would suggest that 'otherness' sells. Yet, at the local level, representation as other is not always utilised. Such a situation reinforces Lukes' (2005, p. 150) observation that 'three-dimensional power does not and cannot produce one-dimensional man. Power's third dimension is always focused on particular domains of experience and is never, except in fictional dystopias, more than partially effective'.

Conclusions

Processes of tourism branding and promotion seek to simplify representations and images, yet the provision of product remains highly complex. In the same way notions of indigenous tourism as itself a category of knowledge and power, are inadequately discussed in the indigenous tourism literature (Hollinshead, 1992 being a notable exception). There is insufficient reflexivity on how the term is applied and the implications of use within certain dominant discourses of economic development 'which plays out through a particular industrial actor-network of academic knowledge production, circulation and reception' (Gibson and Klocker, 2004, p. 425). Few seem to query the implications of its application. For this particular author the category of indigenous tourism is highly problematic. Implicit within its use are conceptualisations of certain interests and not others. Sometimes its utilisation may be advantageous to Aboriginal or First nation groups but other times it takes on a paternalistic or colonial tone. Much of the writing on indigenous tourism is also by those who are not actually Aboriginal. As well meaning as some of this writing might be, it is hard to know to what extent such writings have met the interests of the subjects as compared with the interests of academic and institutional production. However, to problematise the indigenous category further, it is also hard to find research on indigenous tourism that also identifies power relations within indigenous communities and the use and misuse of power relations.

The exercise of cultural power in terms of tourism and the subsequent occupation of cultural space may have a profound effect on cultural identity.

But often the exercise of power with respect to indigenous tourism is based purely on the actions of one set of political actors towards another. However, the exercise of such power is variable over space and at different scales of analysis. Tourism at times silences indigenous voices. While the romantic representation of Aboriginal peoples still holds sway in much tourism promotion, substantial fragmentation is occurring at the local level with respect to tourism. Such fragmentation and subsequent reassertion of identity by ethnic groups who had previously been denied their cultural voice is related to broader processes of culturalisation and localisation within the cultural and economic dynamic of late capitalism and the neo-liberal project. Tourism is an integral component of this dynamic and provides a mechanism to articulate previously silenced voices. Such a situation has substantial implications not only for tourism but also for the longer-term development of indigenous identity and well-being. It is too simplistic to suppose that unwilling and willing compliance to domination are mutually exclusive, one can consent to power and resent the mode of its exercise. Given the binary relationship of tourism to indigenous identity and representation it would therefore seem essential to look beyond tourism in order to understand the economic, socio-cultural and political well-being of First Nations and instead seek explanation in the nexus of interests, values and power.

CHAPTER 22

Conclusions: Key themes and issues in indigenous tourism

Richard Butler and Tom Hinch

Introduction

Concluding a book which has a considerable number of contributions by an even larger number of authors inevitably poses problems of drawing meaningful conclusions from a variety of approaches and interpretations, and this volume is no exception. We do not claim to have covered all aspects of such a wide topic as the relationships between tourism and indigenous peoples; to do so would be presumptuous and inaccurate. We do argue, however, that through our contributors we have presented a reasonably large range of situations and issues relating to this topic which reflects the complexity of the relationship between tourism and indigenous peoples.

In the decade since Butler and Hinch (1996) was published there has been a considerable expansion of indigenous offerings in tourism, and far greater involvement of indigenous peoples in the planning, development and marketing of tourism in their homelands. That is not to say that the situation is universally ideal or even satisfactory. In his chapter, Hollinshead notes the many issues that existed in 1996 are still unresolved such as the way that indigenous peoples are portrayed in the media generally and the tourism media in particular. He argues persuasively for a much greater involvement and empowerment of indigenous peoples in the presentation of their culture, their resources and themselves, as well the ability to correct misleading or incorrect and inappropriate images that still exist. While the situation in this regard has certainly improved over the last decade, problems still exist and unfortunately are likely to remain in a variety of forms as long as external media and agencies continue to be the major proponents of marketing and promotion of indigenous tourism opportunities.

Despite the range of countries covered by the examples contained in this volume, there are still significant parts of the world not represented, in particular South America and parts of Asia and eastern Europe. Similarly there are forms of tourism not included in the discussion, although the examples here range from basic short trips with indigenous guides and interpreters, through community stays to indigenous owned and operated conventional tourism businesses up to mega-casinos. There are sufficient examples and areas included to be able to identify and discuss a number of themes which pervade several of the contributions and would appear to represent ongoing issues which have not yet been resolved. These are discussed below, and in the context of the revised model of indigenous tourism presented in the opening chapter, fall mostly in the boxes entitled Cultural Attraction and Filters, and Indigenous Destinations and Hosts. That is not to say that factors operating in the generating regions and the characteristics of the tourists themselves do not feature in some of the issues and problems summarized in the key themes, but the focus of the book has been on the supply side of tourism, the opportunities offered under the rubric of indigenous tourism, rather than on the demand (tourist) side. Clearly the opportunities need to be appropriate for, and match or create, the market led demand or they will be short lived and quickly disappear. There have been a good number of studies, mostly by government agencies, on the potential and existing market for indigenous tourism offerings, and generally these have shown a limited but strong demand for this form of tourism.

There needs to be a word of caution interjected here. Market research surveys are notorious for presenting positive interpretations on topics, even as McKercher (2006) has pointed out, creating a non-existent demand. If researchers were to add the supposed number of participants in specialized forms of tourism (such as ecotourism, cultural tourism, sports tourism, and visiting friends and relatives, for example), one would end up with a figure many times the actual number of tourists. The reason for this discrepancy is that indicating a desire to participate in a particular form of tourism does not mean that individual is necessarily going to participate in that form of tourism, and it rarely means that they are going to participate in that form of tourism only. Thus counting each would-be participant in every activity gives an inflated total. In reality, many people engage in multiple forms of tourism on a holiday, thus one might engage in an ecotourism day trip, lying on a beach, visiting an indigenous community for a day and renting a car and sightseeing around the destination base. It would be unlikely in such a scenario that the primary reason for visiting that destination would be the indigenous encounter, important and rewarding though it might be. Thus we must accept that to many tourists, an indigenous tourism opportunity is simply one of many possibilities they are offered during their holiday, and it may be taken up casually as simply another attraction to be visited. This should not be taken as degrading or downplaying the importance or significance of such an activity, nor should it be taken as more important than it is to the tourist participant.

It is clear from the comments made by indigenous entrepreneurs reported in Carr's chapter that they fully appreciate the role they are playing and how their tourism offerings fit into the wider realm of tourism in New Zealand. Similarly, many of the participants in the indigenous tourism opportunities discussed in various chapters seem aware that successful tourism visitation is dependent on offering the visitors something which they want to see and experience. The altering of indigenous host behaviour to facilitate these visitor experiences is similar to the adjusted behaviour of someone working in a hotel or other conventional tourist enterprise, who is expected to be courteous and obliging to sometimes rude and inconsiderate visitors. Where it becomes of more significance and a problem, of course, is where the altered behaviour becomes more permanent, and where local attributes, cultural features and resources are lost or converted into something else to serve the needs of tourism. The tourism literature abounds with discussions of the prostitution of art and culture, the changes in traditional activities, the shortening of performances for tourist shows, the creation of artificial and inauthentic artefacts for sale to tourists and the staging of inauthentic events (e.g., weddings, feasts, festivals) for tourist consumption; in short, acculturation and commodification of culture and the abandonment of traditional activities, combined with the demonstration effect on contemporary host behaviour. Much of the discussion of such effects of tourism tends to take the view that tourism is solely responsible for many of these changes and that tourists themselves, by their ignorance and impatience are greatly to blame. This view is at least disputable. Tourism is only one of many influences on indigenous peoples as we have noted earlier (Hinch and Butler, 1996), and while tourism has grown in many Aboriginal areas, so too have other influences. While the negative policies of non-indigenous schooling, language prohibition, enforced cultural abandonment and restrictive legislation have mostly ceased in the last few decades, their influence is still lingering and pervasive in some areas. The advent of modern technology, particularly in the context of telecommunications and computer networks has opened many areas to the vicissitudes of modern, mostly western, society. While it has allowed small tourism operations to communicate to the world market on their own terms and using their own selected images, thus avoiding for the most part the influence of exogenous intermediaries, it has in turn opened such communities to the outside world on a much larger scale than before.

One might also note the fact that tourists generally do not like to be sold something which they discover is inauthentic. Although ignorant at an academic level about indigenous culture (they are not lay anthropologists as McKercher (2002) notes), they do exhibit sensitivity to authenticity. For example, tourists will often reject obviously fake and imported souvenirs, although that does not necessarily mean that they will be willing or able to pay an appropriate price for a genuine artefact. The fact that they may buy a 'model' totem pole or didgeridoo does not mean that they thought these were the original articles but rather that they wanted a low cost reminder of their visit and contact with an indigenous group. Souvenirs for most tourists are reminders or trophies of their holidays (Goss, 2004) and few would seriously contemplate learning to play a genuine didgeridoo when they have returned home. Few tourists to Scotland buy genuine bagpipes which cost several thousand pounds, but they may buy a figurine dressed in tartan with a set of bagpipes as a reminder of their trip. The purchase of the model does not automatically degrade or insult the genuine article and is rarely portrayed as a realistic alternative.

Similarly tourists watching a concert at a local hotel of a community group singing traditional songs or an Indonesian shadow puppet show are unlikely to want to watch a performance that may last several hours. An abbreviated form lasting perhaps an hour while eating a meal allows them the opportunity to witness a genuine art form, albeit in shortened format. Opera singers recording a solitary aria from a full length opera do not view that performance as cultural prostitution, but accept the fact that their audience might want a range of different composers and operas on their CD. What is at issue should not be the abbreviated or amended form of the offering itself, but the appreciation of it by the audience and the effect, if there is one, on the performers themselves. One might be forgiven for thinking that some researchers seem to assume that presenting an altered version of a cultural performance automatically scars the performer and is an act of sacrilege. It may well be the action of a skilled and world-wise artiste understanding their audience and their preferences better than the researcher. Much depends on the setting and the circumstances, and the information given to the audience before and following the performance, as well the marketing and promotion of the opportunity (as Hollinshead has noted).

Key themes

Vulnerability

Despite the growth in number and range of indigenous tourist opportunities and experiences, and the apparent growth in the market for forms of indigenous tourism, one theme which is identifiable in the contributions is the vulnerability of even the most well run and appropriate indigenous tourism operation. Schmiechen and Boyle in their chapter note the fact that despite considerable public sector support, many indigenous tourism operations have short commercial lifespans and fail to achieve permanent success and profitability. The reasons for this are not clear. Certainly the indigenous operators interviewed in Carr's research showed familiarity with the need for modern business practices despite offering an indigenous product and were well able to combine the two worlds in their operations. One reason for the relatively high failure rate of indigenous business in tourism may be misplaced optimism. Selling a tourist experience is different from selling more conventional products such as natural resources. Not only is one dependent on the tourist coming to the supplier to purchase the experience, but also there are a great many external influences that affect that action. The means of access to many areas are dependent on external transportation services, major airlines for example, and one of the reasons some operations in Sarawak were successful was clearly the links with external tourism agencies, as Braken, Devlin and Simmons demonstrate. Political unrest, as for example, was recently experienced in Fiji yet again, mitigates against tourism to the destination in general and indigenous tourism, which is frequently in less accessible areas, in particular. Visiting indigenous peoples is still something of a challenge and an activity which may provoke some trepidation amongst participants. Political unrest or outbreaks of disease or natural calamities may accentuate the risks of visitation to such areas resulting in rapid and even total decline in numbers, and thus income, threatening the viability of the enterprises involved.

In many cases the effects of financial losses due to ceasing tourism operations may not be as severe as they might be in a non-indigenous situation, where tourism may be the only source of income. For example, in several of the indigenous operations discussed in this volume, the income generated from tourism was just one of a number of sources of funds, and tended to be viewed as additional income. In other cases it may be the only form of cash income but the societies involved may be used to existing in an economic framework in which cash is of minor importance. However, viewing tourism as unreliable and/or uneconomic may be a self-fulfilling prophecy in that a reduction of operations in a particular community may undermine the critical mass that is needed for any tourism activity. It may be a long time, if ever, before tourism may be reintroduced in such situations. In other cases it may be that business plans were unrealistic, that forecasts of tourist numbers, often made by external consultants, were overestimates, that necessary infrastructural improvements were not made, or that marketing and promotion were ineffective. Alternatively, the operations themselves may not meet competitive standards in terms of reliability, security or comfort, given an increasingly sophisticated tourist market that is still somewhat ignorant of indigenous affairs. Given the efforts made by an increasing number of governments (see the chapters by Schmiechen and Boyle, Williams and O'Neill, and Nepal, for example) to provide instruction and advice on managing tourism operations, this last reason is much less likely to apply than in earlier years. Despite the presence and efforts of many agencies in assisting indigenous tourism enterprises, however, their longevity in operation is still not assured, and they are likely to remain vulnerable in the future, situated as many are, on the margins of an industry that is itself vulnerable to many influences (Aramberri and Butler, 2005).

Education and training

Education and training have emerged as crucial aspects of successful indigenous tourism operations. Berno, in her chapter, discusses the importance of training not only in, but also about, tourism in situations such as those in the South Pacific. Tourism, travelling for pleasure on holiday, is not a universal concept, despite its practice throughout much of the world. To many people it is an alien or at least a non-experienced concept, and to expect people in that situation to be able to deal with the complexities and vagaries of tourism and tourists at an acceptable and successful level is unrealistic. Indigenous peoples are no different to other people in terms of rarely being conversant with the likely overall impacts of tourism, and it is essential that they are well informed before making a decision on whether to venture into the competitive world of tourism. In many indigenous societies, the decision to become involved in tourism represents a significant step and needs to be discussed at length before a consensus is reached. There is clearly a major role for public sector agencies in particular to play in making information and advice available, and if and when a positive decision is made to engage in tourism, making training, advice and capital available. The process of the creation of appropriate strategies for indigenous involvement in tourism is a topic discussed by Schmiechen and Boyle and by Williams and O'Neill. In these examples, the groups involved in formulating strategies engaged with indigenous groups and representatives to produce a strategy for research and for engagement that would be acceptable to the indigenous groups involved. Perhaps the best example of the importance of education and training is given in the chapter by Colton, which reveals the significance of appropriate training in tourism in terms of enabling a community to become successfully involved in tourism. Unfortunately, most tourism studies and training programmes include little information that is specific to indigenous groups, their beliefs, their culture and ways of operation, as Hollinshead notes.

Linkages

Tourism is an industry which is highly dependent on linkages between its component parts and over the years vertical and horizontal integration in the industry has become common. Indigenous tourism is no different and like many specialized forms of tourism it is particularly dependent upon access to the international tourist market. In the case of indigenous tourism, this link is particularly significant because many indigenous communities are located in relatively isolated or inaccessible areas and it can be difficult for tourists to reach their location. In many cases tourists are introduced to indigenous communities and their opportunities through intermediaries, some whose primary business is to make such linkages. In other cases, these intermediaries may have primary interests in providing accommodation or other services but may offer linkages to indigenous operators as a value added service to their clients. The importance of positive and effective links is made clear in the chapters by Salole and by Braken, Devlin and Simmons. In the Namibian case, the initial development of the camp and the training of indigenous employees was undertaken by the non-indigenous enterprise and the agreement included a buy-out clause for the indigenous community. In the Sarawak situation, the longhouses which have been successful in operating a tourism business have been those with formal arrangements with a non-indigenous organization operating from one of the hotels in the national park. In both cases the non-indigenous organizations were in business before the indigenous enterprises began, and were instrumental in bringing the tourists to the communities.

While the internet and the WWW have both made it easier for small tourist enterprises to interact with potential markets, often on different continents, there is frequently the logistical problem of enabling guests to reach the indigenous communities from the main tourist centres or from the points of access to a country or region such as an airport or port. Other important links include contact and information flows between the enterprises and tourism information centres, the latter often acting as booking agents for indigenous and small-scale enterprises, and also between indigenous groups and arts and cultural bodies, particularly where performance is involved or the sale of cultural artefacts. Such linkages can assist indigenous and other operators to establish the value of goods and services offered, to ensure contact with potential markets and to advise on aspects such as opportunities, seasonal trends and market preferences which small isolated operators may not be in a position to identify. Finally, in many countries in which indigenous tourism is important, such as Australia, Canada and New Zealand, governments have helped establish specific agencies to assist and advise indigenous entrepreneurs in terms of operating procedures and regulations, marketing and financial planning.

Image

Image is of crucial importance to any tourism operation at almost any scale. If tourists do not have a positive image of a destination or an attraction, they will not visit it. If they have no image of a destination at all, then they are unlikely to visit it. Establishing and maintaining a positive and attractive destination image in the tourist market is vital therefore, but such an image, as Hollinshead emphasizes, must be appropriate, accurate and accepted within the indigenous community itself as well as to the tourist market. In the past, as noted in the literature (Albers and James, 1988; Cohen, 1993; Hollinshead, 1996), images of indigenous peoples have often been distorted, negative, racist, sexist and stereotyped, and most often prepared and promoted by external forces. Indigenous peoples were rarely involved in the preparation or approval of such images but were often expected to perform as portrayed in the imagery. While the situation has much improved in most areas, there are still occasions when inappropriate or offensive images are used. A great deal depends on whether the indigenous group is producing the image and controlling the attraction or simply being used as part of a wider offering. In their discussion of the Mongolian traditional festival Naadam, Thompson and O'Gorman note the different images held of, and different reactions to, the festival by indigenous groups and foreign tourists. To the former it is a national celebration with strong cultural and historic overtones; to the tourists it is an authentic cultural festival but their experience is limited and partial. To one group it is sold as part of their heritage, to the tourists it is sold as an indigenous attraction upon which they can gaze on the exotic 'other'. The images that each group has of the event influences their perceptions of, and satis-faction with, the experience they gain. The image projected of indigenous groups varies from country to country; in Taiwan, as Ryan, Chang and Huan note, the 12 tribes are formally recognized but tourism promotion is limited. In Iran, O'Gorman, McLellan and Baum point out that the indigenous presence is subsumed beneath the national religious image that is put forth by the Islamic government of that country, and specific promotion of indigenous attractions does not take place. There is, for all intents, no indigenous image of Iran, only the national religious one. In northern Europe, however, the Sami have developed a fairly strong and clear image as Pettersson and Viken identify, although they note that the activities promoted as Sami vary across the countries involved and do not all meet with universal approval within the Sami people. Some of their respondents argued that it is more a question of being and feeling Sami than appearing Sami and that the same image does not apply to all. There is also a tension between the tourist image of traditional Sami and the contemporary reality. The control of imagery is also partly political, and the role of indigenous groups approved and supported in a country also varies by the political persuasion of the government. Hall discusses the political economy of indigenous tourism and it is clear that politics at all levels, from the smallest community to the nation as a whole, influence not only what is offered but also the image that is used to sell that offering. At the national level, Sofield and Li demonstrate that in China indigenous groups are recognized and promoted for tourism as part of regional tourism development strategies, including the marketing of Tibet with the completion of the high altitude railway line to Lhasa in 2006.

Ownership and control

Clearly these two elements are closely related as ownership normally denotes control, although in tourism such may not always be the case. While an indigenous group may legally own specific resources, they may not have control over them in the sense of the ability to utilize them as they may wish for the development of tourism. Hall in his chapter notes the relationship between control and development through policy and politics, and Hollinshead discusses at length the issues relating to ownership and control of image in the context of indigenous peoples. Increasingly in recent decades indigenous peoples have been regaining control of traditional homelands and resources, most often through legislation at the highest level, as in Canada (Williams and O'Neill), Australia (Hall) and New Zealand (McIntosh and Ryan), and the changes in legislation in the US have paved the way for the establishment of casinos on native reserves (Carmichael and Jones).

The ability of indigenous peoples to enter the tourism business on their own terms and in their own preferred ways is critical for the long term sustainability of indigenous tourism enterprises. The situation described by Colton in his chapter suggests that the process of consultation and information gathering is also of great importance in the establishment of appropriate and complementary forms of tourism, developed at the appropriate scale and rate for the specific community and its resources. Along with control is implied knowledge, both of resources and tourism. The incorporation of local indigenous and ecological knowledge into tourism development by indigenous groups (Butler and Menzies) is shown to add particular attributes of uniqueness and authenticity in the tourism operations, a point also made by respondents discussed in Carr's chapter. While indigenous groups have unique knowledge about their setting, their resources and their culture, and this knowledge may be highly applicable to specific forms of tourism activity (as Butler and Menzies demonstrate), it is also important for them to gain knowledge about tourism in order to not only maximize their potential benefits, but also to avoid undesirable effects of inappropriate development. The importance of education and training has already been noted above and is part of the strategies being developed by those governments desirous of assuring the sustainable development of indigenous-based tourism (Schmiechen and Boyle, Williams and O'Neill).

As tourism enterprises develop and grow, maintaining control may prove difficult for indigenous groups. A business which can be operated and managed by a family group is very different from one which expands to the point that it needs to employ additional people, and needs to tap into a different and larger market. Business and management skills need to be acquired, a fact pointed out clearly by Carr's respondents, and the linkages noted above do not always turn out as well as those discussed by Salole and Braken, Devlin and Simmons. In some cases the associated enterprises make unacceptable demands for changes and operational formats, or, as suggested by Colton, assume control by virtue of investment or external links and knowledge. The tourism literature is replete with issues of dependency in the development of tourism in less developed countries (e.g., Britton, 1981; Mowforth and Munt, 1998; Sharpley and Telfer, 2002) and in many cases indigenous peoples represent less developed populations within what may be otherwise developed countries. They face a range of problems as noted earlier, often stemming from the treatment they have suffered in earlier years by colonizing powers, many of them similar to those faced by populations in developing countries. Interestingly, however, Sofield and Li reject the colonization hypothesis in the context of many indigenous groups in China, where tourism and other forms of economic activity have been developed by the central government, arguing that denying development to such groups would have been denying them an opportunity to improve their economic situation and quality of life. Knowledge is power, and the specific knowledge that indigenous peoples have may not always be sufficient to guarantee them control over their way of life and their resources once they become involved in tourism.

Ideology

Tourism is normally seen as an agent of development, and thus tied to the capitalist system and the free market philosophy. It has benefited greatly from reductions in hindrances to free trade and the opening up of political boundaries to the movement of people. Deregulation of airlines has resulted in lower fares and greater access to travel for many people, as well as increased access to peripheral areas, including those inhabited by indigenous peoples. The long continuous period of growth of international and domestic tourism is evidence of how the spread of world trade and greater mobility of people and capital have benefited this particular industry. These processes have also, of course, brought different ideologies and beliefs into contact with one another. The cash and credit based modern economy as characterized by economies of scale, on large-scale or mass production (even in a post-Fordist age) and freedom of movement of goods and capital; does not always sit easily with indigenous societies. Such modernity contrasts with traditional ethics of sharing, and with non-competitive and subsistence forms of existence, in which travel is undertaken out of necessity, where hospitality may be a natural fact of life from historic times required by a harsh environment (as O'Gorman, McLellan, and Baum note) and where 'serving' visitors for profit is an alien concept, albeit one that has parallels to the common indigenous concept of reciprocity.

As well, within tourism itself, of course there are ideological issues, most notably between green or sustainable tourism and more conventional and traditional forms of tourism. While many governments, in principle and print at least are strongly in favour of a sustainable development approach to tourism; in practice few, if any, have successfully converted their conventional tourism industries to sustainable ones. A very few areas, Bhutan being one, have placed limits on the numbers of tourists permitted, but even in areas where strict conservation regulations exist, breaches of such regulations are often common (as Nepal notes). It remains debatable at best whether the tourism market in general has really become 'greener' or whether it is still mainly driven by price. There is no doubt that many indigenous tourism enterprises rely heavily on the natural resources of their homelands, and on their traditional culture. Seeing something different is a key feature of many holidays, and there are few things more different for most tourists than another people operating in their traditional manner in their homeland, using their traditional knowledge and local resources. Unique values and viewpoints are distinguishing features in most indigenous tourism oper-ations and it is essential to ensure these are maintained and do not succumb to the pressure of the dominant western economic ideology. Preserving such ideologies in the face of a dominant western economic context in which indigenous tourism exists is a major challenge.

Relationships

The final theme is that of relationships, between the indigenous peoples and others, and within the indigenous communities. Good relations with neighbours are essential for the success and acceptance of all tourism businesses, and this is equally if not more true for indigenous operations. The generally long and often conflict-ridden relations between indigenous populations and their colonizing peoples have tended to leave bitterness and animosity to varying levels in both populations, driven by guilt, resentment and dissatisfaction. Attempts by recent and current governments to repair the damage inflicted by earlier policies is sometimes neither successful nor accepted by one or both sides in these issues, resulting in continuing resentment and poor relations. Indigenous tourism operations can be caught in the middle of such difficult relations and suffer as a result. One way in which this problem may be manifest is in the reluctance of non-indigenous domestic populations to patronize indigenous operations, in contrast to the considerable desire of foreign tourists to engage in indigenous tourism during their travels. In many countries visitation to indigenous tourism enterprises is much higher among international tourists than it is among domestic tourists, and the legacy of mistreatment may be a factor in this situation.

The dominant theme in the chapter by Carmichael and Jones is the tension in the relationship between the indigenous owners of the large casinos and their non-indigenous neighbours. While the opinions of respondents in the one community are not generally negative about the indigenous population, in the other community, relations are clearly strained. The effects of the large-scale developments have had major impacts upon the nearby towns and many of these impacts are not seen as positive. Such a situation is somewhat unusual as it is a common feature of indigenous tourism enterprises that they are small-scale and often located at considerable distances from non-indigenous towns and settlements, with the result that their impacts are rarely experienced beyond their immediate surroundings.

Given the importance of the linkages between the indigenous operations and the mostly non-indigenous international operations such as tour operators and transportation providers, relationships are particularly important. Within the indigenous communities themselves, relationships are also an issue. It is often difficult to ensure the survival of businesses if the next generation is not keen or willing to continue them. Traditional crafts and art forms are at risk in many communities because the young generation does not wish to learn the necessary skills, and this is equally true with respect to the passing on of local indigenous knowledge, which as Butler and Menzies indicate, involves tapping into the wisdom of the elders and senior generations for their knowledge of the history of resources and resource use. In societies where history is maintained in oral rather than written form, much of this knowledge is at risk, and inter-generational relations must be kept at a strong positive level to ensure the knowledge and thus unique advantages are passed on to future generations.

Conclusions

Indigenous tourism has come a long way since it simply meant tourists coming to an area to stare at natives posing in traditional dress. The range of enterprises and opportunities has grown rapidly and extensively, as have the communities and areas now open to this type of tourism. Yet one cannot assume that indigenous tourism is guaranteed a successful future. The earlier discussion noted the vulnerability of this form of tourism, based as it is in some of the least accessible areas and proffered by people less versed in business and management techniques than many of their competitors. Many enterprises have done well because they are offering products that are highly desired by a significant segment of modern tourists, that is, things which are unique or rare and prestigious because of this, which are generally environmentally and socially positive, which are different to the modern large-scale corporate international world in which most tourists exist, and which are often located in impressive natural settings with magnificent scenery and wildlife. Some of the most successful of these enterprises have been those which are clearly genuine and in harmony with their setting, offering an experience which cannot be obtained elsewhere. From what we can judge of tourism demand in the future, this sort of attraction is likely to remain highly sought after, especially in a world which is becoming more and more homogenized. That is not to say that there are not problems, some of which have been outlined above. Tourism as an industry is highly vulnerable as a discretionary activity to external shocks, and the likely increasing scarcity of fuel and higher costs of travel threaten the market for those attractions requiring long haul travel from the major tourist generating regions, as do the political efforts of organizations trying to reduce global travel on environmental grounds. Traditional indigenous activities are also under pressure from organizations opposed to hunting and trapping and the fur trade for example. Thus the future for indigenous tourism is uncertain, despite the many positive attributes which it possesses. In the future it is likely to remain a niche form of tourism, mostly small in scale, dependent on mainstream tourism elements for access to and from markets, but of increasing importance to many indigenous communities as a supplementary form of income and perhaps, and as one form of economic and cultural empowerment.

References

ABC (1998). *Promoting the growth of Canada's aboriginal businesses.* Ottawa: Aboriginal Business Canada, Industry Canada.

Aboriginal Tourism Association of British Columbia (ATBC) (2006). *Aboriginal Cultural Tourism Blueprint Strategy for BC.* Vancouver: ATBC.

Aboriginal Tourism Team Canada (ATTC) (1996). *Aboriginal Tourism: Business Planning Guide, Checklist for Success.* Ottawa: ATTC.

Agar, M. (1996). *The Professional Stranger.* London: Academic Press.

AGB McNair (1996). *Aboriginal Culture: Qualitative Research Report: Reference No. Qg4831.* Darwin, NT: Confidential report prepared for the Northern Territory Tourist Commission.

Agrawal, A. (1995). Indigenous and scientific knowledge: some critical comments. *Indigenous Knowledge and Development Monitor*, 3(3), 3–6.

Ahmad, S., Tisen, O.B. and Bennett, E.L. (1999). Wildlife conservation and local communities in Sarawak. *Hornbill*, (3), 223–229. Sarwak: Forest Department.

Ahoy, L. (2000). *Promotion vs Product National Indigenous Tourism Forum Proceedings Report: Tourism – The Indigenous Opportunity.* Canberra: Commonwealth Department of Industry, Science and Resources.

Akha Heritage Foundation Website. Available from: http://www.akha.org/content/projects/howweconductprojects.html (accessed 25 September 2005).

Albers, P. and James, W. (1983). Tourism and the changing photographic image of the Great Lakes Indians. *Annals of Tourism Research*, 10(1), 123–148.

Albers, P. and James, W. (1988). Travel photography: a methodological approach. *Annals of Tourism Research*, 15(1), 1134–1158.

Alipour, H. and Heydari, R.C. (2004). Tourism revival and planning in the Islamic Republic of Iran: challenges and prospects. *Proceedings of Tourism: State of the Art 2; International Conference at The University of Strathclyde*, Glasgow.

Almagor, U. (1985). A tourist's 'vision quest' in an African game reserve. *Annals of Tourism Research*, 12, 31–47.

al-Muqaddasī, M.A. (946/1877). *Kītāb absan al-taqāsīm fı ma'rifat al-aqālīm.* Brill: Lugduni Batavorum.

al-Narshakhī, M.J. (959/1954). *The History of Bukhara, Muhammad Narshakhī* [Translated from a Persian abridgement of the Arabic original by Narshakhī]. Cambridge: Mediaeval Academy of America.

al-Tabarī (838/1989). *Ta'rīkh al-rusul wa al-mulūk. English Selections The History of al-Tabarī.* Albany, NY: State University of New York Press.

Altman, J.C. (1989). Tourism dilemmas for Aboriginal Australians. *Annals of Tourism Research*, 16(4), 456–476.

Altman, J.C. and Finlayson, J. (1991). *Aborigines and Tourism: An Issues Paper Prepared for the Ecologically Sustainable Working Group on Tourism.* Canberra: The Centre for Aboriginal Economic Policy Research, Australian National University.

Altman, J.C. and Finlayson, J. (1993). Aborigines, tourism and sustainable development. *The Journal of Tourism Studies*, 4(1), 38–50.

Anderson, I. (2005). Introduction: the aboriginal critique of colonial knowing. In *Blacklines: Contemporary Critical Writing by Indigenous Australians* (M. Grossman et al., ed.), pp. 17–24. Melbourne: Melbourne University Press.

Andrews, R.C. (1921). *Across Mongolian Plains.* London: Appleton and Co.

Angus Reid Group (1993). *Native Product Analysis.* Yukon: Yukon Tourism and Western Research M.O.U. Committee.

Ap, J. and Crompton, J. (1993). Resident strategies for responding to tourism impacts. *Journal of Travel Research*, 32(1), 47–50.

AP, J. and Crompton, J.L. (1998). Developing and testing a tourism impact scale. *Journal of Travel Research*, 37(2), 120–130.

Ap, J., Var, T. and Din, K. (1991). Malaysian perceptions of tourism. *Annals of Tourism Research*, 18, 321–323.

Aramberri, J. and Butler, R.W. (2005). *Tourism: A Vulnerable Industry.* Clevedon: Channel View Publications.

Arman, S. (1997). Socioeconomy. In *International Tropical Timber Organisation Borneo Biodiversity Expedition Scientific Report*, pp. 168–180. Yokohama: ITTO.

Arthur, W.S. (1991). The Aboriginal Community and Community Enterprise. *Proceedings of the 2nd National Social Policy Conference, Social Policy in Australia: Options for the 1990s*, Sydney, University of New South Wales, pp. 1–10.

Ashley, C. (2000). *The Impacts of Tourism on Rural Livelihoods: Namibia's Experience.* London: Overseas Development Institute Working Paper 128.

Ashley, C. and Jones, B. (2001). Joint ventures between communities and tourism investors: experience in Southern Africa. *International Journal of Tourism Research*, Vol. 3, no. 2, 407–423.

Ashley, C. and Roe, D. (1998). Enhancing community involvement in wildlife tourism: issues and challenges. *IIED Wildfire and Development Series No. 11.* London: IIED.

Ashley, C., Roe, D. and Goodwin, H. (2001). *Pro-Poor Tourism Strategies: Making Tourism Work for the Poor. A review of experience.* Pro-Poor Tourism, London.

Assael, H. (1987). *Consumer Behaviour and Marketing Action.* Boston, MA: Kent Publishing Co.

Ateljevic, I. and Doorne, S. (2002). Representing New Zealand: tourism imagery and ideology. *Annals of Tourism Research*, 29(3), 648–667.

Atkins, P., Simmons, I. and Roberts, B. (1998). *People, Land and Time*. London: Hodder Arnold.

Ayob, A.M. and Yaakub, N.F. (1991). Development and change in Batang Ai, Sarawak: perception of a resettled Iban community. *Sarawak Museum Journal*, XLII(63), 267–282.

Bachrach, P. and Baratz, M.S. (1962). Two faces of power. *American Political Science Review*, 56, 947–952.

Bachrach, P. and Baratz, M.S. (1970). *Power and Poverty: Theory and Practice*. New York: Oxford University Press.

Bah, A. and Goodwin, H. (2003). Improving access for the informal sector to tourism in The Gambia. PPT Working Paper 15-Poor Tourism Partnership, London: ODI.

Barnett, S. (2000). Maori tourism. In *Tourism Management: Towards the Next Millenium* (C. Ryan and S. Page, eds.). Amsterdam: Pergamon.

Barnett, S. (2001). Manaakitanga: Maori hospitality – a case study of Maori accommodation providers. *Tourism Management*, 22, 83–92.

Barrass, T. and Laurie, V. (2006). Long road home: from Terra Nullius to Noongar, the quest for land rights. *The Australian*, September, 27, 13.

Baum, T. (1996). Tourism in Aland: a case study. *Progress in Tourism and Hospitality Research*, 1(2), 111–118.

Baum, T. (1999). The decline of the traditional North Atlantic fisheries and tourism's response. *Current Issues in Tourism*, 2(1), 47–67.

Baum, T. and Conlin, M. (1996). Brunei Darussalam: sustainable tourism development within an Islamic cultural ethos. In *Tourism and Economic Development in Asia and Australiasia* (F.M. Go and C.L. Jenkins, eds.). London: Cassell.

Bauman, Z. (1991). *Modernity and Ambivalence*. New York: Cornell University Press.

Bawden, C.R. (1958). Two Mongolian texts concerning Obo-worship. *Oriens Extremus*, 5(1), pp. 81–103.

BBC (1999a). *World: Middle East – Tourists Kidnapped in Iran*. http://news.bbc.co.uk/1/hi/world/middle_east/420953.stm (accessed 15 October 2006).

BBC (1999b). *My Holidays in the Axis of Evil*. http://news.bbc.co.uk/1/hi/uk2705627.stm (accessed 15 October 2006).

BBC (2003) http://news.bbc.co.uk/1/hi/uk/2705627.stm

BBC (2006a). *Iran 'to Open Atomic Site Tours'*. http://newsvote.bbc.co.uk/mpapps/pagetools/print/news.bbc.co.uk/hi/world/middle   (accessed 15 October 2006).

BBC (2006b). *Today Programme*, 16 September 2006.

Beckett, J.R. (ed.) (1994). *Past and Present: The Construction of Aboriginality*. Canberra: Aboriginal Studies Press.

Becquelin, N. (2004). Staged development in Xinjiang. In *China's Campaign to "Open Up the West": National, Provincial and Local Perspectives* (D.S.G. Goodman, ed.), pp. 22–44. Cambridge: Cambridge University Press.

Beeho, A.J. and Prentice, R.C. (1997). Conceptualising the experiences of heritage tourists. A case study of New Lanark World Heritage Village. *Tourism Management*, 18(2), 75–87.

Bell, M. (1999a). *The Changing Face of Community Development in the North: from the Power Paradigm to the Spirit Paradigm*. Yellowknife: Inukshuk Management Consultants.

Bell, M. (1999b). *Creating Public Government in Nunavut – The Life-Place Model*. Yellowknife: Inukshuk Management Consultants.

Bell, M. (2000). *Recreation: A Tool for Community Development and Capacity Building in Aboriginal Communities*. Thunder Bay, Ontario: Recreation Northwest.

Bennett, E.L. and Shebli, Z. (1999). Sarawak's system of totally protected areas: will it protect Sarawak's biodiversity? *Hornbill*, 3, 38–45. Sarawak: Forest Department.

Bennett, E.L., Nyaoi, A. and Sompud, J. (2000). Saving Borneo's bacon: the sustainability of hunting in Sarawak and Sabah. In *Hunting for Sustainability in Tropical Forests* (J.G. Robinson and E.L. Bennett, eds.), pp. 305–324. New York: Columbia University Press.

Bennett, J. (2005). *Indigenous Entrepreneurship, Social Capital and Tourism Enterprise Development: Lessons from Cape York*. Victoria: La Trobe University.

Berkes, F. (1993). Traditional ecological knowledge in perspective. In *Traditional Ecological Knowledge: Concepts and Cases* (J.T. Inglis, ed.), pp. 1–9. Ottawa: Canadian Museum of Nature and the International Development Research Centre.

Berkes, F. (1999). *Sacred Ecology: Traditional Ecological Knowledge and Resource Management*. Philadelphia, PA: Taylor and Francis Press.

Berma, M. (2000). Iban poverty: a reflection on its causes, consequences and policy implementations. In *Borneo 2000: Politics, History and Development* (M. Leigh, ed.), pp. 482–512. *Proceedings of the Sixth Biennial Borneo Research Conference, Kuching, Sarawak, 10–14 July*. Universiti Malaysia Sarawak and Sarawak Development Institute.

Berneshawi, S. (1997). Resource management and the Mi'kmaq nation. *Canadian Journal of Native Studies*, XVII(1), 115–148.

Berno, T. (1996). Cross cultural research methods in the field – content or context? A Cook Islands case study. In *Tourism and Indigenous Peoples* (R.W. Butler and T. Hinch, eds.), pp. 376–395. London: International Thomson Publishing.

Berno, T. (1999). When is a guest a guest? Cook Islanders conceptualize tourism. *Annals of Tourism Research*, 26(3), 565–675.

Berno, T. (2001). Human resources development for the tourism sector in the South Pacific. Invited paper presented at the *APETIT UN-ESCAP Conference*, Khajuraho, India, 7–10 August.

Bhabha, H. (1994). *The Location of Culture*. London: Routledge.

Blaikie, P. and Brookfield, H. (1987). *Land Degradation and Society*. New York: Methuen.

Blanton, D. (1981). Tourism training in developing countries. *Annals of Tourism Research*, 8,116–123.

Bodley, J.H. (1982). *Victims of Progress*. Palo Alto, CA: Mayfield.

Boissevain, J. (1996). Ritual, tourism and cultural comodification in Malta. In *The Tourist Image: Myths and Myth Making in Tourism* (T. Selwyn, ed.), pp. 105–120. Chichester: Wiley.

Boltvinik, J. (nd). *Poverty Measurement Methods An Overview SEPED Series on Poverty Reduction UNDP*. Available from: www.undp.org/poverty/publications/pov_red/

Bongo Gaino, L.B. (2005). *Samen som Turistattraksjon*. Master Thesis, Finnmark University College, Alta.

Boo, E. (1990). *Ecotourism: The Potential and Pitfalls*. Washington, DC: World Wildlife Fund.

Botterill, D. (1992). Tourism education: changing attitudes – facing the challenge. *In Focus*, 3, 2–3.

Boyle, A. (2001a). Australian Indigenous Tourism Research Strategy Scoping Study. *Workshop Discussion Paper Research Gap Literature Review*, Darwin, NT.

Boyle, A. (2001b). Australian Indigenous Tourism Research Strategy Scoping Study. *Workshop Report*, Darwin, NT.

Boyle, A. (2002). Research and indigenous tourism – cultural collision or collaboration. *Proceeding of the 12th International Research Conference of CAUTHE*, Fremantle, WA.

Britton, S.G. (1981). *Tourism, Dependency and Development: A Mode of Analysis*. Canberra: ANU Press.

Britton, S.G. (1982). The political economy of tourism in the Third World. *Annals of Tourism Research*, 9(3), 331–358.

Brody, H. (1988). *Maps and Dreams: Indians and the British Columbia Frontier*. Vancouver: Douglas & MacIntyre.

Brohman, J. (1996). New directions in tourism for third world development. *Annals of Tourism Research*, 23(1), 48–70.

Brown, D.F. (1999). Mayas and tourists in the Maya world. *Human Organization*, 58(3), 295–304.

Bruner, E.M. (1995). The ethnographer/tourist in Indonesia. In *International Tourism: Identity and Change* (M.-F. Lanfant, J.B. Allcock and E.M. Bruner, eds.), pp. 224–241. London: Sage Publications.

Bryden, J. (1973). *Tourism and Development: A Case Study of the Commonwealth Caribbean*. New York: Cambridge University Press.

Bulstrode, B. (1920). *A Tour in Mongolia*. London: Methuen.

Burchett, C. (1993a). A Profile of Aboriginal and Torres Strait Islander Tourism – its history and future prospects. In Office of Northern Development (Commonwealth of Australia). *Indigenous Australians and Tourism: A Focus on Northern Australia, Proceedings of the Indigenous Australians and Tourism Conference*, Darwin, NT, Australia, June 1993. Canberra: Aboriginal and Torres Strait Islander Commission.

Burchett, C. (1993b). A Profile of Indigenous and Torres Strait islander Tourism – its history and future prospect. *Indigenous Australians and Tourism: A Focus on Northern Australia. Proceedings of the Indigenous Australians and Tourism Conference. Darwin, Canberra, Goanna Print*, 20–25.

Burchett, C. (1993c). *North Australian Aboriginal and Ecological Roadshow – 1993 Report*.Darwin, NT: NTTC.

Burlo, C.D. (1996). Cultural resistance and ethnic tourism on South Pentecost, Vanuatu. In *Tourism and Indigenous Peoples* (R. Butler and T. Hinch, eds.), pp. 255–276. London: Thomson Business Press.

Burns, P. (1992). Going against conventional wisdom. *In Focus*, 3, 8.

Burns, P. (1999). Vaka Pacifica: a regional approach to tourism training in the South Pacific region. *Pacific Tourism Review*, 3, 101–118.

Butler, C.F. (2004). Research TEK for multiple uses. *Canadian Journal of Native Education*, 28 (1–2), 33–48.

Butler, C.F. (2005). *More than Fish: Political Knowledge in the Commercial Fisheries of British Columbia.* Unpublished Ph.D. dissertation. Department of Anthropology, University of British Columbia. Vancouver: British Columbia.

Butler, C.F. (2006). Historicizing indigenous knowledge: practical and political issues. In *Traditional Ecological Knowledge and Natural Resource Management* (C. Menzies, ed.), pp. 107–126. Omaha: University of Nebraska Press.

Butler, R.W. (1980). The concept of a tourist area cycle of evolution: implications for management of resources. *Canadian Geographer*, XXIV, 5–12.

Butler, R.W. and Hinch, T. (eds.) (1996). *Tourism and Indigenous Peoples.* London: International Thompson Business Press.

Buultjens, J. (2004). *Minutes Indigenous Tourism Researchers Meeting*, Brisbane.

Cahill, J. (1988). *Three Alternative Histories of Chinese Painting.* Kansas City: University of Kansas.

Caldecott, J.O. (1988). *Hunting and Wildlife Management in Sarawak.* Gland, Switzerland and Cambridge, UK: IUCN.

Canaday, L. and Zeiger, J. (1991). The social, economic and environmental costs to a gaming community perceived by the residents. *Journal of Travel Research*, 30, 45–49.

Canadian Tourism Commission (CTC) (1998). *A Guide to the Aboriginal Experience: Live the Legacy.* Ottawa: Canadian Tourism Commission.

Carmichael, B.A. (1998). Foxwoods Resort Casino, Connecticut – who wants it? Who benefits? In *Casino Gambling in North America: Origins, Trends and Impacts* (K. Meyer-Arendt and R. Hartmann, eds.), pp. 67–75. New York: Cognizant Communications.

Carmichael, B.A. (2000). A matrix model of resident attitudes and behaviours in a rapidly changing tourism area. *Tourism Management*, 21, 601–611.

Carmichael, B.A. (2001). Casinos, communities and sustainable economic development. In *Tourism, Recreation and Sustainability* (S. McCool and N. Moisey, eds.), pp. 217–232. Wallingford: Oxford CABI.

Carmichael, B.A. (2003). First Nation casino gaming and tourism. In *Tourism, People, Places and Products* (G. Wall, ed.), pp. 177–206. Waterloo: Department of Geography Publication Series, Occasional Paper No. 19.

Carmichael, B.A. and Peppard, Jr., D.M. (1998). The impacts of Foxwoods Resort Casino on its dual host community: Southeast Connecticut and the Mashantucket Pequot tribe. In *Tourism and Gaming on American Indian Lands* (A. Lew and G.A. Van Otten, eds.), pp. 128–144. New York: Cognizant Communications.

Carmichael, B.A., Peppard, D. and Boudreau, F. (1996). Mega-resort on my doorstep: local resident attitudes toward Foxwoods Casino and casino gambling on nearby Indian reservation land. *Journal of Travel Research*, Winter, 9–16.

Carr, A.M. (2004). Mountain places, cultural spaces – interpretation and sustainable visitor management of culturally significant landscapes: a case study of Aoraki/Mount Cook National Park. *Journal of Sustainable Tourism*, 12(5), 432–459.

Carr, A.M. (2006). Lakes, myths and legends: the relationship between tourism and cultural values for water in Aotearoa/New Zealand. In *Lake Tourism: An Integrated Approach to Lacustrine Tourism Systems* (C.M. Hall and T. Harkonen, eds.), pp. 83–100. Clevedon: Channel View Publications.

Carruthers, D. (1914). *Unknown Mongolia*. London: Hutchinson and Company.

Cater, E. (1994). Introduction. In *Ecotourism: A Sustainable Option?* (E. Cater and G. Lowman, eds.), pp. 3–18. Chichester: John Wiley and Sons.

Cave, J. (2005). Conceptualising 'Otherness' as a management framework for tourism enterprise, considerations. In *Indigenous Tourism – The Commodification and Management of Culture* (C. Ryan and M. Aicken, eds.), pp. 261–280. Oxford: Elsevier.

Chang, J. (2006). Segmenting tourists to aboriginal cultural festivals: an example in the Rukai tribal area, Taiwan. *Tourism Management*, 27, 1224–1234.

Chang, J., Wall, G. and Tsai, C.-T. (2005). Endorsement advertising in aboriginal tourism: an experiment in Taiwan. *International Journal of Tourism Research*, 7, 347–356.

Chang, J., Wall, G. and Chu, S.-T. (2006). Novelty seeking at aboriginal attractions. *Annals of Tourism Research*, 33(3), 729–747.

Chen, J.S. and Hsu, C.H.C. (2001). Developing and validating a riverboat gaming impact scale. *Annals of Tourism Research*, 28(2), 459–476.

Cheong, S. and Miller, M. (2000). Power and tourism: a Foucauldian observation. *Annals of Tourism Research*, 27(2), 371–390.

Chin, C.L.M. and Bennett, E.L. (2000). Beside the beaten track: effects of increased accessibility on wildlife and patterns of hunting in Sarawak. In *Borneo 2000, Environment, Conservation and Land. Proceedings of the Sixth Biennial Borneo Research Conference* (M. Leigh, ed.), pp. 29–40, Kuching, Sarawak, Malaysia.

Chi-Ting Chuang (2006). Rukai struggle to keep their culture alive. Taipei Times, Tuesday August 8th, p. 2.

Chithtalath, S. (2006). Community development projects and the status of ethnic minority women in the Moksuk-Tafa area, Bokeo Province, Laos. *Community Development Journal Advance Access*. Available from: http://intl-cdj.oxfordjournals.org/papbyrecent.dtl (Accessed 03 December 2006).

Chow, W.S. (1988). Open policy and tourism between Guangdong and Hong Kong. *Annals of Tourism Research*, 15, 205–218.

Christensen, H. (2000). Economic importance of wild food in a Kelabit longhouse community in Sarawak, Malaysia. In *Borneo 2000, Environment, Conservation and Land. Proceedings of the Sixth Biennial Borneo Research Conference* (M. Leigh, ed.), pp. 356–368, Kuching, Sarawak, Malaysia.

Clayoquot Sound Scientific Panel (1995). *First Nations Perspectives Relating to Forest Practices Standards in Clayoquot Sound*. Victoria: Cortex Consultants.

Cleary, M. and Eaton, P. (1992). *Borneo: Change and Development*. New York: Oxford University Press.

Cohen, E. (1995). Contemporary tourism trends and challenges. In *Change in Tourism* (R. Butler and D. Pearce, eds.), pp. 12–29. London: Routledge.

Cohen, E. (1993). The study of touristic images of native people: mitigating the stereotype of the stereotype. In *Tourism Research: Critiques and Challenges* (D. Pearce and R.W. Butler, eds.). London: Routledge, 36-69.

Colchester, M. (2004). Conservation policy and indigenous peoples. *Cultural Survival Quarterly*, 28, 17–22.

Colmar Brunton (2004). *Demand for Māori Cultural Tourism: Te Ahu Mai – He whao tapoi Māori*. Wellington: Tourism New Zealand and the Ministry of Tourism.

Colton, J. (2000). *Searching for Sustainable Tourism in the Caribou Mountains*. Unpublished doctoral dissertation, University of Alberta, Edmonton, AB.

Colton, J.W. (2005). Motivations for indigenous tourism development in northern Canada. *Journal of Canadian Native Studies*, 15(1), 173–192.

Conference Board of Canada, O'Neil Marketing and Consulting, Spirit Hawk Aboriginal Tourism Advisory Services. (1997). *Aboriginal Tourism Product Identification Project*. Ottawa: Aboriginal Business Canada, Indian and Northern Affairs Canada.

Conlin, M.V. and Baum, T. (1994). Comprehensive human resource planning: an essential key to sustainable tourism in island settings. *Progress in Tourism, Recreation and Hospitality Management*, 6, 259–270.

Connolly, W.E. (1974). *The Terms of Political Discourse*. Oxford: Martin Robertson.

Coombs, H.C., McCann, H., Ross, H. and Williams, N.M. (1989). *Land of Promises: Aborigines and Development in the East Kimberley*. Canberra: Centre for Resource and Environmental Studies, Australian National University.

Cornell, S. and Kalt, J.S. (1990). Pathways from poverty: economic development and institution-building on American Indian reservations. *American Indian Culture and Research Journal*, 14(1), 89–125.

Cornell, S., and Kalt, J.S. (1998). Sovereignty and nation-building: the development challenge in Indian country today. *American Indian Culture and Research Journal*, 22(3), 187–214.

Coull, C. (1997). *A Traveller's Guide to Aboriginal British Columbia*. Vancouver: Whitecap Books/Beautiful British Columbia.

Country Report: Lao PDR. (2006). Travel and Tourism Intelligence.

Cowlishaw, G., Kowal, E. and Lea, T. (2006). Introduction: double binds. In *Moving Anthropology: Critical Indigenous Studies* (T. Lea, E. Kowal and G. Cowlishaw, eds.), pp. 1–16. Darwin, NT: Charles Darwin University Press.

Craig-Smith, S.J. (2005). Tourism education in Oceania. In *Oceania: A Tourism Handbook* (C. Cooper and C.M. Hall, eds.), pp. 362–379. Clevedon: Channel View Publications.

Craik, J. (1997). The culture of tourism. In *Touring Cultures – Transformations of Travel and Theory* (C. Rojek and J. Urry, eds.), pp. 113–136. London: Routledge.

Crang, M. (1999). Knowing, tourism and practices of vision. In *Leisure/Tourism Geographies* (D. Crouch, ed.), pp. 238–256. London: Routledge.

Crang, M. (2004). Cultural geographies of tourism. In *A Companion to Tourism* (A.A. Lew, C.M. Hall and A.M. Williams, eds.), pp. 74–84. Oxford: Blackwell.

Crawshaw, I. (2005). *Aboriginal and Indigenous Australia: An Owner's Manual*. Australia: Cactus Media Publishing.

Crenson, M.A. (1971). *The Un-Politics of Air Pollution: A Study of Non-decision Making in the Cities*. Baltimore, MD: The John Hopkins Press.

Crick, M. (1989). Representations of international tourism in the social sciences: sun, sex, sights, savings, and servility. *Annual Review of Anthropology*, 18, 307–344.

Csargo, L. (1988). *Indian Tourism Overview*. Ottawa: Policy Development Branch, Economic Development Sector, Department of Indian and Northern Affairs.

Curtin, S. (2003). Whale-watching in Kaikoura: sustainable destination development? *Journal of Ecotourism*, 2(3), 173–195.

Da Cruz, M. (2006). Māori culture next big thing in tourism. *New Zealand Herald*, 7 January 2006, p. 7.

Dahl, R.A. (1961). *Who Governs? Democracy and Power in an American City*. New Haven: Yale University Press.

D'Amore, L. (1988). Tourism – the world's peace industry. In *Proceedings of the First Global Conference – Tourism a Vital Force for Peace*, Vancouver, October 1988 (L. D'Amore and J. Jafari, eds.), pp. 7–14. Montreal: Lou D'Amore Associates.

D'Hauteserre, A.M. and Carmichael, B.A. (2005). Abhorrent casino or abhorrent owners: explaining the conflictual relations between surrounding residents and Foxwoods casino and resort. Paper presented at the *New Zealand Hospitality and Tourism Conference*, Wellington, NZ, October 2005.

Daniel, Y.P. (1996). Tourism dance performances: authenticity and creativity. *Annals of Tourism Research*, 23(4), 780–797.

Daniels, M., Bricker, K. and Carmichael, B.A. (2006). Tourism Development and Planning. In *Quality Tourism Experience* (G. Jennings and N. Nickerson, eds.), Butterworth Heinemann, UK: 179–191.

Dann, G.M.S. (1994). "De higher de monkey climb, de more 'e show 'e tail": tourists' knowledge of Barbadian culture. In *Global Tourism Behaviour* (W. Husbands and M. Uysal, eds.), pp. 181–204. New York: The Haworth Press.

Dann, G.M.S. (1996). *The Language of Tourism: A Sociolinguistic Perspective.* Wallingford: CAB International.

Dann, G.M.S. (2000). Differentiating destinations in the language of tourism: harmless hype or promotional irresponsibility? *Tourism Recreation Research,* 25(2), 63–75.

Dashdondov, T.S. (2005). *Mongolian Traditions.* Ulaanbaatar: Montsame.

Dashtseren, B. (2001). *The History and Culture of Mongolia.* Ulaanbaatar: University of Technology and Science. Dasmann 1973.

Dasmann, R.F. 1973. A system for defining and classifying natural regions for purposes of conservation. Morges (Switzerland): International Union for Nature.

Debnam, G. (1984). *The Analysis of Power: A Realist Approach.* London: Macmillan.

Decrop, A. (1999). Triangulation in qualitative tourism research. *Tourism Management,* 20, 157–161.

Decrop, A. (2004). Trustworthiness in qualitative tourism research. In *Qualitative Research in Tourism: Ontologies, Epistemologies and Methodologies* (J. Phillmore and L. Goodson, eds.), pp. 156–169. London: Routledge.

De Kadt, E. (1979). *Tourism: Passport to Development?* New York: Oxford University Press.

Department of Industry, Tourism and Resources (DITR) (2000). *Survey of Indigenous Tourism.* Canberra.

Department of Industry, Tourism and Resources (DITR) (2004a). *A Medium Long Term Strategy for Tourism – Tourism White Paper.* Canberra.

Department of Industry, Tourism and Resources (DITR) (2004b). *Request for Tender: Requirement Business Ready Program for Indigenous Tourism.* Canberra.

Department of Regional Economic Expansion (DREE) (1980). *The Development of Native Tourism In British Columbia.* Ottawa: Department of Regional Economic Expansion, Travel Industry Development Study Agreement.

Desert Knowledge Australia (2005). *Our Outback. Partnerships and Pathways to Success in Tourism.* Brisbane: National Centre for Studies in Travel and Tourism.

Deur, D. and Turner, N.J. (2006). *Keeping it Living: Traditions of Plant Use and Cultivation on the Northwest Coast of North America.* Vancouver: UBC Press.

Din, K.H. (1989). Islam and tourism. Patterns, issues and options. *Annals of Tourism Research,* 16, 542–563.

Dodson, M. (2005). The end in the beginning: re(de)finding aboriginality. In *Blacklines: Contemporary Critical Writing by Indigenous Australians* (M. Grossman et al., eds.), pp. 25–42. Melbourne: Melbourne University Press.

Dogan, H. (1989). Forms of adjustment. Sociocultural impacts of tourism. *Annals of Tourism Research,* 16(2), 216–236.

Doucette, V. (2000). The Aboriginal tourism challenge: managing for growth. *Canadian Tourism Commission Communique,* 4(11), 1.

Downward, P. and Mearman, A. (2004). Triangulation and economic methodology. Paper presented at the *Conference of the International Network of Economic Methodology,* Amsterdam, August.

Dowse, M. (1994). *Tourism studies at the USP. Discussion Paper by the Pacific ACP: EU Bureau for the Tourism Council of the South Pacific and the University of the South Pacific*, Unpublished Manuscript, Suva, Fiji.

Doxey, G.V. (1975). A causation theory of visitor resident irritants: methodology and research inferences. In *The Impact of Tourism, the Travel Research Association 6th Annual Conference Proceedings*, pp. 195–198, September 1975, San Diego, California, CA.

Driver, G.R. and Miles, J.C. (1952). *Code of Hammurabi in English and Akkadian.* Clarendon Press, Oxford.

Eade, D. (2000). *Capacity-Building – An Approach to People-Centered Development.* Oxford: Oxfam GB.

Eadington, W.R. (1995). The emergence of casino gaming as a major factor in tourism markets: policy issues and considerations. In *Change in Tourism: People, Places, Processes* (R. Butler and D. Pearce, eds.), pp. 159–186. London: Routledge.

Eagles, P.F.J. (1997). *International Ecotourism Management: Using Australia and Africa as Case Studies.* Albany: IUCN World Commission on Protected Areas.

Echtner, C.M. (1995). Entrepreneurial training in developing countries. *Annals of Tourism Research*, 22(1), 119–134.

Eder, James F. (1977). "Portrait of a Dying Society: Contemporary Demographic Conditions Among the Batak of Palawan." *Philippine Quarterly Culture and Society*, No 5 Manila.

Edmond, G. (2004). Thick decisions: expertise, advocacy, and reasonableness in the federal court of Australia. *Oceania*, 74(3), 190–330.

Elections BC (2002). *Referendum 2002: Report of the Chief Electoral Office on the Treaty Negotiations Referendum.* Victoria, BC: Elections BC.

Elias, P.D. (1991). *Development of Aboriginal People's Communities.* North York: Captus Press.

Elias, P.D. (1997). Models of aboriginal communities in Canada's north. *International Journal of Social Economics*, 24(11), 1241–1255.

Elliott, R. and Jankel-Elliott, N. (2003). Using ethnography in strategic consumer research. *Qualitative Market Research: An International Journal*, 6(4), 215–223.

Errington, S. (1998). *The Death of Authentic Primitive Art and Other Tales of Progress.* Berkely: University of California Press.

Evrard, O. and Goudineau, Y. (2004). Planned resettlement, unexpected migrations and cultural trauma in Laos. *Development and Change*, 35(5), 937–962.

Fabian, J. (1983). *Time and the Other: How Anthropology Makes Its Object.* New York: Colombian University Press.

Farrington, J., Carney, D., Ashley, C. and Turton, C. (1999). *Sustainable Livelihoods in Practice: Early Applications of Concepts in Rural Tourism.* Overseas Development Institute Natural Resource Perspectives No. 42, London.

Featherstone, M. (1991). *Consumer Culture and Postmodernism.* London: Sage.

Fennell, D. (1999). *Ecotourism: An Introduction*. London: Routledge.

Fennell, D.A. (2002). *Ecotourism Programme Planning*. Wallingford: CABI Publishing.

Ferber, S.R. and Chon, K.S. (1994). Indian gaming: issues and prospects. *Gaming Research and Review Journal*, 1(2), 55–65.

Ferraro, C. (2006). Digeridoos and don'ts. *Sunday Telegraph (London)*, 1 January. Travel, p. 1.

Fielding, N. and Thomas, H. (2001). Qualitative interviewing. In *Researching Social Life* (N. Gilbert, ed.), pp. 123–144. London: Sage.

Finer, J. (2002). Khan do spirit. *Far Eastern Economic Review*, 15 August, pp. 52–53.

Finlayson, J. (1991). *Australian Aborigines and cultural tourism: case studies of Aboriginal involvement in the tourist industry*. Working papers on multiculturalism, (No. 15), Canberra: Office of Multicultural Affairs.

Finlayson, J. (1993). A critical overview of current policies and programs. *Indigenous Australians and Tourism: A Focus on Northern Australia. Proceedings of the Indigenous Australians and Tourism Conference*. Darwin, Canberra, Goanna Print: 76–82.

Finlayson, C. and McCay, B. (2000). Crossing the threshold of ecosystem resilience: the commercial extinction of northern cod. In *Linking Social and Ecological Systems: Management Practices and Social Mechanisms for Building Resilience* (F. Berkes and C. Folke, eds.), pp. 311–337. Cambridge: Cambridge University Press.

FitzGibbon, C.D., Mogaka, H. and Fanshawe, J.H. (2000). Threatened mammals, subsistence harvesting and high human population densities: a recipe for disaster? In *Hunting for Sustainability in Tropical Forests* (J.G. Robinson and E.L. Bennett, eds.), pp. 154–167. New York: Columbia University Press.

Foley, D. (2005). The Heartland chronicles revisited: the casino's impact on settlement life. *Qualitative Inquiry*, 11(2), 296–320.

Foucault, M. (1972). *The Archeology of Knowledge* (translation A.M. Sheridan Smith). New York: Pantheon.

Foucault, M. (1980). *Power/Knowledge: Selected Interviews and Other Writings 1972–1977*. New York: Pantheon Books.

Francis, D. (1992). *The Imaginary Indian: The Image of the Indian in Canadian Culture*. Vancouver: Arsenal Pulp Press.

Fredman, P., Emmelin, L., Heberlein, T.A. and Vuorio, T. (2001). Tourism in the Swedish mountain region. In *Going North* (B. Sahlberg, ed.), pp. 123–146. Östersund: ETOUR.

Freeman, D. (2000). Indigenous Tourism – The Way Ahead. *National Indigenous Tourism Forum Proceedings Report Tourism The Indigenous Opportunity*. Commonwealth Department of Industry, Science and Resources, Canberra.

Frideres, J.S. (1988). *Native Peoples in Canada: Contemporary Conflicts*, 3rd edition. Scarbourough, Ontario: Prentice-Hall Canada Inc.

Frow, J. (1997). *Time and Commodity Culture. Essays in Cultural Theory and Postmodernity*. Oxford: Claredon Press.

Fürer-Haimendorf, C. von (1989). *Exploratory Travels in Highland Nepal*. New Delhi: Sterling Publishers.

Gallie, W.B. (1955–1956). Essentially contested concepts. *Proceedings of the Aristotelian Society*, 56, 167–198.

Gansukh, D. (2003). *The Role and Prospects of the Tourism Industry in Export Trade of Mongolia*. Ulaanbaatar: Ministry of Industry and Trade/Gesellschaft für Technische Zusammenarbeit.

Gansukh, D. (2005). *International Tourism Survey*. Ulaanbaatar: Mongolian Tourism Board.

Gardiner, A.H. (1961). *Egypt of the Pharaohs: An Introduction*. Oxford: Oxford University Press.

Gardner, J.E. and Nelson, J.G. (1988). National parks and native people in Northern Canada, Alaska, and Northern Australia. In *Tribal Peoples and Development Issues: A Global Overview* (J. Bodley, ed.), pp. 334–351. Mountain View, CA: Mayfield Publishing Company.

Gegeo, D.W. and Watson-Gegeo, K.A. (2002). Whose knowledge? Epistemological collisions in Solomon Islands community development. *Contemporary Pacific*, 14(2), 377–409.

Gelder, K. and Jacobs, J.M. (1998). *Uncanny Australia: Sacredness and Identity in a Postcolonial Nation*. Melbourne: Melbourne University Press.

Gellner, E. (1983). *Nations and Nationalism*. Ithaca: Cornell University Press.

Ghimire, K.B. (2001). *The Native Tourist*. London: Earthscan.

Gibson, C. and Klocker, N. (2004). Academic publishing as 'creative' industry, and recent discourse of 'creative economies': some critical reflections. *Area*, 36(4), 423–434.

Giddens, A. (1979). *Central Problems in Social Theory: Action, Structure and Contradiction in Social Analysis*. London: Macmillan.

Goodman, R. (1994). *Legalized Gambling as a Strategy for Economic Development*. Northampton, MA: United States Gambling Study.

Goodman, D.S.G. (ed.) (2004). *China's Campaign to "Open Up the West": National, Provincial and Local Perspectives*. Cambridge: Cambridge University Press.

Goodwin, H. (1998). *Sustainable Tourism and the Elimination of Poverty DFID/DETR*. Available from: www.icrtourism.org/Publications/Povert Paper2.doc

Goodwin, H. (2006). Measuring and reporting the impact of tourism on poverty. In *Proceedings: Cutting Edge Research in Tourism: New directions, challenges and applications*. Surrey: University of Surrey, n. p.

Goodwin, H.J., Kent, I.J., Parker, K.T. and Walpole, M.J. (1997). *Four reports on Tourism, Conservation and Sustainable Development*, Vol. IV, Zimbabwe. Southeast Lowveld. Department for International Development, London.

Goss, J. (2004). The souvenir: conceptualizing the object(s) of tourist consumption. In *A Companion to Tourism* (A.A. Lew, C.M. Hall and A.M. Williams, eds.), pp. 327–336. Oxford: Blackwell.

Government of Canada (1989). *The Canadian Aboriginal Economic Development Strategy*. Ottawa: Government of Canada.

Government of Canada (1997). *Delgamuukw/Gisdaywa v. The Queen*. Ottawa: Supreme Court of Canada.

Graburn, N.H.H. (1997). Tourism and cultural development in East Asia. In *Tourism and Cultural Development in Asia and Oceania* (Y. Shinji, K.H. Din and J.S. Eades, eds.), pp. 194–213. Selangor: Penerbit Universiti Kebangsaan Malaysia.

Gray, A. (1991). Between the spice of life and the melting pot: biodiversity conservation and its impact on indigenous peoples. IWGIA Document No. 70. International Work Group on International Affairs, Copenhagen, pp. 197–207.

Gray, J. (1983). Political power, social theory and essential contestability. In *The Nature of Political Theory* (D. Miller and L. Siedentop, eds.), pp. 75–101. Oxford: Clarendon Press.

Green, R. (2004). Some urge new approach in tribal casino fight, *Hartford Courant*, July 18, 2004, A1. The Section of the paper is A, the page number is 1.

Green, R.C. (1991). A reappraisal of some Lapita sites in the Reef/Santa Cruz Group of the southeast Solomons. In *Indo-Pacific Prehistory* (P. Bellwood, ed.), pp. 197–207 Canberra: Indo-Pacific Prehistory Association.

Grenier, L. (1998). *Working with Indigenous Knowledge: A Guide for Researchers*. Ottawa: International Development Research Centre.

Grinder, B. (1992). Dance carries on traditions. *Windspeaker*, 10(6), 10.

Grossman, M. (2005). Introduction: after aboriginalism power, knowledge and Indigenous Australian critical writing. In *Blacklines: Contemporary Critical Writing by Indigenous Australians* (M. Grossman et al., eds.), pp. 1–16. Melbourne: Melbourne University Press.

Grossman, M. et al. (eds.) (2005). *Blacklines: Contemporary Critical Writing by Indigenous Australians*. Melbourne: Melbourne University Press.

Grünewald, R. (2002). Tourism and cultural revival. *Annals of Tourism Research*, 29, 1004–1021.

Guizhou Yearbook, 1996. *Guizhou Tongji Nianjian* [Guizhou Statistical Yearbook], Beijing: Zhongguo Tongji.

Gupta, A. and Ferguson, J. (1992). Beyond culture: space, identity and the politics of difference. *Cultural Anthropology*, 7(1), 6–23.

Gupta, A. and Ferguson, J. (eds.) (1997). *Culture, Power, Place: Explorations in Critical Anthropology*. Durham and London: Duke University Press.

Gurung, C.P. and Coursey, M. (1994). The Annapurna Conservation Area project: a pioneering example of sustainable tourism? In *Ecotourism: A sustainable option*? (E. Cater and G. Lowman, eds.), pp. 177–194. Chichester: John Wiley.

Gurung, H. (1980). *Vignettes of Nepal*. Kathmandu: Sajha Prakashan.

Guzzini, S. (2000). A reconstruction of constructivism in international relations. *European Journal of International Relations*, 6(2), 147–182.

Guzzini, S. (2001). The significance and roles of teaching theory in international relations. *Journal of International Relations and Development*, 4(2), 98–117.

Hackel, J.D. (1999). Community conservation and the future of Africa's wildlife. *Conservation Biology*, 13(4), 726–734.

Hadwiger, D. (1996). State governors and American Indian casino gambling: defining state-tribal relationships. *Spectrum*, Fall, 16–25.

Hakopa, H. (1998). The Māori World View. Unpublished Manuscript, Political Science Lecture, University of Otago, Dunedin.

Hall, C.M. (1994). *Tourism and Politics: Policy, Power and Place*. New York: John Wiley & Sons.

Hall, C.M. (2000a). Tourism, national parks and Aboriginal peoples. In *Tourism and National Parks* (R.W. Butler and S.W. Boyd, eds.), pp. 57–71. Chichester: Wiley.

Hall, C.M. (2000b). *Tourism Planning*. Harlow: Pearson.

Hall, C.M. (2006). Tourism, governance and the (mis-)location of power. In *Tourism, Power and Space* (A. Church and T. Coles, eds.). London: Routledge.

Hall, C.M. and Tucker, H. (eds.) (2004). *Tourism and Postcolonialism*. London: Routledge.

Hall, S. (ed.) (1997). *Representation: Cultural Representations and Signifying Practices*. London: Sage.

Hao Ke Ming (1987). *Zhongguo Gaodeng Jiaoyu Jiegou Yanjui* (A Study of China's Higher Education Structure) [In Chinese]. Beijing: Renmin Chubanshe.

Haralambopoulos, N. and Pizam, A. (1996). Perceived impacts of tourism: the case of Samos. *Annals of Tourism Research*, 22(3), 503–526.

Harlow, B. (1987). *Resistance Literature*. New York: Methuen.

Harris, M. and Wearing, S. (1999). An approach to training for indigenous ecotourism development. *World Leisure and Recreation*, 41(2), 9–17.

Harrison, D. (1992). Tourism to less developed countries: the social consequences. In *Tourism and the Less Developed Countries* (D. Harrison, ed.), pp. 19–34. London: Belhaven Press.

Harrison, D. and Schipani, S. (2007). Lao tourism and poverty alleviation: community-based tourism and the private sector. *Current Issues in Tourism* (in press).

Haywood, M., Reid, D., Wolfe, J. and Nightingale, M. (1993). Enhancing hospitality and tourism education and training in Canada's Northwest Territories. In *Canadian Outbound Travel Market Product/Market Match* (M. Johnson and ISTC (1992)). Ottawa: Industry, Science and Technology of Canada.

Hechter, M. (1975). *Internal Colonialism: The Celtic Fringe in British National Development*. London: Routledge.

Hegarty, J. (1990). Challenges and opportunities for creating hospitality and tourism education programs in developing countries. *Hospitality and Tourism Educator*, 2(3), 12–13, 40–41.

Heide, S. von der (1988). *The Thakalis of Northwestern Nepal*. Kathmandu: Ratna Pustak Bhandar.

Henderson, J. (2003). Managing tourism and Islam in Peninsular Malaysia. *Tourism Management*, 24, 447–456.

Hicks, J. (2004). On the application of theories of 'internal colonialism' to Inuit societies. Presentation to the *Annual Conference of the Canadian Political Science Association*, Winnipeg, 5 June 2004.

Higham, J.E.S. and Carr, A.M. (2002a). Profiling tourists to ecotourism operations. *Annals of Tourism Research*, 29(4), 1168–1171.

Higham, J.E.S. and Carr, A.M. (2002b). Ecotourism visitor experiences in Aotearoa/New Zealand: challenging the environmental values of visitors in pursuit of pro-environmental behaviour. *Journal of Sustainable Tourism*, 10(4), 277–294.

Higham, J.E.S. and Carr, A.M. (2003). The scope and scale of ecotourism in New Zealand: a review and consideration of current policy initiatives. In *Ecotourism: Policy and Planning* (D.A. Fennell and R.K. Dowling, eds.), pp. 235–255. Oxon, UK: CABI Publishing.

Higham, J.E.S., Carr, A.M. and Gale, S. (2001). *Profiling visitors to New Zealand Ecotourism Operations. He tauhokohoko ngä whakaaturanga a ngä manuhiri ki rawa whenua o Aotearoa*. Research Paper No. 10, Department of Tourism, University of Otago.

Hinch, T. (1995). Aboriginal people in the tourism economy of Canada's Northwest Territories. In *Polar Tourism: Tourism in the Arctic and Antarctic Regions* (C.M. Hall and M.E. Johnston, eds.), pp. 115–130. New York: John Wiley & Sons.

Hinch, T. (1998). Tourists and indigenous hosts: diverging views on their relationship with nature. *Current Issues in Tourism*, 1(1), 120–124.

Hinch, T. and Butler, R. (1996). Indigenous tourism: a common ground for discussion. In *Tourism and Indigenous Peoples* (R. Butler and T. Hinch, eds.), pp. 3–21. London: International Thompson Business Press.

Hinch, T. and Colton, J. (1997). Harvesting tourists on a cree trap line. In *Conference Proceedings Trails in the Third Millennium: Cromwell, New Zealand* (J.E.S. Higham and G.W. Kearsley, eds.), pp. 115–124. Dunedin: University of Otago.

Hinch, T.D. (1994). Aboriginal tourism in Alberta: a community perspective. In *Planning for Aboriginal Cultural Tourism* (W. Jamieson, ed.), pp. 45–57. Calgary, Alberta: Centre for Liveable Communities, University of Calgary.

Hinch, T.D. (2001). Indigenous territories. In *The Encyclopedia of Ecotourism* (D. Weaver, ed.), pp. 345–358. Oxon, UK: Cab International.

Hinch, T.D. and Delamere, T.A. (1993). Native festivals and tourism attractions. *Journal of Applied Recreation Research*, 18, 131–142.

Hinch, T.D., McIntosh, A.J. and Ingram, T. (1999). Managing Maori tourist attractions in Aotearoa. *World Leisure and Recreation Journal*, 41(2), 21–24.

Hinkson, M. (2005). New media projects at Yuendumu: towards a history and analysis of intercultural engagement. In *The Power of Knowledge: The Resonance of Tradition* (L. Taylor et al., eds.), pp. 157–168. Canberra: Aboriginal Studies Press.

His Majesty's Government (HMG) of Nepal (2000). *Nepal Tourism Statistics*. Kathmandu, Ministry of Tourism and Civil Aviation, Nepal.

Hiwasaki, L. (2000). Ethnic tourism in Hokkaido and the shaping of Ainu identity. *Pacific Affairs*, 73(3), 393–412.

Hoffmann, J. (1988). *State, Power and Democracy: Contentious Concepts in Practical Political Theory*. New York: St. Martin's Press.

Holbig, H. (2005). The emergence of the campaign to open up the west: ideological formation, central decision making and the role of the provinces. In *China's Campaign to "Open Up the West": National, Provincial and Local Perspectives* (D.S.G. Goodman, ed., 2004), pp. 4–21. Cambridge: Cambridge University Press.

Hollinshead, K. (1988). 'First-blush of the Longtime: the market development of Australia's living Aboriginal heritage', in Travel and Tourism Research Association, Tourism Research: Expanding Boundaries: *Proceedings of the 19th Annual Conference, Montreal, Canada, June 1988*, pp. 183–98. Salt Lake City: University of Utah.

Hollinshead, K. (1992). 'White' gaze, 'red' people – shadow visions: the disidentification of 'Indians' in cultural tourism. *Leisure Studies*, 11, 43–64.

Hollinshead, K. (1996). Marketing and metaphysical realism: the disidentification of Aboriginal life and traditions through tourism. In *Tourism and Indigenous Peoples* (R. Butler and T. Hinch, eds.), pp. 308–347. London: International Thomson Business Press.

Hollinshead, K. (1998a). Tourism, hybridity and ambiguity: the relevance of Bhabha's 'third space' cultures. *Journal of Leisure Research*, 30(1), 121–156 [Special Issue on Race, Ethnicity and Leisure].

Hollinshead, K. (1998b). Tourism and the restless peoples: a dialectical inspection of Bhabha's halfway populations. *Tourism, Culture and Communication*, I(1), 49–77.

Hollinshead, K. (1998c). Disney and commodity aesthetics: a critique of Fjellman's analysis of 'distory' and the 'historicide' of the past. *Current Issues in Tourism*, 1(1), 58–119.

Hollinshead, K. (2002a). Being Transported Downunder: Spiritual Alchemy and the Pied Piety of Australia. Presentation at the *International Sociological Association's World Congress of Sociology*, Brisbane, Australia, Unpublished.

Hollinshead, K. (2002b). *Tourism and the Making of the World: Tourism and the Dynamics of Our Contemporary Tribal Lives*. Honors Excellence Lecture. The Honors College, Miami, Florida, Florida International University.

Hollinshead, K. (2002c). Tourism and the ancestral now: holding-the-country traditionally, carrying-the-country transitionally. Presentation at the *International Sociological Association's World Congress of Sociology*, Brisbane, Australia, Unpublished.

Hollinshead, K. (2006). Spirituality and the communicative power of tourism: the projection of dynamic Aboriginal life: the corrective projection of transitionality. *Conference Proceedings, Tourism: The Spiritual Dimension*, The University of Lincoln, 5–7 April.

Hollinshead, K. (In preparation (a)). Tourism and new collective effervescence: the rekindling of Aboriginality B A critique of a New Lonely Planet

Publication, and of the power of representation in/of tourism. Paper being prepared for *Current Issues in Tourism*.

Hollinshead, K. (In preparation (b)). 'Worldmaking' and the transformation of place and culture: the enlargement of Meethan's analysis of tourism and global change. Manuscript submitted to the *Journal of Tourism and Cultural Change*.

Holmes, S. (1988). Gag rules or the politics of omission. In *Constitutionalism and Democracy* (J. Elster and R. Slagstad, eds.), pp. 19–58. Cambridge: Cambridge University Press.

Hon, D. (1990). Sarawak tourism potential. *Sarawak Gazette*, 12–16 October.

Honey, M. (1999). *Ecotourism and Sustainable Development: Who Owns Paradise?* Washington, DC: Island Press.

Hong, E. (1987). *Native of Sarawak: Survival in Borneo's Vanishing Forests*. Kuching, Malaysia: Institut Masyarakat.

Hopkins, R. (2004). *South Pacific: Facts and Figures of Tourism*. Available from: (http://www.spto.org/spto/export/sites/spto/tourism_resources/presentations/spto_speeches/2004_facts_x_figures.pdf (accessed 30 October 2006).

Horowitz, S.L. (1998). Integrating indigenous resource management with wildlife conservation: a case study of Batang Ai National Park, Sarawak, Malaysia. *Human Ecology*, 26(3), 371–403.

Horton. D. (ed.) (1994). *The Encyclopaedia of Aboriginal Australia: Aboriginal Torres Strait Islander History, Society and Culture*, Vol. 1. B A to L. Canberra: Aboriginal Studies Press.

Hough, J.L. and Sherpa, M.N. (1989). Bottom up vs. basic needs: integrating conservation and development in the Annapurna and Michiru Mountain conservation areas of Nepal and Malawi. *Ambio*, 18, 434–441.

Hsu, C.H. (1999). Social impacts of Native American gaming. In *Legal Casino Gaming in the United States: The Economic and Social Impact* (C.H. Hsu, ed.). New York: Hayworth Press. 221–232.

Hudman, L.E. and Hawkins, D.E. (1989). *Tourism in Contemporary Society*. Englewood Cliffs: Prentice Hall.

Huggins, J. (2005). Always was always will be. In *Blacklines: Contemporary Critical Writing by Indigenous Australians* (M. Grossman et al., eds.), pp. 60–65. Melbourne: Melbourne University Press.

Humphrey, A. and Humphrey, E. (2003). *A Profile of Four Communal Area Conservancies in Namibia, Torra, Khoadi/Hoas, Mayuni, Salambala*, Commissioned by the WILD Project.

Husbands, W. (1994). Visitor expectations of tourism benefits in Zambia. In *Global Tourism Behaviour* (W. Husbands and M. Uysal, eds.), pp. 21–38. New York: The Haworth Press.

Hyland, J.L. (1995). *Democratic Theory: The Philosophical Foundations*. Manchester: Manchester University Press.

ibn Abd Al-Hakam, A. (1014/1922). *Kitāb Futūh Misr wa-ahbārihā*. New Haven, CT: Yale University Press.

ibn Anas, M. (1999). *al-Muwatta' lil-Imām Mālik ibn Anas*. Dār al-Hadīth, al-Qāhirah.

IMF and IDA (1999). Poverty Reduction Strategy Paper: Operational Issues Washington, DC.

Indigenous New Zealand Aotearoa, http://www.inz.Māori.nz/(accessed 12 March 2006).

Indigenous Tourism Leadership Group (2003). *Response to "The 10 Year Plan for Tourism" – A Discussion Paper*. Canberra: Indigenous Tourism Leadership Group.

Information Office of the State Council (IOSC) (2005). White Paper: *Regional Autonomy for Ethnic Minorities in China*. Beijing: IOSC.

Ing, R. (1990). The effects of residential schools on Native childrearing practices. *Canadian Journal of Native Education*, 18(Suppl.), 67–118.

Ingram, G. (2005). A phenomenological investigation of tourists' experience of Australian indigenous culture. In *Indigenous Tourism. The Commodification and Management of Culture* (C. Ryan and M. Aicken, eds.), pp. 21–34. Oxford: Elsevier.

Ingram, T. (1996). *Māori Tourism Development: A Strategic Plan and Policy for Ministry of Māori Development*. Wellington, NZ: Te Puni Kokiri.

Ingram, T. (1997). Tapoi Tangata Whenua: Tapoi Māori ki Aotearoa – Indigenous Tourism: Regio nal Māori Tourism in Aotearoa. In *Conference Proceedings Trails in the Third Millenium: Cromwell, New Zealand* (J.E.S. Higham and G.W. Kearsley, eds.). Dunedin, University of Otago.

Industry, Science and Technology Canada (ISTC) (1992). *Canadian Outbound Travel Market Product/Market Match*. Ottawa: Industry, Science and Technology Canada.

Industry, Science and Technology Canada (ISTC) (1996). *Promoting the Growth of Canada's Aboriginal Businesses: New Directions 1996*. Ottawa: Industry, Science and Technology Canada.

Integrated Rural Development and Nature Conservation (IRDNC) (2002). Information sheet, January, Integrated Rural Development and Nature Conservation, Windhoek.

International Union of Official Travel Organizations (IUTO) (1963). *Conference on International Travel and Tourism*. Geneva: United Nations.

Iran Touring and Tourism Organisation (ITTO) (2002). *Tourism Management and Impact Analysis*. Teheran: National Tourism Development Office.

Ite, U.E. (1996). Community perceptions of the Cross River National Park, Nigeria. *Environmental Conservation*, 23(4), 351–357.

Jacobsen, T. (1970). *Toward the Image of Tammuz and Other Essays on Mesopotamian History and Culture*. Cambridge: Harvard University Press.

Jacobsohn, M. (2001). Namibia's Kunene Region: a new vision unfolds. In *Once We Were Hunters. A Journey with Africa's Indigenous People* (P. Weinberg, ed.), pp. 122–146. Cape Town: David Philip.

Jamieson, W., Goodwin, H. and Edmunds, C. (2004). *Contribution of Tourism to Poverty Alleviation, Pro Poor Tourism, and the Challenge of Measuring*

Impacts. Bangkok: Transport Policy and Tourism Section, Transport Division UN ESCAP.

Jamison, D. (1999). Tourism and ethnicity: the brotherhood of coconuts. *Annals of Tourism Research*, 26, 944–967.

Jampen, M. (2000). Dynamische Entwicklung der touristischen Ubernachtungsbetribe in der Annapurna Conservation Area, Nepal, Diplomarbeit. Masters Thesis, Universität Bern, Switzerland.

Jarrett, R.L. (1993). Focus group interviewing with low-income minority populations: a research experience. In *Successful Focus Groups. Advancing the State of Art* (D.L. Morgan, ed.), pp. 184–201, Newbury Park: Sage.

Jaworski, A. and Pritchard, A. (eds.) (2005). *Discourse, Communication and Tourism*. Clevedon, England: Channel View Publications.

Johnston, A. (2000). Indigenous peoples and ecotourism: bringing indigenous knowledge and rights into the sustainability equation. *Tourism Recreation Research*, 25(2), 89–96.

Johnston, A.M. (2006). *Is the Sacred For Sale: Tourism and Indigenous Peoples*. London: Earthscan.

Joint NGO's Statement on Tourism (2004). Working Group 1, Agenda Item 19.7 COP7, Kuala Lumpur, 9–20 February 2004.

Jones, B. (2001). The evolution of a community-based approach to wildlife management. In *African Wildlife and Livelihoods* (D. Hulme and M. Murhpree, eds.), pp. 160–176. Oxford: James Currey Ltd.

Jones, J.L. (2003). *Modifying the Tourism Impact Attitude Scale (TIAS) to Explore Casino Impacts and Resident Attitudes*. Unpublished Doctoral Dissertation. Storrs, CT: University of Connecticut.

Joppe, M. (1996a). Sustainable community tourism development revisited. *Tourism Management*, 17(7), 475–479.

Joppe, M. (1996b). Sustainable community tourism development revisited. *Journal of Native Education*, 18(Suppl.), 3–63.

Kabzińska-Stawarz, I. (1987). 'Eriin gurvan nadaam' – 'Three Games of the Men' – In Mongolia. *Ethnolgia Polona*, 13, 45–89.

Kabzińska-Stawarz, I. (1991). *Games of Mongolian Shepherds*. Warsaw: Polish Academy of Sciences.

Kadt, Emmanuel de (1990). 'Making the alternative sustainable: Lessons from development for tourism', Discussion Paper, No. 272, Institute of Development Studies, University of Sussex, Brighton.

Kanara-Zygadlo, F., Shone, M., McIntosh, A. and Matunga, H. (2005). A value-based approach to Maori tourism: concepts and characteristics. In *Understanding the Tourism Host-guest Encounter in New Zealand: Foundations for Adaptive Planning and Management* (D.G. Simmons and J.R. Fairweather, eds.), pp. 109–133. Christchurch: EOS Ecology.

Kapiti Island Alive. Available from: http://www.kapitiislandalive.co.nz/ThePeople.htm (accessed 15 March 2006).

Kauffman, P. (2000). *Travelling Aboriginal Australia: Discovery and Reconciliation*. Flemington, Victoria, British Columbia: Hyland House.

Kearsley, G.W., McIntosh, A.J. and Carr, A.M. (1999). Māori myths, beliefs and values: products and constraints for New Zealand Tourism. In *Tourism Industry and Education Symposium Proceedings, Reports and Proceedings Jyvaskyla Polytechnic No. 5* (E. Arola and T. Mikkonen, eds.), pp. 292–302. Finland: Jyvaskyla Polytechnic.

Keelan, N. (1996). Māori heritage: Visitor management and interpretation. In *Heritage Management in New Zealand and Australia* (C.M. Hall and S. McArthur, eds.), pp. 195–201. Melbourne: Oxford University Press.

Keller, C.P. (1987). Stages of peripheral tourism development: Canada's Northwest Territories. *Tourism Management*, 8(1), 20–32.

Kelly, M. (2005). *Atiik Askii: Land of the Caribou. Building Community Partnerships for the Northwestern Manitoba Regional Tourism Strategy.* Ottawa: Minister of Indian Affairs and Northern Development.

Kessler, C. (1992). Pilgrim's progress: the travellers of Islam. *Annals of Tourism Research*, 19, 147–153.

Kim, C. and Lee, S. (2000). Understanding the cultural differences in tourist motivation between Anglo-American and Japanese tourists. *Journal of Travel and Tourism Marketing*, 9(1/2), 153–170.

Kim, S.-S., Prideaux, B. and Kim, S-H. (2002). A cross cultural study on casino guests as perceived by casino employees. *Tourism Management*, 23, 511–520.

King, B. (1994). Tourism higher education in island microstates: the case of the South Pacific. *Tourism Management*, 15, 267–272.

King, B. (1996). A regional approach to tourism education and training in Oceania: progress and prospects. *Progress in Tourism and Hospitality Research*, 2(1), 87–101.

King, B. and Berno, T. (2002). Tourism and civil disturbances: an evaluation of recovery strategies in Fiji 1987–2000. *Journal of Hospitality and Tourism Management*, 9(1), 46–60.

King, D.A. and Stewart, W.P. (1996). Ecotourism and commodification: protecting people and places. *Biodiversity and Conservation*, 5(3), 293–305.

Kirch, P.V. (1997). *The Lapita Peoples.* Oxford, Blackwell Publishers.

Kirshenblatt-Gimblett, B. (1998). *Destination Culture: Tourism, Museums and Heritage.* Berkeley: University of California Press.

Knightley, P. (2001). *Australia: Biography of a Nation.* London: Vintage.

Koch, E. and Massyn, P. (eds.) (2001). *African Game Lodges and Their Contribution to Rural Livelihoods.* Johannesburg: Report Commissioned by the Ford Foundation.

Kokubo, M. and Haraguchi, Y. (1991). *Mission Report on Advisory Services for Hotel Management and the Promotion of Conventions in Mongolia.* Ulaanbaatar: Economic and Social Commission for Asia and the Pacific.

Kraijo, A. (1997). Agriculture or forestry: a case study in Ghandruk, Nepal, of the motivation of villagers to give up agricultural production and to plant trees. Thesis, submitted to the Faculty of Public Administration and Public Policy, University of Twenthe, The Netherlands.

Krippendorf, J. (1990). *The Holiday Makers: Understanding the Impact of Leisure and Travel*, 3rd edition. Oxford: Heinemann.

Kuhn, R. and Duerden, F. (1996). A review of traditional environmental knowledge: an interdisciplinary Canadian perspective. *Culture*, 16(1), 71–84.

Kwmae, R.C. (1997). Tourism education and training in the Caribbean: preparing for the 21st century. *Progress in Tourism and Hospitality Education Research*, 3, 189–197.

Lang Research (2000). *Travel Activities and Motivation Survey – Aboriginal Tourism Report*. Canada: Lang Research.

Langdon, S.J. (2006). Tidal pulse fishing: selective traditional Tlingit salmon fishing techniques on the west coast of the Prince of Wales Archipelago. In *Traditional Ecological Knowledge and Natural Resource Management* (C. Menzies, ed.), pp. 21–46. Omaha: University of Nebraska Press.

Langton, M. (2005a). Introduction: culture wars. In *Blacklines: Contemporary Critical Writing by Indigenous Australians* (M. Grossman et al., eds.), pp. 81–91. Melbourne: Melbourne University Press.

Langton, M. (2005b). Aboriginal art and film: the politics of representation. In *Blacklines: Contemporary Critical Writing by Indigenous Australians* (M. Grossman et al., eds.), pp. 109–126. Melbourne: Melbourne University Press.

Langton, M. and Palmer, L. (2003). Modern agreement making and indigenous people in Australia: issues and trends. *Australian Indigenous Law Reporter* 1.

Lao National Tourism Administration. Available from: http://www. tourism-laos.gov.la/about-lnta.htm (accessed: 20 May 2006).

Lao National Tourism Administration (2004). National Ecotourism Strategy and Action Plan 2005–2010. Lao National Tourism Authority. Vientien. *LNTA Website*. Available from: Ecotourism Laos. http://www.ecotourismlaos.com/activities/ akha_experience.htm (accessed 25 September 2006).

Lao PDR Country Report (2005, nd) prepared by LNTA for UNESCAP in August/September 2005.

Laos expanding eco-tourism niche: Official hope to protect tribal culture, 14 May 2004. Available from: http://www. cnn.com. (accessed 24 June 2005).

Lasswell, H.D. (1936). *Politics: Who Gets, What, When, How*? New York: McGraw-Hill.

Latour, B. (1999). *Pandora's Hope: Essays on the Reality of Scientific Studies*. Cambridge: Harvard University Press.

Lattimore, O. (1941). *Mongol Journeys*. London: Jonathan Cape.

Laxson, J.D. (1991). How we see them: tourism and native Americans. *Annals of Tourism Research*, 18(3), 365–391.

Lee, B. (1992). Colonialization and community – implications for 1st Nations Development. *Community Development Journal*, 27(3), 211–219.

Lee, C.K., Lee, Y.K. and Wicks, B.E. (2004). Segmentation of festival motivation by nationality and satisfaction. *Tourism Management*, 25(1), 61–70.

Leiper, N. (1990). *Tourism Systems*. Department of Management Systems, Occasional Paper No. 2. Palmerston North, New Zealand: Massey University.

Leiper, N. (1995). *Tourism Management*. Collingwood, Vic.: TAFE Publications.

Lennox Island Aboriginal Ecotourism (2004). http://www. lennoxisland. com/liae/ home.htm. (accessed October 2004).

Leung, H. and Chan, K.W. (1986). Chinese regional development policies: a comparative reassessment. Paper presented at the *Annual Meeting of the Canadian Asian Studies Association*, Winnipeg, Canada. Cited in Oakes, T. (1999). Selling Guizhou: cultural development in an era of marketization. In *The Political Economy of China's Provinces* (H. Hendrischke and C.Y. Feng, eds.), pp. 27–67. London and New York: Routledge.

Lew, A. and Van Otten, G.A. (1998). *Tourism and Gaming on American Indian Lands*. New York: Cognizant Communications.

Lewis, A. (2005). Rationalising a tourism curriculum for sustainable tourism development in small island states: a stakeholder perspective. *Journal of Hospitality, Leisure, Sport and Tourism Education*, 4(2), 4–15.

Li, D. (2000). Seek truth from fact. *Qiushi* 288, 1 June 2000, pp. 22–25.

Li, F.M.S. (2006). "*Tourism Development, Empowerment and the Tibetan Minority*: Jiuzhaigou National Nature Reserve" in Managing World Heritage Sites (2006). A. Leask and A. Fyall. Butterworth Heinemann: London. 226–238.

Li, F.M.S. and Sofield, T.H.B. (1994). Tourism and socio-cultural change in rural China. In *Tourism: The State of the Art* (A. Seaton, ed.), pp. 854–867. Chichester: Wiley.

Liang. F. (1993). Guizhou's Ordinance Industry Turns Civil. *Beijing Review*, 11–17 October, p. 13. Cited in Oakes, T. (1999). Selling Guizhou: cultural development in an era of marketization. In *The Political Economy of China's Provinces* (H. Hendrischke and C.Y. Feng, eds.), pp. 27–67. London and New York: Routledge.

Liu, A. and Wall, G. (2006). Planning tourism employment: a developing country perspective. *Tourism Management*, 27, 159–170.

Long, D.A. and Dickason, O.P. (1996). *Vision of the Heart – Canadian Aboriginal Issues*. Toronto: Harcourt Brace & Company.

Long, P.T. (1995). Casino Gambling in the United States – 1994 status and implications. *Tourism Management*, 16(3), 189–197.

Long. P.T., Clark, J. and Liston, D. (1994). *Win, Lose or draw? Gambling with America's small towns*. Washington, DC: The Aspen Institute.

Long, S.A. (2002). *Disentangling Benefits, Livelihoods, Natural Resource Management and Managing Revenue from Tourism: The Experience of the Torra Conservancy, Namibia*. DEA Research Discussion Paper, No. 53, November, Directorate of Environmental Affairs, Windhoek.

Lukes, S. (1974). *Power: A Radical View*. London: MacMillan.

Lukes, S. (1986). Introduction. In *Power* (S. Lukes, ed.), pp. 1–18. Oxford: Basil Blackwell.

Lukes, S. (2005). *Power: A Radical View*, 2nd edition. London: Palgrave MacMillan in association with the British Sociological Association.

Lundgren, J.O. (1995). The Tourism Space Penetration: processes in Northern Canada and Scandinavia: a comparison. In *Polar Tourism* (C.M. Hall and M.E. Johnston, eds.), pp. 43–62. Chichester: Wiley.

Lyngnes, S. and Viken A. (1998). *Samisk Kultur og Turisme på Nordkalotten*. Rapport, Oslo: NMH/BI.

Lyttleton, C. and Allcock, A. (2002). Tourism as a Tool for Development: UNESCO – Lao National Tourism Authority Nam Ha Ecotourism Project, External Review.

MacCannell, D. (1976). *The Tourist: A New Theory of the Leisure Class*. New York: Shocken Books.

MacCannell, D. (1992). *The Empty Meeting Grounds: The Tourist Papers*. London: Routledge.

MacCannell, D. (1994). Tradition's next step. In *Discovered Country. Tourism and Survival in the American West* (S. Norris, ed.). Albuquerque: Stone Ladder Press. 161–179.

MacCannell, D. (1999). *The Tourist – A new Theory of the Leisure Class*, 3rd edition. Berkeley: University of California Press.

MacGregor, J. (1993). Traditional ecological knowledge; an opportunity for Native Tourism. *Expanding Responsibilities: A Blueprint for the Travel Industry. Proceedings of the 24th Annual Conference of the Travel and Tourism Research Association*, 13–16 June 1993. Whistler, B.C.

MacHattie, B. and Wolfe-Keddie, J. (2000). *Mi'kmaq of a Sacred Bay – Lennox Island Aboriginal Ecotourism Strategy: Ten Year Strategic Planning Process 1999–2009*. University of Guelph, Guelph, Ontario.

Mackerras, C., Pradeep T. and Young, G. 1994. *China Since 1978. Reform, Modernization and Socialism with Chinese Characteristics*. New York: Longman Cheshire.

Mackerras, C. (2003). *Ethnic Minorities and Globalisation*. London: Routledge Curzon.

Mackerras, C. (2006). Western development policy. *The China Journal*, Issue 56, 165–167.

Mackerras, C., Pradeep, T. and Young, G. (1994). *China Since 1978. Reform, Modernization and Socialism with Chinese Characteristics*. New York: Longman Cheshire.

Malan, J.S. (1995). *Peoples of Namibia*. Pretoria: Rhino Publishers.

Malinowski, B. (1922). *Argonauts of the Western Pacific*. London: Routledge-Keegan.

Malkki, L.H. (1996). National Geographic: the rooting of peoples and the territorialization of national identity among scholars and refugees. In *Culture, Power, Place: Explorations in Critical Anthropology* (A. Gupta and J. Ferguson, eds.), pp. 52–74. Durham and London: Duke University Press.

Mana (2005). *Maori in Tourism*, Issue 66, October/November, 25.

Martin, A. (1997). *Assessment of Special Interest Market Draft Stage 1 Report*. Darwin, NT: NTTC.

Mason, P. (2003). *Tourism Impacts, Planning and Management*. Amsterdam: Butterworth Heinemann.

Mate, S. (2006). Demand for Aboriginal tourism experiences exceeds supply. *Aboriginal Times*, March/April, 20–21.

Mathison, S. (1988). Why Triangulate? *Educational Researcher*, March, 13–17.

Mattson, L., Butler, C. and Menzies, C.R. (2004). *Informal Economy Report for the North Coast LRMP*. Smithers, BC: Ministry of Sustainable Resource Management.

Matunga, H. (1995). *Māori Recreation and the Conservation Estate*. Christchurch: Centre for Māori Studies and Research, Lincoln University.

McBride, J.M., Macdonell, G., Smoke, C. and Sanderson, C. (2002). *Rebuilding First Nations: Tools, Traditions and Relationships*. Burnaby: Simon Fraser University, Community Economic Development Centre.

McIntosh, A., Smith, A. and Ingram, T. (2000). *Tourist experiences of Maori culture in Aotearoa, New Zealand*. Research Paper No. 8. Dunedin: Centre for Tourism, University of Otago.

McIntosh, A.J. (2004). Tourists' appreciation of Maori culture in New Zealand. *Tourism Management*, 25, 1–15.

McIntosh, A.J. and Johnson, H. (2004). Exploring the nature of the Maori experience in New Zealand: views from hosts and tourists. *Tourism: An International Interdisciplinary Journal*, 52(2), 117–129.

McIntosh, A.J., Hinch, T. and Ingram, T. (2002). Cultural identity and tourism. *International Journal of Arts Management*, 4(2), 39–49.

McIntosh, A.J., Zygadlo, F. and Matunga, H. (2004). Rethinking Maori tourism. *Asia Pacific Journal of Tourism Research*, 9(4), 331–351.

McIntosh, R., Goeldner, C.R. and Ritchie, J.R.B. (1994). *Tourism, Principles, Practices and Philosophies*, 7th edition. Englewood Cliffs, NJ: Prentice Hall.

McKercher, B. (2002). Towards a classification of cultural tourists. *International Journal of Tourism Research*, 4, 29–38.

McKercher, B. (2006). Phantom demand: how some research 'proves' demand when none really exists. Paper presented at *"Culture, Tourism and the Media" the 5th DeHaan Tourism Management Conference*, University of Nottingham, Nottingham, 12 December 2006.

McKercher, B. and Du Cros, H. (2002). *Cultural Tourism: The Partnership between Tourism and Cultural Heritage Management*. New York: The Haworth Hospitality Press.

Medina, L.K. (2003). Commoditizing culture – tourism and Maya identity. *Annals of Tourism Research*, 30(2), 353–368.

Medlik, S. (1989). *University Studies in Tourism*. Report by Prof. S. Medlik within the Pacific Tourism Development Programme, financed by the European Economic Community, July. Suva, Fiji: Tourism Council of the South Pacific.

Meethan, K. (2001). *Tourism in Global Society: Place, Culture, Consumption*. Basingstoke, Hampshire: Palgrave.

Menzies, C.R. (2004). Putting words into action: negotiating collaborative research in Gitxaała. *Canadian Journal of Native Education*, 28(1–2), 15–32.

Menzies, C.R. (2006). Ecological knowledge, subsistence, and livelihood practices: the case of the pine mushroom harvest in Northwestern British Columbia. In *Traditional Ecological Knowledge and Natural Resource Management* (C. Menzies, ed.), pp. 87–106. Omaha: University of Nebraska Press.

Mercer, D. (1995). Native peoples and tourism: conflict and compromise. In *Global Tourism, the Next Decade* (W.F. Theobald, ed.), pp. 124–145. Oxford: Butterworth-Heinemann.

Mercer, D. (2005). The 'new pastoral industry'?: tourism in indigenous Australia. In *Global Tourism*, 3rd edition (W.F. Theobald, ed.), pp. 140–162. Oxford: Butterworth-Heinemann.

Meredith, M.E. (1993a). *A fauna survey of Batang Ai National Park, Sarawak, Malaysia*. Unpublished report. Wildlife Conservation Society, New York.

Meredith, M.E. (1993b). *Draft Management Plan for Batang Ai National Park 1993–1995*. Unpublished Draft Management Plan. Wildlife Conservation Society, New York.

Merton, R.K., Fiske, M. and Kendall, P.L. (1956). *The Focused Interview*. New York: Free Press.

Meyer Arendt, K. and Hartmann, R. (1998). *Casino Gambling in North America: Origins, Trends and Impacts*. New York: Cognizant Communications.

Middleton, V.T.C. (1997). Sustainable tourism: a marketing perspective. In *Tourism and Sustainability* (M.J. Stabler, ed.), pp. 129–142. CAB International: Wallingford.

Middleton, V.T.C. (1998). *Sustainable Tourism: A Marketing Perspective*. Oxford: Butterworth-Heinemann.

Millar, C. and Aiken, D. (1995). Conflict resolution in aquaculture: a matter of trust. In *Coldwater Aquaculture in Atlantic Canada*, 2nd edition (A. Boghen, ed.), pp. 617–645. Moncton: Canadian Institute for Research on Regional Development.

Miller, G. (2000). *Is it Culture or is it Business? National Indigenous Tourism Forum Proceedings Report: Tourism – The Indigenous Opportunity*. Canberra: Commonwealth Department of Industry, Science and Resources.

Milne, S. (2005). *The Training Needs of the South Pacific Tourism SME Owners & Managers – 2005*. Suva, Fiji: South Pacific Tourism Organisation.

Milne, S., Grekin, J. and Woodley, S. (1998). Tourism and the construction of place in Canada's Eastern Arctic. In *Destinations: Cultural Landscapes of Tourism* (G. Ringer, ed.), pp. 101–120. London: Routledge.

Milne, S., Nickles, S. and Wenzel, G. (1991). Inuit perceptions of tourism development, the case of Clyde River Baffin Island, N.W.T. *Etudes Inuit Studies*, 15(1), 157–169.

Milne, S., Ward, S. and Wenzel, G. (1995). Linking tourism and art in Canada's eastern Arctic: the case of Cape Dorset. *Polar Record*, 31, 176.

Ministry of Road, Transport and Tourism (2005). *The Yearbook of Mongolian Tourism Statistics, 2005 Edition*. Ulaanbaatar: Ministry of Road Transport and Tourism.

Ministry of Tourism (2004). *Measurement of Maori in tourism. Te ahu mai – He tatau tapoi Maori. Summary Report*, October 2004. Wellington, NZ: Ministry of Tourism.

Mitchell, I., Hall, C.M. and Keelan, N. (1992). The cultural dimensions of heritage tourism in New Zealand: issues in the development of Maori culture and heritage as a tourist resource. In *Ecotourism: Incorporating the Global Classroom* (B. Weiler, ed.), pp. 271–280. Canberra: Bureau of Tourism Research.

Mokken, R.J. and Stokman, F.N. (1976). Power and influence as political phenomena. In *Power and Political Theory: Some European Perspectives* (B. Barry, ed.), pp. 33–54. London: John Wiley.

Montagu, I. (1956). *Land of Blue Sky: A Portrait of Modern Mongolia*. London: Dennis Dobson.

Moore, S. (2000). *Gaps – What We Need to Know. National Indigenous Tourism Forum Proceedings Report: Tourism – The Indigenous Opportunity*. Canberra: Commonwealth Department of Industry, Science and Resources.

Moreton-Robinson, A. (2006). Afterword B How white possession moves: after the word. In *Moving Anthropology: Critical Indigenous Studies* (T. Lea, E. Kowal and G. Cowlishaw, eds.). Darwin, NT: Charles Darwin University Press. 219–232.

Morgan, D.L. (1996). Focus Groups. *Annual Review of Sociology*, 22, 129–152.

Morriss, P. (1987). *Power: A Philosophical Analysis*. Manchester: Manchester University Press.

Morrissey, P. (2005a). Aboriginality and corporatism. In *Blacklines: Contemporary Critical Writing by Indigenous Australians* (M. Grossman et al., eds.), pp. 52–59. Melbourne: Melbourne University Press.

Morrissey, P. (2005b). Afterword: moving, remembering, singing our place. In *Blacklines: Contemporary Critical Writing by Indigenous Australians* (M. Grossman et al., eds.), pp. 189–193. Melbourne: Melbourne University Press.

Morse, J. (2000). *International Demand. National Indigenous Tourism Forum Proceedings Report: Tourism – The Indigenous Opportunity*. Canberra: Commonwealth Department of Industry, Science and Resources.

Moscardo, G. and Pearce, P.L. (1999). Understanding ethnic tourists. *Annals of Tourism Research*, 26(2), 416–434.

Mowforth, M. and Munt, I. (1998). *Tourism and Sustainability: New Tourism in the Third World*. London: Routledge.

Muecke, S. (2004). Ancient and Modern: Time, Culture, and Indigenous Philosophy. University of New South Wales Press, Sydney.

Müller, D. and Pettersson, R. (2001). Sami tourism in northern Sweden. *Scandinavian Journal of Hospitality and Tourism*, 1(1), 5–19.

Müller, D. and Pettersson, R. (2005). What and where is the indigenous at an indigenous festival? Observations from the winter festival in Jokkmokk, Sweden. In *Indigenous Tourism: The Commodification and Management of Culture* (C. Ryan and M. Aicken, eds.), pp. 201–218. Oxford: Elsevier.

Müller, D. and Pettersson, R. (2006). Sami heritage at the winter festival in Jokkmokk, Sweden. *Scandinavian Journal of Hospitality and Tourism*, 6(1), 54–69.

Murphy, P.E. (1985). *Tourism, a Community Approach*. London: Methuen.

Nadasdy, P. (2003). *Hunters and Bureaucrats: Power, Knowledge, and Aboriginal-State Relations in the Southwest Yukon*. Vancouver: University of British Columbia Press.

Nam Ha Phase II: A Situation Analysis and Review of the Project Document (2005). SNV.

Namibia Holiday and Travel (2003). *The Official Namibian Tourism Directory*, Windhoek: Venture Publications.

Namibian Association of CBNRM Support Organization (NASCO) (2006). Windhoek.

Nash, D. (1989). Tourism as a form of imperialism. In *Hosts and Guests: The Anthropology of Tourism*, 2nd edition (V.L. Smith, ed.), pp. 37–52. Philadelphia, PA: University of Pennsylvania Press.

Native Council of Canada (1987). *An Inventory of Métis and Non-status Indian Tourism Opportunities*. Ottawa: Native Council of Canada.

Naughton, B. (1988). The third front: defense industrialization in the Chinese interior. *China Quarterly*, 115, 366.

Neale, G. (1998). *The Green Travel Guide*. London: Earthscan Publications Ltd.

Nehrt, L.C. (1987). Entrepreneurship education in Bangladesh: a beginning. *Journal of Small Business Management*, 25, 76–78.

Neis, B. et al. (1999). Fisheries assessment: What can be learned from interviewing resource users? *Canadian Journal of Fisheries and Aquatic Sciences*, 56, 1949–1963.

Nepal, S.K., Kohler, T. and Banzhaf, B. (2002). *Great Himalaya: Tourism and the Dynamics of Change in Nepal*. Berne: Swiss Foundation for Alpine Research.

Neudorfer, C. (2006). Community-Based Tourism in Laos: Challenges and Opportunities for Local Communities. *Juth Pakai*, Issue 6, pp. 6–14.

New Zealand Māori Tourism Council (NZMTC) (2005). *2005 Conference Report*, Wellington, NZMTC.

Nichols, M., David, G. and Grant Stitt, B. (2002). Casinos as a Catalyst for Economic Development, Tourism Economics, 8(1), 59–75.

Nickerson, N. (1995). Tourism and Gambling Content Analysis. *Annals of Tourism Research*, 22(1), 53–66.

Nielsen, A.C. (2002). *New Zealand Product: Potential and Actual Visitor Feedback from Key Markets. Report Prepared for Tourism New Zealand*, November 2002. Wellington, NZ: A.C. Nielsen.

Norkunas, M.K. (1993). *The Politics of Memory: Tourism, History, and Ethnicity in Monterey, California*. Albany, NY: State University of New York Press.

Northern Territory Tourist Commission (NTTC) (1995). *National Aboriginal Tour Operators Forum Proceedings*. Alice Springs.

Northern Territory Tourist Commission (NTTC) (1996). *Aboriginal Tourism Strategy*, Darwin, NT.

Northern Territory Tourist Commission (NTTC) (2000). *Survey of Indigenous Tourism, Final report*, March. Australian Tourist Commission and Aboriginal Tourism Australia.

Northern Territory Tourist Commission (NTTC) and Northern Territory Office of Aboriginal Development (1994). *Aboriginal Tourism in the Northern Territory – A Discussion Paper*, Darwin, NT.

Noss, A. (2000). Cable snares and nets in the Central African Republic. In *Hunting for Sustainability in Tropical Forests* (J.G. Robinson and E.L. Bennett, eds.), pp. 282–304. New York: Columbia University Press.

Nott, C., Davis, A. and Roman, B. (forthcoming). Communal area conservancies in Namibia, Torra Conservancy, Economic Sustainability and Biodiversity.

Notzke, C. (1999). Indigenous tourism development in the Arctic. *Annals of Tourism Research*, 26(1), 55–76.

Notzke, C. (2004). Indigenous tourism development in Southern Alberta, Canada: tentative engagement. *Journal of Sustainable Tourism*, 12(1), 29–54.

Notzke, C. (2006). *The Stranger, the Native and the Land: Perspectives on Indigenous Tourism*. Concord, Ontario: Captus Press Inc.

Nussbaum, M.C. (2000). *Women and Human Development: The Capabilities Approach*. Cambridge: Cambridge University Press.

Nyaoi, A. and Bennett, E.L. (2002). *Does Nature Tourism Reduce Hunting Pressure in Tropical Forest in Sarawak* (Draft, for submission to ORYX). Unpublished.

Nygren, A. (1999). Local knowledge in the environment-development discourse: from dichotomies to situated knowledges. *Critique of Anthropology*, 19(3), 267–288.

O'Grady, R. (1981). *Third World Stop Over: The Tourism Debate*. Geneva: World Council of Churches.

O'Neil, B. (ed.) (1996). *Aboriginal Cultural Tourism: Checklist for Success*. Ottawa: Aboriginal Tourism Team Canada.

O'Neil Marketing and Consulting et al. (2005). *Blueprint Strategy: Market Literature Review*. Victoria, Aboriginal Tourism BC.

O'Regan, T. (1990). Māori control of the Māori heritage. In *The Politics of the Past* (P. Gathercole and D. Lowenthal, eds.), pp. 95–106. Cambridge: University Press.

Oakes, T. (1993). Tourism in Guizhou: the legacy of internal colonialism. In *Tourism in China. Geographical, Political and Economic Perspectives* (A.A. Lew and L. Yu, eds.), pp. 203–222. Boulder: Westview Press.

Oakes, T. (1999). Selling Guizhou: cultural development in an era of marketization. In *The Political Economy of China's Provinces* (H. Hendrischke and C.Y. Feng, eds.), pp. 27–67. London and New York: Routledge.

Office of Northern Development (Commonwealth of Australia) (1993). *Indigenous Australians and tourism: a focus on Northern Australia. Proceedings of the Indigenous Australians and Tourism Conference*, Darwin, NT (June 1993). Canberra: Office of Northern Development B Dept. of Industry, Technology, and Regional Development.

Office of the Premier (2006). *News Release: $4 Million Preserves Haida Culture and Builds Tourism*. Office of the Premier/Skidegate Band Council, 13 July.

Olsen, K. (2003). The touristic construction of the "Emblematic" Sámi. *Acta Borealia*, 20, 3–20.

Olsen, K. (2006). Making differences in a changing world: The Norwegian Sami in the tourist industry. *Scandinavian Journal of Hospitality and Tourism*, 6(1), 37–53.

Opermann, M. (2000). Triangulation – a methodological discussion. *International Journal of Tourism Research*, 2, 141–146.

Oppenheim, A.L. (1967). *Letters from Mesopotamia: Official, business, and private letters on clay tablets from two millennia*. Chicago: University of Chicago Press.

Oppenheim, F.E. (1981). *Political Concepts: A Reconstruction*. Oxford: Basil Blackwell.

Osherenko, Gail (1988). *Sharing Power with Native Users: Co-Management Regimes for Native Wildlife*. Ottawa: Canadian Arctic Resources Committee.

Oula, T. (2005). *A Best Practice Community Based Tourism Programme in the Lao PDR: Trekking in Nammat Kao and Nammat Mai (Financial Benefits and Income Distribution)*.

Page, E. (1978). Michael Hechter's internal colonial thesis: some theoretical and methodological problems. *European Journal of Political Research*, 6(3), 295–317.

Parker, B. (1992). Aboriginal tourism: from perception to reality. In *Community and Cultural Tourism. Conference proceedings of the Travel and Tourism Research Association – Canada* (L.J. Reid, ed.), pp. 14–20. St Catherines, ON: Department of Recreation and Leisure Studies, Brock University.

Parker, B. (1993). Developing aboriginal tourism, opportunities and threats. *Tourism Management*, 14(4), 400–403.

Pearce, P., Moscardo, G. and Ross, G.F. (1996). *Tourism Community Relationships*. Oxford, UK: Elsevier Science Ltd.

Pearce, P.L. (1995). From culture shock and culture arrogance to culture exchange: ideas towards sustainable socio-cultural tourism. *Journal of Sustainable Tourism*, 3(3), 143–154.

Pêcheux, M. (1982). *Language, Semantics and Ideology: Stating the Obvious* (H. Nagpal, trans.). London: Macmillan.

Peck. J.G. and Lepie, A.S. (1989). Tourism development in three North Carolina coastal towns. In *Hosts and Guests: the Anthropology of Tourism*, 2nd edition (V. Smith, ed.), pp. 203–222. Philadelphia, PA: University of Pennsylvania Press.

Pegg, C. (2001). *Mongolian Music, Dance and Oral Narrative*. Washington, DC: University of Washington Press.

Perdue, R.R., Long, P.T. and Kang, Y.S. (1999). Boomtown tourism and resident quality of life: the marketing of gaming to host community residents. *Journal of Business Research*, 44, 165–177.

Perry, G. (2000). *Domestic Demand – Where is it? National Indigenous Tourism Forum Proceedings Report: Tourism – The Indigenous Opportunity*. Canberra: Commonwealth Department of Industry, Science and Resources.

Pettersson, R. (2002). Sami tourism in Northern Sweden: measuring tourists' opinions using stated preference methodology. *Tourism and Hospitality Research*, 3(4), 357–369.

Pettersson, R. (2003). Indigenous cultural events: the development of a Sami winter festival in Northern Sweden. *Tourism*, 51(3), 319–332.

Pettersson, R. (2004). Sami Tourism in Northern Sweden: Supply, Demand and Interaction. ETOUR. Doctoral Thesis. Östersund. *Scientific Book Series* V 2004:14.

Pfister, R.E. (2000). Mountain culture as a tourism resource: Aboriginal views of the privileges of storytelling. In *Tourism and Development in Mountain Regions* (P. Godde, M.F. Price and M.F. Zimmermann, eds.), pp. 115–136. Oxon: CABI Publishing.

Pforr, C. (2006). Tourism administration in the Northern Territory in the era of the Country Liberal Party governance 1978–2001. *Australian Journal of Public Administration*, 65, 61–74.

Picard, M. (1993). Cultural tourism in Bali: national integration and regional differentiation. In *Tourism in South-East Asia* (M. Hitchcock, V.T. King and M.J.G. Parnwell, eds.), pp. 71–98. London: Routledge.

Piner, J.M. and Paradis, T.W. (2004). Beyond the casino: sustainable tourism and cultural development on Native American lands. *Tourism Geographies*, 6(1), 80–98.

Pitcher, M.J. (1999). Tourists, tour guides and true stories: Aboriginal cultural tourism in the Top End. Doctoral Dissertation, Northern Territory University, Darwin.

Pitcher, M.J, van Oosterzee, P. et al. (1999). *Choice and Control: The Development of Indigenous Tourism in Australia*. Darwin, NT: Centre for Indigenous Cultural and Natural Resource Management.

Pitterle, S. (2000). *Where to Now? National Indigenous Tourism Forum Proceedings Report: Tourism – The Indigenous Opportunity*. Commonwealth Department of Industry, Science and Resources, Canberra.

Poon, A. (2000). Namibia, *Country Reports*, No. 4. Travel and Tourism Intelligence.

Poonwassie, A. and Charter, A. (2001). An Aboriginal worldview of helping: empowering approaches. *Canadian Journal of Counseling*, 35(1), 63–73.

Price Waterhouse Coopers (2000). *Demand for Aboriginal Cultural Tourism Products in Key European Markets 2000*. Ottawa: Aboriginal Tourism Team Canada and Canadian Tourism Commission.

Project Development Facility (2005). *Global Environmental Facility (GEF). Achieving the Millennium Development Goals: A GEF Progress Report*. GEF, Washington DC.

Pro-Poor Tourism Partnership (PPTP) (2005). Annual Register Pro-Poor Tourism Partnership, London: PPTP.

Raento, P. and Berry, K. (1999). Geography's spin of the wheel of American gaming. *The Geographical Review*, 89(4), 590–595.

Rankin, S.N. (2006). The enunciatory present. Review of Bhabha, Homi (2004). *The Location of Culture*. London: Routledge 16 February 2006. http://www.amazon.com/Location-Culture-Routledge-Classics/dp/0415336392 (accessed 20 August 2006).

Reisinger, Y. and Turner, L. (1997). Cross-cultural differences in tourism: Indonesian tourists in Australia. *Tourism Management*, 7(4), 79–106.

Research Resolutions Consulting (2001). *Demand for Aboriginal Tourism Products in the Canadian and American Markets*. Ottawa: Aboriginal Tourism Team Canada.

Research Resolutions Consulting (2004). *Opportunities for BC: Activity-Based Tourists in Canada*. Victoria, BC: Tourism BC.

Richter, L.K. (1989). *The Politics of Tourism in Asia*. Honolulu: University of Hawaii Press.

Ritter, W. (1975). Recreation and tourism in Islamic countries. *Ekistics*, 236, 56–59.

Roberts, M., Norman, W., Minhinnick, N., Wihongi, D. and Kirkwood, C. (1995). Kaitiakitanga: Māori perspectives on conservation. *Pacific Conservation Biology*, 2(1), 7–20.

Robinson, J.G. and Bennett, E.L. (2000). Carrying capacity limits to sustainable hunting in tropical forests. In *Hunting for Sustainability in Tropical Forests* (J.G. Robinson and E.L. Bennett, eds.), pp. 13–30. New York: Columbia University Press.

Robinson, M. and Boniface, P. (eds.) (1999). *Tourism and Cultural Conflicts*. Wallingford: CABI Publishing.

Roehl, W.S. (1994). Gambling as a tourist attraction. In *Tourism: the State of the Art* (A.V. Seaton, C.L. Jenkins, R.C. Wood, P.U.C. Dieke, M.M. Bennett, L.R. MacClellan and Smith, R, eds.), pp. 156–168. Chichester: John Wiley and Sons.

Roehl, W.S. (1999). Quality of life issues in a casino destination. *Journal of Business Research*, 44, 223–229.

Rogers, R. (1995). *The Oceans are Emptying: Fish Wars and Sustainability*. Montreal: Black Rose Books.

Rooke, B. (1993). Finance – the Umorrduk experience. *Indigenous Australians and Tourism: A Focus on Northern Australia. Proceedings of the Indigenous Australians and Tourism Conference*, pp. 38–39, Darwin, Canberra, Goanna Print.

Ross, H. (1991). Controlling access to environment and self: Aboriginal perspectives on Tourism. *Australian Psychologist*, 26(3), 176–182.

Ross, S. and Wall, G. (1999). Ecotourism: towards congruence between theory and practice. *Tourism Management*, 20, 123–132.

Rossiter, D. and Wood, P. (2005). Fantastic topographies: neo-liberal responses to Aboriginal land claims in British Columbia. *The Canadian Geographer*, 49(4), 352–366.

Royal Commission On Aboriginal Peoples (1996). *People to People; Nation to Nation. Highlights from the Report of the Royal Commission on Aboriginal Peoples*. Ottawa: Minister of Supply and Services.

Ruddle, K. (1994). Local Knowledge in the Folk Management of Fisheries and Coastal Marine Environments. In *Folk Management in the Worlds Fisheries: Lessons for Modern Fisheries Management* (C. Dyer and J.R. McGoodwin, eds.), pp. 161–166. Niwot: University Press of Colorado.

Ruotsala, H. (1995). Lapplandsturismens Janusansikte. *Nord Nytt*, 59, 55–64.

Ryan, C. (1997). Māori and tourism, a relationship of history, constitutions and rites of tourism. *Journal of Sustainable Tourism*, 5(4), 257–278.

Ryan, C. (1999). Some dimensions of Maori involvement in tourism. In *Tourism and Cultural Conflicts* (M. Robinson and P. Boniface, eds.), pp. 229–245. UK: CABI Publishing.

Ryan, C. (2002). Tourism and cultural proximity: examples from New Zealand. *Annals of Tourism Research*, 29(4), 952–971.

Ryan, C. (2005). Tourist-host nexus – research considerations. In *Indigenous Tourism – the Commodification and Management of Culture* (C. Ryan and M. Aicken, eds.), pp. 1–11. Oxford: Elsevier.

Ryan, C. and Aicken, M. (1995). *Indigenous Tourism : the Commodification and Management of Culture*. Amsterdam: Elsevier.

Ryan, C. and Crotts, J. (1997). Carving and tourism: a Maori perspective. *Annals of Tourism Research*, 24(4), 898–918.

Ryan, C. and Huyton, J. (2000a). Who is interested in Aboriginal tourism in the Northern Territory, Australia? A cluster analysis. *Journal of Sustainable Tourism*, 8(1), 53–88.

Ryan, C. and Huyton, J. (2000b). Aboriginal tourism – a linear structural relations analysis of domestic and international tourist demand. *International Journal of Tourism Research*, 2, 15–29.

Ryan, C. and Huyton, J. (2002). Tourists and aboriginal people. *Annals of Tourism Research*, 29(3), 631–647.

Ryan, C. and Higgins, O. (2006). Experiencing cultural tourism: visitors at the Maori Arts and Crafts Institute, New Zealand. *Journal of Travel Research*, 44(3), 308–318.

Ryan, C. and Trauer, B. (2005a). Visitor experiences of indigenous tourism – introduction. In *Indigenous Tourism. The Commodification and Management of Culture* (C. Ryan and M. Aicken, eds.), pp. 15–20. Oxford: Elsevier.

Ryan, C. and Trauer, B. (2005b). Conceptualisation and aspiration. In *Indigenous Tourism – The Commodification and Management of Culture* (C. Ryan and M. Aicken, eds.), pp. 219–222. Oxford: Elsevier.

Ryan, C., Hughes, K. and Chirgwin, S. (2000). The gaze, spectacle and ecotourism. *Annals of Tourism Research*, 27(1), 148–163.

Ryan, C., Scotland, A. and Montgomery, D. (1998). Resident attitudes to tourism development – a comparative case study between Rangitikei, New Zealand and Bakewell, United Kingdom. *Progress in Tourism and Hospitality Research*, 4, 115–130.

Ryan, M. (1988). Postmodern politics. *Theory, Culture and Society*, 5(2–3), 560–561.

Saarinen, J. (1999). The social construction of tourist destinations: the process of transformation of the Saariselkä tourism region in Finnish Lapland. In *Destinations, Cultural Landscapes of Tourism* (G. Ringer, ed.), pp. 154–173. London: Routledge.

Saarinen, J. (2001). *The Transformation of a Tourist Destination: Theory and Case Studies on the Production of Local Geographies in Tourism in Finnish Lapland*. Oulu: Oulu University Press.

Saffery, A. and Sugar, O. (2003). *International Tourism Survey 2002 – Report of Results*. Ulaanbaatar: Mongolian Tourism Association/USAID.

Saffu, K. (2003). The role and impact of culture on South Pacific entrepreneurs. *International Journal of Entrepreneurial Behaviour and Research*, 9(2), 55–73.

Sagging, E., Noweg, G.T., Abdullah, A.R. and Mersat, N.I. (2000). In *Borneo 2000: Language, Management and Tourism. Proceeding of the Sixth Biennial Borneo Research Conference*, July 2000 (M. Leigh, ed.), pp. 423–439, Kuching, Sarawak.

Salisbury, R. (1986). *Homeland for the Cree: Regional Development in James Bay 1971–81*. Kingston: McGill-Queens University Press.

Salole, M. (2003). *Torra Conservancy and Tourism Development: Merging Two Disparate Worlds in Rural Namibia*, MSc Dissertation, Guildford: University of Surrey.

Sara, M.N. (2001). *Reinen – et Gode fra Vnden: Reindriftens Tilpasningsformer i Kautokeino*. Karasjohka: Davvi Girji.

Satzewich, V. and Wotherspoon, T. (1993). *First Nations: Race, Class, and Gender Relations*. Toronto: Nelson.

Saville, N.M. (2001). *Practical Strategies for Pro-Poor Tourism: Case Study of Pro-Poor Tourism and SNV in Humla District, West Nepal*. PPT Working Paper 3. London: Pro-Poor Tourism Partnership.

Schanzel, H. and McIntosh, A.J. (2000). An insight into the personal and emotive context of wildlife viewing at the Penguin Place, Otago Peninsula, New Zealand. *Journal of Sustainable Tourism*, 8(1), 36–52.

Schattsneider, E. (1960). *Semi-sovereign People: A Realists View of Democracy in America*. New York: Holt, Rinehart and Wilson.

Scheyvens, R. (2002). *Tourism for Development*. Harlow, England: Prentice Hall.

Scheyvens, R. (2003). Local involvement in managing tourism. In *Tourism in Destination Communities* (S. Singh, D.J. Timothy and R.K. Dowling, eds.). Wallingford: CAB International.

Scheyvens, R. (1999). Ecotourism and the empowerment of local communities. *Tourism Management*, 20, 245–249.

Schipani, S. (nd). *An Assessment of Independent Tourists or 'Backpackers' in Luang Namtha, Lao PDR*. Available from: http://www.unescobkk.org/file admin/user_upload/culture/namha/An_Assessment_of_International_ Tourists_or_backpackers.pdf (accessed 20 July 2006).

Schipani, S. and Marris, G. (nd). Monitoring Community Based Eco-tourism in the Lao PDR: The UNESCO-NTA Lao Nam Ha Ecotourism Project Monitoring Protocol. Available from: http://www.unescobkk. orgfileadmin/user_upload/culture/namha/Monitoring_ecotourism_in_ Lao_PDR.pdf (Accessed: 20 July 2006).

Schipani, S. (2003). *An Assessment of the Community-Based Ecotourism Potential in Sing District, Luang Namtha, Lao PDR*.

Schipani, S. (2006a). *The Nam Ha Ecoguide Service in Luang Namtha: Organizational Structure and Direct Financial Benefits Generated by Community-based Tours in Luang Namtha, Lao PDR*. Lao National Tourism Administration, Vientien.

Schipani, S. (2006b). *Ecotourism as an Alternative to Upland Rubber Cultivation in the Nam Ha National Protected Area, Luang Namtha, Lao PDR*. Lao National Tourism Administration, Vientien.

Schipani, S. and Marris, G. (nd). *Monitoring Community Based Ecotourism in the Lao PDR: The UNESCO-NTA Lao Nam Ha Ecotourism Project Monitoring Protocol*. Available from: http://www.unescobkk.org/fileadmin/ user_upload/culture/namha/Monitoring_ecotourism_in_Lao_PDR.pdf (accessed 20 July 2006).

Schmiechen, J. (1996). *Special Interest Tourism – Not for Profits in Tourism Conference Report*. Darwin, NT: NTTC.

Schmiechen, J. (1997). *Special Interest Tourism – Not For Profits in Tourism Conference Report*, Darwin, NT: NTTC.

Schmiechen, J. (2000). *Aboriginal Tourism – The Indigenous Difference – Forming new partnerships*. Presentation to WA Aboriginal Tourism Operators Forum, Broome, April 2000.

Schmiechen, J. (2004). *Lake Eyre Basin Heritage Tourism – Future Directions*. Adelaide: Lake Eyre Basin Coordinating Group.

Schmiechen, J. (2005a). *Indigenous Tourism Research Issues Paper*. Alice Springs: CDU.

Schmiechen, J. (2005b). *Indigenous Tourism Research Agenda*. Alice Springs: CDU.

Secretariat of the Convention on Biological Diversity (2004). *Guidelines on Biodiversity and Tourism Development: International Guidelines for Activities Related to Sustainable Tourism Development in Vulnerable Terrestrial, Marine and Coastal Ecosystems and Habitats of Major Importance for Biological Diversity and Protected Areas, including Fragile Riparian and Mountain Ecosystems* (CBD Guidelines). Montreal: Secretariat of the Convention on Biological Diversity.

Serruys, H. (1974). *Kumiss Ceremonies and Horse Races: Three Mongolian Texts. Asiatische Forchungen No 37*. Wiesbaden: Otto Harrassowitz.

Shackley, M. (2001). *Managing Sacred Sites*. London: Continuum.

Shackley, M. (ed.) (1998). *Visitor Management: Case Studies from World Heritage Sites*. Oxford: Butterworth-Heinemann.

Sharpley, R. (2002). The challenges of economic diversification through tourism: the case of Abu Dhabi. *International Journal of Tourism Research*, 4, 221–235.

Sharpley, R. and Telfer, D. (2002). *Tourism and Development: Concepts and Issues*. New York: Channelview Books.

Shohat, E. and Stam, R. (1994). *Unthinking Eurocentrism: Multiculturalism and the Media*. London: Routledge.

Shum, K. (2005). *Tourism in Muang Sing: A Summary of Tourists' Perspectives*. A report paper. Available from: www.hotelschool.cornell.edu/chr/pdf/showpdf/chr/research/casestudies/Shum_LaosReport_TourismResearch.pdf (accessed 15 September 2006).

Sidu, J. (2000a). Perception of the community living adjacent to the Lanjak-Entimau Wildlife Sanctuary (LEWS) towards its conservation and management. In *Development of Lanjak-Entimau Wildlife Sanctuary as a Totally Protected Area, Phase I and Phase II, Scientific Report* (E. Soepadmo and P.P.K. Chai, eds.), pp. 192–207. Kuching, Malaysia: Percetakan Nasional Malaysia Berhad.

Sidu, J. (2000b). Socio-economic survey of the longhouse communities in the vicinity of LEWS. In *Development of Lanjak-Entimau Wildlife Sanctuary as a Totally Protected Area, Phase I and Phase II, Scientific Report* (E. Soepadmo and P.P.K. Chai, eds.), pp. 161–174. Kuching, Malaysia: Percetakan Nasional Malaysia Berhad.

Silver, I. (1993). Marketing authenticity in third world countries. *Annals of Tourism Research*, 20, 302–318.

Sim, J. (1998). Collecting and analysing qualitative data: issues raised by focus group. *Journal of Advanced Nursing*, 28(2), 345–352.

Simons, M. (2000). Aboriginal heritage art and moral rights. *Annals of Tourism Research*, 27, 412–431.

Simpson, K. (2001). Strategic planning and community involvement as contributors to sustainable tourism development. *Current Issues in Tourism*, 4(1), 3–41.

Simpson, L.R. and Driben, P. (2000). From expert to acolyte: learning to understand the environment from an Anishinaabe point of view. *American Indian Culture and Research Journal*, 24(3), 1–19.

Simpson, P. and Wall, G. (1999). Consequences of resort development. A comparative study. *Tourism Management*, 20, 283–296.

Sinclair, D. (1992a). Land: Māori view and European response. In *Te Ao Hurihuri: Aspects of Māoritanga* (M. King, ed.), pp. 65–84. Auckland: Reed Books.

Sinclair, D. (1992b). Land since the treaty. In *Te Ao Hurihuri: Aspects of Māoritanga* (M. King, ed.), pp. 85–105. Auckland: Reed Books.

Sindiga, I. (1999). *Tourism and African Development: Change and Challenge of Tourism in Kenya*. Aldershot: Ashgate Publishing Ltd.

Singh, S. et al. (eds.) (2001). *Aboriginal Australia and the Torres Strait Islands: Guide to Indigenous Australia*. Melbourne: Lonely Planet Publications.

Smith, C. and Ward, G.K. (2000). *Indigenous Cultures in an Interconnected World*. Vancouver: University of British Columbia Press.

Smith, M.K. (2003). *Issues in Cultural Tourism*. London: Routledge.

Smith, V.L. (1996). Indigenous tourism and the 4 H's. In *Tourism and Indigenous Peoples* (R.W. Butler and T. Hinch, eds.), pp. 283–307. London: Routledge.

Smith, V.L. (2001). Tourism change and impacts. In *Hosts and Guests Revisited; Tourism Issues of the 21st Century* (V.L. Smith and M. Brent, eds.), pp. 107–121. New York: Cognizant Communication Corporation.

Snellgrove, D. (1981). *Himalayan Pilgrimage: A Study of Tibetan Religion by a Traveller Through Western Nepal*. Boston, MA: Shambhala Publications Inc.

Snow, S.G. and Wheeler, C.L. (2000). Pathways in the periphery: tourism to indigenous communities in Panama. *Social Science Quarterly*, 81(3), 732–749.

Sofield, T.H.B. (1991). Sustainable ethnic tourism in the South Pacific: some principles. *Journal of Tourism Studies*, 2(1), 56–72.

Sofield, T.H.B. (1996). Anuha Island Resort, Solomon Islands: a case study of failure. In *Tourism and Indigenous Peoples* (R. Butler and T. Hinch, eds.), pp. 176–202. London: International Thompson Business Press.

Sofield, T.H.B. (2002). Australian Aboriginal ecotourism in the Wet Tropics Rainforest of Queensland, Australia. *Mountain Research and Development*, 22(2), 118–122.

Sofield, T.H.B. (2003). *Empowerment for Sustainable Tourism Development*. London: Elsevier Science and Pergamon.

Sofield, T.H.B. and Li, F.M.S. (1998). "China: Tourism Development and Cultural Policies". *Annals of Tourism Research*, Volume 25, no. 2, , pp. 362–392.

South Pacific Forum Secretariat (1998). *Session 5 Background Paper: Key Issues Constraining Tourism Development in Forum Island Countries*. Nadi, Fiji: Pacific Islands Forum Secretariat.

South Pacific Tourism Organisation (SPTO)(2002). *Regional Tourism Strategy for the South and Central Pacific*. Suva, Fiji: SPTO.

Spivak, G.C. (1987). *In Other Worlds: Essays in Cultural Politics*. London: Methuen.

Squires, N. (2005). *Aborigines Seek Return of Tribal Justice*. London: *Daily Telegraph*.

Stafford Group, te Hau, H. and McIntosh, A. (2001). *A Study of Barriers, Impediments and Opportunities for Maori in Tourism – He matai tapoi Maori*. A report prepared for the Office of Tourism and Sport and Te Puni Kokiri, June 2001.

Stansfield, C. (1996). Reservations and gambling: native Americans and the diffusion of legalized gaming. In *Tourism and Indigenous peoples* (R. Butler and T. Hinch, eds.), pp. 129–149. London: International Thompson Business Press.

Stevens, S. (1997). Introduction. In *Conservation through Cultural Survival: Indigenous Peoples and Protected Areas* (S. Stevens, ed.), pp. 1–8. Washington, DC: Island Press.

Stokowski, P.A. (1993). Undesirable lag effects in tourist destination development. *Journal of Travel Research*, 32, 35–41.

Stokowski, P.A. (2004). Gaming and tourism. In *A Companion to Tourism* (A.A. Lew, C.M. Hall and A.M. Williams), pp. 399–409. Oxford: Blackwell.

Strang, V. (1997). *Uncommon Ground: Cultural Landscapes and Environmental Values*. New York: New York University Press.

Sullivan, H. (ed.) (1984). *Visitors to Aboriginal Sites: Access, Control and Management: Proceedings of the 1983 Kakadu Workshop, Australian National Parks and Wildlife Service (ANPWS)*. Canberra: ANPWS.

Sunday Times (2006). Nuclear Tourists. *The Sunday Times*, 8 October 2006.

Swain, M.B. (2004). (Dis)embodied experience and power dynamics in tourism research. In *Qualitative Research in Tourism: Ontologies, Epistemologies, and Metodologies* (J. Phillimore and L. Goodson, eds.), pp. 102–118. London: Routledge.

Swain, M.B. (1993). Women producers of ethnic arts. *Annals of Tourism Research*, 20, 32–51.

Swinwood, M. (1998). *Aboriginal Themes in Tourism: Walking Between Two Worlds*. Ottawa: Canadian Tourism Commission.

Szuchman, P. (2001). Ecotourism Award. Preserving Paradise. Our winners serve the environment, locals, and responsible travelers. *Conde Nast Traveler*, June, pp. 70–74. London: Conde Nast Publications.

Tacey, D.J. (1995). *Edge of the Sacred: Transformation in Australia*. Blackburn, Victoria: Harper Collins.

Tahana, N. and Opperman, M. (1998). Māori cultural performances and tourism. *Tourism Recreation Research*, 23(1), 23–30.

Tai Tokerau Maori Tourism Association (1998). Let's Take a Journey, Whangarei, Pre-Press Studio.

Tanner, A. (1979). *Bringing Home Animals: Religious Ideology and Mode of Production of the Misstassini Cree Hunters.* St. John's: ISER Books.

Taylor, G. (1995). The community approach: does it really work? *Tourism Management*, 16(7), 487–489.

Taylor, J.P. (2001). Authenticity and sincerity in tourism. *Annals of Tourism Research*, 28(1), 7–26.

Taylor, L., Ward, G.W., Henderson, G., Davis, R. and Wallis, L.A. (eds.) (2005). *The Power of Knowledge: The Resonance of Tradition.* Canberra: Australia Studies Press.

Te Awekotuku, N. (1981). The Sociocultural Impact of Tourism on the Te Arawa People, Unpublished PhD Thesis, University of Waikato, Hamilton.

Technical Assistance for the Commonwealth of Independent States (TACIS) (1998). *International Visitor Survey.* Ulaanbaatar: TACIS.

Telfer, D.J. (2002). Tourism and regional development issues. In *Aspects of Tourism: Tourism and Development – Concepts and Issues* (R. Sharpley and D.J. Telfer, eds.), 112–148. Clevedon: Channel View Publications.

Thakali, S. (1997). *Local Level Institutions for Mountain Tourism and Local Development – The Annapurna Experience.* Lalitpur: International Centre for Integrated Mountain Development.

Thaman, K. (1993). Culture and curriculum in the South Pacific. *Comparative Education*, 29(3), 249–260.

Thaman, K. (1997). Education for human resource development in the Pacific Islands. In *Roundtable Proceedings on Sociocultural Issues and Economic Development in the Pacific Islands, Volume II.* Suva, Fiji: Asian Development Bank.

Thaman, K. (2000). Towards a new pedagogy: Pacific cultures in higher education. In *Local Knowledge and Wisdom in Higher Education* (G.R. Teasdale and Z. Ma Rhea, eds.), pp. 43–50. Oxford: Pergamon.

Thaman, K. (2004). Le'o e peau: towards cultural and cognitive democracy in sustainable development in Pacific Island communities. Keynote address, *Islands Conference*, Kinmen Island, Tawain, 1–5 November 2004.

The Stafford Group (2001). *He Matai Tapoi Māori: A Study of Barriers, Impediments and Opportunities for Māori in Tourism.* Wellington: Ministry of Māori Development and the Office of Tourism and Sport.

Theuns, H.L. and Go, F. (1992). "Need led" priorities in hospitality education for the third world. *World Travel and Tourism Review*, 2, 293–302.

Thomas, A. (1992). Non-governmental organisation and the limits to empowerment. In *Development, Policy and Public Action* (M. Wuyts, M. McIntosh and T. Hewitt, eds.), pp. 117–146. Oxford: Oxford University Press.

Thompson, W.N. and Dever, D.R. (1994). A sovereignty check on Indian gaming. *Indian Gaming Magazine*, 5(5), 5–7.

Thomson, S. and Baden. S. (1993). *Women and Development in Laos*. Report prepared for Women, Health and Population Division. Brighton: Australian International Development Assistance Bureau, Institute of Development Studies.

Tisen, O.B. (2004). Conservation and Tourism: A Case Study of Longhouse Communities in and Adjacent to Batang Ai National Park, Sarawak, Malaysia. A thesis submitted in partial fulfilment of the requirements for the degree of Master of Parks, Recreation and Tourism Management, New Zealand, Lincoln University.

Tisen, O.B., Ahmad, S., Bennett, E.L. and Meredith, M.E (1999). *Wildlife conservation and local communities in Sarawak, Malaysia*. Paper presented at the *Second Southeast Asia Regional Form of the IUCN World Commission for Protected Areas*, Pakse, Lao PDR, 6–11 December 1999.

Tisen, O.B. and Meredith, M. (2000). Participation of local communities in management of totally protected areas. *Hornbill*, 4, 42–49. Sarawak: Forest Department.

Tosun, C. (2000). Limits to community participation in the tourism development process in developing countries. *Tourism Management*, 21, 613–633.

Tosun, C. and Jenkins, C. (1998). The evolutions of tourism planning in third world countries: a critique. *Progress in Tourism and Hospitality Research*, 4, 101–114.

Touraine, A. (1990). The idea of revolution. In *Global Culture: Nationalism, Globalization, and Modernity* (M. Featherstone, ed.), London: Sage. 121–142.

Tourism Australia (2005). *The Aussie Experience Kit*. Tourism Australia, Canberra: Sydney.

Tourism Canada (1988). *The Native Tourism Product: A Position Paper*. Ottawa: Tourism Canada.

Tourism Council of the South Pacific (TCSP) (1992). *Pre-feasibility Study of Tourism Training Facilities and Institutional Frameworks in the South Pacific*. Suva, Fiji: Tourism Council of the South Pacific.

Tourism Council of the South Pacific (TCSP) (1995). *Human Resources Development and Training Needs Assessment Study*, pp. 4–11. Suva, Fiji: Tourism Council of the South Pacific.

Tourism Council of the South Pacific (TCSP) (1999). *Proposals for the restructuring of the Human Resource Development Division and review of industry training requirements*. Suva: TCSP.

Tourism New Zealand (TNZ) (2003a). *Tourism New Zealand 3 Year Strategic Plan 2003–2006*. Wellington: Tourism New Zealand.

Tourism New Zealand (TNZ) (2003b). *New Zealand's Ideal Visitor: The Interactive Traveller*. Wellington: Tourism New Zealand.

Tourism Research Australia (2004). *Tourism Research Report*, 6(1), Canberra: Tourism Research Australia.

Tourism Queensland (2000). *Special Interest Unit New Product Research – A Research Report*. Marketing and Communications Research. Brisbane.

Town of Montville (2004–2006). *History. Town of Montville.* Available from: http://www.townofmontville.org (accessed 5 September 2006).

Tremblay, P. et al. (2005). *Assessing Demand for Indigenous Tourism: International Comparisons. A Report for the Northern Territory Tourist Commission,* pp. 117–118. Darwin, NT: CDU.

Tsai, Wen-Ting (2006a). From the streets to the villages – The Indigenous Peoples' movement turns 20. *Taiwan Panorama,* 31(3), 7–18.

Tsai, Wen-Ting (2006b). And what is your name? Reclaiming a heritage. *Taiwan Panorama,* 31(3), 19–23.

Tuffin, B. (2005). *Ecoclub Interview,* year 6, issue 68. Available from: http://www.ecoclub.com/news/068/interview.html (accessed 20 September 2006).

Turner, L. and Ash, J. (1975). *The Golden Hordes: International Tourism and the Pleasure Periphery.* London: Constable.

Turner, P. (1993). Where to now? Summary of workshops, overviews and findings. *Indigenous Australians and Tourism: A Focus on Northern Australia. Proceedings of the Indigenous Australians and Tourism Conference.* pp. 83–85. Darwin, Canberra: Goanna Print.

Tuuluntie, S. (2006). The dialectic of identities in the field of tourism. The discourses of the indigenous Sami in defining their own and the tourists' identities. *Scandinavian Journal of Hospitality and Tourism,* 6(1), 25–36.

Ulva's Guided Walks. Available from: http://www.ulva.co.nz/ (accessed March 2006).

United Nations (UN) (1999). United Nations Commission on Sustainable Development Seventh Session, 19–30 April 1999, Agenda item 5 E/CN.17/1999/L.6. Available from: www.un.org/esa/sustdev/sdissues/tourism/tourism_decisions.htm

United Nations General Assembly (UN GA) (2000). United Nations Millennium Declaration 55/2.

University of the South Pacific (2006). *The Vision, Mission and Values for a Regional University of Excellence.* Available from: http://www.usp.ac.fj/index.php?id=newstaff_usp_mission (accessed 30 October 2006).

United Nations World Health Organisation (UNWTO) (2006). *Compendium of Tourism Statistics.* Madrid: World Tourism Organisation.

Upitis, A. (1989). Interpreting cross-cultural sites. In *Heritage Interpretation: Volume 1 Natural and Built Environment* (D. Uzzell, ed.), pp. 142–152. New York: Belhaven Press.

Urry, J. (1990). *The Tourist Gaze: Leisure and Travel in Contemporary Society.* London: Sage.

UWIP Website (2006). Available from: http://www.uwip.org/ index.phd?t=art4&p=a (accessed 28 September 2006).

Uzzell, D. (1996). Creating place identity through heritage interpretation. *International Journal of Heritage Studies,* 1(4), 219–228.

Van Aalst, I. and Daly, C. (2002). International visitor satisfaction with their New Zealand experience: the cultural tourism product market – a summary of studies 1990–2001. Unpublished report. Wellington: Tourism New Zealand.

Van Den Berghe, P. and Ochoa, J.F. (2000). Tourism and nativistic ideology in Cuzco, Peru. *Annals of Tourism Research*, 27(1), 7–26.

Van Den Berghe, P. (1994). *The Quest for the Other*. Seattle: University of Washington Press.

Veal, A.J. (1997). *Research Methods for Leisure and Tourism*, 2nd edition. London: Prentice Hall.

Venn, C. (2006). *The Postcolonial Challenge: Towards Alternative Worlds*. London: Sage.

Victurine, R. (2000). Building tourism excellence at the community level: capacity building for community-based entrepreneurs in Uganda. *Journal of Travel Research*, 3(38), 221–229.

Viken, A. and Müller, D. (2006). Introduction: Tourism and the Sami. *Scandinavian Journal of Hospitality and Tourism*, 6(1). (Special Issue: Tourism and the Sami), 1–6.

Viken, A. (1997a). Turismens Visualitet og Estetisering av Sameland. *Sosiologi i Dag*, 27(1), 49–72.

Viken, A. (1997b). Sameland tilpasset turistblikket. In *Turisme. Fenomen og Næring* (J.K.S. Jacobsen and A. Viken, eds.), pp. 174–180. Oslo: Universitetsforlaget.

Viken, A. (2000). Turismens Essensialiserende Effekt – Samisk Kultur i Lys av en Tiltakende Turisme. In *Kulturens Mmaterialisering: Identitet og Uttrykk*. (S.R. Mathisen, ed.), pp. 25–52. Kristiandsand: Høgskoleforlaget.

Viken, A. (2002). Turismens Sameland; Tradisjoner i Transformasjon. *Utmark*, 1, www.utmark.org.

Viken, A. (2006). Tourism and Sami identity: an analysis of the tourism-identity nexus in a Sami community. *Scandinavian Journal of Hospitality and Tourism*, 6(1), 7–24.

Viken, A., Midtgard, M.R., Bakken, T. and Broch, T. (1998). *Innovasjoner i samisk reiseliv*. Report. Alta, Finland: Finnmarksforskning.

Walker, R. (1990). *Ka Whawhai Tonu Matou. Struggle Without End*. Auckland: Penguin Press.

Walker, R. (1992). The relevance of Māori myth and tradition. In *Te Ao Hurihuri: Aspects of Māoritanga* (M. King, ed.), pp. 171–184. Auckland: Reed Books.

Wallerstein, I. (1990). Culture as the ideological battleground of the modern world-system. In *Global Culture: Nationalism, Globalization, and Modernity* (M. Featherstone, ed.), 31–55. London: Sage.

Wallheimer, B. (2006). Casinos power economy, attract millions. *Norwich Bulletin*. Available from: http://www.norwichbulletin.com, June 14 (retrieved 12 September 2006).

Walsh, E. (2001). Living with the myth of matriarchy: the Mosuo and tourism. In *Tourism, Anthropology and China* (C.B. Tan, C.H.C. Sidney and H. Yang, eds.), Studies in Asian Tourism, No. 1, pp. 93–124. Bangkok: White Lotus Press.

Wang, N. (1999). Rethinking authenticity in tourism experience. *Annals of Tourism Research*, 26(2), 349–370.

Wang, N. (2000). *Tourism and Modernity: A Sociological Analysis*. Oxford: Pergamon Press.

Warren, J.A.N. and Taylor, C.N. (1994). *Developing Eco-tourism in New Zealand*. Wellington: NZ Institute for Social Research and Development.

Warren, J.A.N. and Taylor, C.N. (2001). *Developing Heritage Tourism in New Zealand*. Wellington: Centre for Research, Evaluation and Social Assessment.

Warry, W. (2000). *Unfinished Dreams: Community Healing and the Reality of Aboriginal Self-Government*. Toronto: University of Toronto Press.

Weaver, D.B. (2001). *The Encyclopedia of Ecotourism*. Oxon, United Kingdom: CABI.

Weaver, D. and Opperman, M. (2000). *Tourism Management*. Australia: Wiley.

Webb, C. and Kavern, J. (2001). Focus groups as research method: a critique of some aspects of their use in nursing research. *Journal of Advanced Nursing*, 33(6), 798–805.

Weinig, P. (2006). *Mongolian International Tourism Survey 2005 – Report of Results*. Ulaanbaatar: Economic Policy Reform and Competitiveness Project/Mongolian Tourism Association, United States Agency for International Development.

Wells-Dang, A. and Buasawan, S. (2006). Economic Integration and Social Development of Ethnic Minority Communities in Laos: Case Studies from Luang Namtha and Savannakhet. *Juth Pakai*, Issue 6, 16–26.

White, S., Williams, P.W and Hood, T. (1998). Gearing up for aboriginal tourism delivery: the case of FirstHost. *Journal of Hospitality and Tourism Education*, 10(1), 6–12.

Whitford, M., Bell, B. and Watkins, M. (2001). Indigenous tourism policy in Australia: 25 years of rhetoric and economic rationalism. *Current Issues in Tourism*, 4, 2–4, 151–181.

Whyte, A.L.H., Marshall, S.J. and Chambers, G.K. (2005). Human evolution in Polynesia, *Human Biology*, 77(2), 157–177.

Wigsten, J. (2005). *Personal Communication with Mr. Jan Wigsten, Director of Nomadic Journeys Incoming Tour Operator*. Ulaanbaatar.

Wilderness Safaris (WS) (2006). Available from: www.wilderness-safaris.com/news/detail.jsp?newsitem-id=8727 (accessed 18 June 2006).

Wildlife Conservation Society and Sarawak Forest Department (WCS & FD) (1996). *A Master Plan for Wildlife in Sarawak*. Kuching, Sarawak: Wildlife Conservation Society and Sarawak Forest Department.

Wilkinson, S. (1999). Focus groups. A feminist method. *Psychology of Women Quarterly*, 23, 221–244.

Williams, J. (1997). Mauri and the traditional Māori environmental perspective. *Environmental Perspectives*, University of Otago, 1(4), 3–4.

Williams, P.W. and Stewart, K. (1997). Canadian aboriginal tourism development: assessing latent demand from France. *The Journal of Tourism Studies*, 9(1), 25–41.

Williams, P.W. and Richter, C. (2002). Developing and supporting European tour operator distribution channels for Canadian Aboriginal tourism development. *Journal of Travel Research*, 40, 404–415.

Williams, P.W. and Dossa, K.B. (1999). *Aboriginal Tourism Markets: An Analysis of Germany, Japan and Canada.* Vancouver: Aboriginal Tourism Association of B.C. and Centre for Tourism Policy and Research.

Williams, P.W. and Dossa, K.B. (1995). *Native Tourism Travel Market Analysis.* Ottawa: Canadian Tourism Commission, Aboriginal Tourism Directorate.

Wimmer, A. (1997). Who owns the State? Understanding ethnic conflict in post-colonial societies. *Nations and Nationalism*, 3(4), 631–666.

Winson, A. (2006). Ecotourism and sustainability in Cuba: Does socialism make a difference? *Journal of Sustainable Tourism*, 14(1), 6–23.

Wolf, J. et al. (1991). *Indigenous and Western Knowledge and Resource Management Systems.* Guelph: University School of Rural Planning and Development, University of Guelph.

Wong, V., Pride, D. and Bouton, R. (1999). Taiwan Aboriginal Singers Settle Copyright Lawsuit. *Billboard*, July, 1999. 111(31), 14–16.

Wood, K. (2005). *Pro-poor Tourism as a Means of Sustainable Development in the Uctubamba Valley, Northern Peru.* ICRT: University of Greenwich Occasional Paper.

World Bank (2005). *World Development Indicators 2005.* Washington, DC: World Bank.

World Tourism Organization (2002). *Tourism and Poverty Alleviation.* Madrid: World Tourism Organization.

World Tourism Organization (2006). *International Tourism up by 5.5% to 808 million Arrivals in 2005.* Available from: http://www.world-tourism.org/newsroom/Releases/2006/january/06_01_24.htm (accessed 30 October 2006).

World Tourism Organization (2006). Available from: http://www.world-tourism.org/regional/south_asia/states/iran/iran.htm (accessed 19 October 2006).

Wuttunee, W. (1992). *In Business for Ourselves.* Montreal: McGill-Queen's University Press.

Wyrostok, N.C. and Paulson, B.L. (2000). Traditional healing practices among First Nations students. *Canadian Journal of Counseling*, 34(1), 14–24.

Yankelovich, D. (1974). *The Yankelovich Monitor.* New York: Daniel Yankelovich.

Yea, S. and Noveg, G.T. (2000). The reality of community: women's roles on Iban Longhouse Tourism in Sarawak, *Borneo Review,* Malaysia, Kotu Kinabulu (Sabah). Cited in Yea, S. (2002). On and off the ethnic tourism map in Southeast Asia: the case of Iban longhouse tourism, Sarawak, Malaysia. *Tourism Geographies* 4(2), 173–194.

Yong, P. and Basiuk, R. (1998). *The Ulu Ai Longhouse Project.* Nomination for ASTS/Smithsonian Magazine Environment Award.

Yu, L. and Goulden, M. (2006). A comparative analysis of international tourists' satisfaction in Mongolia. *Tourism Management*, 27, 1331–1342.

Yunnan Province Government (1999). *General Policy Statement on the Construction of Yunnan Province into a Great Province of Nationalities Cultures.* Kunming: Yunnan Province Government Information Office.

Zeppel, H. (1998). Land and culture: sustainable tourism and indigenous peoples. In *Sustainable Tourism – A Geographic Perspective* (C. Hall and A. Lew, eds.), pp. 60–75. New York: Addison Wesley Longman Ltd.

Zeppel, H. (1993). Getting to know the Iban: the tourist experience of visiting an Iban longhouse in Sarawak. In *Tourism in Borneo: Issues and Perspectives* (V.T. King, ed.), pp. 59–66. Williamsburg: Borneo Research Council.

Zeppel, H. (1996). Partners, participants or performers: Iban involvement in longhouse tourism (Sarawak, Borneo). In *Pacific Rim Tourism 2000: Issues, Interrelations, Inhibitors Conference Proceedings* (M. Oppermann, ed.), pp. 368–377. Rotorua, New Zealand: Centre for Tourism Studies, Waiariki Polytechnic.

Zeppel, H. (1999). *Aboriginal Tourism in Australia: A Research Bibliography*. Australia: CRC for Sustainable Tourism.

Zhang, G. and Lew, A. (2003). Introduction: China's tourism boom. In *Tourism in China* (A. Lew, L.Yu, J. Ap and G. Zhang, eds.), pp. 3–12. New York: Haworth Hospitality Press.

Zinder, H. (1969). *The Future of Tourism in the Eastern Caribbean*. Washington, DC: Zinder & Associates.

Zygadla, F.K., McIntosh, A., Matunga, H.P., Fairweather, J.R. and Simmons, D.G. (2003). *Māori Tourism. Concepts, Characteristics and Definition*, Report No. 36, Lincoln University, Tourism Recreation Research and Education Centre. Loncoln.

Subject index

Accommodation: 46, 49, 54, 92, 94, 117, 119,
    125, 132, 133, 153, 169, 179, 198, 212,
    236, 253, 262, 225
Agriculture: 11, 129, 130, 131, 132, 149, 150,
    236, 256, 273
Assimilation/Assimilate: 19, 191, 221, 230,
    235, 266, 268, 269, 280, 292, 299
Authentic/Authenticity: 45, 48, 49, 52, 53,
    55, 76, 78, 81, 82, 83, 85, 115, 116, 125,
    126, 134, 139, 160, 169, 170, 172, 173,
    174, 175, 180, 182, 185, 189, 197, 198,
    199, 213, 246, 248, 264, 278, 279, 280,
    290, 293, 303, 321, 322, 326, 327

Commodification/Commodify: 85, 160,
    170, 180, 183, 184, 185, 186, 196, 303,
    306, 321
Community:
  Community resources: 18, 19, 20, 21,
    25, 46, 48, 51, 62, 77, 78, 92, 94, 123,
    146, 147, 166, 204, 206, 207, 214,
    217, 221, 224, 225, 226, 239, 240, 243,
    244, 245, 277, 279, 280, 282, 285, 321,
    322, 320
  Community impacts: 20, 21, 24, 38, 49,
    69, 78, 86, 87, 89, 90, 91, 92, 93, 94, 95,
    96, 97, 103, 104, 107, 108, 109, 129, 134,
    139, 142, 152, 154, 157, 193, 195, 204,
    209, 210, 211, 215, 216, 217, 218, 219,
    221, 222, 223, 224, 225, 226, 227, 228,
    229, 230, 231, 232, 233, 235, 236, 323,
    329
  Community planning: 4, 10, 11, 12, 16, 20,
    22, 23, 25, 32, 34, 41, 42, 43, 44, 45, 47,

48, 49, 50, 51, 52, 55, 56, 64, 65, 72, 85,
    86, 92, 93, 94, 96, 104, 109, 126, 129, 134,
    146, 149, 153, 155, 196, 208, 209, 210,
    211, 212, 215, 216, 217, 219, 220, 221,
    224, 225, 226, 227, 229, 230, 231, 233,
    238, 239, 240, 241, 242, 244, 245, 248,
    288, 293, 295, 296, 297, 298, 299, 300,
    308, 309, 310, 311, 313, 321, 324, 325,
    326, 327
Conservation: 14, 16, 19, 21, 22, 23, 26, 86,
    87, 88, 89, 119, 130, 131, 132, 135, 141,
    142, 143, 147, 149, 154, 155, 156, 157,
    206, 207, 208, 209, 211, 213, 215, 217,
    218, 219, 235, 237, 238, 239, 242, 243,
    244, 245, 246, 280, 288, 329
Consultation: 60, 61, 62, 63, 65, 67, 70, 104,
    147, 226, 327
Costume/Dress/Clothing/Garb: 53, 132,
    133, 137, 166, 171, 178, 183, 186, 192,
    193, 195, 197, 254, 263, 270, 279, 316,
    317, 322, 330
Culture:
  Cultural resources: 5, 6, 8, 25, 27, 41, 42,
    45, 46, 48, 49, 51, 52, 54, 55, 56, 59, 66,
    68, 72, 74, 75, 77, 78, 79, 81, 82, 83, 84,
    85, 89, 90, 93, 105, 115, 124, 126, 130,
    134, 135, 140, 142, 148, 159, 160, 162,
    163, 164, 165, 170, 177, 179, 181, 182,
    183, 186, 189, 193, 197, 198, 199, 200,
    201, 224, 225, 226, 228, 233, 239, 240,
    241, 248, 252, 254, 256, 263, 264, 266,
    267, 270, 274, 275, 276, 277, 278, 279,
    280, 282, 283, 284, 285, 286, 288, 293,
    306, 316, 320, 329

Cultural impacts: 33, 55, 75, 80, 104, 115, 134, 135, 136, 137, 154, 160, 161, 174, 180, 181, 183, 187, 190, 196, 198, 201, 223, 224, 225, 228, 230, 231, 235, 252, 253, 271, 276, 277, 278, 279, 280, 301, 302, 304, 321, 327

Cultural filters: 2, 6, 7, 8, 9, 10, 12, 32, 35, 37, 38, 46, 48, 75, 76, 77, 78, 79, 80, 81, 82, 83, 94, 118, 124, 125, 126, 134, 135, 136, 138, 174, 178, 179, 180, 182, 183, 185, 186, 187, 189, 190, 193, 195, 197, 198, 199, 200, 201, 214, 241, 252, 255, 269, 274, 277, 278, 279, 289, 292, 294, 295, 298, 301, 302, 321, 322, 325

Diet: 144, 146, 154, 156, 275

Education: 14, 19, 32, 33, 34, 35, 36, 37, 38, 39, 48, 60, 64, 66, 67, 81, 86, 90, 91, 102, 103, 105, 106, 116, 117, 135, 147, 151, 171, 199, 204, 214, 223, 225, 238, 243, 254, 266, 269, 272, 274, 283, 324, 327

Economic development: 9, 16, 19, 26, 36, 45, 48, 62, 70, 72, 74, 85, 86, 87, 92, 97, 99, 132, 191, 195, 208, 209, 221, 223, 225, 226, 227, 228, 229, 231, 232, 269, 266, 268, 269, 272, 288, 309, 311, 313, 317

Elders: 11, 19, 20, 46, 53, 55, 65, 182, 183, 192, 217, 218, 223, 227, 228, 230, 231, 232, 244, 280, 330

Empowerment: 29, 33, 34, 36, 37, 38, 89, 90, 91, 92, 131, 215, 216, 218, 221, 222, 223, 227, 228, 229, 235, 244, 248, 249, 279, 289, 320, 331

Entrepreneur/Entrepreneurial: 2, 9, 37, 38, 39, 41, 43, 48, 51, 55, 61, 65, 117, 133, 138, 175, 177, 179, 183, 184, 199, 228, 243, 244, 274, 313, 321, 325

Ethics: 85, 223, 307, 311, 328

Exchange: 3, 48, 59, 66, 70, 81, 86, 130, 134, 135, 136, 166, 264, 268, 279

Festival/Festivals: 8, 42, 45, 49, 50, 51, 160, 162, 164, 165, 166, 167, 168, 169, 170, 171, 172, 173, 174, 175, 184, 193, 275, 321, 326

First Nations: 4, 14, 16, 18, 22, 24, 25, 26, 27, 55, 204, 220, 221, 225, 226, 227, 229, 230, 231, 232, 233, 313, 314, 317, 318

Food: 10, 23, 24, 25, 26, 46, 48, 51, 77, 82, 86, 89, 91, 93, 115, 124, 132, 133, 146, 147, 153, 157, 165, 170, 177, 211, 213, 214, 227, 228, 230, 270, 285

Globalisation: 2, 17, 33, 180, 261, 277, 300

Government:
  Local: 7, 9, 42, 45, 86, 89, 94, 99, 119, 131, 191, 199, 204, 223, 242, 314, 312
  Other (state, region, national, etc.): 2, 7, 9, 17, 18, 19, 32, 35, 41, 42, 43, 47, 49, 59, 60, 64, 69, 76, 81, 85, 86, 87, 89, 90, 93, 94, 95, 99, 105, 116, 117, 119, 125, 129, 130, 131, 132, 133, 134, 135, 137, 138, 139, 147, 156, 157, 164, 191, 192, 195, 197, 198, 199, 200, 201, 204, 206, 207, 208, 209, 210, 221, 225, 228, 229, 230, 232, 237, 238, 242, 243, 245, 248, 252, 253, 258, 259, 261, 262, 263, 264, 266, 267, 270, 271, 272, 274, 275, 276, 278, 279, 289, 290, 293, 299, 306, 309, 310, 311, 312, 313, 317, 321, 324, 325, 326, 327, 328, 329

Harvest/Harvesting: 19, 20, 21, 22, 23, 24, 25, 26, 27, 54, 90, 142, 146, 147, 148, 149, 150, 152, 154, 155, 156, 157, 177, 182, 192, 193, 197, 226, 229, 238

Hospitality: 3, 8, 60, 109, 116, 164, 210, 211, 215, 218, 227, 253, 256, 262, 328

Identity: 5, 9, 114, 115, 116, 118, 119, 120, 123, 124, 125, 126, 127, 174, 178, 182, 183, 191, 192, 201, 223, 231, 233, 262, 277, 279, 280, 283, 288, 295, 298, 299, 300, 301, 306, 316, 317, 318

Intellectual property: 7, 123

Knowledge: 4, 14, 15, 16, 17, 18, 19, 21, 25, 27, 29, 31, 35, 38, 61, 62, 66, 69, 72, 76, 77, 78, 134, 135, 140, 151, 187, 194, 206, 210, 216, 219, 222, 223, 232, 235, 252, 269, 284, 301,308, 309, 315, 316, 317, 328, 329, 330
  Environmental/Ecological Knowledge 13, 14, (15–27)
  Indigenous Knowledge 13, 14, (15–27), 46, 70, 119, 120, 123, 230, 283, 294, 329, 330, 377

Traditional Ecological Knowledge 13, 14, (15–27)

Traditional Knowledge 13, 14, (15–27) 222, 223, 228, 230, 231, 301

Labour: 20, 32, 34, 38, 89, 134, 145, 147, 150, 152, 192, 214, 261

Land/lands:
General: 3, 10, 11, 17, 18, 22, 25, 32, 56, 67, 86, 88, 89, 90, 99, 113, 115, 121, 125,143, 145, 146, 148 150,196, 207, 223, 224, 225, 231, 232, 233, 235, 237, 253, 266, 286, 300, 320, 327, 329

Claims/Rights: 10, 11, 16, 17, 19, 32, 49, 52, 55, 63, 64, 93, 96, 99, 102, 104, 108, 115, 119, 120, 122, 125, 127, 136, 145, 146, 148, 149, 150, 155, 190, 207, 210, 211, 225, 248, 298, 309, 310, 311, 312, 314, 316

Traditional: 11, 16, 42, 55, 56, 64, 9, 97, 99, 102, 104, 115, 118, 119, 120, 127, 139, 149, 150, 207, 209, 225, 236, 237, 285, 296, 299, 309, 312

Minorities: 85, 129, 130, 131, 132, 134, 135, 136, 139, 140, 199, 200, 208, 243, 248, 258, 262, 263, 265, 266, 267, 268, 269, 270, 271, 272, 273, 274, 275, 276, 277, 278, 280, 312

Media: 7, 9, 68, 103, 125, 182, 189, 195, 199, 200, 215, 252, 261, 262, 264, 282, 300, 302, 309, 320

Museums: 25, 42, 45, 77, 179, 275, 316

Parks:
Cultural: 185, 194, 195, 197

National/Provincial: 66, 86, 122, 130, 141, 142, 143, 144, 147, 149, 150, 154, 155, 156, 157, 207, 213, 242, 310, 311, 316, 325

Planning: 14, 18, 19, 20, 26, 27, 29, 33, 34, 35, 36, 41, 43, 44, 47, 49, 54, 56, 72, 79, 88, 91, 92, 93, 103, 104, 108, 126, 127, 132, 138, 154, 209, 214, 216, 218, 219, 223, 226, 230, 233, 235, 239, 242, 243, 244, 245, 256, 263, 308, 309, 310, 312, 320, 325

Policy: 9, 14, 34, 41, 43, 49, 60, 65, 70, 74, 82, 85, 87, 89, 101, 116, 117, 130, 138, 146, 164, 200, 211, 216, 223, 248, 266, 267,

268, 269, 270, 272, 274, 275, 278, 296, 306, 308, 309, 311, 312, 327

Poverty: 3, 10, 72, 84, 85, 86, 87, 88, 89, 92, 94, 99, 130, 131, 132, 134, 135, 138, 139, 140, 153, 215, 219, 224, 270, 273

Power: 5, 17, 19, 36, 41, 55, 72, 86, 88, 96, 98, 104, 107, 166, 167, 191, 195, 212, 216, 218, 242, 243, 244, 245, 246, 248, 249, 262, 271, 275, 278, 281, 283, 288, 292, 293, 294, 301, 303, 304, 305, 306, 307, 308, 309, 310, 311, 312, 313, 314, 315, 316, 317, 318, 328

Religion/Spirituality: 77, 79, 83, 89, 148, 166, 167, 253, 254, 255, 259, 263, 253, 254, 255, 259, 278, 301

Residents (attitudes, impacts): 25, 34, 72, 96, 97, 100, 102, 103, 104, 105, 107, 108, 109, 114, 137, 147, 148, 149, 150, 151, 152, 153, 154, 155, 156, 157, 195, 204, 208, 210, 211, 212, 216, 217, 235, 279

Resource:
Cultural: 27, 55, 114, 115, 139, 146, 147, 153, 157, 180, 206, 224, 255, 266, 269, 270, 306, 310, 316, 328, 330

Human: 29, 30, 31, 34, 35, 47, 60, 89, 92, 93, 106, 155, 207, 210, 262, 329

Natural: 5, 11, 20, 23, 24, 27, 55, 70, 87, 90, 91, 115, 119, 127, 132, 139, 142, 144, 146, 147, 149, 152, 155, 156, 157, 162, 164, 204, 206, 207, 210, 211, 223, 226, 238, 239, 240, 241, 243, 255, 269, 272, 273, 311, 312, 316, 323, 329

Management: 8, 10, 14, 16, 17, 18, 19, 20, 62, 63, 64, 69, 70, 85, 93, 94, 96, 107, 119, 123, 132, 142, 143, 144, 232, 224, 232, 238, 242, 244, 245, 309, 320, 321, 327

Rights: 5, 156
Aboriginal/Indigenous: 16, 17, 27, 88, 226, 235, 270, 288, 296, 300, 310, 313, 314

Legal: 6, 7, 10, 32, 100, 108, 116, 144, 154, 155, 157, 208, 210, 262, 310, 311, 312, 314, 316

Traditional: 20, 119, 145, 146, 149, 209, 210, 216, 225, 235, 263, 288

Sovereignty: 16, 19, 96, 98, 99, 103, 105, 108, 223, 224, 229, 232

Sport: 21, 22, 23, 24, 45, 46, 162, 164, 165, 166, 167, 168, 170, 171, 172, 173, 174, 175, 255, 275, 321

Territory/Territories: 16, 21, 22, 23, 24, 59, 61, 65, 66, 67, 68, 88, 162, 221, 253, 254, 266, 277, 285, 297, 309

Threats: 2, 33, 103, 108, 137, 138, 182, 199, 215, 256

Tour: 23, 24, 25, 26, 51, 122, 139, 135, 139, 169, 171, 242

  Companies/Packages: 9, 65, 152, 155, 175, 193, 194, 209, 213, 215, 215, 228, 256, 258, 263

  Guides: 75, 92, 131, 306

  Operators: 8, 44, 45, 47, 48, 51, 53, 66, 79, 93, 94, 116, 129, 134, 152, 156, 162, 163, 167, 168, 169, 171, 175, 185, 215, 213, 256, 262, 330

Tradition/Traditional: 3, 11, 18, 19, 20, 21, 23, 24, 32, 34, 35, 37, 39, 41, 42, 44, 48, 51, 52, 53, 56, 66, 67, 78, 79, 81, 100, 104, 114, 115, 116, 118, 119, 120, 121, 122, 123, 124, 125, 129, 131, 133, 136, 139, 142, 145, 146, 147, 148, 149, 150, 152, 153, 154, 155, 156, 157, 162, 163, 164, 165, 166, 167, 168, 169, 170, 171, 174, 177, 178, 179, 180, 182, 183, 184, 185, 186, 193, 197, 198, 201, 207, 208, 210, 211, 216, 222, 223, 224, 225, 227, 228, 230, 231, 235, 238, 239, 242, 244, 245, 248, 253, 263, 273, 275, 276, 277, 279, 280, 282, 284, 285, 288, 290, 294, 295, 298, 299, 300, 301, 310, 316, 317, 321, 322, 326, 327, 328, 329, 330, 331

  Traditional Communities (check against communities)

  Traditional Knowledge (check against knowledge)

  Traditional lands (check against land/lands)

Activities/Management: 5, 10, 11, 16, 18, 19, 23, 25, 42, 65, 78, 89, 118, 124, 125, 133, 142, 146, 147, 149, 150, 152, 156, 157, 177, 185, 197, 201, 230, 238, 245, 275, 321, 331

Food/Resources: 14, 21, 24, 89, 115, 124, 153, 154, 157, 177, 211, 224, 225

Lifestyles/culture: 14, 23, 26, 27, 32, 34, 35, 37, 42, 50, 51, 52, 53, 54, 55, 64, 67, 77, 81, 83, 85, 115, 116, 121, 125, 129, 131, 136, 137, 142, 145, 146, 147, 148, 154, 155, 156, 157, 162, 163, 164, 167, 168, 169, 180, 183, 184, 185, 186, 192, 193, 195, 198, 208, 223, 225, 230, 231, 235, 275, 276, 279, 284, 298, 310, 317, 322, 326, 329, 330

  Rights: 24, 119, 149, 235, 239, 310

Training: 14, 28, 29, 30, 31, 32, 33, 34, 35, 36, 37, 38, 39, 45, 48, 49, 54, 64, 66, 68, 70, 89, 91, 94, 106, 116, 132, 133, 135, 192, 204, 208, 211, 213, 214, 218, 223, 228, 240, 242, 262, 313, 324, 325, 327

Values: 14, 26, 27, 35, 42, 49, 50, 52, 54, 55, 64, 77, 83, 114, 115, 116, 123, 124, 126, 127, 142, 143, 145, 157, 182, 184, 185, 186, 193, 208, 213, 217, 226, 260, 261, 263, 277, 284, 285, 287, 298, 303, 306, 307, 308, 310, 311, 317, 318, 329

Voice: 2, 4, 10, 14, 29, 60, 65, 69, 70, 118, 124, 126, 181, 182, 219, 225, 248, 249, 295, 296, 302, 310, 313, 318

Wilderness: 21, 22, 23, 26, 48, 53, 162, 164, 184, 207, 227, 295

Wildlife: 23, 26, 27, 48, 49, 67, 90, 114, 117, 120, 122, 141, 142, 143, 144, 146, 147, 148, 149, 150, 151, 156, 207, 208, 209, 213, 215, 217, 226, 285, 330